Emotions of Normal People

By

WILLIAM MOULTON MARSTON

*Lecturer in Psychology at Columbia University
and at New York University*

LONDON
KEGAN PAUL, TRENCH, TRUBNER & Co. Ltd.
NEW YORK: HARCOURT, BRACE AND COMPANY.
1928

PRINTED IN GREAT BRITAIN BY THE DEVONSHIRE PRESS, TORQUAY

To

MY TEACHERS AND COLLABORATORS

My Mother
Claribel Moulton Waterman
Elizabeth Holloway Marston
Marjorie Wilkes Huntley
Olive Byrne

CONTENTS

LIST OF FIGURES

EMOTIONS OF NORMAL PEOPLE

CHAPTER I

NORMALCY AND EMOTION

ARE you a "normal person"? Probably, for the most part, you are. Doubtless, however, you have occasional misgivings. Your "sex-complexes", your emotional depressions, or your "hidden fears" seem to you, at times, distinctly abnormal. And so psychology might adjudge them. On the other hand, you undoubtedly experience milder fears, furies, petty jealousies, minor hatreds, and occasional feelings of trickery and deception which you have come to regard as part of your *normal* self. And psychology aids and abets you in this notion, also. In fact, many psychologists at the present time frankly regard "fear" and "rage", not only as *normal* emotions, but even as the "major" emotions. By some writers[1] "choc", or emotional shock is suggested as the one element essential to normal emotion. Some psychological experimenters have compelled women subjects to cut off the heads of live rats, proudly presenting reaction data thus obtained as a measure of normal emotional response to an adequate stimulus. One of the most eminent investigators of emotion[2] goes so far as to advocate retention of "fear" and "rage" in normal human behaviour, for the purpose of supplying bodily strength and efficiency ! This suggestion seems to me like recommending the placing of tacks in our soup for the sake of strengthening the lining of the alimentary canal. I do not regard you as a "normal person", emotionally, when you are suffering from fear, rage, pain, shock, desire to deceive, or any other

[1] D. Wechsler, *The Measurement of Emotional Reaction*, New York, 1925, Chapter X.
[2] W. B. Cannon, *Bodily Changes in Pain, Hunger, Fear and Rage*, New York and London, 1920, Chapter XV.

emotional state whatsoever containing turmoil and conflict. Your emotional responses are "normal" when they produce pleasantness and harmony. And this book is devoted to description of normal emotions which are so common-place and fundamental in the every-day lives of all of us that they have escaped, hitherto, the attention of the academician and the psychologist.

Normal Emotions are Biologically Efficient Emotions.

If, as psychologists, we follow the analogy of the other biological sciences, we must expect to find normalcy synony-mous with maximal efficiency of function. Survival of the fittest means survival of those members of a species whose organisms most successfully resist the encroachments of environmental antagonists, and continue to function with greatest internal harmony. In the field of emotions, then, why should we alter this expectation ? Why should we seek the spectacularly disharmonious emotions, the feelings that reveal a crushing of ourselves by environment, and consider these affective responses as our *normal* emotions ? If a jungle beast is torn and wounded during the course of an ultimately victorious battle, it would be a spurious logic indeed that attributed its victory to its wounds. If a human being be emotionally torn and mentally disorganized by fear or rage during a business battle from which, ultimately, he emerges victorious, it seems equally nonsensical to ascribe his conquering strength to those emotions symptomatic of his temporary weakness and defeat. Victory comes in proportion as fear is banished. Perhaps the battle may be won with some fear still handicapping the victor, but that only means that the winner's maximal strength was not required.

I can still remember vividly the fear I once experienced, as a child, when threatened, on my way to school, by a half-witted boy with an air-gun. I had been taught by my father never to fight ; so I ran home in an agony of fear. My mother told me, "Go straight by F——. Don't attack him unless he shoots at you, but if he does, then go after him". I was an obedient child, and followed orders ex-plicitly. I marched up to F—— and his gun with my face set and my stomach sick with dread. F—— did not shoot. I have known, ever since that well-remembered occasion, that fear does *not* give strength in times of stress. Part of the strength with which I faced F——'s air-gun came from my own underlying *dominance*, newly released from artificial control. But most of it belonged to my mother, and she was able to use it in my behalf because I *submitted* to her. *Dominance* and *submission* are the " normal ", strength-giving emotions, not " rage ", or " fear ".

Present Emotion Names are Literary Terms, Scientifically Meaningless

Yet my initial researches in emotion were not concerned with normal, biologically efficient emotions. I began to try to measure the bodily symptoms of deception in the Harvard Psychological Laboratory, in 1913,[1] and later continued this work in the U.S. Army, during the war,[2] and in some court cases.[3] But the more I learned about the bodily symptoms of deception, the more I realized the futility of trying to measure complex conflict-emotions, like " fear ", " anger ", or " deception ", without in the least knowing the normal, fundamental emotions which appeared in the process of being melodramatically baffled in laboratory or court-room torture situations.

What does the average teacher of psychology mean when he glibly rattles off the words " fear ", " rage ", " anger ", and " sex-emotion " ?[4] Almost any literary light of the Victorian era, if asked to define these words, would have answered, readily enough : " They are names for emotions possessing distinctive conscious qualities, experienced by everybody, every day. These easily recognized, primitive emotions constitute the very backbone of literature." I submit that the backbone of literature has been transplanted intact into

[1] For reports of these researches see : W. M. Marston, " Systolic Blood Pressure Symptoms of Deception," *Jr. Exp. Psy.*, 1917, vol. 2, p. 117. W. M. Marston, "Reaction Time Symptoms of Deception," *ibid*, 1920, vol. 3, pp. 72-87. W. M. Marston, "Negative Type Reaction Time Symptoms of Deception," *Psy. Rev.*, 1925, vol. 32, pp. 241, 247.

[2] R. M. Yerkes, " Report of the Psy. Committee of the National Research Council," *Psy. Rev.*, 1919, vol. 26, p. 134.

[3] W. M. Marston, " Psychological Possibilities in the Deception Tests," *Jour. Crim. Law and Crim.*, 1921, vol. XI, pp. 552-570. W. M. Marston, " Sex Characteristics of Systolic Blood Pressure Behaviour," *Jour. Exp. Psy.*, 1923, vol. VI. 387-419.

[4] The substance of the following paragraphs appeared originally in an article by the writer, entitled " Primary Emotions," *Psy. Rev.*, and is reproduced with the kind permission of its editor, Prof. H. C. Warren.

psychology, where it has proved pitifully inadequate. The whole structure of our recently christened "science", in consequence, remains spineless in its attempted descriptions of human behaviour. Most teachers of psychology, it would seem, are still unable to define these time-worn emotional terms with greater exactness or scientific meaning than that employed by literary men of the last century.

Nor can the average teacher be blamed. Theorists and researchers upon whom the teacher must depend for his scientific concepts have written many hundreds of thousands of words on the subject of emotions, without attempting definite, psycho-neural description of a single basic, or primary emotion. On the other hand, nearly all writers seem to accept the old, undefined literary *names* of various "emotions" without question; each writer then giving these terms such connotation as they may happen to hold for him, individually.

Consider, for example, the term "fear". This word seems to find its way, unquestioned, into nearly every emotions research reported to the literature of psychology and physiology. What does it mean? The James-Langeites say "fear" is a complex of sensations, perhaps largely visceral, perhaps not; perhaps the same in all subjects, but probably differing importantly in different individuals. Surely the unfortunate teacher of psychology can extract little comfort from such vague guess-work. Besides, the physiologists have proved, with their customary thoroughness, that the condition of consciousness traditionally termed "fear" in popular and literary parlance, cannot be composed characteristically of sensory content.[1]

What then of the physiologists? They use the term "fear", it appears, quite as blithely and trustfully as do the James-Langeites. Cannon uses the word "fear" throughout the entire course of his extremely valuable work entitled, *Bodily Changes in Pain, Hunger, Fear and Rage.*

But how does he differentiate it from "rage", or from "pain"? He points out physiological similarities, but no measurable differences between these "major emotions". Cannon assumes that the so-called sympathetic division of the autonomic nervous system is always activated by the "fear"

[1] For summary of investigations touching this point see W. M. Marston, "Motor Consciousness as a Basis for Emotion," *Jour. Abn. and Soc. Psy.*, vol. XXII, July-Sept., 1927, pp. 140-150.

pattern. But he cites various other effects of " fear ", such as nausea, weakness, vomiting, etc., which would be ascribed, by many writers, to vagus impulses. Moreover, "rage ", " pain ", and other " major emotions " also discharge characteristically into the sympathetic, as Cannon himself emphasizes.[1] So we are left, again, high and dry in our search for any specific meaning for the famous word " fear ".

What must be done is to give up attempts to define conflict-emotions, and go down to the very roots of biologically efficient behaviour and discover the simple, normal emotions that lie buried there. This book attempts that task. It attempts to describe the emotions of *normal* people, and *people are not normal when they are afraid, or enraged, or deceptive.* When the simplest normal emotion elements are revealed, it becomes a comparatively easy matter to put them together into normal compound emotions—in real life or in the psychological laboratory. It becomes comparatively easy, moreover, to detect—and to remove--*the reversed interrelationships between normal emotion elements which are responsible for these conflicts and thwartings in " fear ", " rage ", " jealousy " and the other abnormal states.*

In What Terms can " Normal Emotions " be Described ?

But a person who calls himself a psychologist is in a peculiar position these days. Before he can write about the psychology of emotion, or intelligence, or, in fact, about the psychology of any human behaviour, he must define what he means by psychology. The introspectionistic psychologists, now considered unscientific, regarded any exposition as psychological which described its phenomena in subjective or introspective terms. Now the introspectionists are pushed into the background. In their place we find a great variety of teachers and researchers all naming their diverse methods and observations " psychology ". We have, for instance, in the field of emotions, the physiologists, the neurologists, the physiological psychologists, the behaviourists, the endocrinologists, the mental-tester-statisticians, the psycho-analysts, and the psychiatrists. Each of these types of worker confesses himself to be a psychologist, and, moreover, each maintains that his are the only psychologically worth-while results. Psychology

[1] W B Cannon, *Bodily Changes in Pain, Hunger, Fear, and Rage,* New York and London, 1920, pp. 277-279

to-day, like Europe in the Middle Ages, is being fought over by feudal barons who have little in common save tacit acceptance of the rule that spoils shall be taken whenever and however possible.

In what terms, then, can we describe simple, normal emotions, with any expectation that one or all of psychology's warring factions may regard our terminology with aught but disdain ? I once made the mistake of using the term " will-setting " in a discussion of bodily emotion mechanisms ; and, although several American psychologists of various sorts strove manfully to read the article in question, all gave it up in the end. I once asked Dr. Watson a question containing, stupidly enough, the word " consciousness ". " I'm sorry ", said Watson, in a tone of genuine regret, " I *don't* understand what you mean, and so I can't answer your question." I once remarked to an eminent psycho-analyst, that I had enjoyed the play " Outward Bound ". " O ho ! " this friend triumphed. " So you have an Oedipus complex ! " then added, plaintively, " When *are* you going to learn psycho-analytical terms ? You might have told me about that Oedipus, instead of letting it out of the bag in that round-about fashion ! " In the first two instances I thought I had said something, but found I had not. In the last instance, I did not think I had said anything, but found that I had committed myself irretrievably. What is one to do in describing normal emotions ?

Only this. One may try, at least, to " reinterpret and correlate the old fog signals ", as Ogden aptly puts it,[1] and so correct some " errors in manipulating the logos " by an attempted application of " the science of orthology ". Which means, of course, that we first have to find out what the various types of psychological writers really are talking about, each in his own peculiar dialect. And then we have to devise a sort of psychological Esperanto, defining each new term, as we use it, with meticulous exactitude. The task is not an easy one. But to induce the different types of researchers in psychology of emotion to unite their efforts toward describing *normal primary emotions* would be worth any amount of effort. Each of the varieties of psychologist named has something vital to contribute to this central problem, if he would only get over his language difficulty and play the game.

[1] C. K. Ogden, Editorial : " Orthology ", *Psyche*, July, 1927.

CHAPTER II

MATERIALISM, VITALISM AND PSYCHOLOGY

OUR problem is : What are the underlying desires, or wishes, that lead some scientists to insist upon mechanistic conceptions, and others equally eminent, to espouse some form of scientific vitalism ? For in psychology, as in other sciences, a materialistic or vitalistic bias may be found at the root of nearly all factional schools, or contentious groups. Sometimes, of course, the underlying desire relates solely to the advancement of the personal fortunes of the workers concerned ; and such purely egoistic motives probably play a considerable part in the evolution of every scientific doctrine. In addition to this, however, originators and promulgators of conceptual systems of thought, nearly always possess hidden desires to push science in this direction or that, " for science's own sake ". The goal selected is the one that accords most closely with the basic emotional set of the scientific agitator. And the emotional sets of scientists may be classified, broadly, into two elementary groups, materialistic and vitalistic.

The Mechanistic Set

Mechanists are " hard-boiled ". They are chronic sceptics, and must be shown. They pretend to base all their conclusions upon material evidence, and seldom observe that their own aggressive disbeliefs in the existence of this or that are based upon temperamental rejection of the very proffered evidence which their creed holds sacred. Their rationalization of their own emotional bias runs something like this : Science is the study and exposition of material causation. " Material " means always " cruder, less complex forms of energy ". Therefore, true science is the study of the influence of simpler energy units upon more complex energy units. And, since we can account for everything we have experienced in this way, why waste time imagining that there exists any other type of

7

cause or causation ? The mechanistic doctrine is pithy, succinct, and easily understood. Like the emotional set of its adherents, the mechanistic doctrine is aggressive, self-assured, and makes for rapid and decisive action. Scientific results, like other types of reward, are attained by action. Materialism, therefore, has proved itself a very useful agent in turning man's intellect from arm-chair speculation, to laboratory research.

The Vitalistic Set

Vitalism seems to associate itself very intimately with religion, and religion might be defined as an emotional police force for morals. The vitalist's basic emotional set is subtler, more complex, and harder to define than is that of the mater-ialist. It seeks a more ultimate good for the self, and, at the same time, desires opportunity to dispense loftier cheer to others. If mere physical fact interferes, at any point, with vitalism's sacred purposes, then escape is taken to the heights of imagination, where no physical facts exist. Nor do these occasional excursions prove wholly futile. Often the fugitive from reality returns to earth with new and usable inspiration. Physical facts frequently turn out to be chameleons, changing to richer and more varied colours under more vivid illum-ination.

In rationalizing his underlying desires for science, the vitalist remains true to form, starts with a priori assumptions, and ultimately descends to facts. He assumes, to begin with, that physical phenomena cannot adequately be accounted for as mere results of physical causes. Therefore, it seems, we must further assume the existence of a first cause, or super-physical influence of unknown attributes. Granting the existence of such an ultra-material agent, it is easy to assert that " He " produces, emanates, or *is* physical consciousness. From this point on, the vitalist descends into the same world with the materialist. Only, vitalistic causation proceeds in an opposite direction. Consciousness is a more complex, more ultimate form of being than is organic matter ; which, in turn, is more complex and potent than are inorganic energy units. Complex energy forms are regarded by the vitalist as more compelling than the cruder units. It is held, therefore, that higher energy units are the causes, and that simpler energy units are effects. " God made man in His own image ", and set him to rule over the beasts of the field. The beasts, in turn, rule the vegetables, and so on down the line. Science is conceived of by the vitalist as a study and description of the causal influences of the higher upon the lower, the more complex upon the simpler, the more conscious upon the less animate. This doctrine is utterly repellant to many scientists, because it bases itself, initially, upon sheer, unproved assumption, and because, with equal naîveté, it ignores countless instances, appearing in every day life, wheie determinative influences are exercised by cruder forms of matter upon human consciousness itself, which the vitalist regards as the highest known form of energy.

Existence of Mechanistic-Type Causes and Vitalistic-Type Causes

On the other hand, physical scientists who desire, unselfconsciously, to uplift their fellow humans, endure with difficulty the thought that the destiny of mankind rests supinely in the power of the unbound electron. Mechanistic determinism is abhored just as whole-heartedly by many a man of letters who sees no logical escape from its tentacles, as it is by "fundamentalist" preachers who see in the triumph of materialism a prospective loss of their own bread and butter. Most dreaded of all mechanistic tenets, apparently, is Darwinian evolution. That monkey has made man in his own image is felt to be a degrading thought. Why? Because such a conclusion is taken to mean that man, once made, continues to be controlled by the same elementary forces which originally produced him. But biological evolution, even if true, entails no such implications. Monkey (or the common ancestor), may have caused man to evolve into his present form ; but man, on the other hand, can now create new types of monkeys at will, by exercising a controlling influence over their breeding habits. And this is the very type of causation idealized by the vitalists. Man, the complex, sets causes in motion which influence the nature of monkey, the simpler animal. Moreover, while the materialistic supposition that monkey originally created man is beyond our present powers of verification, the influence exercised by man over monkey can be observed, any day, in the laboratory. In this argument, at least, we must concede that the vitalists' variety of causation is more solidly upheld by facts than is the méchanistic type of cause raised by materialists to epic grandeur in the saga of biological evolution. We must admit that while the vitalists begin their theorizing with fictional flights, the materialists conclude their doctrines with an almost equally speculative sublimation of their underlying emotional set. Also, in justice to both, it may be said that the vitalistic account of causation is just as much an accurate observation of physical fact, as is the mechanistic account. Simpler energy units constantly influence more complex units, and may, under favourable conditions, control their behaviour, while more intricate assemblages of force, by virtue of new attributes derived from their complexity, as constantly compel comliance from cruder types of matter, and do, under our very eyes, completely regulate the simpler energy forms.

·-Physical science must and does include both mechanistic and vitalistic types of causation.

Science Must Describe Both Types of Causes

We do not know as a matter of actual observation how organic forms of energy originate. We do know, however, that such energy units exist, and that any life-possessing unit exercises spontaneous influences over inorganic matter throughout its life span. These influences are in every sense vitalistic-type causes. Even inorganic matter may spontaneously generate causes of this same type. Radio-active metals, for instance, emanate energy particles regardless of the nature of the environment in which these emanations take place. Physical science, without doubt, is held accountable for a full description of these phenomena.

At the same time, life-possessing units of matter, such as plants and animals, are constantly undergoing modification as a result of stimuli which impinge upon their organisms from the less complex material units of their environment. Simple, but intensely energized forces like wind or waves may destroy plant or animal organisms altogether ; or such forces may influence in conclusive manner the growth or movements of the more complex animal and plant organisms. In the case of inorganic matter, acids or single chemical elements vastly less complex in themselves than the radio active metals, may attack and destroy the latter, or may hasten or retard the radio activity. These are mechanistic-type causes acting determinatively upon energy units more complex than themselves.

Interaction of Mechanistic Type and Vitalistic-Type Causes

In addition to such wholly separable types of causation, science has still to deal with the interaction of vitalistic and mechanistic causes. It is in the discussion of influences interacting between complex and simple energy units that the greatest confusions and conflicts of scientific analysis arise. For instance, let us suppose that science is called upon to describe the plant growing in a field. It can be shown definitely that the soil is delivering a continuous series of chemical stimuli to the plant. It is equally ascertainable that the plant reacts to these stimuli with a series of reactions peculiar to its own inherent nature. Some of these plant responses will result in the delivery of counter stimuli to the soil and some will not. Those influences which are exercised by the plant over the soil will, for the most part, alter the soil in ways determined by the chemical power of the plant. In so far, therefore, as soil and plant interchange influences, it may fairly be said that the more complex units of energy composing the plant will dominate the interplay of causal forces.

But, as we have noted, there will be many changes in the plant, as a result of reactions to soil stimuli, which will not direct any influence back toward the earth. Were these plant changes directed by the soil to its own ultimate benefit, then we might clearly assume that the simpler form of energy was in causal control of the more complex energy unit. That is to say, if the soil were able to use the more complex energy of the plant to effect its own enlargement, simply by stimulating the plant to act according to the plant's own principles of action, we might conclude that, after all, the balance of control lay with the simpler unit of energy. This would amount to philosophical admission that mechanistic causation holds the balance of power. But such does not appear to be the case. Though stimulated to action by the soil, the plant reacts with its own energy according to its own innate principles of action, and with reaction tendencies designed for its own ultimate benefit. With innate power to develop spontaneously throughout its own life cycle, with a balance of power of interaction capable of changing the soil more radically than the soil can change it, and, finally, with a structure designed in such a way as always to react for its own benefit when stimulated to action by the soil, we are forced to conclude that the plant is a more potent generator of effective causes than is the soil. In short, a close logical analysis of influences interacting between complex and simple energy units would seem to show that the responses of the simpler unit are dependent to a greater extent upon the causal control of the more complex form of matter, than are the reactions of the latter upon the former. If a balance is to be struck, then, upon the basis of empirical observation, between vitalistic and mechanistic types of causation, we should be obliged to concede to the vitalistic causes the final balance of power. But science is not called upon to strike any such balance; it is merely required to describe both types of causation, neglecting neither the one nor the other.

Complex Matter-Units Possess Greatest Causal Power

In the large, we may put the matter somewhat as follows. Science finds, in this world, units of energy of varying complexity. It finds that the complex units are capable of exerting spontaneous influences upon the simpler units, and vice versa. It finds that simple and complex units customarily interact, each causing changes in the other. The balance of power, on the whole, in this interchange of causal influences, lies with the more complex energy accretions. Even supposing, by way of illustration, that lead was once responsible for the evolution of uranium, it seems now the fact that radio-active metal can create lead under our own observation; while lead, if it still possesses evolutionary power, manifests it in too small a degree to be detected with available instruments. Perhaps inorganic compounds, millions of years ago, evolved plant structures. But now, at least, vegetable growths alter the entire composition of their nurturing soils, in the course of a few seasons; while the ability of the chemical influence of the soil to change the fundamental characteristics of plant life is extremely uncertain. Monkey-like primates may have given rise, in the long ago, to genus homo; but there is now little comparison between the influence that man is capable of exerting over ape behaviour, and that which monkeys may bring to bear upon man. It seems to be a principle of nature that *once a more complex form of energy appears, it forthwith possesses greater causal power over simpler forms of energy than the simpler forms possess over it.*

But the mere fact that a quantitative majority of causations are of vitalistic type, does not in the least mean that science can neglect the huge, co-existing volume of mechanistic-type causations. Both aspects of causal description are required in all sciences. In physics, for example, which seeks to describe the most ultimate, or elementary reaction tendencies of matter, the attempt is now being made to resolve all complex masses into ultra-simple proton and electron systems. The influence of each proton-electron microcosm, then, must be traced in its most far-reaching effects upon the physical behaviour of the macrocosmic mass of which it forms a single unit. The causal influences of the total mass, on the other hand, upon its constituent proton-electron systems, and upon other free-lance proton-electron systems, must be described.

Chemistry, starting with already complex units of matter, the atom and the molecule, seeks to describe the causal effects of atoms upon molecules, and of molecules upon their constituent atoms, and upon other atoms, free or in other molecular systems of combination. Complexly organized groups of molecules, also, are studied by chemistry, which attempts to trace the influences which single molecules exercise upon organic and inorganic compounds, and the causal effects of such compounds upon the simpler, molecular units.

From chemistry we step over the border line between inorganic and organic matter into the field of the sciences which deal with living organisms. In botany an attempt is made to analyze plant structures into cellular units. The effects of these units, together with the influences of still simpler inorganic units upon complex plant structures is then considered. Slightly more important, perhaps, is the description of the manner in which plants utilize and react upon their environment. In the general science of biology, which serves as an introduction to the more highly specialized physiological sciences, it is interesting to note that animal organisms are classified into phyla, genera, and species, upon the basis of the type of action which each animal exerts upon its environment, rather than according to the effect which inorganic or vegetable environment exerts upon the animal. Both aspects of scientific description are important in biology, however, as we have seen them to be in the other sciences.

With the advent of the highly specialized physiological sciences, we find a group of studies whose special object is analysis and description of man himself. Animal organisms below the complexity level of man are, of course, constantly utilized in the physiological laboratory ; but such animal subjects are studied in order to apply the knowledge thus gained to further understanding of man. In other words, the purpose of the physiological sciences has become frankly vitalistic as to type of causation emphasized. It is desired to know how man reacts upon and utilizes animals less complex than himself, as well as to learn the influences which he is able to wield over his vegetable and inorganic environments. This underlying purpose of the human scientist appears greatly to disturb mechanistic -minded writers and investigators, and the repeated attempt is made to assert the equal scientific importance of animal and botanical results regardless of their ultimate bearing upon analyses of man's own creative tendencies. Similarly, attempts are frankly made by materialistically biased persons to assert that man's behaviour is determined in its entirety by the influences exerted upon it by units of energy simpler than man himself.

The truth of this assertion may be tested by examination of the nature of the nervous impulses by which, it is generally conceded, man's bodily conduct is initiated and controlled. Nerve impulses were formerly thought of as electrical disturbances. The energy travelling along a given nerve was conceived of as an outside force imposed upon the nerve by an environmental or physiological stimulus ; that is, by a stimulus less complex in energy organization than the nerve itself. Neurologists have subsequently discovered, however, that the nature of a nervous impulse is wholly dependent upon the potential energy already contained within the nerve fibre. A nervous impulse is now described as a series of explosions,[1][2] dependent for their intensity and volume, not upon the intensity of the physical stimulus, but rather upon the intrinsic structure of the particular nerve fibre stimulated. The

[1] K Lucas, *The Conduction of the Nerve Impulse*, London, 1917, p 23.
[2] A Forbes, " The Interpretation of Spinal Reflexes in Terms of Present Knowledge of Nerve Conduction, " *Physiological Reviews*, vol ii, July, 1922, p 367 : " It has been likened to the burning of a train of gunpowder, in contrast with the transmission of a sound wave whose energy comes entirely from its initiating source This fact, now well established, should put an end to all efforts to explain the nerve impulse simply·as a transient current of electricity conducted along the fibre on the same principle as in an insulated wire ; the dynamics of the two modes of conduction are fundamentally different,"

function of the physical stimulus is limited to an initial release of nervous energy accumulations more complex than itself. In no sense is the nervous impulse determined by, or causally dependent upon the less complex physical stimulus to which it responds, except in the single particular that the physical stimulus is responsible for the origin of the nervous impulse. Once the nervous impulse appears, it proceeds to operate on its own energy and according to its own rules of behaviour, like all other complex forms of energy. The mechanistic thinker assumes that causal responsibility for the origin of the more complex form of energy implies subsequent control of the more complex unit throughout its life span. Only if such continuous control were exercised by the simpler over the more complex could this world be regarded as uniformly mechanistic. As a matter of fact, however, the moment a more complex energy unit, such as the nervous impulse, is called into being, it forthwith assumes control of its own behaviour, and, to a considerable extent also, it exercises control over the behaviour of the stimulus energy unit.

The analysis of human emotions hereinafter set forth will, I trust, clearly show that man, the most complex of unit organisms, is similarly independent of, and influential over, the environmental stimuli which initially call into being his responses.

Assignments of the Sciences

Psychology is the youngest and most undeveloped of the specialized, man-describing sciences. What is psychology's peculiar assignment ? What especial group of energy units must psychology examine, both with respect to the influences exerted upon these units by simpler forms of matter, and with respect to manipulations of simpler forms by the units described by psychology ? Physiologists, as we have seen, undertake to examine the effects of environment upon bodily tissues and organs. They also seek to discover the actions of the organs themselves upon the various vegetable and mechanical forces of matter which they contact. Neurology, which is also a comparatively new branch of science, is particularly interested in the effects of bodily organs and tissues upon the net-work of neurons constituting the so-called nervous system. More particularly is neurology interested in the influences exerted by nervous impulses over the various organs and tissues of the body. Is there any stabilized form of energy more complex than the nervous impulse ? The common sense answer to this question is " Yes, Consciousness ".

Psychology's Assignment

Physiologists, neurologists, psycho-physiologists and possibly psycho-analysts, substantially agree with this answer. All these types of investigators assume, either tacitly or explicitly, that consciousness is a manifestation of energy which exists and reacts as a unit separate from mere intra-neuronic disturbance. If this separate existence of the phenomenon consciousness be conceded, then psychology's especial task must be the description of this most complex form of energy. And psychology, like all other sciences, must proceed to the analysis and description of both causal aspects of its subject ·.natter. The effects of nerve impulses upon consciousness must be discovered and analyzed. None-the-less importantly must the influences of consciousness upon nervous impulses be studied Through the mediumship of its influence upon nervous energy consciousness will, of course, act upon bodily tissues, and through the mediumship of bodily tissues, consciousness will be found ultimately to influence the organism's physical environment. To leave out any of these essential causal media which are interposed between consciousness and physical environment must be to leave a gap in the totality of scientific description. Such gaps usually make for inaccuracy. Therefore, it would seem sensible for psychology to base itself first of all upon neurology, relying upon the description of nerve impulse behaviour furnished by workers in that field. Thus may psychology find more or less ready-made its points of departure and application.

If psychology's assignment be consciousness, and if consciousness lies in immediate contact with nervous energy, then the physiological changes which can be discovered in bodily organs and the observable physical movements of the body itself may be utilized for psychology's purposes in two ways. In the first place, bodily movements may be regarded as possibly symptomatic of a preceding psycho-neural cause. The proof of the existence of this primary, conscious-cause should not, as will later be set forth in detail, depend upon introspective observations. Definitive, objective criteria, based upon known structures and functions of the particular mechanisms of consciousness, should be used always in deciding whether observed body changes or movements are the result of consciousness or not. In the second place, if such a change or movement is not the result of consciousness, it might still prove of interest to psychology as a causal originator of consciousness. That is to say, measurable bodily changes and movements may represent the simpler energy unit causes of the generation of consciousness, or they may represent causes of its modification. ˖Again we must emphasize the fact that bodily changes may or may not influence consciousness, and that the issue of whether consciousness has, in fact, been changed is to be decided as far as possible upon objective, rather than upon introspective data.

In summary, then, measurable bodily changes and observable bodily movements may be of value to the psychological investigator in one of two ways. First, it is possible that the psychologist may use the bodily change as an indicator of pre-existing consciousness. In that case consciousness is treated as a vitalistic-type cause, the effect of which is the bodily movement. Or, secondly, measured modifications may prove of value to the investigating psychologist as indicators of the consciousness which is to follow. In this case the bodily changes represent a mechanistic type cause of which the alteration of consciousness is a predictable result.

Types of Causes Emphasized by Different Schools of Emotion Investigators

With such a preliminary view of psychology as that just outlined, we find ourselves in a position to consider the various aspects of psychology's task in which different types of workers specialize.

Psycho-Physiologists

The psycho-physiologists may be regarded as investigators who are trying to make careful laboratory measures of intra-bodily changes. More especially do we find this type of researcher emphasizing the mechanictically causal aspect of his data. That is, the psycho-physiologist seems especially concerned with trying to describe the consciousness resulting from the physiological changes measured. Following this bias, perhaps, psycho-physiological workers have long striven in vain to prove that bodily changes constitute mechanistic-type causes of resulting sensations, and that these sensations are emotion (James-Lange theory).

On the other hand, a limited number of psycho-physiological researchers have tried to utilize physiological measures as symptoms, or indicators of previously existing emotional causes. Association reaction-time tests, systolic blood-pressure deception tests, and galvanometric emotion-detecting tests may be listed as investigations of this type. Bodily changes, thus regarded, are tacitly treated as results of emotion impulses acting as vitalistic-type causes. Though physiological psychologists have been severely handicapped by the senseless assumption that all consciousness is, in its final essence, composed of sensation, they have, on the whole, shown no prejudicial bias toward limiting the use of their results by regarding them either as exclusively mechanistic-type causes or as exclusively vitalistic-type causes. In short, the psycho-physiologists, for the most part, have made their bodily measurements, or they have recorded their subjects' introspections as carefully, and they have refrained from dogmatic assertion as to the type of causal conception, if any, existing between their two sets of data.

Mental-Tester-Statisticians

It is more difficult to place the mental-tester-statistician within the field of psychology as we have attempted to outline it. One is tempted to believe, at times, that this type of person is not working in the field of psychology at all. Yet even if this conclusion were justified, it would still remain true that the statistical-testing type of result is throwing invaluable side lights upon many strictly psychological problems. It is difficult to find intrinsic psychological meaning in the statement that Thomas Brown has made an army alpha score of 200. There exists, so far as I know, no available key to the different elements of consciousness involved in securing 200 on that particular test, nor is there an extant compendium detailing the psycho-neural mechanisms of causation employed by the subject in obtaining this unusually high score. The prevailing mental test meaning of the score is merely that Thomas Brown has complied with and dominated an arbitrarily fixed set of tasks considerably more effectively than several million other persons have been able to do. If one would utilize this result in a truly psychological analysis of

Brown, one must guess what psycho-neural mechanisms were called into play in this particular individual by the tasks imposed. Such an application of a test score to psychology is not as difficult as it sounds. After a little practical experience with tests, one comes to realize that certain characteristics of consciousness such as speed of reaction and finesse of compliance emotion are necessary to the making of a high test score. This is the sort of rough and ready analysis of test results into heterogeneously named " mental traits " at which mental test specialists become extremely expert. To a genius like Thorndike, for example, who has spent many years in analyzing mental test results, the psychologically suggestive values of test tabulations are tremendous, if one may judge from his theoretical contributions to the psychology of learning. Accepting, then, this suggestive value of mental tests, rather than the statistical formulation of their results, as the chief psychological value of this method of investigation, we may regard mental test procedures as specializing in the vitalistic-type of psychological causation. The bodily performances of the persons tested are treated as symptomatic of consciousness energy and nervous energy acting as vitalistic-type causes of the behaviour measured.

Behaviourists

John B. Watson states[1] that in 1912 the behaviourists decided either to give up psychology or else to make it a natural science. Many people are now inclined to believe that Watsonian behaviourists have carried out not one but both of these threats. Certainly Watson's mechanistic bias, backed by his extraordinarily keen scientific observation, has accomplished wonders in converting psychology into an objective science. But, at the same time, there is considerable evidence that Watson himself has given up psychology altogether. In his latest text, he defines the subject matter of human psychology as " the behaviour or activities of the human being "[2] but he explicitly excludes consciousness from human behaviour and activity. If Watson should succeed in this bob-tailing of psychology, he would have talked himself out of a job. For neuronic activity has been assigned to the neurologist, body tissue activity to the physiologist, and classification

[1] J B Watson, *Behaviorism*, New York and London, 1925, p 16.
[2] J. B. Watson, *ibid.*, p. 3.

of gross bodily behaviour of all animals, including man, to the general biologist. It might be possible, of course, for psychology to appropriate to itself the last-named function of biology in so far as it relates to the genus homo. In such case psychology would act as a sort of clearing house for the facts of neurology and physiology, with a department for the release of composite motion pictures of whole human beings in action. But behaviourists, as a matter of fact, have not behaved as though acting upon such a concept of their scientific task. Watson, for instance, has reported to the literature many carefully controlled experiments in which he sought to analyze and explain the intra-bodily mechanisms by which the final gross actions were brought about. Watson himself, of course, is now devoting himself to business, and his recent expressions of lack of interest in attempting to describe the more intricate bodily mechanisms of response (particularly those of the central nervous system) are probably attributable to his personal lack of time for laboratory experimentation, rather than to any radical shift in scientific attitude. On the whole, then, we may conclude that the Watsonian type of behaviourism is merely a mechanistically motivated attempt to turn psychology into objectively scientific channels by the simple expedient of eliminating whatever type of subject matter the behaviourists feel themselves incapable of describing. That the phenomenon eliminated chanced to be consciousness is unfortunate for "behaviourism", not for psychology.

If, then, we dare to assume, in the very teeth of the behaviouristic tempest, that consciousness is a very complex but stabilized form of energy which must be included in the "activities of the human being", we may conclude that Watson and his allies would be especially interested in the control which physical environment and bodily tissues exercise over consciousness. Watson insists that only mechanistic-type causes exist He regards the central nervous system as a mere off-shoot of the other bodily tissues which control it completely ; and he furthermore states that the responses of both bodily tissues and nervous system are wholly at the mercy of the physical environment, just as Atalanta found herself wholly at the mercy of the golden apples.[1] Almost

[1] J. B. Watson, *Psychology from the Standpoint of a Behaviorist*, 1919, Philadelphia and London, p. 3.

in the next paragraph, however, Watson attempts to show how the human race can throw off its thraldom to religious and social convention and other environmentally determined influences. He has recently maintained that no more children should be brought into the world until parents have learned enough about them to regulate each child's life according to the principles of the child's own nature, physical, mental, and emotional. Surely no more striking faith in the potencies of vitalistic-type causation can be found than this statement ! If human consciousness were truly controlled by less complex energy forms of the environment, such dreams for human self-regulation would be sheer madness. The actively potent cause in the programme which Watson advocates is the complex human consciousness of parents, which, when it has been made still more complex by added knowledge, Watson hopes can control and modify the simpler consciousness of the child. It was not really the apples which over-powered Atalanta, but the more complex consciousness of Milanion who dropped the apples. It seems to me probable, therefore, in light of this unintentional self-revelation on Watson's part, that we may, after all, expect the master " behaviourist " to lay fully as much emphasis upon analysis of vitalistic-type causes as upon purely mechanistic descriptions. These two aspects of any science are, of course, inseparable. And it is not reckless to predict that the behaviourists of to-day may be transforned completely into the psycho-physiologists of to-morrow if procedures for objective examination and description of consciousness can be perfected.

Psycho-Analysts

Lastly, we may consider, briefly, the causal emphasis to be found in the doctrine of psycho-analysis. The psycho-analysts seem to take an especial interest in the control which various conflicting and distorted elements of consciousness exercise over human conduct. This clearly is a vitalistic-type of causation. Yet when we penetrate one step further into the psycho-analytical teachings, we discover that the offending conscious elements themselves are regarded as being the product of still another type of entity, the libido. If, then, the libido turns out to be a mass of unconscious, physical, or physiological energy, the whole foundation of the psycho-analytical system must be regarded as thoroughly mechanistic.

If, on the other hand, the libido is discovered to partake of the nature of consciousness itself, we might conclude that a vitalistic theme of causation runs back into the very heart of the psycho-analytical doctrine.

The effects which physical objects and environmental situations are supposed to have upon the emotional consciousness of children constitute instances of purely mechanistic-type causation. That is to say, the psycho-analysts teach that the emotional consciousness of young children is peculiarly susceptible to being controlled, perverted, and mis-directed by irresistible effects produced upon it by less complex forms of matter in the physical environment. As the individual grows older his consciousness is thought to be less susceptible to damage or perversion from such causes, although when the libido meets with environmental enemies, these outside antagonists may exercise more control over the subject's consciousness than does the libido itself. On the whole, we may characterize psycho-analysis as a system of thought which assumes a continuous state of bodily conflict between the vitalistic-type causes, having their origin in the libido or in consciousness itself, and the mechanistic-type causes springing from environmental stimuli. The psycho-analyst's avowed intention is to ally himself with the self-controlling conscious causes existing in a subject, for the purpose of defeating the, mechanistic, environmental causes. These material influences are to be brought, if possible, into harmony with the human being's own nature. We may, perhaps, draw a general conclusion that the psycho-analyst believes psychology to be a study of the conflict between vitalistic-type causes and mechanistic-type causes, in so far as such causes relate to consciousness.

Summary

It may be well to summarize the causal emphasis of investigators making the most important contributions to psychology of emotions as follows : Psychologists who seek to make simultaneous laboratory examination of consciousness as reported introspectively, and of physiological changes in the subjects' body as measured by instruments of precision, are usually interested equally in mechanistic-type causes and vitalistic-type causes. These workers need not, and often do not, commit themselves very definitely as to whether consciousness has caused bodily change, or bodily change has controlled consciousness. No fault can be found with this position, though a hope may be expressed that psycho-physiologists may manifest a little more boldness in the causal interpretation of their results, once consciousness has come to be definitely recognized as a form of physical energy.

Mental-tester-statisticians, working by a method which produces psychologically suggestive results of considerable value, may be said to seek causes of vitalistic-type in so far as test results are regarded as revelatory of existing consciousness or conscious tendencies.

Watsonian behaviourists, though ostensibly and aggressively mechanistic in their present propaganda, are found, nevertheless, to possess the most practical interest of all in vitalistic-type causation. For these behaviourists maintain that human beings, who are the most complex of physical energy units, possess the ability wholly to free their own behaviour from environmental control.

The psycho-analyst takes especial interest in the relations existing between mechanistic-type causation and vitalistic-type causation. The existing relationship between these antithetical types of causal influence is conceived by the psycho-analyst to be one of conflict, and this conflict he would resolve in favour of the vitalistic-type causes. Of all classes of thinkers contributing to the problem of emotional theory, the psycho-analyst seems to be alone in his explicit recognition of the simultaneous existence of both types of causation, and of the scientific necessity for psychology to deal with both.

Psychology of Emotion Tentatively Defined

Applying our conclusions with regard to mechanism, vitalism, and psychology to the psychology of emotions, we may suggest a tentative definition of our prospective field of research. *Psychology of emotion is the scientific description of affective consciousness.* " Scientific description ", as hereinbefore set forth, must include discovery and exposition of both mechanistic-type and vitalistic-type causes and their interactions within the field defined.

Concretely, we may expect to trace the origin of emotion to mechanistic-type causes ; that is, to nerve impulses, thence to bodily changes and, ultimately, to environmental stimuli. These three types of cause constitute simpler forms of energy than does consciousness itself. We may also expect to find that many elements of emotional consciousness are terminated by these same mechanistic-type causes. Unfortunately, also, we may feel rather sure that the conditioning of emotional consciousness upon environmental stimuli will be found under the control, for the most part, of mechanistic-type influences. That is to say, we shall find that the quality of emotional consciousness which responds to and reacts upon a given environmental stimulus frequently has been determined by chance repetition of that stimulus, or by the conditions under which the stimulus first happened to be presented to the subject, by his inanimate environment. If such be the case, the inanimate object, or simpler form of energy, is exercising complete control over the nature of the emotional response, and indirectly over the subsequent type of influence exerted back again upon environment by the emotional consciousness evoked. This type of causation remains predominantly mechanistic throughout.

On the other hand, we must be prepared to regard bodily expressions of emotional consciousness as vitalistically caused by the conscious energy itself. In other words, we must not forget that physical or physiological behaviour which we regard as symptomatic of emotional consciousness, is truly a result of the physical causation set up by the emotion energy. Emotional consciousness is to be regarded as a vitalistic-type cause whenever it expresses itself by modification of simpler forms of energy such as nerve impulses, bodily tissues, or unconscious objects of environment. We may expect, furthermore, to find emotional consciousness acting as a vitalistic-type cause over its own less complex units. Larger and more complex units of emotional consciousness may causally control simpler units of consciousness by the round-about method of compelling nerve impulses, and, through their mediation, compelling environmental stimuli to manufacture new units of emotional consciousness made to order, as it were. Thus we find that the complete control of one's own emotional conditioning advocated by Watson may be brought about by vitalistic-type causation controlling and using to its own purposes mechanistic-type causes. This method, rather than the method of mutual conflict between two existing units of emotional consciousness each acting as a vitalistic-type cause, seems to constitute the natural means of emotional self-control.

In short, emotional consciousness, acting as a vitalistic-type cause, may not only definitely influence nerve impulses, bodily states, and environmental forces, but it may also influence these simpler energy units in such a way that their powers of mechanistic-type causation shall be utilized to prolong or terminate the existing vitalistic-type cause—emotional consciousness.

This detailed analysis of scientific causation as it appears in the psychology of emotion is intended as a preliminary determination of the requirements which any sensible theory of emotions must meet if it is to serve as a skeleton for research I may say, at this point, that I have not found the task of meeting these requirements an easy one. But when the re-.quirements are eventually met I believe that the resulting psychological structure should prove acceptable to all the divers cults of research contributors to the psychology of emotions. The benefit of such a truce in the present psychological civil war would be great, for it is only by the establishing of a common working hypothesis that any substantial portion of these divers research contributions can be given meaning for all.

CHAPTER III

The Psychonic Theory of Consciousness[1]

The question, " What is consciousness ? " has been asked, but not answered, since the first dawnings of speculative thought. The present age, however, can boast of a new question all its own : " Does consciousness exist ? " To one whose common-sense life has been spent outside the intellectual fantasies of academic shades this question might seem ludicrous. Nevertheless, professors of the older school are beginning to experience a considerable degree of bepuzzlement when confronted with the task of convincing a healthfully sceptical younger generation that there is such a thing as consciousness.

" What is it ? " ask the student readers of Watson. " Where is it ? Prove to me that consciousness exists ! "

In vain does the instructor insist that " everyone knows what consciousness is, because everyone is conscious " ; that " many phenomena which cannot be ' kicked ' (seemingly the prescribed behaviouristic test for recognizable being), can yet definitely be shown to exist."

" Very well ", reply the students, " show us, then."

Objective evidence of the existence of consciousness must necessarily be indirect evidence, just as is the case with electricity, Hertzian waves, and even disturbances of propagation in nervous tissue. No wireless wave, electric current, or nerve impulse is in itself sufficiently tangible to be made subject to observation by human senses aided by such instruments as are at present available. The effects of these various forces upon observable materials, however, are accepted not only as proofs of the existence of the forces under

[1] " The Psychonic Theory of Consciousness " made its first appearance in the *Journal of Abnormal and Social Psychology for July*, 1926. The theory was amplified in an article appearing in *Psyche* for July, 1927. Portions of both articles are reproduced in this chapter, and the author makes grateful acknowledgment to the editors for their kind permission to reprint the material.

examination, but also as scientifically descriptive criteria by which the nature of the unseen causes may be determined. Thus, an electric current may actuate a voltmeter or an ammeter ; a Hertzian wave may produce differences of conductivity within an audion tube ; and a nervous impulse may result in easily recorded contractions of a strip of muscle fibre.

If, then, examination of consciousness is approached with similar objectivity, we must assume that consciousness itself, or the physical mechanism used to produce it, constitutes a definite, physical force, capable of registering its presence and nature by causing changes in some observable material. Further, this force, consciousness, if it exists anywhere, is to be found in the more complex reactions of the normal, adult, human being. In terms of the preliminary analysis of causation arrived at in our last chapter, we are now called upon to prove that a vitalistic-type cause called consciousness actually exists in some part of the human organism and that this supposedly complex form of energy exerts a measurable influence upon simpler energy units, within the body itself, capable of observation with the unaided senses or with laboratory instruments.

Most of the human family have observed, without the aid of a psychologist, that some human activities seem to the subjects themselves to be more conscious than others. Habitual responses, such as walking, twirling a watch fob, or swinging a stick, often do not seem to be accompanied by any consciousness whatever. On the other hand, the making of momentous decisions which may occupy many hours, days, or weeks, exemplify the type of human action which seems to include the greatest relative amount of consciousness. The question as to whether or not habitual actions are, in truth, totally devoid of consciousness may be regarded at the moment as purely academic. If our subjects unanimously report more of the phenomenon called consciousness in one sort of behaviour than in another, and if there are objectively observable effects which seem to proceed *pari passu* with the increase in consciousness, this constitutes scientifically acceptable proof that consciousness is a material force acting upon our bodies as a vitalistic-type cause. In exactly the same way, the fluctuating needle of the voltmeter is accepted as offering scientific proof of the invisible presence of an electric current acting as a vitalistic-type cause over the materials of the instrument. Should this causally effective force, consciousness, be identified later with nervous energy in some part of the brain, it would still remain a vitalistic-type cause, that is, a more complex form of energy than the materials moved. Moreover, when psychology has properly performed its task, we shall hope to find physical consciousness explicitly described in terms of physical energy units.

Our first question, then, is : What changes in bodily behaviour characteristically accompany this reported consciousness ?

Proofs of Consciousness

1. The more conscious a reaction is, the slower it is.

It has frequently been observed that the more conscious an action is, the longer is the observable delay between reception of environmental stimuli and appearance of overt bodily responses. As already noted, habitual actions occur very quickly after contact with the stimulus ; whereas, in the making of momentous decisions, overt activity may be delayed for days or weeks. Reflexes like the knee jerk, where no accompanying consciousness can be detected by the subject himself, manifest a still shorter reaction time than the habitual responses ; while certain " thinking " activities, which may persist over a period of many hours, and which are recognized as intensely conscious throughout the entire period, may never manifest a detectable ultimate response. One observable effect of consciousness upon bodily behaviour, then, would seem to be a lengthening of the time interval between stimulus and response.

2. The more consciousness accompanying a response, the longer it persists after the stimulus is removed.

Quite in contrast to the first-mentioned result of the influence of conscious energy upon bodily behaviour is a second equally common effect. Strictly reflex, or habitual actions, tend to cease very quickly after the removal of the environmental stimulation that brought them about. For instance, a machine operator in a factory does not continue to press down the stopping lever of his machine after the machine has stopped. One does not continue to make watch-fob-twirling movements when dressed in pyjamas, nor to swing the legs in a walking movement after stretching oneself out in an easy chair. On the other hand, if a greater amount of consciousness is attached to a given action, the action is likely to persist for a much longer period after complete removal of the effective stimulus. Suppose a young man has responded to the stimulus of a chance remark that he is " mentally abnormal " by deciding, after some weeks of cogitation, to become a psychiatrist (an actual case which came to my attention in clinic). He begins to act upon this remark within a few months by entering a medical school, but long years of training must follow before he can even begin to analyze his own personality. During these years he may not once have encountered any repetition of the suggestion that he is mentally unbalanced, but his original reaction, which was initially accompanied by intense and prolonged " consciousness " of both emotional and intellectual varieties, has persisted without abatement throughout a period of years after the disappearance of the environmental stimulus. Probably most physiological authorities would agree that such a tremendously extended response represents not a single reaction, but a long series of reactions. Since most of these responses are centrally initiated, and all are unified to accomplish a single purpose, the original stimulus must have evoked a large volume of energy somewhere in the central nervous system which continued to control behaviour for a long period of years. In conformance with this idea, R. S. Woodworth[1] in his theory of " tendencies to action " and " preparatory reactions " holds that " damned up energy " may exist in the central nervous system for periods of months and years, escaping in tiny rivulets as the dam is punctured by appropriate environmental stimuli.

3. The more conscious a response is, the less its rhythm corresponds with the rhythm of the stimulus.

Habitual or reflex actions show a much closer correspondence between the rhythm of end effect and the rhythm in which the stimulus is received than do more conscious responses. In the swinging of a cane or regulation of a semi-automatic machine, the rhythms of bodily response are adjusted automatically to the rhythms of stimulation. This type of adjust-

---

[1] R. S. Woodworth, *Psychology*, New York, 1925, pp. 82-84.

ment is still more marked in such highly reflex activities as
skilled chorus dancing, playing the piano, or using a type-
writer.   On the other hand, the more conscious the action
becomes, the more the automatic correspondence between
rhythm of stimulus and rhythm of response tends to be broken
up.   Let the dancer become suddenly aware of her steps, the
typist of the keys, the pianist of his notes, and the established
rhythm is shattered.   Grace dissolves into jerky awkwardness,
speedful accuracy into hesitant blundering and rhythmic
harmony to lagging dissonance.   " Introverted " persons, or.
those customarily given to expressing a great deal of "self-
consciousness " while reacting to a stimulus, are notoriously
awkward   in   games   or   physical   exercises   requiring   close
approximation of the rhythm of bodily responses to the rhythm
of an environmental stimulus.   Their physical actions are
jerky, and indiscriminately slower or quicker than the rhythm
of the physical stimulus to which they are attempting to adapt
their own rhythms of action.   The increased consciousness
seems to interfere with the correspondence between rhythm
of stimulation and rhythm of response.

4.   The more conscious a response is, the less its intensity
corresponds with the intensity of the stimulus.

Within limits, the intensity of simple reactions, involving
little consciousness, corresponds rather closely with the
intensity of the physical stimulation.   A vocalist unconsciously sings louder if the volume of the piano accompaniment
is increased.   Small adjustments in the reactions of walking
are made " unconsciously " in response to differences in intensity of pressure stimulation presented by the path along
which one is walking.   A slight up grade which increases the
intensity of the pressure upon the feet and also increases the
intensity of muscular pressure upon the proprioceptive sense
organs, is " unconsciously " followed by corresponding
increase in the intensity of muscular exertion.   But in responses which are reported as involving a great deal of consciousness, there may be little or no correspondence between
the intensity of the stimulus and the intensity of reaction
to the stimulus.   In the case of the young psychiatric student
just considered, the chance remark concerning his possible
abnormality constituted a stimulus of slight intensity indeed.
The same remark, or similar ones, had probably been made
concerning nearly all of this young man's friends with no

particular effect, yet in the specific case cited it released a volume of energy regarded as "conscious", which was probably many thousands of times as intense as the stimulus, and which was also more intense than reactions to other stimuli much more intense than this stimulus. On the other hand, instances might be cited where increase of consciousness decreases intensity of response as compared with the intensity of the stimulus—as when the singer thinks "The piano is too loud—I will sing pianissimo and force him to follow". Or the reduction in intensity of the response may be a positive inhibition—this in turn to be accounted for by the positive agency of some active force within the organism. An example of an effect of this sort is to be found in the total elimination of overt actions which is caused by "pausing to think" after experiencing an irritating stimulus. One child may slap another child's face with considerable strength. Remembering the nursery adage of "count ten before you strike back", the assaulted youngster finds that by the time he had counted ten he does not feel inclined to strike back at all. Voluntary increase of consciousness seems to have eliminated reaction to an intense stimulus altogether. Consciousness, then seems, on the whole, to alter markedly the correspondence between intensity of stimulus and intensity of respose.

, 5. The more consciousness attaches to subliminal stimuli, the greater is their tendency to summation.

A stimulus evoking little or no consciousness, so far as the subject is able to observe, and which is too weak to produce a response, is not apt to bring about the reaction toward which it tends, even though the "unconscious" stimulus be repeated a large number of times. For instance, during my first two years of residence in New York City, I passed the Metropolitan Museum, riding in buses or automobiles, probably a hundred times or more, without making any move toward entering the building. On one of my earliest trips up-town a companion had pointed out the Museum, and I had formed a habit of looking toward that side of the street in passing. But my subsequent visual sensations, though they controlled eye movements, evoked no thoughts or emotions concerning the building or its contents. In short, visual perception of the Metropolitan Museum constituted an almost "unconscious" stimulus, of too slight intensity to arouse the reaction of entering the building, toward which it tended ; and constant repetition of this stimulus failed to bring about the final response.   After more than two years of residence in the city, a guest from another part of the country chanced to expatiate, in my presence, upon the wonders of the Metropolitan Museum. This stimulus, though it intrigued my interest temporarily, and was accompanied by many fully conscious thoughts and feelings, also proved too weak a stimulus to result in a Museum-seeing reaction.   More than a month later another friend expressed enthusiasm concerning the Metropolitan, arousing still more consciousness concerning it.   This stimulus, added to the first highly conscious stimulus, sent me to the Museum. It seems to me highly improbable that the numerous habitual-view stimuli entered into the final summation of energy which brought about the response, or that another two years of viewing the building almost daily would have resulted in my entering it.   One may argue, of course, that the two descrip-tions, by friends, of the museum's contents, were more intense stimuli than were mere views of the outside of the building ; and so they were.   But the point to be noted here is merely that two stimulations which evoked much consciousness added themselves together to provoke a certain response, while a hundred little-conscious stimuli failed to bring about the same result.   Many other instances of the same sort, from every-day life, might be cited.   A person may gaze " unconsciously " at a store, as he walks by it, every day for months, without entering.   A " window ticker " may then appear in the show-window, and the subject may become conscious of a momentary wonder as to how the thing works.   Next day this same consciousness concerning the ticker may again occur.   On the third or fourth day the individual is likely to enter the store and purchase the cigarette or other article advertised by the ticker.   It is not our present task to speculate as to *how* the additional consciousness was aroused by the advertising device ; it is our present purpose to note that consciously experienced stimuli tend to add themselves together more quickly and effectively, upon repeated presentation, to evoke the reaction toward which they tend, than do stimuli " un-consciously " contacted.

6.   The more conscious a response is, the more subject it is to fatigue.

The more consciousness accompanies any activity, the more quickly fatigue sets in, no matter whether the response is one of " thinking ", or one of violent physical exertion. Many a distance runner has found himself miraculously refreshed by some sudden roadside occurrence that " takes his mind off " his own movements. His fatigue, in other words, becomes less when the consciousness attached to his own running is lessened. A person whose continuous occupation is " thinking " along scientific lines may learn to increase his attention-span, correspondingly diminishing his mental fatigue, by ceasing to introspect upon his own thinking while he is doing it, thus cutting possibly in half the volume of consciousness accompanying his mental activity. Eventual physical fatigue is inevitable, of course, as a result of muscular fatigue products generated in the course of strenuous exercise or work ; but the tirelessness of a well-trained and hardened body is amazing when the muscular tasks undertaken are regarded as mere matters of course, and are performed, as far as the subject can tell, unconsciously. The endurance feats of the American Indian, and the astonishingly continuous exertions of the pioneer type of person, in all lands, are illustrations in point. Where much consciousness is, there much fatigue will be, also ; and the limits of endurance of unconscious activities, of all sorts, are difficult to determine.

7. The more conscious a reaction is, the more variable is the threshold value of its stimulus.

Another easily observable effect which consciousness seems to have upon responses to which it attaches is to render less predictable the exact intensity of environmental stimuli necessary to bring about the reactions in question. Simple reflex reactions can usually be evoked by physical stimuli of approximately the same intensity. There is a margin of variability even here. The knee jerk, for example, as Carlson[1] finds, shows marked increase of excitability, with presumable lowering of threshold stimulus intensity, during strong hunger contractions of the empty stomach. Nevertheless, even the difference caused by hunger pangs in the stimulus intensity necessary to call forth the patellar reflex, could not be measured outside the physiology laboratory.

[1] A. J. Carlson, *The Control of Hunger in Health and Disease, p.* 85, Chicago, 1919.

Activities more complex than the simple reflex but still reported to be unconscious are definitely conditioned upon a specific intensity of stimulus. The unconscious response to the legend naming the destination of the street car or 'bus may frequently fail to occur if the electric illumination of the sign be reduced only slightly. Persons frequently fail to stop a street car because the letters of the legend on the front of the car are smaller than those to which they have accustomed themselves to respond. Machine operators who depend upon a certain sound in the machine they are operating to set off a reaction of shifting gears, may fail to perform the required act if the sound has slightly less than the customary volume. A housewife, using an electric coffee percolator, and depending for a signal that the coffee is done upon a certain sound made by the bubbling water, may fail to turn off the electric current at the proper moment if the crucial bubbling sound be less intense than usual.

On the other hand, where the activity is more highly conscious, it is impossible to name a fixed intensity of stimulus which will invariably set off a given reaction. Consider, for example, responses which necessitate a great deal of consciousness such as a decision to play tennis or to take a two hundred mile automobile ride. Upon one occasion a normal subject may assent immediately to a casual suggestion that the tennis be played or that the trip be undertaken. Next day, perhaps, no amount of persuasion or even moderate financial inducement would evoke the reaction of playing tennis or driving the car. Should these very reactions become habitual, as a part of the subject's professional duties or principal life activity, his consciousness concerning the actions would be tremendously reduced, also the margin of variability of the intensity of stimulus to which he responded. Again, it is necessary to call attention to the fact that we are not considering at the moment the psycho-neural mechanisms by which these differences are brought about. The significant point seems to be that when a large amount of consciousness attends a given response it may be evoked at one time by a stimulus of very low intensity and at another time it may require an exceedingly intense stimulus ; while if an action is habitual or " unconscious " it is brought about upon all occasions by stimuli of nearly equal intensity.

8. The more conscious a response is, the more readily it can be inhibited.

Highly conscious actions are more easily susceptible to inhibition than are responses carrying little observable consciousness. A love response, for example, which may have occupied the consciousness of a young woman for many days or weeks, is frequently completely inhibited by a chance frown or impatient gesture on the part of the loved one. The most fiercely aggressive purposes of an adult human male, carrying with them both prolonged and intense consciousness, may similarly be interrupted easily by inhibition at a crucial point, even though the intruding stimulus be of no greater intensity than the disapproval of a partner or the absence from the city of another individual concerned in the enterprise. On the other hand, habitual responses such as walking or finding one's way to one's place of business through crowded traffic of a great city, may fail to be inhibited or impaired in the slightest degree even by the most intense variety of stimulus such as business failure, or the loss of a loved member of one's family. They are inhibited only when brought into consciousness by the loud honk of an approaching motor. If an adult eats food with his knife, he can only overcome such a fixed habit by making himself fully aware of his act every time he performs it. If 'a person is performing a task which requires him to think out every move, a single suggestion on the part of another may suffice to inhibit the response altogether. Consciousness, then, seems to be associated with ready inhibition of response.

9. The more conscious two or more responses are, the more they tend to facilitate or to interfere with one another.

There is, we find, another characteristic propensity of conscious behaviour which very closely resembles the ease of inhibiting just considered. Reactions of a simple reflex type to which little consciousness is attached do not seem to be markedly influenced by other responses which may happen to be simultaneously taking place. Highly conscious reactions, however, are readily facilitated or impeded by the addition of further conscious elements of behaviour. An interesting experiment, frequently performed by students of psychology, is to train oneself to write automatically while performing arithmetical sums, or while carrying on trivial conversation with another person. When this ability has been acquired, we have a situation where two reflex processes, each as slightly conscious as it is possible to make them, proceed simultaneously without any observable influence one upon the other. Similar effects of the same sort are found in every day life. A person with very little social training can converse readily on superficial subjects, while dropping sugar or lemon in his tea. An automobile driver is required to manipulate the wheel with one hand, turn on the lights, perhaps, with the other hand, regulate the accelerator by pressing down with his right foot, and let in the clutch by raising his left foot from the floor of the car. Frequently he must perform all these actions simultaneously and without mutual influence one upon the other.

What happens when the response is necessarily accompanied by a great deal of consciousness ? Suppose that a couple of research students are deep in discussion of the apparatus required for a given experiment. Another student brings into the room a piece of apparatus which he has used in his own work. Inspection of his apparatus requires the initiation of a new and complicated group of reactions on the part of both students concerned in the original discussion. Yet their inspection responses will be sure to combine in some way with the discussion already going forward. The new apparatus may harmonize with the plans tentatively evolved. In that case a very noticeable increase in the vigour and volume of the discussion will immediately occur. Or, as the apparatus is inspected, it may present hitherto unsuspected difficulties in the procedures under consideration. In that case the new set of reactions produced conflict with the preceding responses, the conflict manifesting itself to the casual observer in the form of hesitation, argument, and disagreement. There is little likelihood that inspection of the newly-presented apparatus can proceed simultaneously with the preceding discussion or that it even can alternate with this discussion without influencing it by way of facilitation or conflict or both. When responses already going forward attach to themselves much consciousness, it usually will be found impossible to undertake a new set of conscious responses simultaneously. If the super-added reactions fail to inhibit the preceding conscious behaviour altogether, which is always likely, the new reactions will combine with the old either by enhancing their efficiency ɔr by introducing obvious conflicts. Whether this result is due to what has traditionally been called " increase of associative connections " *pari passu* with increase of consciousness, ɔr whether it is to be explained by some more explicit neurological mechanism, the fact remains that the more conscious any two reactions are, the more likely they are to inhibit one another, to facilitate one another by alliance, or to diminish one another's efficiency by conflict.

10. The more conscious a response is, the more easily it is abolished or enhanced by drugs.

Highly conscious responses may be abolished completely by the use of drugs, while reflex reactions of low order involving little consciousness proceed with only slight diminution under moderate dosages of anaesthetic. In taking ether, the responses carrying the largest amount of consciousness are first abolished. The " unconscious " reactions proceed substantially undiminished after the patient has taken all the anaesthetic he is able voluntarily to inhale.

Other drugs, such as various forms of morphia and Indian hemp, in certain appropriate dosages, produce tremendous enhancement of the most highly conscious reactions while having a negligible effect upon the more unconscious types ɔf behaviour. The highly imaginative writings of DeQuincy may be cited as examples of intensely conscious responses greatly enhanced, according to DeQuincy's own report, by appropriate drugs. These same drugs at advanced stages of their influence upon the body may abolish or inhibit the habitual reactions, also ; but the first effect to appear as well as the most quantitatively marked influence seems to be exercised upon the most highly conscious activities of the subject.

W. W. Smith has shown[1] that moderate doses of alcohol produce what he calls an " all or none " effect upon the emotional responses of his subjects. That is, the highly affective reactions carrying with them a great deal of consciousness require a much more intense stimulus to set them off. When, however, these highly conscious responses are evoked, their intensity is out of proportion to the intensity of the stimulus. We have already noted that conscious emotions were subject to greater variability of effective stimulus intensity and also to less close correspondence with stimulus intensity than are

[1] W. W. Smith, *The Measurement of Emotion*, ch. viii., p. 124.

the little conscious, or " unconscious " responses. Smith's work, therefore, seems to indicate that the influence of small amounts of alcohol is markedly apparent in those responses to which is attached the larger amount of consciousness. Drugs, then, whatever be the direction of their effect upon the body, appear to exercise their influence more clearly upon the reactions involving most consciousness.

In summary, there are ten easily observable objective changes in human behaviour appearing simultaneously with the reported increase of consciousness, namely :

1. Longer period between application of the physical stimulus and appearance of bodily response.

2. Persistence of bodily responses after the physical stimulus has been removed.

3. Less correspondence between the temporal rhythm or intervals manifest in the reaction, and the time intervals at which the environmental stimulus is received.

4. Less correspondence between the intensity of the final bodily response and the intensity of the stimulus.

5. Increased tendency for several stimuli, each too weak to arouse the response by itself, to add themselves together and jointly evoke the reaction toward which they tend.

6. Greater fatiguability.

7. Greater likelihood that the same reactions will occur, at different times, in response to stimuli of different intensity.

8. Increased tendency to be inhibited by stimuli of comparatively slight intensity.

9. Increased tendency to combine with, or to conflict with, simultaneously imposed responses.

10. Increased susceptibility to the influences of drugs.

These ten behaviour variances, then, may be shown to appear in human behaviour *pari passu* with the reported appearance of consciousness. Like the sparks from Ben Franklin's kite-string they reveal a specific but as yet undescribed type of energy. Is this energy identical with consciousness ?

There is, of course, a logical possibility, not to be overlooked, that the effects noted may be ascribable to the same vitalistic-type cause that simultaneously produces consciousness, instead of the effects being ascribable to consciousness itself acting as a vitalistic-type cause. Elaboration of this logical issue, however, is largely academic. All the effects noted must be attributed, because of their positive nature, to some form of potent energy ; and it is more of a philosophical than a psychological issue to decide whether this potent energy *causes* consciousness or *is* consciousness. The later form of expression seems, for scientific purposes, more simple and accurate.

If there exists, then, a describable form of energy somewhere within the human organism capable of influencing behaviour in the ways noted, and if this potent form of energy is always found appearing simultaneously with consciousness, we may state, for psychological purposes at least, that *the form of energy thus discovered is consciousness.* Should consciousness turn out to be an energy by-product of the primarily potent form of force producing effects enumerated, then we should find inevitably a new series of observable effects which the energy by-product, consciousness, exercises, both over the parent energy directly, or over the physical behaviour results supposed to be produced jointly with consciousness, indirectly.

Consider an analogous situation. During electrolysis of water, two sets of physical phenomena are readily observable— the giving off of hydrogen gas, and the formation of bubbles on the electrodes. For a time, after the current is turned on, these two sets of changes run parallel to one another, and during that initial period the mistake might be made of attributing one phenomenon to the causal agency of the other, instead of considering both as results of a common cause, the electric current. But, after a short time, the formation of bubbles interferes, slightly, with the passage of the current, so that the more bubbles are formed, the less hydrogen is given off. This change in relationship reveals, at once, that a common cause of both phenomena must be sought. So far as my own researches reveal, there is no indication of a change in the parallel relationship between symptomatic behaviour and consciousness, which might suggest that both are attributable to a common cause. In short, granted a complete correspondence between symptomatic behaviour effects, and the appearance of consciousness without subsidiary variance, there is strong likelihood that consciousness and the primarily potent energy cause of the behaviour symptoms are identical. When the nature of this energy is discovered, it can definitely be described, like any other form of energy.

Consciousness Is Not Intra-neuronic Energy

What, then, is the nature of this conscious-energy ? Where is it to be found ? The simplest suggestion, in answer to these questions, seems to be that consciousness, in its physical aspect, is merely intra-neuronic energy. When physiologists, who naturally tend toward this hypothesis, are asked to account for the presence of much consciousness in some responses, and little or no consciousness in others, they reply that only in the more highly evolved portions of the brain is there a sufficient accumulation of nervous energy, or a sufficient intensity, or some other attribute of nervous energy, to produce consciousness. A few theorists may, perhaps, suggest that somewhere in the brain is a special kind of nerve cell capable of manufacturing conscious energy ; but, so far as reported to the literature, no new type of brain cell, differing basically from neurones in other parts of the central nervous system, has been discovered. Such a suggestion, therefore, represents sheer imaginative speculation, and need not be resorted to until all known sources have failed to yield a trace of identification of any known form of energy with consciousness. What, then, of the physiologist's proposition that a sufficient mass of nerve impulses, *per se*, may constitute consciousness ?

Does nerve trunk conduction actually correspond with consciousness ? There are many difficulties in the way of such a theory.

First, and most important, we find that the ten types of effect upon human behaviour enumerated above as probable results of consciousness, do not find their physical basis in intra-neuronic phenomena at all. They are, rather, attributable to synaptic influence. The ten varieties of end-effect mentioned, together with several other similar effects, are listed by Sherrington[1] as inhering in reflex-arc conduction only, and not in simple nerve-trunk conduction at all. Sherrington further shows that the salient characteristic of reflex conduction is the fact that synapses are interposed in the total nerve impulse circuit. It is at these synapses that phenomena occur producing the effects reviewed. That is to say, the fewer synapses in any nervous circuit, the less prominently may we expect the effects which we have seen to be typical of consciousness to appear.

[1] C. S. Sherrington, *The Integrative Action of the Nervous System*, p. 14.

The simple reflex acts, characterized by least consciousness, would contain, on the other hand, by far the greatest proportion of intra-neuronic disturbances, or simple impulses of conduction within the nerve trunk, and by far the fewest synapses. If these nerve trunk impulses truly constitute consciousness, as some physiologists maintain, there is a complete contradiction between evidence and theory. Where least consciousness actually appears, the greatest proportion of nerve trunk activity is to be found, and vice versa. It seems impossible, therefore, to define consciousness as the totality of changes, or energy within simple nerve tisŝue, since this does not contain the mechanisms for the effects most characteristic of consciousness in our every-day experience.
. In the second place, the same nerve trunks may be used for several purposes, that is, to convey impulses ultimately associated with two or more diverse varieties of consciousness. By the all-or-none law, each nerve fibre must respond *in toto* if it reacts at all. If, then, different units of consciousness ultimately appear due to ultimately diverse paths over tiny lengths of nerve trunk in the brain, could they escape marked resemblances, one to the other, when the greater portion of their purely intra-neuronic constituents had been identical? Pain impulses, for example, seem to travel during the first part of their circuit, at least, over identical sensory neurones with cold, pressure, auditory, visual, and many other types of afferent excitations, modally distinct in consciousness one from the other.

This point[1] has been adversely criticised by A. Forbes,[2] of Harvard Medical School, who cites the work of Adrian and Zotterman. C. J. Herrick,[3] however, states, " From this it would appear that most sensory nerves may, upon occasion, function as pain nerves." Herrick holds that the painful quality of consciousness is superadded to the ordinary sensory consciousness of the receptor apparatus stimulated, unless the stimulation is excessively strong ". Moreover, according to both physiological and psychological theories of vision, and other senses, excitations ultimately producing different sensations may originate in the same sense organ, thus making the

[1] The argument under discussion was advanced more briefly by the writer in " The Psychonic Theory of Consciousness," *Journ. Abnormal and Social Psychology*, July, 1926.
[2] In a letter to the writer.
[3] C. J. Herrick, *Introduction to Neurology*, 1920, p. 277.

long, afferent conductor paths to the higher centres identical. But no part of this identity seems to be left in the final sensory consciousness.

On the motor side, the term, " final common path ", speaks for itself. All motor impulses must travel final common paths with impulses originating from many different sources, so that all must have large identical elements of intra-neural excitement. Physiologists, to be sure, might attempt to avoid this further problem by denying the existence of such a thing as motor consciousness altogether, even though, in so doing, they introduce an inconsistency into their conception of consciousness by maintaining that half the nerve impulses of the body (motor nerves) are not conscious, while the other half (sensory impulses) are conscious. Without pursuing further, at this time, the arguments for and against motor consciousness, we may emphasize the fact that the lack of similarity in various sensory elements of consciousness initially employing identical afferent nerve paths still stands as evidence against the physiological theory that nerve-trunk excitement *is* consciousness.

In the third place, different neurons appear frequently to be used in manufacturing identical elements of consciousness. Centrally aroused sensation such as, for example, " memory " of the colour red, or of muscle sensations in the legs or arms, or of the tone of a violin, may be consciously no whit different from the originals of these remembered sensations when the sensations were evoked directly by environmental stimulation of appropriate sensory nerves. Yet we know that nervous impulses cannot travel backward down the afferent paths so that the actual nerve impulses responsible for the remembered sensations must differ greatly from the intra-neuronic impulses which brought about the original sensations themselves. If consciousness consisted of the actual totality of nervous impulses concerned, in each case, then a remembered red sensation might be expected to differ substantially from red sensations which resulted from nerve impulses travelling up the optic nerve. Granted that both environmentally aroused red and the remembered red sensation utilized the same final sensory paths in the visual centres of the brain, there would still be the entire amount of optic nerve trunk energy possessed by the original sensation but not by its memory. Is it probable to suppose that this added increment of energy, if this energy were consciousness itself, would add nothing to the totality of consciousness in the original red sensation ?

This proposition might indeed contain greater probability were it not that the optic tract nerve trunks are of great length as compared to the microscopic lengths of conducting fibres in the higher centres of the brain. If each unit of nerve impulse energy is conscious, it is hard to see how the very short conductor tracts of the cerebral centres could contribute a greater total amount of simple nerve impulse energy than could the long afferent nerve trunks ; and it is still more difficult to guess how the relatively tiny conductor trunks in the brain could contribute enough nerve impulses to obscure altogether the quantity of intra-neuronic energy contribued by the afferent nerve trunks. If, as previously noted, the presence of large identical units of nerve energy in the manufacture of different sensations does not make these different sensations in the least similar, no more does the presence of a considerable volume of nerve trunk energy in connection with a given sensation seem to cause the sensation to differ in the least from an identical sensation manufactured without a similar volume or locale of nerve trunk participation.

In the fourth place, although there seems to be a mnemonic factor intrinsic in the behaviour of a single neurone in forming habitual junctions with neighbouring cells[1] there clearly could exist no structural changes within the nerve itself which could actually constitute the process of functional conjunction, since this process by definition takes place in the synapse, externally to the intra-cellular protoplasms of all neurones concerned. Thus no train of consciousness could be consecutive or continuous, if it were regarded as being constituted by the changes within any nerve cell in a reflex arc, for whenever any nervous impulse passed from neurone to neurone the propagation of energy between the cells would be of a totally different nature[2] and so it would no longer be included in our

[1] C. J. Herrick, *Neurological Foundations of Animal Behavior*, New York, 1924, p. 112.

[2] C. S. Sherrington states : " . . . the intercalation of a transverse surface of separation or membrane into the conductor must modify the conduction," and : " It (the synaptic membrane) would be a mechanism where nervous conduction, especially if predominantly physical in nature, might have grafted upon it characters just such as those differentiating reflex-arc conduction from nerve-trunk conduction." *The Integrative Action of the Nervous System*, p. 17.

definition of "consciousness". Moreover, since all facilitations and conflicts between impulses seeking to use a common neural path must occur for the most part in the synapses between the antagonistic neurones and the cell which both sets of impulses are seeking to enter, such alliances and antagonisms could find no counterpart among "conscious" phenomena, were the latter confined to intra-neural activities. Yet frequently reported "feelings of conflict", "conscious thwartedness", and, on the other hand, "relief" and "feelings of harmony" seem most probably to depend upon these very extrinsic relationships between opposed and allied nerve impulses which we have been considering.

Finally, we know that different rhythms of stimulation, simultaneously applied, and using the same final common path to evoke the same muscular response, do not interfere with each other or break up the existing rhythm of response.[1] This would indicate that two separate nervous impulses, though they may use the same neurones simultaneously, do not fuse or combine in any way within the conductor nerve cells. If this be so, then identification of "consciousness" with intra-neuronic change would leave totally unaccounted for all those "psychological" fusions, alterations, and recombinations of "conscious" elements which are continually reported by nearly all observers. If such fusions actually do occur, as supposed, at the synapses, no possible change within the individual neurones in any reflex chain could ever give them "conscious" representation.

Consciousness is Synaptic Energy

We have seen, during the foregoing brief review, that there exist substantial objections to the definition of consciousness in terms of nervous impulses. We have, therefore, the question still with us : What is consciousness ? Before discussing the intra-neuronic theory of consciousness, ten types of effect which consciousness seems to have upon human behaviour were mentioned. These ten types of influence were cited as proof that an active energy is generated somewhere in the human organism possessing the attributes of consciousness. During discussion of the first of our reasons for rejecting the intra-neuronic theory, the fact was disclosed that, although

[1] C. S. Sherrington, *The Integrative Action of the Nervous System,* p. 188.

the ten types of conscious influence do not have their causal origin in nerve impulses of conduction, their origin is attributed by neurological authorities to whatever happens at the synapse. Sherrington lists some thirteen of fourteen phenomena as characteristic of synaptic influence upon nerve conduction as follows[1] :

1—latent period

2—after discharge

3—loss of correspondence between rhythm of stimulus and rhythm of end effect

4—interference with grading of intensity

5—temporal summation

6—fatiguability

7—variability of threshold value of the stimulus

8—inhibition

9—mutual facilitation and conflict of impulses (treated separately in Sherrington's original work)

10—increased susceptibility to drugs : also, irreversibility of direction of nerve impulses, marked refractory period, " bahnung ", shock, dependence upon blood circulation.

It will be noted that the first ten synaptic influences listed correspond to the ten influences consciousness exerts over human behaviour. It is quite easy, also, to discover close correspondence between consciousness and the other synaptic influences mentioned. Such discussion of these further correspondences is omitted in order to avoid too technical an excursion into neurological subject matter.

While human reactions, from the simplest to the most complex, probably depend upon reflex arc conduction, each arc containing, according to Sherrington,[2] at least three neurones and, therefore, two synapses, the more complex the reaction, the more complex must be the reflex arcs involved. That is, the more synapses have to be passed in any response, the more must be the synaptic phenomena under consideration. As the complexity of the arc is increased, the greater will be the volume of synaptic energy as compared to the volume of simple nerve trunk energy. And, as we have observed, the greater

[1] C. S. Sherrington, *The Integrative Action of the Nervous System*, p. 14.

[2] "The reflex-arc consists, therefore, of at least three neurones," Sherrington, *ibid*, p. 55.

the complexity of the reaction the more consciousness is to be found accompanying it. Simple reflexes and habitual actions are brought about by a maximum of nerve trunk energy and a minimum of synaptic energy. Simple reflex responses contain little, or no, consciousness, which the subject himself can observe. Complex subjective responses involve a maximum of synaptic energy, and a minimum of nerve trunk activity. These are the responses which are uniformly regarded as containing a maximum amount of consciousness.

The intra-neuronic theory supposes that consciousness appears only in the higher centres of the brain, because in no other place is to be found sufficient concentration of nerve impulse energy which is regarded as a physical basis for consciousness. "The higher centres" referred to, however, are located in the grey matter of the brain, and the grey matter is characterized chiefly by the enormous number of synaptic connections which are there operative. The grey matter is, in fact, chiefly composed of microscopically small neurones, each forming a large number of synapses with many similar neurones. The cerebral centres, therefore, where some physiologists suppose consciousness to be, are composed almost entirely of synaptic junctures.

Granted that the physical basis of consciousness lies in the higher centres, made up chiefly of tremendous numbers of synaptic connections, this fact, together with the evidence offered that the effects of consciousness on human behaviour are also synaptic, lead to the conclusion that *consciousness is to be identified with synaptic energy.*

Concept of the Psychon, and of the Psychonic Impulse

"Synaptic energy" is, however, a somewhat vague term. Specific types of energy are customarily defined by describing the type of matter within which the energy in question takes its origin. "Matter" is a word that is somewhat out of vogue, since it is now the fashion to conceive of matter itself in ultimate terms of energy. Nevertheless, if one understands by the word "matter" a form of energy so permanently established that it gives rise to a comparatively uniform sort of experience, it remains a very convenient word to use in a discussion such as the one we are now undertaking.

All physical science assumes that there is some sort of matter, moving. Description of any connected series of changes in any form of matter and its movement may aptly be termed a study of its " behaviour " in that particular level of complexity. Physics seeks to present basic descriptions of the behaviour of matter in its most elementary forms, the proton and the electron, and to trace the behaviour propensities of larger material masses back to the interaction of proton and electron systems, within the atom. Chemistry begins where physics stops, and deals with the laws of behaviour of the atom and the molecule, each containing varying numbers of protons and electrons. Chemistry deals especially with the laws controlling the combinations of atoms and molecules into more complex forms of matter. Biology deals with the behaviour of still more complex matter units, usually called " living organisms " of various sorts. Biology includes botany, which describes the type of living organisms called " plants " ; and zoology, which deals with another type of living organism called " animals ". Animals are matter-units of such extreme complexity, that their component parts become subject matter for several specialized sciences. Physiology specializes in describing certain parts of the animal termed " bodily organs ", and their behaviour. Neurology selects matter-units called " nerves ", upon which the behaviour of many bodily organs largely depends, and attempts to describe the behaviour of these nerves or neurones. If, then, there exists no further type of matter-unit capable of modifying neuronic behaviour, psychology, for all I can see, is out of a job. Should I become convinced of this state of facts I should feel compelled to consider psychologists in the same relation to neurologists as are carpenters to architects, and I should, for my own part, try to escape the fixed limits of craftmanship by studying my way into the ranks of my immediate intellectual superiors.

But, if, as suggested, there exists still another sort of matter unit beyond the neurone, capable of undergoing its own particular series of changes called " conscious " or " psychical " changes, and capable of modifying, by these changes, the behaviour of neurones, then, and then only is psychology truly justified in assuming a definite place among the physical sciences by the side of physiology and neurology.

Neurologists inform us that a specific conductive structure does exist at the synapses in all types of nervous systems evolutionally above those of the coelenterates. " It is generally

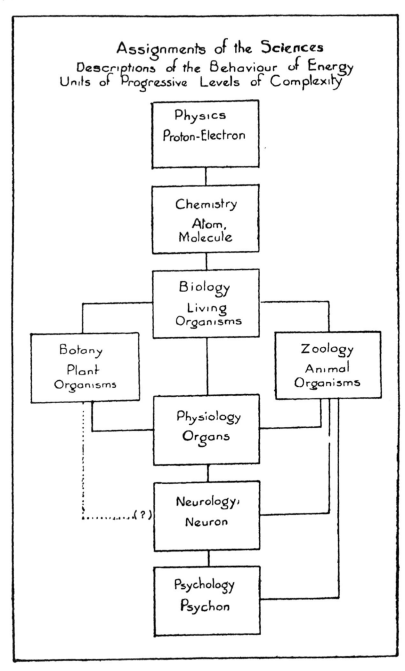

Figure I

admitted ", says Sherrington,[1] " that there is not actual confluence of the two cells together, but that a surface separates them ; and a surface of separation is physically a membrane. . . . It would be a mechanism where nervous conduction, especially if predominantly physical in nature, might have grafted upon it characters just such as those differentiating reflex arc conduction from nerve trunk conduction."

" In most groups of animals above the coelenterates ", says Herrick,[2] " the cells of which the nervous system is com- -posed (or some of them) are related to each other quite differ- ently from those seen in the meshwork of protoplasmic strands which compose the nerve net . . . there is a membrane separating the neurones. The presence of such a barrier at the synaptic junction does not imply that the neurones are not in protoplasmic continuity, for the separating membrane itself is living substance. What it does indicate is that there is a change in the physico-chemical nature of the conducting substance at the synaptic barriers. Langley has termed this barrier ' junctional tissue ', and of its great physiological importance there can be no doubt."

Physiologists, then, agree that there exists a special type of matter unit at the synapse capable of giving rise to a special type of energy which differs, in essential respects, from the nervous impulse. Neurological authorities, however, are not in such close agreement concerning the physical description of this junctional tissue. In the case of the giant Mauthner's cells, synapses between these cells and adjacent neurones can be seen and studied under the microscope by means of pre- parations in which the material has been fixed and stained. G. W. Bartelmez originally reported[3] that the knob-like endings of the axone fibres of the eighth nerve were seen in contact with the surface of the adjacent cell. Bartelmez saw a distinct plasm, or membrane, over the root fibres ; and, where the lateral dendrite was cut squarely, a smaller mem- brane could be distinguished around it. There is little delay at this synapse, yet Bartelmez found that two synaptic membranes forming a junction by contact with one another

[1] C. S. Sherrington, *Integrative Action of the Nervous System*, p. 16.
[2] C. J. Herrick, *Neurological Foundations of Animal Behavior*, 1924, pp. 104, 114, 115.
[3] G. W. Bartelmez, "Mauthner's cell and the Nucleus Motorius Tegmenti," *Jour. Comparative Neurology*, 1915, vol. 25, pp. 87-128.

Figure 2 THE SYNAPSE
(From Bartelmez, *Jour. of Comp. Neurol.*)

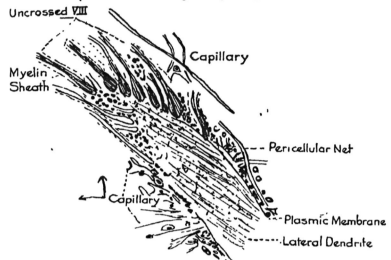

PART A.—" The detail of the VIIIth nerve endings, and pericellular net of the lateral dendrite of Mauthner's cell, drawn from a single section of an adult Ameiurus brain fixed in osmic-Zenker and stained with iron hematoxylin . . . The section passes obliquely through the base of the lateral dendrite, and shows the bulb-like endings of the VIIIth root fibres, and the fine meshed neuropil of the pericellular net on its surface."

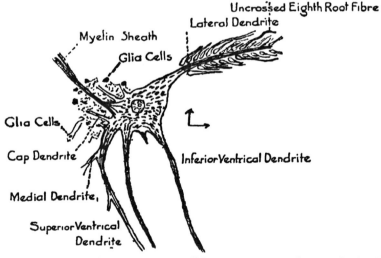

PART B.—" The right Mauthner's cell from a young Ameiurus male, fixed in a formol-osmic-Zenker and stained with iron hematoxylin. A semidiagrammatic reconstruction of ten sections, 5μ thick, magnified 250 diameters, to show the relations of dendrites and axone to the cell body and the two striking synapses of the cell, viz., the endings of the VIIIth root fibres (Uncrossed VIII) upon the lateral dendrite, and the axone cap covering the medial surface of the cell. Only four of the cap dendrites are shown."

had to be energized before conduction could continue through the recipient neurone. Marui, who used different fixing and staining solutions, reported,[1] on the other hand, that he was able to trace tiny connective fibres emerging through the outer membrane of the club endings, and that he traced these minute, protoplasmic threads into contact, at least, with the adjacent neurone. Says Marui, " it is clearly shown that the intra and extra cellular neural fibres communicate with each other ".

Bartelmez, in still a later paper[2], criticized Marui's technique on the ground that he had used formol in the staining solution, and that the use of this fixative was responsible for the false appearance of intercellular fibres. Such connecting filaments, Bartelmez regards, therefore, as arte-facts. Sherrington[3] in a recent citation propounds a theory of synaptic phenomena which seems to assume the existence of a membrane similar to that described by Bartelmez. Forbes,[4] on the other hand, has propounded a theory of the synapse based upon the idea that the various synaptic phenomena are results of nerve impulses in adjacent neurones being compelled, at the synapses, to communicate their energy through intercellular fibres of much smaller dimensions than the nerve trunk fibres. This view would be in accord with Marui's description of the physical appearance of junctional tissue, rather than with the view of Bartelmez. The exact structural description of the connective synaptic tissue must, it would seem, be left in some doubt for the present. I believe that it will make little difference to the theory of consciousness, herein proposed, whether the junctional tissue be thought of as a pair of sheet electrodes formed from the surface membranes of adjacent fibres, or whether the junctional tissue may eventually be described by comparison to the Tungsten filaments of electric lamps. Whichever observation may turn out to be most accurate, the evidence for placing consciousness at the synapse remains unchanged.

[1] K. Marui, *Jour. of Comparative Neurology*, Vol. 30, pp. 127-158.
[2] G. W. Bartelmez, " The Morphology of the Synapse in Vertebrates," *Archives of Neurology and Psychiatry*, Vol. 4, pp. 122-126.
[3] C. S. Sherrington, " Remarks on Some Aspects ot Reflex Inhibition." 1925. *Proc. Royal Soc.*, VCII, 519.
[4] A. Forbes. " The Interpretation of Simple Reflexes in Terms of Present Knowledge of Nerve Conduction," *Physiological Reviews*, Vol. II, No. 3, July, 1922, pp. 361-414.

In view of all the evidence, I submit the suggestion that *the totality of energy generated within the junctional tissue between any two neurones, whenever the junctional membrane is continuously energized, from the emissive pole of one adjacent cell to the receptive pole of the next, intrinsically constitutes consciousness.*

In expounding this theory during lectures, I have found it very convenient to employ a single term descriptive of any particular unit of junctional tissue which may be under discussion. Neurology, the science of nervous behaviour, dubs its structural unit the "neurone". Following this analogy, I have ventured to term the structural unit of psychology, which, as a science, must surely undertake the study of "psychical" or "conscious" behaviour, the "psychon".

Propagation of energy upon any psychon, or unit of junctional tissue, is definitely dissimilar in nature to the passage of nervous energy through individual neurones. Following the neurological analogy to its logical completion, therefore, we may term *any wave of physico-chemical excitation initiated within a psychon, a "psychonic impulse"*.

It is clearly established by neurologists that the principal function of the neurone is conduction. It is my suggestion that *the principal function of the psychon is consciousness.* Whatever conduction of energy may occur across a psychon seems incidental to the modifying major effect of impeding, regulating, and generally psychon's that energy in the course of its passage. The Tungsten filament in an electric light bulb conducts, to be sure, a certain amount of electrical energy from electrode to electrode ; but the principal function of the filament is, nevertheless, illumination. Thus, while we may probably regard the psychon as a certain sort of conductor of inter-neuronic energy, we may adequately describe its chief property only, I believe, as the generation of consciousness.

CHAPTER IV

Motor Consciousness as the Basis of Feeling and Emotion

The importance to psychology as a whole of obtaining a tangible psycho-neural hypothesis of emotion can hardly be exaggerated. At the moment, investigators in the field of emotions find themselves at sea between the Scylla of James-Langeism, and the Charybdis of youthful-minded adventurers in psychological research who would persuade us to hoist the Jolly Roger, abandon all theories, and all previous results and undertake statistical correlations of how all people react under all possible circumstances. These young pirates urge the irrefutable thesis that no knowledge is absolute, and themselves conclude that any attempted formulation of disconnected emotional data into anything resembling scientific law must be nothing short of maudlin.

Such new-found insistence upon the sanctity of unrelated fact is commendable in so far as it places just emphasis upon objectivity of research method. But the history of psychology's elder sisters among the sciences, and even of psychology herself, reveals a certain dependence upon constructive theory. The laws of Newton, for example, have received important modification at the hands of Einstein and others ; yet who can doubt the central importance of Newton's hypothesis to the growth of physics, and allied sciences ? The atomic theory may be inadequate as a formulation of present-day chemical data ; yet modern chemistry has climbed to its present height upon the scaffolding of that same atomic theory. So it is with the James-Lange theory of emotions. Psychology may be just at the point of outgrowing it, but must we abandon ourselves, forthwith, to an orgy of unscientific disorganization ?

Clearly, efforts are being made to drive the psychology of emotion in that direction. There is a certain self-important ease and nonchalance to be obtained by the method of putting out one's research results bare of theoretical analysis that has its appeal. And there is less danger of being contradicted. Yet, if psychology is to become the same sort of science that neurology and physiology are, for example, it seems to be necessary for somebody to take a chance and construct basic theories.

Physiologists' Disproof of James-Lange Theory

James' theory of emotion received two radically different formulations at his hands. The first formulation was contained in the simple statements : " We are afraid because we run away. We are angry because we attack." With this theory duly qualified, I am in entire agreement, and this book will be devoted to an attempted elucidation thereof.

When faced with the necessity of explaining his radical-sounding thought, however, James slipped over into an entirely different theory of emotion which agreed, substantially, with that of Lange. It is easy to see how James was forced into this contradictory transition. He had observed, introspectively and objectively, that bodily changes " followed directly the perception of the exciting fact ", and that " awareness of these changes as they occur, *IS* the emotion ". But when called upon to state how we could be aware of the changes occuring in our organism, as they occur, James found only sensory terms in existence with which to describe the awareness in question. If we didn't have sensations of the immediately resulting bodily changes, how could we become conscious of them at all ? So James was compelled to suppose that the initial bodily changes stimulated somatic sensory end organs, in muscles and viscera, setting up a second series of reflex arcs productive of bodily sensations. Shrewdly forecasting, perhaps, the reports of Lennander[1] and others concerning the paucity of visceral sensory mechanisms, James did not place the same emphasis upon visceral sensation as content of emotion as did Lange. Nevertheless, he accepted both visceral and kinaesthetic sensations as characteristic constituents. In so doing, we may note that James denied his primary thesis that " emotion *IS* the awareness of these bodily changes *AS THEY OCCUR* ". If emotion is made up of

[1] K. G. Lennander, " Leibschmerzen, ein Versuch, einige von ihnen zu erklaren," *Grenzgeb. d. Med. u. Chir.*, 1906, vol. XVI, 24.

sensation, then the important sensations are those set up as a result of initial bodily changes, and these sensations can only occur *after* the primary bodily changes. The refutation of this sensory-content formulation of the James-Lange theory, then, could be accomplished by showing that emotion persists after the sensations of which it was said to be composed have been eliminated.

Sherrington's Results

This work was undertaken by Sherrington[1], who performed appropriate spinal transections upon dogs, eliminating visceral and most kinaesthetic sensations following emotional stimulation of the animals. Behaviouristic evidences indicated that the dogs' emotions remained unchanged. One animal was stimulated with dog-meat, a stimulus never applied to this dog prior to operation. Evidences of what Sherrington calls " disgust " immediately appeared. Neither memory of previous sensations nor previous conditioning of symptomatic behaviour could have taken place in this instance. Sherrington concluded that emotion might be supplemented by sensations of bodily changes, but was not essentially composed of such sensory content.

Goltz's Results

· Goltz proved, conversely, that all emotions but " rage " did disappear after decerebration of dogs,[2] an animal preparation permitting the sensations of which emotion is composed, according to James-Lange, to remain, but abolishing the higher correlation and motor centres. No pleasure, sex response, or even appetitive enjoyment of food could be aroused in an animal thus prepared. From various supplementary data, Goltz concluded that " rage ", also, was a product of the central nervous system, but at a lower level than that required for the other emotions.

Work of Langley and of Cannon

Another approach to the problem of determining the rôle that visceral sensations play in making up emotion was made

[1] C. S. Sherrington, " Experiments on the Value of Vascular and Visceral Factors for the Genesis of Emotion," *Proc. Roy. Soc.*, 1900, LXVI, 390.

[2] F. Goltz, "Der Hund ohne Grosshirn," *Arch. fur d. gesam. Physiol*, 1892, vol. LI, 570.

possible by the work of Langley,[1] who described the " autonomic " innervation of the viscera. Langley's description indicated that if any part of the viscera were adequately innervated, large allied areas must undergo identical changes, and would, of course, produce identical sensations.

Cannon[2] was the first to apply this neurological fact to criticism of the James-Lange theory. After proving experimentally that practically identical visceral changes did, in fact, occur during " rage ", " pain ", and " fear " responses of animal subjects, Cannon pointed out that the conscious qualities differentiating these " major emotions " could not possibly depend upon sensory differences which did not exist. Cannon concluded, as had Sherrington, Goltz, and others, that emotional " response is a *pattern reaction* . . . in which impulses flash through peculiarly co-operating neuron groups of the central nervous system, suddenly, unexpectedly, and in a manner not exactly reproducable by volition. . ."

To an unprejudiced mind, not " brought up on " the James-Lange theory in its commonly accepted formulation, these physiological results would seem conclusive refutation of the idea that emotion consists of sensation. One loophole, however, has been pointed out frequently in discussion, by those who still cling to the sensation theory. Though any given emotion, experimentally tested, can be shown not to depend upon sensation, may not the emotion have been built up, originally, by compounding of sensations containing minute differences from other major emotional compounds, and subsequently remembered in connection with that type of stimulus ? If so, the sensation compounds must have been manufactured prior to birth. For Watson has shown[3] that human infants are inherently equipped to manifest at least three responses of an emotional nature, " rage ", " fear ", and " love ", without passing through any preliminary learning process.

Unsolved Problem

Thus we return, perforce, to James' simpler statement of

[1] J. N. Langley, " Sympathetic and Other Related Systems of Nerves " ; Schafer's *Textbook of Physiol.*, vol. II, 616-697, 1900 ; also *Ergebnisse der Physiologie*, Wiesbaden, 1903, vol. II, 818.

[2] W. B. Cannon, *Bodily Changes in Pain, Hunger, Fear and Rage*, 1920, N.Y.

[3] J. B. Watson and Rosalie R. Watson, " Studies in Infant Psychology," *The Scientific Monthly*, 1921, 493-515.

his own theory : We feel in a given way because we act in a given way. And our awareness of our reaction *as it occurs IS* the emotion. Unless we choose, like Watson, to deny that " awareness " or " consciousness " constitutes a physical phenomenon which psychologists are called upon to describe, we find ourselves squarely faced with the same problem that forced James into that untenable sensory-content formulation of his theory which we have just discussed.

The problem is : `How can awareness of reaction *as it occurs* be described in psycho-neural terms ?

Motor Consciousness Theory

Does anyone know why it has become so uniformly the fashion to assume that all consciousness is sensory in its ultimate nature ? Is not the denial of the existence of motor consciousness the real bugbear from which Watsonian behaviourists are fleeing in their insatiable insistence upon the importance of the motor aspect of behaviour ? Watson, for instance, inveighs with particular emphasis against " such elements as *sensations*, and their ghosts, the *images* ". " This thing we call consciousness ", he says, " can be analyzed only by *introspection*—a looking in on what goes on inside of us ". And it is true, of course, that many very basic presumptions of present-day psychology have been adopted by tacit assumption upon originally faulty introspective evidence. Perhaps the non-existence of motor consciousness may turn out to be one of these unwarranted, introspective limitations upon psychological theory. We have already, in fact, reviewed a considerable line of emotional evidence plainly pointing to unmistakable affective awareness of reactions *as they occur*. Let me defy Watson's categorical statement that consciousness can be analyzed only by introspection, by attemping an objective analysis of the case for the existence of motor consciousness on the basis of the previously suggested objective description of consciousness itself.

We concluded, in the preceding chapter, that inter-neuronic energy, supposed by Sherrington and other neurologists to possess entirely different characteristics from the disturbances propagated within the individual neurones, may be called " psychonic energy ". The further suggestion was advanced that there is considerable evidence for tentative acceptance of the hypothesis that *psychonic energy is consciousness*. •

Before continuing with this hypothesis, it might be said that the objective evidence for the existence of motor consciousness would not be any the less striking if we were to adopt other physical theories of the nature of consciousness, such as the physiological idea that consciousness inheres in every propagated neural disturbance. The general plan and structure of the central nervous system, and other points to be considered in favour of motor consciousness would remain equally applicable. Let us consider these points of objective evidence very briefly.

Proofs of Existence of Motor Consciousness

1. Biologically, motor function is primary and sensory and connector mechanisms secondary. Parker says[1] : " To state this conclusion in the terms used in the earlier part of this discussion, sponges may be said to have among their cell combinations effectors, but no receptors or adjustors. They mark the beginnings of the neuromuscular mechanism in that they possess the original and most ancient of its constituents, muscle, around which the remainder of the system is supposed subsequently to have been evolved." " This last conclusion is reinforced ", says Herrick, " by citing a number of cases in the higher animals where muscle may act independently of nerves, as in the human iris." Forbes,[2] in fact, has gone so far as to point out that muscle possesses capacity for the " single type of disturbance which seems to be a phenomenon common to muscle and nerve fibres."

It would be most unexpected, though of course not impossible, to find that the motor element, of which sensory and connector tissues remain but slightly divergent modifications, should itself completely fail of representation in the product, consciousness.

2. Motor neurones, in the central nervous system of human beings, are distinguishable from sensory neurones both as to cell structure and as to type of synaptic organization.[3] Motor

---

[1] Quoted by C. J. Herrick, *Neurological Foundations of Animal Behavior*, New York, 1924, p. 86. Quotation by Herrick, following taken from *same page*.
[2] A. Forbes, " The Interpretation of Spinal Reflexes in Terms of Present Knowledge of Nerve Conduction," *Physiological Review*, 1922, Vol. II, 361-414.
[3] C. J. Herrick, *ibid.*, p. 237.

cells have been shown to possess larger cell bodies, with a richer supply of chromophilic substance. In fixed and stained preparations, this substance is seen arranged in definite, discreet granules, and not diffusely, evidently for the sake of facilitating more rapid and powerful nervous discharge. The motor pathway, moreover, contains a minimum number of subsidary synapses, the large and powerful groups of motor impulses thus sweeping onward to their appropriate organs of discharge with a minimum number of interruptions, once these impulse groups have won the right of way at the central synapses. The motor cells, in short, are constructed for carrying larger and more powerful units of energy ; while the sensory tracts seem designed to carry smaller but more variegated impulse groups.

What reason is there to suppose that the smaller units of psychonic energy constitute consciousness, while the larger, simpler units do not ? Or, if consciousness is thought of as inherent in the nerve impulses themselves, why should more powerful accumulations of such impulses be supposed to have lost the conscious characteristic ? Moreover, the contrast between motor and sensory impulse characteristics, just emphasized, naturally suggests the corresponding contrast between the powerful but comparatively simple sweep of " major " emotions consciousness, and the less insistent but more variegated awareness of discreet sensations. If we find two types of neurone, two types of synaptic arrangement, and two types of impulse groups, what objective reason can be found for granting consciousness to one and denying it to the other ?

3. Again, motor phenomena may occur independently of sensory stimulation. Any given impulse or battery of impulses may be blocked at its entrance to a common motor path, not by rival impulse groups, but by the previously existing chemico-physical conditions within the nervous material itself. If sensation is the sole element of consciousness, such phenomena could never attain conscious representation, for they could only result in absence of sensation on the arc of stimulation. Is such an absence of awareness of motor obstruction compatible with the commonly observed ability of the subject verbally to report them accurately ?

4. Affective states accompanying motor discharge give

every evidence of being far more diverse than the ensuing sensations of resulting bodily changes could possibly be.[1] Conversely, many investigators report great diversity of bodily changes (with necessarily corresponding diversity of sensory awareness of these changes) resulting from motor discharge accompanied by approximately uniform emotional states.[2] The emotional consciousness, in both classes of cases, is evidenced by verbal report, and also by observed *motor attitude*, *or set* of the subjects, both human and animal. It is amusing to note the confidence with which various experimenters purporting to be utter disbelievers in consciousness, name a given emotion, and assume its existence in the subject solely on the basis of a motor attitude naturalistically observed without instruments of precision of any sort. Can it be that these cynical objectivists are depending upon their own *introspection* ?

If, however, we assume such reports to offer some degree of objective evidence in favour of the existence of emotional consciousness radically differing from resultant sensations, but closely agreeing with the motor attitudes, or pattern of the primary response, it becomes exceedingly difficult to correlate such emotional states either with sensations or with the conscious relationships between sensations. It is very easy, on the other hand, to account for such emotional consciousness if we are willing to correlate it with " motations ", or simple units of motor consciousness and their inter-relations in the primary motor pattern.

5. Affective tone may, apparently, be changed by altering the motor set, without the slightest change in associated sensations. In a series of experiments upon myself lasting over a period of ten years, I have three times succeeded in eliminating altogether the unpleasantness of severe toothache by changing my " subconscious ", or " unconscious " motor set from one of resistance to one of complete acceptance of the stimuli imposed. Each time, this change of motor set has been objectively evidenced by faintness, pallor, and drops

---

[1] W. B. Cannon, *Bodily Changes in Pain, Hunger, Fear and Rage*, 1920, New York.

[2] C. Landis, " Studies of Emotional Reactions," *Jour. Comp. Psy.*, 1924, Vol. IV, 447-509. (And other studies, all uniformly negative in findings).

in systolic blood pressure ; possibly to be accounted for by an opening of vagus channels of motor discharge hitherto closed against the pain stimuli. Twice the full unpleasantness returned upon resumption of resistant motor set.

Boring[1] and Carlson[2] both mention subjects in whom the unpleasantness of hunger pangs was absent. Instead appeared faintness, and passivity of motor attitude, nausea taking the place of food-seeking responses. I studied a subject of this type for three years, and succeeded in retraining her in such a way that hunger pangs now appear with very intense unpleasantness. The change in the subject's motor attitude, from passivity to extreme food-seeking activity, which has accompanied this restoration of unpleasantness, is very marked, and is, to some extent, verified, also, by systolic blood pressure readings. Another preliminary experiment, performed in 1926 under my direction, was the change in attitude of a number of subjects toward stimulation with hydrogen sulphide, presented at all times in a perfume bottle as a new type of perfume.[3] No pleasantness could be induced. But one subject, owner of a restaurant, so far lost unpleasantness, following change of motor attitude from resistance to acceptance, that he failed to understand why several customers left his lunch room after the bottle had been freshly opened during meal hour. Olfactory fatigue or sensory adaptivity can be excluded because of the length of the interval, twenty-four hours between stimulations.

All these results are very difficult (although perhaps not altogether impossible) to account for on the basis of changes in sensory consciousness alone. But the simple, obvious, explanation would seem to be found in the assumption that there exists a basic awareness of motations and their inter-relationships. Conflicts of motation, evidenced by resistant motor set, seem unpleasant : while removal of motor conflict seems to result in corresponding removal of unpleasant consciousness.

[1] E. G. Boring, " Processes Referred to the Alimentary and Urinary Tracts : A Qualitative Analysis," *Psy. Rev.*, 1915, vol. XXII, 306-331, at p. 320.
[2] A. J. Carlson, *The Control of Hunger in Health and Disease*, Chicago, Second Edition, 1919, p. 92 ff.
[3] Experiment performed by Tufts student, in 1925-1926, not yet published.

6. I have pointed out elsewhere[1] that the work of Head and Holmes[2] furnishes striking evidence of the dependence of effective consciousness upon freedom of motor outlet, and consequent increase in the number of motor conflicts and alliances taking place in the central nervous system.   When the inhibitory effect of the cerebrum is removed, through thalmic lesion, over-reaction and increase of effective consciousness simultaneously occur.   I spent nearly a year trying to work out an explanation of this and similar phenomena without departing from the fashionable assumption that consciousness is made up of sensations and their inter-relations, and nothing else.   Herrick and other neurologists have spent a much longer period upon the same problem, faced with the same bugaboo of denial of motor consciousness.[3]   Yet adoption of some such simple platform as the psychonic theory of consciousness not only permits, but necessitates, acceptance of motor consciousness as the true basis of feelings and emotions. By doubling the number of psycho-neural elements of consciousness accepted as basic, we do much more than halve our resulting complexities of psychological theory.   All rouud-about influences of motor set upon sensation vanish from discussion, and motation may be treated with the same objective simplicity as sensation.

But we have still to face the big guns of current psychological opinion, for psychology, at the moment, unequivocally denies the existence of motor consciousness in any form. Whence arises this attitude ?

Motor Consciousness Not Previously Identified with Affection

The ostensible reason for denying the existence of motor consciousness, as customarily given in the older days of psychology when it was thought necessary to discuss the issue at all, was the lack of introspective proof that discernable elements of motor consciousness could be identified in connection with resultant bodily movements.   That is, in response to a given sensory stimulus, and with kinaesthetic sensations

---

[1] W. M. Marston, " Thoery of Emotions and Affection Based Upon Systolic Blood Pressure Studies," *Am. Jour. Psy.*, 1924, vol. XXXV, p. 496 ff.

[2] H. Head and G. Holmes, " Sensory Disturbances from Cerebral Lesions," *Brain*, 1911, vol. 34, p. 109.

[3] C. J. Herrick, *Introduction to Neurology*, Phil., Second Ed., 1920 ; see especially pp. 284-290.

eliminated in one way or another, an arm or a leg might be moved, yet the subject, who was, of course, prevented from visual observation of his own movement, remained unable to say whether or not any part of him had been moved. To be sure, the results of some of these experiments were seriously questioned ; and cases, equally valid, at least, were cited by Wundt and others wherein certain paralyzed patients reported " innervation feelings " resulting from will to move the paralyzed members. ˙In these cases no actual movement or kinaesthetic sensations of movement were possible.[1]

Similarly doubtful reports concerning observation of, or failure to observe the " innervation feeling " or supposed unit of pure motor consciousness, have been printed from time to time. But, of late years, the issue has given way to other controversies of more simple and immediate interest, and psychology has gone on, serenely, putting up as best it might with a single basic category of consciousness, sensation, into which all conscious experiences have been squeezed, no matter how distorted they become in the process. It is small wonder that many psychologists have found some comfort in assuming that meaning, intent, and purpose, and other conscious elements of obviously motor character must depend upon an immaterial basis[2], since all available material basis has been pre-empted by the greedy presumption of sensation, and to define motor experience in sensory terms is an agony no accurate introspectionist cares to endure.

Actually, psychologists seem to have failed to find motor consciousness, all these years, simply because they did not know what they were looking for, and consequently did not recognize motation as such, when it was repeatedly thrust upon their attention. From earliest known speculations concerning the nature of feeling tone, or affection, come repeated assertions that feeling tone inheres in sensation, or that the affective qualities of pleasantness and unpleasantness are integral parts of sensory experience. So close has the introspectively observed union between feeling tone and sensation proven, that it has defied successfully the attempts of the most severe logical analysis to pull it apart. Curiously

---

[1] For brief summary and discussion of this early controversy, see E. B. Titchner, *Text Book of Psychology*, New York, 1912, p. 169 ff.

[2] Wm. McDougall, for instance, holds that meaning, value, purpose. and unity of consciousness have no physical correlates in the brain, W. McDougall, *Body and Mind*, 1918, pp. 175, 271, 298, etc.

enough, it seems not to have accurred to these psychological analysts to perceive, in feeling tone, the simplest possible manifestation of motor consciousness, under normal conditions.

Motation has been thought of as a *sensory awareness of movement*, and has, therefore, been sought in the impossible form of consciousness of passage of motor nerve impulses engaged in skeletal muscular innervations. Psychology has been looking for a sort of *motor-nerve sensation*, informing the subject whenever a motor impulse shall have passed over the nerve trunk under examination. Such awareness, if found, would still be sensory in nature. And were such an element of consciousness as an "innervation feeling" actually to be discovered, it must prove something of a mixture of imagined kinaesthetic sensations informative of movement, and sensory awareness of the object resisting movement (whether a limb of the subject's own body, or an environmental object). Such a composite experience would not, by any means, justify separate classification as a basically unique type of motor consciousness, since all its constituent elements would be sensory. Psychology, it seems, has been searching for a new type of being in the guize of a three-legged man, not realizing that, were such a person found, he would represent merely a monstrosity of the race already known.

Emotional Stimuli are Central, Never Environmental

There is, in addition, a psychological reason for psychology's absorption in sensation to the exclusion of motation. The stimulus to sensation is an obvious, environmental one; while the stimulus to motation, assuming motation to be integrative, psychonic energy in the motor centres, is a hidden, inaccessable stimulus. The particular motor impulses which, in synaptic juncture, form motation, flow from a stimulus concealed within the central nervous system and consisting of the resolution of sensory impulses evoked in the sensory centres by the initial, easily observed environmental stimulus. It is a commonly recognized fact that, while a given environmental stimulus always evokes virtually the same sensation on all occasions, these sensations may, at one time, be followed by feelings of pleasantness, and upon another occasion, by feelings of unpleasantness. The motor impulses evoked on either occasion can not be directly observed, though we have noted, earlier in this chapter, the possibility of indirect proof that different motor impulses are, in fact, evoked whenever different affective tones result.

It is not altogether surprising, therefore, that psychology, like Tito Melema in George Eliot's *Romola*, has taken the seemingly easiest way out of a difficult problem, by denying all claims for recognition emanating from the hidden source of its supply. Thus have psychologists unconsciously sought, by ignoring the central motor impulse situation altogether, to obtain a false simplicity of scientific description which should define feelings and emotions in terms of sensory consciousness.

Despite its present, fancied security, however, psychology cannot hope ultimately to escape the problem of determining the basic principles of both sensory and motor integration. It is by these integrative processes that the initial afferent impulses, mechanistically caused by environment, are manufactured into psychonic sensory energy units or sensations. It is by the now hidden attributes of these centrally produced sensation units that all forms of connective integrations, and motor integrations, are vitalistically caused.

Analysis of Intervening Factors Between Environmental Stimulus and Bodily Movement

The central, psychonic energy stimuli, which act upon the efferent nerves by exciting motor impulses within them, possess individual characteristics as distinctive and as definitely discoverable as those now attributed to sensory stimuli. They constitute intermediate, vitalistic-type causes in the total chain of causation connecting environmental stimulus with final bodily behaviour. Their nature and, consequently, their influences upon motor discharge are not determined predictably by the nature of environmental stimuli which indirectly evoke them, because there are too many intervening causes which are shaped, primarily, by the integrative laws of the subject organism, and by the condition of the organism when stimulated. If all these variables were known, then a complete psycho-neural description would have to include the following items :

1—Mechanistic-type causes ;
    (a) environmental stimulus, causing
    (b) afferent, sensory, nerve impulses, causing
    (c) sensations, i.e. psychonic impulses in sensory centres, causing

2—Vitalistic-type causes ;
- (d) thoughts, i.e. psychonic impulses in connector centres, causing
- (e) motations, i.e. psychonic impulses in motor centres, causing
- (f) efferent, motor, nerve impulses, causing
- (g) bodily behaviour.

The older, introspectionistic schools of psychology were inclined to skip from cause (d), thoughts, to cause (f) motor impulses, amalgamating cause (e), motations, with one or more of the foregoing units. It will hardly do, now-a-days, even for psycho-physiologists, to consider causes (c) and (d), since both are damned by introspective colourings ; so that a wider gap is now left, nearly all psycho-physical accounts jumping from cause (b), sensory impulses, to cause (f), motor impulses. In such accounts sensation and motations, both, are usually treated as occurring somewhere along the line of sensory excitations in the central nervous system. But the Watsonian behaviourists are the nimblest jumpers of all. They skip jubilantly from cause (a), the environmental stimulus, to final result (g), bodily behaviour. What a world of psychological trouble they think they are saving themselves ! But what unbridgable gaps would be left in the causal chain between stimulus and response, if these behaviourists really followed their own descriptive formula ! It would be like throwing a few drops of acid into a huge vat full of unknown, seething chemicals, and then analysing a sample of the vat mixture to determine the control which the acid-stimulus had exercised over the original contents of the vat.

The fault of the fathers of psychology, the introspectionists, lay not in trying to describe too many causes in the psycho-neural chain, but rather in omitting one very crucial cause, motation. For, as we have seen, the motor nerves and synapses possess a unique structure and organization of their own, and therefore require analysis and description as a basic type of cause in the total picture. " In short ", says Herrick,[1] " in both reflex and deliberative (including voluntary) reactions we may say that the nature of the neural process is abruptly changed when it ' turns the corner ' from the afferent to the efferent limb of the arc."

[1] C. J. Herrick, *Neurological Foundations of Animal Behavior*, New York, 1924, pp. 235-6,

Reviewing psychology's attitude in denying motor consciousness, we may compare it to that of a little child who is able to appreciate the causal connection between his own toys and Santa Claus, or the delivery man who brought them to him, yet is utterly unable to understand where the new baby came from. He thinks someone must have brought it, as his toys were brought, and he is speciously satisfied when told the doctor delivered his little sister. Psychology has been able, so far, to connect its sensations with causes that it can see and touch, yet it seems unable to connect its feelings with causes that are hidden and inaccessible. So psychology is satisfied with the suggestion that its feelings are brought, ready-made, by the same general type of agent already known, that is, the environmental stimulus. And, psychology further reasons, anything thus obtained, including emotion, must be a kind of sensation.

When psychology grows up, it will learn that there exist certain end-products manufactured exclusively at home. It will learn that, in the study of sensation, the stimulus is outside the body, while the response, sensory consciousness, is within ; but that, in the study of motation (emotion), the stimulus, connector-motor consciousness, is within the body, and the response, bodily behaviour, is outside. Both types of stimuli, and both types of responses must be described with equal objectivity. But easily observed environmental stimuli to sensation must be treated as causes, while readily measured bodily responses to motation must be treated as effects. If these underlying causal relationships are clearly understood and accepted, psychology should have a comparatively easy time of it figuring out the unknown quantities in both equations.

Summary

To summarize, I have tried in this chapter to set at naught the professional taboo upon motor consciousness. Analysing consciousness objectively according to either the psychonic or physiological theories, there are no less than six types of evidence tending toward the conclusion that motor consciousness must exist, constituting an equally important classification with sensory consciousness. Since the motor mechanisms of the central nervous system differ essentially in structure and organization from the sensory mechanisms, the suggestion has been made that motor consciousness in its physical machinery must be studied as a distinct and separate cause within the total psycho-neural picture. We have tried faithfully to set forth in order the series of causes which connect the environmental stimulus with the final bodily response. We have found one link in this chain of causation, motor consciousness has been ignored, so far, by all schools of psychology. Upon enquiry as to the probable reason for psychology's odd conduct in this matter, it has seemed most probable that motor consciousness has not been recognized because it has never seemed to occur to anyone to identify it with feelings and emotion. Psychology has been searching " innervation feelings " and sensation-like awareness of movement upon the chance of finding motor consciousness concealed somewhere therein. But, of course, it was not there. *Motor consciousness is affective consciousness.* The simplest units of motation or motor consciousness are the feelings of pleasantness and unpleasantness ; while next in the complexity series of motations come the primary emotions.

At the beginning of this chapter our analysis of physiological refutations of the James-Lange theory showed that by far the most important and pressing problem in psychology of emotions is the same problem that James first recognized and then answered erroneously. That problem is, how can awareness of motor response as it occurs be described in psycho-neural terms ? This chapter has proposed a new answer to this problem. We are conscious of our motor responses as they occur through motor consciousness, motation, or affective consciousness which are all synonymous terms. Motor, or affective consciousness is psychonic energy released within the psychonic, or connective tissues of the motor synapse of the central nervous system.

CHAPTER V

Integrative Principles of Primary Feelings

DENIAL of the existence of motor consciousness has brought psychology to an impasse in the field of theory of feeling tone, just as it has hampered the adequate development of theory of emotion. Wundt's[1] tridimensional theory of feeling tone, propounded in 1896, constitutes the only radical departure from general agreement that pleasantness and unpleasantness are the only two primary feelings. Wundt supposed that there were six primary feelings : pleasantness and unpleasantness, excitement and depression, tension and relaxation. Wundt's theory was based almost altogether upon introspection, probably accurate enough as far as it went, but not linking up the four extra feeling tone elements with definite psycho-neural mechanisms proving them to be primary feelings.

Titchener, also highly versed in introspection, maintained that " excitement and depression, tension and relaxation are general names for a very large number of different affections."[2]   That is, Titchener's own introspection led him to believe that the extra feelings named by Wundt, did, in fact, exist, but that they should be treated as complex affective experiences rather than primary feeling tones.   The only type of objective data advanced by Wundt in support of this suggestion consisted of studies (including measurements of physiological changes supposedly symptomatic of six affective primaries) designed to show that all six alleged primary feelings, as introspectively reported, occurred independently of one another, and especially independently of any connection with pleasantness and unpleasantness.   S. Hayes,[3] and others,

---

[1] W. Wundt, *Grundzüge der Physiologischen Psychologie*, ii, 1902, p. 263.
[2] E. B. Titchener, *A Text-book of Psychology*, New York, 1912, p. 251.
[3] S. P. Hayes, " A Study of Affective Qualities." Ph.D. Thesis Cornell. *Am. Jour. Psy.*, 1906, XVII, pp. 358-393.

published studies precisely refuting the results of Wundt in
this particular, tending to show that the four additional feeling
tone experiences were either intimately associated with
pleasantness and unpleasantness, or else were still more complex experiences not independently correlated with any
objective criterion which could be set by experimental conditions. The whole controversy gradually petered out ; and
with the decline of introspectionists' supremacy very little
has been heard of any list of primary feelings containing other
elements than pleasantness and unpleasantness. We may,
therefore, confine our attention for the present to a discussion
of the original pair of feeling tone primaries for the existence
of which there seems to be ample evidence of an objective
nature.

Primary Feelings are Pleasantness and Unpleasantness Originating in Motor Alliances and Conflicts

Theories of the physiologists and neurologists seem to be
fairly well in agreement that unpleasantness is associated
with conflicts or mutual interferences between nerve impulses,
while pleasantness is characterized either by an absence of
conflict or by a free unimpeded flow of impulses in the central
nervous system. C. J. Herrick[1], whose opinion may be taken
as fairly representative of the physiologists, says, " The normal
discharge then, of definitely elaborated nervous circuits
resulting in free unrestrained activity is pleasurable, in so far
as the reaction comes into consciousness at all (of course, a
large proportion of such reactions are strictly reflex and have
no conscious significance). Conversely, the impediment to
such discharge, no matter what the occasion, results in a
stasis in the nerve centres, the summation of stimuli and the
development of a situation of unrelieved nervous tension which
is unpleasant until the tension is relieved by the appropriate
adaptive reaction." And again, " The unrelieved summation
of stimuli in the nerve centres, involving stasis, tension, and
interference with free discharge of nervous energy, gives a
feeling of unpleasantness which in turn (in the higher types of
conscious reaction at least) serves as a stimulus to other
associative nerve centres to participate in the reaction until

[1] C. J. Herrick, *Introduction to Neurology*, 1920, Phila. and London,
pp. 286-287.

finally the appropriate avenue for an adaptive response is opened and the situation is relieved. With the release of the tension and free discharge, the feeling tone changes to a distinctly pleasurable quality." It may be noted that Herrick does not specify in which type of nerve centres, sensory or motor, the unrelieved summation of stimuli or the normal discharge of impulses is presumed to occur in order to evoke unpleasantness or pleasantness. Herrick says, however, in a neighbouring passage, that such a stasis may be brought about by the conflict of two impulses for the same final common path. Such mutual facilitation and interference of nerve ,impulses must be presumed to occur in some appropriate connector or motor centre of the central nervous system.

The work of Head and Holmes[1] clearly indicates that whatever changes in nerve impulse behaviour are to be associated with increases of pleasantness and unpleasantness are to be found chiefly upon the motor side of the various reflex arcs involved. These authors studied human subjects suffering from thalamic lesion. The most important effect of the lesion in these cases was to remove a considerable proportion of the normal inhibitory influence exercised by the cerebral hemispheres over the motor discharge. The behaviour changes as noted by Head and Holmes consisted of exaggerated physical reactions to sensory stimuli with parallel increase in the pleasantness or unpleasantness which was felt in connection with the sensation experienced. There seemed to be no change in the sensory threshold nor any significant alteration of any part of the purely sensory reaction. The whole effect, in short, was upon the motor side rather than the sensory, and it was this increase in the number and degree of motor alliances and interferences which corresponded exactly with the increase of pleasantness and unpleasantness as reported by the subjects.

As a result of this research and other similar data accruing to psychology from the medical sciences, it is generally assumed that the free flow of nervous energy as well as the mutual conflicts and interferences between nervous impulses which the physiologists and neurologists definitely correlate with affective tone, are to be looked for primarily in the motor centres rather than in the sensory centres. R. S. Woodworth,

[1] H. Head and G. Holmes, " Sensory Disturbances from Cerebral Lesions," *Brain*, 1911, vol. 34, p. 109.

for instance, expresses his interpretation in this fashion,[1] " Putting this fact into neural terms, we say that pleasantness goes with a neural adjustment directed towards keeping, towards letting things stay as they are ; while unpleasantness goes with an adjustment towards riddance." A "neural adjustment towards letting things stay as they are " must consist of a free flow of unobstructed motor impulses, all in alliance, because all are directed toward a unified behaviour pattern of the whole organism which .is meeting with no opposition. An " adjustment toward riddance " must with equal certainty consist of a motor set rather than sensory set ; and carries, also, suggested implication that there is some motor conflict with the object which the individual would rid himself of. Motor sets, then, seem to be regarded as neurologically responsible for primary feelings rather than sensory sets.

How Do Motor Alliances and Conflicts Reach Consciousness ?

This result confronts psycho-physiological theory of feelings with the same problem faced by the theory of emotions considered in the last chapter. The p:oblem is : If our primary feelings of pleasantness and unpleasantness depend upon alliances and antagonisms between nerve impulses in the motor centres, how does this motor phenomenon ever reach consciousness ?

Theories That Feeling Is an Integral Part of Sensation

Two different methods have been used in attempting the impossible task of getting motor phenomena into consciousness in terms of sensation. The first method, employed by many psychologists of the older school, consisted of setting up the simple hypothesis that feeling is merely an integral part of sensation. Pleasantness or unpleasantness would then be referred to as aspects of sensory experience, and we should be compelled to assume there is no sensation free from affective tone. This assumption would not be so far from the truth, but it is far more difficult to account for the changes in feeling tone which a given sensation may undergo without any change whatsoever in the sensory stimulus. The change in feeling seems to accompany a change in motor response to the sensation experienced, rather than to inhere in the sensory conscious-

[1] R. S. Woodworth, *Psychology*, New York, 1925, p. 178.

ness itself. There remains also, the extreme difficulty of finding any neurological mechanism by which a motor effect that takes place *after* could be reflected back in such a way that it could become an integral portion of the sensory event which had gone before and which might well have been completed by the time the motor phenomenon occurred.

During my own approach to the problem, being awed, at the time, by Psychology's current taboo on motor consciousness, I worked for the better part of an academic year in trying to discover in the literature of either psychology or neurology feasible mechanisms by which motor conflicts and alliances could be conceived of as adding feeling tone to their preceding sensations. The best expedient which I was able to hit upon was to suppose that a motor blockage might cause the sensory impulse blocked to increase its intensity in the sensory centres, above the upper limen of qualitatively distinct sensory consciousness ; while mutual facilitation of motor impulses might be supposed to result in a drop of intensity in the sensory impulses below the lower limen of sensation. This theory only defined pleasantness and unpleasantness as near-sensations (that is, supra-liminal and sub-liminal sensory awareness), but it was the best I could do in warping motor phenomena into sensory terms. I thought the suggestion a rather ingenious one, at the time I worked it out, but after some two years of observation and experiment I found that there was just one trouble with the theory. It wasn't so. Feelings, and the motor phenomena upon which they depend, simply cannot be defined even in near-sensory terms. They distinctly occur *after* the sensation is completed, and with entire independence of it. I was driven, after thus disproving my own theory, to abandon altogether, as most psychologists had done before me, any attempt to regard affective tone as an integral aspect of sensation.

Theories That Visceral Sensations Are Also Feelings

The second method, a modern one, by which even at the present moment, many psychologists are striving to drag motor phenomena into consciousness in terms of sensation, is the arbitrary appropriation of certain sensations, usually visceral ones, to constitute feeling tone *ipso facto*. Just why visceral sensations are so generally thought to possess especial affective value would be very hard to say. One reason probably is that these sensations were for a long time much less definitely known and recognized than are the sensations having their origin at the surface of the body. It was not until 1912 that Cannon and Washburn succeeded in identifying stomach sensations with hunger,[1] while the works of Carlson,[2] Boring[3] and others in experimental examination of sensations from the alimentary tract are also the work of the present generation. These experimenters have definitely shown that visceral receptors are meagre but specific, responding to extremes of temperature, pressure and pain. They evoke recognizable sensations. They do not evoke feelings. If, according to the James-Lange champions, primary feelings and emotions are composed entirely of visceral sensations, how is it possible to account for the fact that visceral sensations possess double characteristics, being felt both as sensations and also as feelings, while other sensations produced by corresponding receptor mechanisms from the external surface of the body, possess but the single characteristic of sensation ?

However, such a slight peculiarity in the psycho-physiological make-up might not deter the energetic psychologist from pursuing this visceral-affection theory, were it not for other and more insurmountable difficulties. Unfortunately for James-Lange addicts, there does exist definite experimental evidence which precludes the theoretical revamping of visceral sensations into feeling-tone consciousness. As noted in the last chapter, Cannon has shown (following Langley's description of the autonomic innervation of the viscera) that visceral changes resulting from motor discharge from the central nervous system occur in large and uniform patterns. That is to say, the autonomic motor nerves which influence the viscera operate on the principle of a non-synaptic nerve net. If one portion of the viscera, therefore, is altered in a certain way, all the visceral regions controlled by that section of the nerve net are similarly and simultaneously influenced. Cannon has shown that as a result of this situation, different emotions and affective states produce identical visceral changes. If the

[1] W. B. Cannon and A. L. Washburn, " An Explanation of Hunger," *Am. Jr. of Physiology*, 1912, vol. XXIX, pp. 442-445.

[2] A. J. Carlson, *The Control of Hunger in Health and Disease*, Chicago, 1916, Ch. VII, p. 101, *The Sensibility of the Gastric Mucosa*.

[3] E. G. Boring, " The Sensations of the Alimentary Canal," *Am. Jour. Psychology*, 1915, vol. XXVI, pp. 1-57.

changes in the viscera are identical, how can the sensations resulting from these changes be different ? Cannon states that they cannot be : and concludes that, " It would appear the bodily conditions which have been assumed by some psychologists to distinguish emotions from one another must be sought for elsewhere than in the viscera."[1]

One would think that the physiologists' conclusion in this matter would be accepted as final, but a few psychologists, driven on, apparently, by the frantic urge to squeeze feeling tone into sensation by hook or by crook, have persisted to the last ditch in trying to find some loop hole in the physiologists' dictum. One such attempt is that of Allport, who says :[2] " The cranio-sacral division of the autonomic, . . . innervates those responses whose return afferent impulses are associated with the conscious quality of pleasantness. The sympathetic division produces visceral responses which are represented in consciousness as unpleasantness." This idea is precisely what Cannon believed his results had disproved. But Allport attempts to use his own version of Cannon's results to support the visceral affection hypothesis. Allport quotes Cannon as stating that pleasant toned emotions result in motor discharge through the cranial and sacral branches of the autonomic nervous system, and that all unpleasant emotions uniformly discharge into the viscera through the sympathetic (thoracio-lumbar) division of the autonomic system. I am sure that Allport had no intention of deliberately misinterpreting Cannon's results, and so we cannot but suppose that Allport, in his visceral-affective zeal, *over*-interpreted Cannon's work in a rather surprising way. For Cannon states[3] : " In terror, rage, and intense elation, for example, the responses in the viscera seem too uniform to offer a satisfactory means of distinguishing states which in man, at least, are very different in subjective quality." Terror, rage, and intense elation according to Cannon result in sympathetic motor discharge, as do also emotions producing sexual orgasm, and " anxiety, joy, grief, and deep disgust."[4]

[1] W. B. Cannon, *Bodily Changes in Pain, Hunger, Fear and Rage*, New York and London, 1920, p. 280.
[2] F. Allport, *Social Psychology*, Cambridge, 1924, p. 90.
[3] W. B. Cannon, *Bodily Changes in Pain, Hunger, Fear and Rage*, New York and London, 1920, p. 280.
[4] W. B. Cannon, *Bodily Changes in Pain, Hunger, Fear and Rage*, New York and London, 1920, p. 279.

Can we believe that Allport regards intense elation, joy, and the climax of sexual emotion as unpleasant emotional states ? If not, then Allport's theory that sensations caused by sympathetic motor impulses constitute unpleasantness finds itself contradicted. Similarly, Cannon emphasizes the fact that various intensely unpleasant emotions, such as extreme fear, may result in sacral motor discharge causing evacuation of the bladder and colon. In this observation of Cannon's, Allport must find singularly little support for the second part of his theory which identifies pleasantness with sensations caused by sacral-cranial discharge.

The acme of ingenuity in visceral-affection theories has been reached by W. W. Smith.[1] It must first be explained that Smith names his affective elements "positive feeling tone" and " negative feeling tone ", defined as those feelings which promote or delay, respectively, associative recall of memorized words. These feelings, he says, are " very close to " pleasantness and unpleasantness. Smith begins discussion by committing himself " four-square " to the James-Lange theory of emotion, and further presupposes that all affective states are composed of nothing but " endo-somatic sensations ". His problem then is : *What* endo-somatic sensations constitute positive feeling tone, and of what sensations is negative tone composed ? Smith's answer, like that of so many others, is based upon the motor-impulse situation ; and, like the others mentioned, he identifies positive feeling tone with harmonious motor discharge from co-operating " ideas ", and negative affective tone with conflicting motor discharge from opposed " ideas ".

Then comes Smith's bid for the rôle of miracle-worker. He attempts to translate these harmonious and conflicting motor impulses into sensory consciousness in an extremely novel way. The motor impulses, he says, are subliminal ; yet they have the extraordinary ability to evoke, in some way difficult to comprehend, the visceral sensations which constitute the actual conscious content of positive or negative feeling. If the " subliminal innervations of the physiological mechanisms ", says Smith, are incompatible, " endo-somatic sensations are thereby generated which, when perceived, give rise to one variety of affective tone " (negative). Relative

[1] W. W. Smith, *The Measurement of Emotion*, New York and London, 922.

relief from this war of the subliminally evoked endo-somatic sensations gives positive affective tone, which " is in the nature of a contrast effect ". Astounding doctrine ! Allport may have revised Langley and Cannon to suite himself by insisting that identical visceral sensations can be different according to the pleasantness or unpleasantness of the emotions that cause them, but Smith has gone him one better. Smith assumes not only that a nerve-net type of conductor is capable of effecting differential visceral changes, but he also appears to suggest that subliminal motor impulses, playing about within this nerve-net, can somehow rise above their own categorical limitations and produce end-effects more emotionally potent than could be brought about by the most intense supra-liminal impulses. Long life to this theory ! May it survive as a monument to future generations symbolizing the heights of acrobatic mentality scaled by man in the brave though futile cause of glorifying his visceral sensations !

Unsolved Problem

It can be seen, even from the above abbreviated review, that many authorities are in substantial agreement as to the physical basis underlying pleasantness and unpleasantness. Yet, despite this fundamental agreement that feeling tone depends upon alliance or conflict of motor set, both methods of translating motor impulses into sensory consciousness have fallen flat. On the one hand, the facts do not support the assumption that motor phenomena can retroactively imbue preceding sensations with their own attributes. On the other hand, motor discharge which is admittedly linked with strong affective tone, has been found by the physiologists to be incapable of producing sensations sufficiently potent or diverse to correspond in any way with the associated feelings of pleasantness and unpleasantness. The problem of getting affective or motor discharge into consciousness remains unsolved.

Feeling Tone is Motor Consciousness, or Motation

My own solution has already been suggested in the last chapter. I have ventured to step in where angels fear to tread. I have entered the gates of motor consciousness long guarded by psychology's sacred taboo. Once one has entered this forbidden territory, however, one finds the building materials for affective and emotional theories ready-cut and prepared for immediate use. Accepting the conclusion agreed upon by the authorities cited, that motor facilitations and conflicts underlie pleasantness and unpleasantness, I have only to select appropriate units of psychonic energy necessarily generated in the motor centres where these motor impulses are integrated and, behold ! these items of motor consciousness *are* pleasantness and unpleasantness. If one accepts the existence of motor consciousness, then, there is no necessity for devising a round-about way of accounting for our affective awareness of the result of motor discharge. The awareness has already occurred at the psychons where the motor impulses in question had their origin.

Integrative Principles of Pleasantness and Unpleasantness

Connector nerve impulses arrive at certain original motor psychons from various associative centres of the brain, and are there integrated into specifically directed motor impulses. These specific motor impulses in turn, are obliged to form several sets of subsequent psychonic connections with each other and with motor impulses previously occupying the paths which they seek to enter. At all the psychons in this series, between the highest motor centres of the brain and the final common nerve paths leading to the muscles or glands innervated, integrative relationships of alliance or antagonism may exist between the various motor nerve disturbances combined at the psychons in question. Each of these synaptic combinations of motor impulses, therefore, must be expected to give rise to one of the two primary elements of motor consciousness, pleasantness or unpleasantness, as well as to form complex varieties of motation corresponding with superadded complexities of impulse relationship.

According to this suggestion, the mutual facilitation of any two motor impulses on a motor psychon constitutes, ipso facto, conscious pleasantness. Antagonism between two or more motor impulses within any motor psychon constitutes conscious unpleasantness.

Causal Attributes of Pleasantness and Unpleasantness as Primary Elements of Motation

Pleasantness and unpleasantness, according to the theory proposed, are the primary elements of motor consciousness,

But primary elements, as here used, must not be taken to mean an element or unit from which all more complex motation can be derived. It seems to me a mistake in conceptual understanding of causation, for instance, to think of water as composed of nothing but hydrogen and oxygen. Or, to put it the other way, it seems a mistake to think of hydrogen and oxygen as containing within themselves all the materials from which water is made. The correct view seems rather to be that the simpler energy units composing the atoms of hydrogen and oxygen possess the capacity, when brought into more complex relationship by the combination of hydrogen and oxygen in certain quantitative proportions, to generate a still more complex stabilization of energy ; namely, water. This more complex energy form contains, it is true, atoms of hydrogen and oxygen, but it contains, also, additional energy units which are its own and which did not exist before in either the hydrogen atom or the oxygen atom or in both. This concept is but another application of our fundamental analysis of physical science into mechanistic-type and vitalistic-type causes. The hydrogen and the oxygen, acting as mechanistic causes, create water which thereupon, as a vitalistic-type cause, possesses powers not resident in either of its so-called elements. In the same way, for the sake of clarity of thought and removal of prejudice against the general concept of " primary elements ", it seems advisable to think of pleasantness and unpleasantness as simple, integrative units, the constituent units of which may combine in still more complex ways, forming still more complex units of affective tone. Such complex, affective units, therefore, while all of them may contain pleasantness or unpleasantness, or both, must be expected to possess new attributes of motation which are actually not present in pleasantness and unpleasantness *per se.*

Possible Objections To Proposed Theory of Pleasantness and Unpleasantness

What are the objections to the hypothesis that pleasantness and unpleasantness are based upon simple facilitation and conflict of impulses ? One objection sometimes argued, maintains that unpleasantness can not be based upon motor conflict because some of our swiftest reactions are intensely unpleasant. The argument is taken that swift actions could not result from motor conflicts and that, therefore, we find intense unpleasantness present without corresponding motor interference. This objection, however, like so many of our present psychological difficulties, is based upon failure to work out clearly the nerve impulse situation which is under discussion. While it is certainly true that swiftness of re-action does not result from the motor conflict element of preceding integration, it is also true that nearly all swift action taken in an emergency *causes* motor conflicts. If, for example, one is walking serenely along a country lane, "day dreaming" of pleasant experiences to come, and if a car, rushing down from behind, honks its horn, the startled dreamer may leap off the road in record time. There existed no dimunition of the motor impulses which succeeded in gaining outlet and which resulted in the jump. But what of the impulses which had been controlling the body and mind a moment before ? The large volume of motor discharge which had successfully found outlet just before the horn sounded, was interrupted, and rudely cut off altogether from motor outlet by the jumping impulses. A motor conflict, therefore, must have existed, and the very intensity of the successful motor discharge bears testimony to the fact that the previously existing motor setting was interrupted by force rather than by harmonic readjustment. Such instances of swift and efficient action under stress of danger seem to offer evidence tending to identify unpleasantness with motor conflict, rather than offering any evidence against such identification.

Conversely, the objection has been urged that pleasantness cannot depend upon positive facilitation since its resulting emotions appear to be of slow, easy-going variety, like the stroll down a country lane mentioned. This objection, again, seems not fully to grasp the exact neurological relationships involved. The relationship of mutual facilitation between impulses simultaneously passing over a given psychon is not to be confused with the intensity of the resulting motor excitation within the final efferent paths. Forbes and Gregg have, in fact, shown that the normal limit of excitation in any individual nerve fibre is quickly reached and that an intense stimulus thereafter super-imposes a sort of secondary rhythm upon the normal disturbance within the nerve.[1]   Thus,

---

[1] A. Forbes and A. Gregg, " Electrical Studies in Mammalian Reflexes," *Am. Jour. of Physiology*, vol. XXXIX, Dec. 1915, pp.

it seems clear that complete mutual facilitation of motor impulses free from secondary interference impulse waves can only occur if the impulses in alliance are of notably low intensity. The swiftness and decision of muscular movement is a product not of the completeness of facilitation existing at any motor psychon, but rather of the intensity of the successful motor impulses which contract the muscles used. It is, in short, the completeness with which two motor impulses blend, that is to be thought of as fixing the degree of pleasantness of which we are conscious. The intensity of motor discharge has nothing to do with the matter, except that it will become increasingly difficult for two or more motor impulses to effect complete alliance in proportion as the intensity of either impulse is increased. In other words, the more swift and abrupt any physical action becomes the more difficult it will be to make this action completely pleasant.

Another objection sometimes raised to the identification of pleasantness with free and unimpeded discharge of motor impulses rests upon the argument that practising any reaction makes it more smooth-running, and free from synaptic obstruction. The more habitual a given action becomes, therefore, the more unimpeded must be the motor discharge which produces it. Yet, such actions, it is said, are not more pleasant than less practised responses, but rather tend to become increasingly indifferent in feeling tone. The initial fallacy in this argument is that free discharge of motor impulses is by no means synonymous with mutual facilitation of impulses at the junctional psychons. While it is true that habitual actions attain a maximum freedom of motor discharge, it is not true that habitual actions are the product of

232-233. " When a mammalian nerve trunk, such as the sciatic or one of its major branches (popliteal or peroneal) in the cat, is stimulated with single induction shocks of graded intensity, and the resulting action currents are recorded monophasically with the string galvanometer, the magnitude of the electrical response normally increases with increasing stimuli until the latter have reached a value in the neighbourhood of 40 Z units ; with further increase in strength of stimulus no further increase in response occurs so long as this retains the form typical of a simple action current record, in short there is a limiting maximal value to the action current. When the increase in the strength of induction shock is carried far enough (usually about 200 Z in round numbers) the electrical responses no longer appear as simple curves, but show deformation which becomes increasingly marked as the strength of shock is further increased."

G

a maximal amount of facilitation between different groups of motor impulses. Quite the contrary. The more habitual an action becomes the more it tends to approximate the lower reflexes of the body. That is, those reflexes which employ a minimum number of synapses and maintain a continuously unimpeded discharge of energy across a single motor synapse, might be expected, according to the psychonic theory of consciousness, to produce a minimum of consciousness of any sort. While responses requiring motor impulse combinations at hundreds, or perhaps thousands of motor synapses might be expected to result in a maximal amount of facilitation (pleasantness) or interference (unpleasantness). The indifference of habitual actions, therefore, again offers positive proof for the theory proposed and seems in accord with it at every point.

The statement that the mere practicing of given responses renders them indifferent or less pleasant is far from fact. Such a proposition would suggest that the " dud " at golf enjoys his strokes more than does the finished master of the game ; or that one derives more pleasure from the first tennis practice of a season than from the execution of a perfect return after months of practice. Such simply is not the case. The more perfectly practised a given movement is the greater pleasantness one derives from it *provided that the consciousness attaching to the action in question is not itself diminished ;* that is, providing the movement is not accomplished by a more mechanical type of psycho-neural reflex containing a smaller number of synapses and psychons.

An objection which has been raised especially to the motor consciousness aspect of the theory proposed brings forward the suggestion that it would seem likely that most motor impulses would be able to gain final discharge without being compelled to form synaptic relationships of facilitation or interference with any motor impulses seeking to occupy a common path. If this were so, it is asserted, we should expect nearly all our reactions to cause a feeling tone of indifference whereas, as a matter of fact, nearly all human responses not habitual or " unconscious " are felt to be noticably pleasant or unpleasant. I would agree certainly, that a totally indifferent response is of comparatively rare occurrence and that, therefore, our motor consciousness theory must be prepared to account for the appearance of mutual facilitations or conflicts of motor impulses in connection with a vast majority of responses. The opinion of Sherrington might be quoted[1] to the effect that it seems to him questionable whether a relationship of complete indifference could obtain between any two co-existing motor excitations because of the complexity and close interconnection of the entire synaptic structure of the central nervous system, especially the brain. However, since this issue is a very important one it may be well to discover, if possible, a fundamental condition in the functioning of the nervous system taken as a unit which would account for the expectation that nearly all motor impulses must form synaptic facilitations or antagonisms before reaching final efferent discharge. Such a fundamental reason may be sought in an examination of the continuous, or tonic discharges which persist throughout the life of the organism.

Constant Tonic Discharge Renders All Responses Initially Pleasant or Unpleasant

Recent neurological researches have tended to emphasize the importance of the tonic motor mechanisms which act continuously against the forces of environment to maintain posture and preparedness for adaptive action. Speaking of decerebrate rigidity, a condition affecting the same mechanisms as those concerned in tonic discharge, Sherrington writes[2]: " The muscles it predominantly affects are those which in that attitude (i.e. the one maintained by tonic reflexes) antagonize gravity. In standing, walking, running, the limbs would sink under the body's weight but for contraction of the extensors of hip, knee, ankle, shoulder, elbow ; the head would hang, but for the retractors of the neck ; the tail and jaw would drop, but for their elevator muscles. These muscles counteract a force, gravity, that continually threatens to upset the natural posture. The force acts continuously and the muscles exhibit continued action, *tonus*. . . .

" Two separable systems of motor innervation appear thus controlling two sets of musculature : one system exhibits

[1] " In presence of the arcs of the great *projicient receptors* and the *brain* there can be few receptive points in the body whose activities are totally indifferent one to another. Correlation of the reflexes from points widely apart is the crowning contribution of the brain towards the nervous integration of the individual."   C. S. Sherrington, *Integrative Action of the Nervous System*, p. 147.

[2] C. S. Sherrington, *Integrative Action of the Nervous System*, p. 302.

those transient phases of heightened reaction which constitute reflex movements ; the other maintains that steady tonic response which supplies the muscular tension necessary to *attitude*. Starting from the tonic innervation as initial state, the first step in movement tends to be flexion and involves under ' reciprocal innervation ' an inhibition of the extensor excitation then in progress. This will be involved whether the excitation be *via* local reflex or *via* the motor cortex. . . .

" And the tonic system will, on inhibition of it passing off, contribute a return movement to the pre-existing pose, thus having its share in alternating movements and in compensatory reflexes. These two systems, the tonic and the phasic reflex systems, co-operate exerting influences complimental to each other upon various units of the musculature."

Thus it is evident that *every* phasic, or transitory group of motor impulses which succeeds in winning through to motor outlet, and thus influencing bodily behaviour, must first conflict with (inhibit) the existing tonic discharge, or else facilitate (co-operate with) the continuous tonic impulses. And this same facilitation or antagonism must occur, according to Sherrington, no matter what level of reflex centres may be employed by the phasic impulses, from lowest (local reflex) to highest (motor cortex). If, then, pleasantness and unpleasantness are generated, in the form of psychonic motor energy, upon each occasion that relationships of alliance or antagonism occur in the motor centres, we must assume that some pleasantness or some unpleasantness will precede every final bodily response ; since, prior to each final response, the motor-impulses setting it off are compelled to ally themselves with, or to antagonize the pre-existing tonic discharge.

This result seems to accord precisely with the facts of experience as cited in the criticism of the motation theory of feeling now being discussed. I should like to add, however, that where a minimum of synaptic juncture between phasic and tonic impulses occur, and where the response is also devoid of any considerable interrelationship between phasic impulses, the pleasantness or unpleasantness may be so slight as to escape the observation of the subject. Also, in the type of reaction where interrelationships of connector impulses predominate, with little motor energy escaping into final efferent paths, we should anticipate little observable affective tone. If " thinking " is based upon this connector-correlation type of neural picture, then its apparent emotional indifference might stand accounted for.

Summary

In summary, there seems to be excellent neurological authority for the assumption that pleasantness is in some way attached, either to free, unimpeded discharge of impulses in the central nervous system, or to positive, mutual facilitation of impulses. Similar authority indicates that unpleasantness is connected with central blockage, stasis, or mutual interference of impulses. The work of Head and Holmes, corroborating this conclusion, also indicates that the facilitations and interferences of impulses running parallel with affective tone must occur in the motor centres rather than upon the sensory side of the central nervous system. Marked over-reactions, that is, motor exaggerations, accompanied increase of pleasantness and unpleasantness, while no alterations in the sensory integrations or receptor mechanisms were found.

Psychology, then, has long been faced with the problem : How do we become conscious of the alliances and conflicts of motor impulses ? The first attempt to answer sought to regard feeling as a true aspect of sensation, and to establish some psycho-neural mechanism by which motor phenomena might retroactively influence their preceding sensations. But no such mechanism seems to exist. Other attempts to solve this problem have sought to set aside special groups of sensations, supposedly caused by the initial motor impulses in question, with the assertion that these sensory units enter consciousness not as sensations, but as affective tone. Visceral sensations have been the ruling favourites among those selected. But visceral sensations, sparse and feeble at best, cannot be evoked selectively by motor discharge from the central nervous system, because the autonomic nerve net, excitable only in large sections, intervenes between the central nervous system and the viscera. The same visceral sensations accompany pleasant and unpleasant emotions.

The psychonic theory of consciousness answers the problem squarely, and without circuminvention. It holds that we become conscious of motor alliances and conflicts *at the time they occur, in the motor synapses*. A relationship of mutual facilitation between two or more motor impulses, once formed upon a motor psychon, *is* pleasantness. A relationship of motor antagonism, similarly formed, *is* unpleasantness. Examination of the evidence advanced by several types of objections to the theory proposed reveals the fact that all this data is closely in accord with the theory.

CHAPTER VI

INTEGRATIVE PRINCIPLES OF PRIMARY EMOTIONS

IN the last chapter it was suggested that all phasic motor impulses are compelled to combine with, or to conflict with, the tonic motor impulses continuously discharging in a pattern which may be called, for convenience, our natural reflex equilibrium.[1] In the manufacture of pleasantness and unpleasantness we had supposed a qualitatively simple relationship to exist between phasic and tonic impulses. That is, a simple one-to-one relationship. If this ultimately simple, one-to-one relationship existed in fact, we should have no variable in the equation except the degree of alliance or antagonism existing between tonic and phasic impulses. In such a theoretically simplified equation, we might expect to find sheer pleasantness or sheer unpleasantness without any further complicating factors due to the quantities of the two units brought together. But the moment we consider a combination of tonic and phasic impulses where one group or the other clearly predominates in quantity, a new set of integrative relationships appears.

Referring back to the same situation appearing in chemistry, we may note that a one-to-one comparison between various chemical atoms reveals merely a contrast or similarity between the internal constituents of the atoms examined, but the moment we vary the number of one or the other atoms brought together, a new set of phenomena appears which must also be described. That is, we must note the properties of two atoms of hydrogen brought in contact with one atom of oxygen. This new set of phenomena are termed chemical compounds, and for each type of atom combined with another type of atom, a long series of compounds might be arranged according

---

[1] " Reflex equilibrium," as a term descriptive of the condition to which the central nervous system returns after the tonic discharge has been disturbed by an intercurrent reflex, is used by Sherrington. C. S. Sherrington, *Integrative Action of the Nervous System*, p. 203.

to the number of atoms used in each compound. The entire series of all possible compounds between all types of atoms might be so arranged as to show at one end of the series the compound resulting from the smallest possible quantity of atoms possessing the greatest possible attraction for one another, while at the opposite extreme of the series might lie compounds containing a maximal quantity of atoms having the greatest repulsion one for the other.

The problem before us with respect to integrative combinations of quantitatively varying intensities of tonic and phasic impulses is first of all, to discover the general principle of the changes resulting from the intensity variant in each combination. That is, to put it more concretely, it is important to discover, if possible, what effect will be wrought in the total intensity of tonic discharge by greater or lesser intensities of allied and antagonistic phasic impulses. We have already noted the effect which the alliance or antagonism of a phasic group or impulses will have upon the tendency of the tonic impulses to ally themselves with, or antagonize the phasic group. We may look, in the second place, for the influences which the relative intensities of the phasic group may exercise over the intensity of the total tonic discharge. In order to discover these basic principles of integration, it will be necessary to examine the nature of the tonic reflexes and their mechanisms of reinforcement, and diminution.   '

The Tonic Mechanisms   •

In the last chapter we noted that the tonic reflexes were designed to counteract environmental influences such as gravitation, atmospheric pressure, etc., which if not counteracted, would abolish the posture and attitude necessary to the life and activity of the organism. Appropriate receptors, or sense organs, therefore, connect with tonic motor centres discharging into those muscles designed to react selectively to the forces which must be offset. The semi-circular canals, and probably other types of receptors of the type affected by gravitational influence, respond quickly to changes in the position of the head. Motor discharge evoked by sensations of equilibrium normally contracts the muscles necessary to hold the head and body in the required state of balance. This is the normal or reflex equilibrium of the tonic mechanism, and increases in the gravitational pull, or any similar influence exerted upon the body by phasic reflexes moving the body off balance, would immediately increase the intensity of stimulation of the semi-circular canals. There would follow, through the tonic centres, compensatory increase in motor discharge which should continue until the body has been restored to its normal balance.

We may also consider another and different type of tonic mechanism which operates independently of the balancing reflexes just considered. Sherrington shows[1] that there exist certain proprioceptor sense organs in the skeletal muscles of the body stimulable by the tension within the muscle itself. These stimulations result in motor discharge back into the muscle itself with the result that the muscle is increasingly stimulated to contraction. Suppose, for example, that an experimental animal in a condition of decerebrate rigidity is placed in a holder so that the outstretched limbs and tail do not receive artificial support, but are held rigidly extended by the tonic reflexes under discussion. If, now, the experimenter moves one of the limbs forcibly in a direction opposed to that in which it is held by the extensor contractions due to tonic motor discharge, the extensor contraction can be shown to increase in intensity. When the pressure is removed, the limb returns to a more extreme position than that in which it was originally held.

This same result has been shown to occur if the limb is moved in a position opposed to that brought about by tonic discharge through the agency of an intervening reflex electrically stimulated, thus demonstrating that the phenomenon may be produced either by passive manipulation of the limb or by phasic reflex movement of the limb in an anti-tonic direction. If the afferent nerves from the limb in question be severed, the efferent discharge is diminished or abolished altogether, indicating that the enhancement of tonic discharge is dependent upon sensory impulses rising from the muscles. of the limb as they are increasingly tensed by the pressure exerted against them. Probably when the movement is produced by phasic reflex stimulation there is some integrative equivalent of this mechanical effect also operative. Forbes, Campbell, and Williams[2] have measured, by means of the

[1] C. S. Sherrington, *Integrative Action of the Nervous System*, pp. 300 ff.
[2] A. Forbes, C. J. Campbell, and H. B. Williams, " Electrical Records of Afferent Nerve Impulses from Muscular Receptors," *American Journal of Physiology*, 1924, vol. LXIX, pp. 238-303.

galvanometer, the action currents resulting from increased tension of the muscles in reflex contraction, and have shown that one battery of proprioceptive afferent impulses is evoked as a result of reflex contraction of the muscle, and that a second battery of afferent impulses is evoked as the muscle contraction meets increased opposition from the load it is trying to move.

Importance of Tonic Mechanisms

We may consider briefly the extent to which the entire operation of the central nervous system depends upon the interaction between tonic and phasic systems of reflex nerve excitation.

The psycho-neural concept which looked upon the brain and spinal cord as mere separately strung telephone wires with a switch key to be turned on at the synapses, is passing rapidly. Herrick says[1] " but the concept of the reflex is not a general master key competent to unlock all the secrets of brain and mind, as all seem to suppose, and it has of late been subjected to very searching physiological analysis ". And again, " all the parts of each such reflex system are so intimately and variously connected with one another and with parts of other systems by collateral branches of the nerve fibres and by correlation neurones that anatomical mechanisms are provided for innumerable modifications of any typical or primary reflex pattern. Which, if any, of these cross connections will be activated in any particular response will be determined by the aggregate of external and internal factors at the moment operating ".

By far the most important of the internal factors operating at any moment are the various units of tonic energy continuously exciting large tracts of the brain, spinal cord, and peripheral nerve trunks. It has long been known that the cerebellum is chiefly concerned with maintaining the constant tonic motor discharge necessary to keep the body in its natural state of equilibrium. The cerebellum has been called primarily the " balancing brain ". " Its cortex ", says Herrick,[2] " seems to be a great reservoir of latent nervous energy which

---

[1] C. J. Herrick, *Neurological Foundations of Animal Behavior*, pp. 234-6.
[2] C. J. Herrick, *Neurological Foundations of Animal Behavior*, p. 242.

may be tapped for discharge into any neuromotor apparatus as needed. Its stabilizing influence may be compared with the action of a gyroscope on a large steamship, ensuring the steady progress of the vessel in its course by compensating the buffeting of wind and waves."

Sherrington has proved that not only is the cerebellum to be regarded chiefly as an organ of tonic discharge, but also, that certain centres of the brain stem are concerned with maintaining tonic motor outflow. Sherrington found that decerebrate rigidity which seems to represent a state of natural reflex equilibrium with the normal inhibitory regulation removed cannot be abolished by ablation of the cerebellum.[1]

Lashley has found[2] that the cerebral cortex itself, may be largely concerned with maintaining tonic discharge. He says, " A normal function of the stimulable cortex is to supply a sub-stratum of facilitating impulses which act in some way to render the final common paths excitable by the more finely graduated impulses ", (which emanate from phasic reflexes).

These few quotations from recent writings and research reports will serve to show that the concept long held by many psychologists with regard to the central nervous system as an inert mass of conducting material within which the environment could cause phasic reflex excitations to play about with no other control than that exercised by other phasic excitations which happen to be simultaneously aroused, is no longer tenable. A more apt metaphor would represent the central nervous system as a powerful dynamo generating energy at high and rather regular speed throughout the life of the organism. Phasic excitations aroused by the environment from time to time are to be thought of as passing hands upon the rheostat switches controlling this dynamo. One phasic influence increases the speed of the generator, others may slow it down. Some phasic impulses may reduce the response in conductors already energized by the dynamo while others may increase such excitations. But unless the mechanical and chemical laws of the planet itself be abrogated, (that is, unless gravitation, temperature, air pressure, etc., cease to exert their natural influences upon the organism) the great dynamo

---

[1] C. S. Sherrington, *Integrative Action of the Nervous System*, p. 302.
[2] K. S. Lashley, " The Relation between Cerebral Mass Learning and Retention," *Journal of Comparative Neurology*, August, 1926, vol. 4.

of the central nervous system may be expected to grind out its daily and hourly quota of tonic motor discharge, pretty much regardless of minor changes and influences of the particular environment in which the organism is placed.

What the transient phasic reflexes do very largely determine is the particular outlet through which the energy generated by the dynamos shall be brought into contact with environment.

Herrick says[1] " What particular motor centres will receive the nervous impulses discharged from the cerebellum is apparently determined less by what is going on in the cerebellum than by what systems are in actual function in the rest of the nervous system . . . The circuits acting in the brain stem tend to capture and utilize the cerebellar discharge."

Lashley has reported evidence tending to show a result quite astounding to the older telephone connection theory of action. By eliminating the cerebral motor cortex in an animal trained to certain definite motor habits, Lashley found that impulses to particular muscles do not leave through the pyramidal tracts from the so-called motor area of the cerebrum.[2] He concluded in a later research that the phasic motor impulses descending from the cortex by extra pyramidal paths thus produce the " finer shades of adaptive movement ".[3] Which may mean, as far as one is entitled to guess from incomplete results, that the motor area itself is chiefly concerned with routing tonic discharge continuously to the so-called voluntary muscles all over the body, thus maintaining all these different muscles in a more or less stabilized condition of continuous excitation. Whenever this reflex equilibrium might be changed in such a way that one muscle receives a larger increment of tonic energy than other muscles, an adaptive bodily movement would result. The phasic or transient environmental stimulus would then constitute merely a hand on the lever shifting the tonic outflow slightly from one muscle to another. This effect might be accomplished within the nervous system either by increasing the tonic outflow itself at an appropriate synapse, or by

[1] C. J. Herrick, *Brains of Rats and Men*, Chicago, 1926.

[2] K. S. Lashley, " The Retention of Motor Habits after Destruction of the so-called Motor Area in Primates," *Archives of Neurology and Psychology*, 1924, vol. XII, p. 249.

[3] K. S. Lashley, " The Relation between Cerebral Mass, Learning and Retention," *Journal of Comparative Neurology*, August, 1926, vol. 41.

facilitating the transmission of energy through a nerve path and synapse common to phasic and tonic motor impulses.

Recent researches, on the whole, appear to describe the constant tonic motor energy as a rather uniformly stabilized mass of motor discharge which may " capture ", or " be captured by " the transient motor energy units called phasic impulses.

This " capture " of tonic motor discharge by phasic impulses, or the " capture " of phasic excitations by tonic impulses, takes place, necessarily, at motor synapses appropriate to the psycho-neural level of the response ultimately manifest. Psychons in all these centres must be in a continuous condition of excitation, prior to the reception of phasic impulses, as a result of the constant out-flow of tonic motor energy.   According to the psychonic theory of consciousness, therefore, there exists a certain residuum of motor (affective) awareness, in all animals above the coelenterates (that is, animals possessing synaptic nerve mechanisms), from before birth until after death (at least as " death " is now defined by medical certification).   Normally, this residual motation should be felt as mild, pervasive pleasantness, since motor impulses from different tonic mechanisms, and from different tonic centres must be supposed normally to be in closely ordered alliance, thus affording a certain constant increment of mutual facilitation at common psychons.   The existence of such a continuous background of pleasantness in the normal individual is in close accord with results (experimental, clinical analysis, and introspective report) from a great majority of the subjects, friends, and students whom I have studied.   It appears to be the basis of " *joie de vivre* ".   Experience of its existence seems to restrain from suicide most of the persons still alive, (at least, those who have not been restrained by dread of the suicidal instruments, as suggested by Watson[1]).

Concepts of " Motor Self " and " Motor Stimuli "

The total of psychonic (synaptic) excitation, existing at any given moment in the subject organism as a result of reflex tonic motor discharge, may be called, for convenience, the " motor self ".   Definition of this term does not include any phenomena not objectively described or indicated.

Phasic motor impulses forming psychonic (synaptic) con-

[1] J. B. Watson, *Behaviorism*, New York, 1925, pp. 147-8.

junction with tonic motor excitations may conveniently be termed " motor stimuli ", and are to be regarded as being in exactly the same relation to the motor self as are afferent impulses to the organism's sensory mechanisms. *Motor stimuli thus objectively defined, are not to be confused, under any circumstances, with environmental stimuli, which may be defined as objects or forces acting upon the organism's sensory receptors.*

Principles of Response of Motor Self to Motor Stimulus

Using the terminology just defined, then, we may summarize the possible relationships so far worked out between the motor self and the motor stimuli as follows : Motor stimuli may first of all either ally themselves with, or antagonize the motor self within motor psychons at any level in the central nervous system. Such motor stimuli will evoke, in return, corresponding alliance or antagonism from the motor self. The resulting situation, which is referred to by neurologists as mutual facilitation or conflict of impulses, will thereupon enter consciousness as pleasant or unpleasant motation. This motation, if pleasant, will be added to the normal, pre-existing pleasantness constituting the motor self ; or if unpleasant, it will diminish or supersede the normal pleasantness of the motor self.

But, as noted, it is exceedingly difficult to find a situation where this relationship of mutual facilitation or antagonism exists all by itself without some superadded effect upon the existing intensity of the motor self. It would require a motor stimulus of exactly the same intensity as the motor self[1] to bring about an ultimately simple relationship of alliance with no other relationship existing between stimulus and reagent. Since intensity differences, then, between motor stimuli and motor self will be found in most cases to exist, our analysis showed that this second general type of complicating relationship might usually be found added to the simple pleasantness or mutual facilitation.

---

[1] It is necessary to emphasize the fact that this one to one relationship might not consist of absolute equalities of intensity, but rather of equal intensities *relative* to the reacting power of tonic and phasic impulses, the former being more easily interrupted than the latter, according to Sherrington. Comparisons between intensities of tonic and phasic excitations should always be understood as including this qualification with regard to the relativity of the measure.

Motor Self and Antagonistic Motor Stimuli (Inferior and Superior)

Let us attempt to discover, then, in the first place, the general principle of reaction manifested by the motor self in changing its intensity or volume, in response to inferior or superior intensity or volume of an antagonistic stimulus. "Inferior" and "superior" as used in the discussion to follow must be taken to mean "intensity or volume of motor stimulus inferior to existing intensity or volume of *the motor self*," and "intensity or volume of the motor stimulus superior to the existing intensity or volume of the motor self". We have already noted, during our brief consideration of the regulative tonic mechanisms, that the tonic discharge may be increased or decreased as a reaction to opposition influences exerted upon the balance of the body or upon tension of the muscle tonically innervated. Such a change of body balance or muscular tension, no matter by what influence this change is brought about, tends to *increase* the intensity of tonic motor discharge. It is to be assumed in all instances of this increase of tonic discharge which we have so far considered, that the intensity of the motor stimulus was *inferior* to the intensity of whatever rival tonic motor impulses might have successfully retained possession of the disputed final common path to the muscle in dispute. For if such had not been the case, how could the increased tonic discharge have been measured by means of the increased contraction of the muscle in question ?

That is to say, if an opposed motor stimulus tries to reach the flexor muscle over a final common efferent path held at the moment of stimulation by tonic impulses which are using the final common path to reach antagonistic extensor muscles, and if we find as a result of intervention of the phasic motor stimulus that the contraction of the extensor is heightened, we must assume that *the tonic impulses or motor self were able to hold full control of the entrant psychon* to the final common path. *This would seem to mean that the motor stimulus was less intense or powerful than the already existing tonic discharge.* Had the motor stimulus been of superior intensity to the motor self, it would have dispossessed the tonic impulses of their control over the entrant psychon to the final common path and we should have observed a contraction of the flexor muscles instead of an enhanced contraction of the extensors.

We may assume, then, that *a motor stimulus of inferior intensity results in an increase of the motor self.*

In the experiment reported by Sherrington where an increased load placed upon the extensor muscles of the dog by physical pressure exerted by the experimenter upon the limb in a flexor direction, it is true that the physical superiority of an antagonistic stimulus failed to dispossess the motor self of its hold upon the efferent paths to the extensors. But a *physically* superior force could not, of course, possess any integrative power or significance whatever, unless it gave rise to intervening phasic reflexes which this particular brief movement of the limb did not do. When a phasic reflex of greater intensity than the tonic discharge was evoked by electric stimulation, the tonic discharge into the extensors was diminished, during the persistence of the intervening reflex, to the point where it exerted no observable power of dimunition over its successful phasic rival.[1] The fact, then, appears to be that a successful intervening *phasic reflex of superior intensity to the existing tonic discharge results in a dimunition of that same tonic discharge (and motor self)* throughout the persistence of the superior motor stimulus.

We find, then, that the general rule of intensity relationship between motor self and motor stimulus seems to be as follows :

(1) *An antagonistic motor stimulus of inferior intensity to the motor self evokes an increase of intensity from the motor self as reagent.*

(2) *An antagonistic motor stimulus of superior intensity to the motor self evokes a decrease of intensity from the motor self as reagent.*

Motor Self and Allied Motor Stimuli (Inferior and Superior)

We still have to consider whether the same principle of change of strength by the motor self holds good for motor stimuli allied to the motor self, since both types of motor

---

[1] " Post-inhibitory rebound " was later found by Sherrington to have no correlation with the amount of tonic activity inhibited, and therefore is not attributed solely to a continued cumulative increase of tonic energy during the interim that the intervening stimulus is in control of the final common path. It evidently represents however a secondary central reaction to the intervening motor stimulus which occurs as a result of primitive integration occuring in the absence of the animal's cerebral hemispheres. Post-inhibitory rebound is to be interpreted, perhaps, as a subsequent resurgence of tonic energy rather than an increase in the motor self while the superior motor stimulus is in control,

stimuli so far considered have been antagonistic in the effect upon the final common path. The experiments of Forbes, Campbell and Williams, already cited, indicate that an intervening reflex *allied* to the tonic discharge in its end effect upon the muscle jointly innervated, would tend to have the same effect of *increasing* the tonic discharge or motor self that occurred, as we have already seen, as a result of intervention by an antagonistic motor stimulus of inferior intensity. So far as one can tell, the motor stimulus evoked in experiments of the type mentioned would be of equal or inferior volume to the pre-existing motor self, if evoked from a normal animal in the natural way. When a greater load is placed upon any muscle already in a state of tonic contraction (as in the case where the dog's leg was passively moved by Sherrington in an anti-tonic direction) the same effect is produced upon the increase of tonic discharge as would be produced ultimately by intervening allied phasic reflexes of inferior volume.

Sherrington describes the reflex neuro-muscular situation, in the matter of tonic reinforcement, as follows[1] :—The extensor muscle of the knee, in the instance discussed, constituted the effector organ into which the tonic impulses were discharged. When this muscle was passively stretched by attaching appropriately calibrated weights, afferent impulses were evoked from receptor organs in the muscle fibres. These excitations entered the cord, and efferent, tonic reinforcement impulses emerged from the cord, and travelled back, over the efferent axone trunk, to the muscle which gave rise, originally, to the reflex. A greater number of individual muscle fibres were stimulated to contraction, as a consequence of this motor discharge, than were previously working. Thus the antagonistic weight imposed upon the muscle was compensated for, and the muscle as a whole resumed nearly the same position as before the weight was imposed.

The individual muscle fibres, it is held, cannot undergo partial contraction. Each fibre contracts to its maximum or not at all. Therefore, tonic reinforcement must always take the form of bringing more individual muscle fibres into play. It is supposed that individual axon fibres, in the efferent nerve, innervate individual muscle fibres. Therefore,

---

[1] This data is reproduced from notes taken by the writer at a lecture delivered by Sir Charles S. Sherrington, before the New York Academy of Medicine, New York City, October 25, 1927,

H

the total muscle contraction depends upon the number of individual muscle fibres maximally contracted ; this depends upon the number of individual axone fibres excited (maximally or not at all by the all-or-none law of nerve conduction) ; and this depends, in turn, according to Sherrington, upon the amount of nervous excitation which reaches the motor centre where the efferent fibres receive their stimulus to excitation.

Sherrington has evidence that each motor fibre has an individual, synaptic threshold of excitation, within the motor centre. The afferent reinforcement disturbance, when it arrives at this motor centre, " grips " its maximum number of motor fibres immediately, then loses its grip on those fibres having the highest synaptic thresholds, and continues to activate, for some time, the motor fibres with lower thresholds.

Suppose, then, that an allied motor impulse, of less strength than the existing tonic discharge, arrives at the same motor centre from some other source within the higher centres of the central nervous system. This allied motor stimulus, by definition, is not able to " grip " as many of the individual efferent nerve fibres as are already being activated by the total tonic excitation at the centre. Yet there is an unused margin of potential tonic excitation coming into the centre over the afferents from stretched muscle fibres. This potential increment is not able, by itself, to become kinetic, psychonic (inter-neuronic) excitation, because it is unable to pass the synaptic thresholds of the efferent fibres which remain to be activated. This potential, unused increment of tonic energy should be released, however, by the mutual facilitation between it and its new ally, the phasic, allied motor stimulus of inferior strength. As a result, the potential tonic increment will become active, psychonic impulses, crossing to the hitherto dormant motor fibres of comparatively high threshold, thus *increasing the motor self by an increment equal to the strength of the allied, inferior, motor stimulus.*

Suppose, on the other hand, that the allied motor stimulus which arrives at the common motor centre is *superior* in strength to the existing motor self, or tonic excitation actually crossing the efferent reinforcement synapses. Exactly the same release of the potential tonic increment may initially occur. But as soon as the superior ally grips its full quota of efferent fibres, a new type of phenomenon must result. More individual axon fibres will be excited, and more individual muscle fibres will be contracted than the total, compensatory tonic reinforcement calls for. That is, compensation for the weight constantly imposed upon the muscle will be carried beyond the point where compensation is complete. If 25 per cent. of all muscle fibres are needed for complete compensation, and 35 per cent. of the total number of fibres are actually shortened by the superior, allied motor stimulus, then the tension imposed by the load on the muscle will be distributed between a larger number of individual fibres, and each fibre will undergo correspondingly diminished tension.

Parallel with the diminution of tension in each muscle fibre activated, the intensity of stimulation of the proprioceptive sensory organ within each muscle fibre will be decreased, and total afferent reinforcement excitation sent to the motor centre, will diminish by a corresponding amount. Following this diminution, a smaller number of efferent nerve fibres will be gripped by the tonic excitement, *per se ;* and, *pari passu,* the total strength of psychonic excitation of tonic origin will suffer decrement. Since this psychonic excitation is synonymous with the motor self, we find that *an allied motor stimulus of superior strength ultimately decreases the motor self by a decrement equal to the amount of the ally's superiority.*

The clearest indication that such a theoretically predictable result does, in fact, occur is to be found in the apparent diminution of muscular tonicity and other bodily resultants of tonic discharge during " sexual " (love) passion. There are easily observable signs of bodily lassitude and weakness, especially in women subjects, at the same time that the passion itself is felt as most intense and pervasive. This weakening of the self in order to surrender utterly to a loved one of superior strength is aptly described in Sappho's immortal lines :

" For when I see thee but a little, I have no utterance left, my tongue is broken down, and straightway a subtile fire has run under my skin, with my eyes I have no sight, my ears ring, sweat pours down and a trembling seizes all my body ; I am paler than grass, and seem in my madness little better than one dead."[1]   Such a description would indicate that tonic-type motor discharge (" sweat ", etc.) is present, but that the motor self proper is progressively weakened (" little better than one dead ").

[1] Second Sapphic fragment, H. T. Wharton, *Sappho,* London, Reprint of Fourth Edition, 1907, p. 65.

Moreover, systolic blood pressure records taken during love excitement sometimes show a progressive and extensive drop at a short interval prior to the sexual orgasm. Such drops in systolic blood pressure perhaps indicate that the strength of the heart beat, which is tonically maintained, has been diminished not by inhibition but by general diminution of the tonic outflow of motor self.

However such cardio-vascular phenomena may be interpreted, the decrease of muscular tonicity all over the body seems unmistakably symptomatic of lessening of tonic discharge. This decrease of the motor self does not occur immediately upon initiation of love excitement, nor does it occur very frequently with male subjects, or even with extremely passionate women subjects, except under maximally favourable conditions. The phenomenon seems to depend upon the passing of a certain threshold in the volume of phasic motor discharge produced by the entire love situation stimulus. When this volume of motor stimuli has become sufficiently great, the symptoms of decrease in the motor self interest themselves, sometimes rather suddenly. May it not be the case that this phenomenon occurs at the time that the total volume of sexual motor discharge exceeds the volume of allied tonic impulses ?

If our foregoing analysis is correct, then we find that *the motor self follows a general principle of increasing its volume' of intensity in response to a motor stimulus of less strength than itself regardless of whether the motor stimulus be allied or antagonistic to the motor self,* and that *the motor self decreases its volume of intensity when reacting to a motor stimulus of greater strength than itself, regardless of whether the motor stimulus be allied or antagonistic to the motor self.*

Differences Between Psychonic Relationships of Motor Self to Allied and to Antagonistic Stimuli

"It should be noted at this point, however, that the actual phenomena occuring upon the motor psychons where the increase or decrease of the motor self is integrated, must be thought of quite differently when the increase or decrease is accompanied by facilitation, than in the case where the change in volume or intensity is coupled with mutual antagonism between motor self and motor stimulus. When the motor stimulus is antagonistic to the motor self, the victor in the conflict wins a right of way across the disputed psychon into the final common path, but there seems to be no neurological evidence that the victor in such a conflict possesses power to compel the vanquished impulse to change its rhythm or impulse rate in such a way as to conform to and facilitate the impulse rate of the victorious antagonist. In the conflict under discussion, however, the motor self attains almost precisely the same result because it reinforces itself in the process of winning its victory by an increment as great as the strength of the vanquished opponent. Thus, although the weaker antagonist is not actually made over into the nature and pattern of its conqueror, the victor is increased in strength or volume in its own nature or pattern by an increment identical in strength with the vanquished stimulus.

The result which occurs when the motor stimulus is the victor is not precisely the same as in the case just considered. When the motor stimulus wins through into the disputed common path, it has no mechanism for self reinforcement[1] and remains, therefore, of exactly the same strength it was in the first place. The diminution of the motor self in this case rather represents a readjustment of tonic discharge to permit the victorious phasic impulse to hold its own, specific course, than a general defeat of the motor self proportionate to the victory of the stimulus. In short, there is a conceded victory for the motor stimulus without any enhancement of the latter. This is followed by a readjustment of the motor self which, if the integration is completed, restores harmony to the entire integrative picture. By means of this adjustment, all parts of the motor self save that interrupted, and also the motor stimulus may follow their own paths without mutual interference.

In the case of a real alliance between the motor self and the motor stimulus, however, each continues in union with the other, no matter which ally is in quantitative supremacy. When the motor self decreases in reaction to an allied motor stimulus of superior volume, it does not step aside, as it were, and permit the victorious motor stimulus to continue on its way unimpeded. The decreased motor self, even though made smaller by the presence of the victorious motor stimulus,

---

[1] According to a recent statement by Sherrington, during the lecture referred to above, the flexor muscle of the knee, an anti-tonic muscle, possesses no mechanism for progressive self reinforcement.

must continue to facilitate the victor across the common psychons, and into the final common path. This relationship, therefore, seems to represent nearly the converse of the antagonistic integration wherein the motor self was reinforced in victory by the quantitative equivalent of its opponent. Yet, in victory, the enlarged motor self could maintain no further relationship with its vanquished opponent, while in allied defeat the diminished motor self must continue to maintain tributary union with its victorious ally..

In the case where the motor self was found to increase as a result of union with a weaker ally, this same continued contact between superior and inferior members of the alliance is found to exist. This integrative situation would be nearly, though not quite, the converse of that antagonistic integration wherein the motor self was diminished, and subsequently made a forced adjustment to the right of way won by its opponent. In the latter instance, the motor self, following its readjustment, might recover its internal harmonization of motor discharge, and the victorious impulses themselves, if of sufficient volume, might separately facilitate one another. But this would not affect any psychonic juncture between motor self and the victorious opponent. In the converse allied integration, however, the victoriously enlarged motor self would continue to receive tributary facilitation from its increased ally throughout the duration of the relationship.

The " Emotion Circle " of Integrative Relationships Between Motor Self and Motor Stimuli

If the above is a correct description of the basic integrative principles involved, we now have a complete analysis of the self-regulatory mechanisms by which the tonic motor discharge, or motor self, readjusts itself upon coming into contact with phasic reflexes, or motor stimuli at entrant psychons to final common paths leading to those muscles which are continuously used to keep the body in its normal posture. According to this analysis, we find that two separate integrative principles appear to operate regardless of how one of these principles may be combined with the other. The two principles may be stated as follows :

1. Alliance and antagonism of motor stimuli toward the motor self evoke corresponding alliance and antagonism from the motor self.

2. Inferior intensity of volume of the motor stimulus evokes increase of intensity or volume from the motor self ; and superior volume or intensity of the motor stimulus evokes decrease of intensity or volume from the motor self.

Thus, an antagonistic motor stimulus may possess either inferior or superior intensity, and the motor self may respond by *an attitude of antagonism plus either increase or decrease of its own intensity.* An allied motor stimulus, similarly, may possess either inferior or superior volume to that of the motor self, and the motor self should thereupon react by *an attitude of alliance plus either an increase or a decrease of its own strength.*

It is convenient to think of the strength of the motor self, plus the strength of the motor stimulus, as representing a constant or balanced equation. Whatever intensity or volume value is thereafter removed from one side of this equation, must be added to the other side to keep the equation balanced ; and whatever intensity or volume value is subtracted from one side must similarly be added to the other side to balance the equation again.

If, now, we combine in every way possible the two sets of integrative relationships above described, we shall have a continuous series of motor stimuli, and a corresponding series of motor self responses, each varying from its predecessor in the series by a just noticeable quantitative difference in degree of harmony, and in degree of intensity or volume difference. Such a continuously graded series of motor stimuli and motor self responses are represented in an accompanying diagram.

The entire series is represented in circular form, just as the just distinguishable colour sensation series may be represented schematically in circular form, and is frequently termed the " colour circle " or " colour pyramid. " The four primary colours placed at the four corners of the base of the colour pyramid represent turning points in the entire series where a given type of colour change has reached its maximum. Thereafter the alteration of hue begins to shift in a new direction.

In exactly the same way, the points D, I, S, and C represent nodal points in the integrative emotion series. At each of these points one type of change in one of the two sets of integrative relationships reaches its maximum and begins to change.

Thus, the point D at the top of the diagram represents a maximal value of antagonism between motor stimulus and

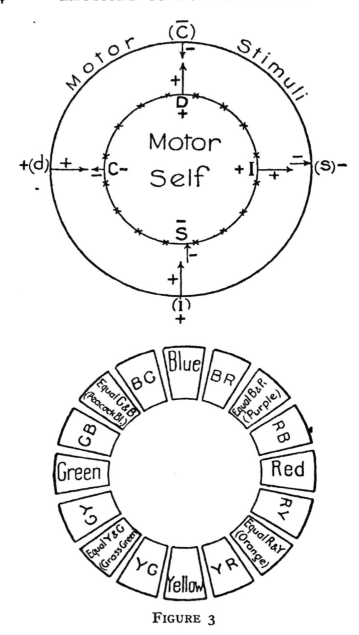

·" The Emotion Circle and the Colour Circle "[1]

[1] Note : These terms for intermediate colours are from Munsell. (See A. H. Munsell, *A Colour Notation*, p. 35).

FIGURE 3.—The capital letters D, I, S, C, indicate responses of the motor self. A plus (+) sign near one of these letters, inside the Motor Self, indicates an *increase* of the Self during response ; while a minus (—) sign indicates a *decrease*.

Arrows between Motor Self and Motor Stimuli indicate relationship between these two elements during response. Relative length of arrows indicates preponderance of one or other element, (also indicated by plus or minus sign near arrow). Arrows pointing in opposed directions indicate antagonism between Self and Stimulus ; arrows pointing in parallel directions indicate alliance.

The small letters (c), (s), (i), (d), indicate the type of Stimulus adequate to evoke each response ; the Stimulus (c) being in the same relationship to the Self as the Self is to its stimulus at C, etc. A minus (—) sign near a small letter indicates a *decrease* of the Stimulus as a result of the Self's action upon it ; while a plus (+) sign indicates an *Increase*.

The Colour Circle is placed with the four nodal points of colour, blue, red, yellow, and green, in positions corresponding to the four nodal points of emotion, dominance, inducement, submission, and compliance. An identity of integrative principles has been suggested by preliminary research in naive associations between primary colours and primary emotions (see *Psyche*, October, 1927, p. 4).

The points marked " × " on the Motor Self circle suggest just-distinguishable differences of response, in between nodal points D, I, S, C, comparable to violet, purple, carmine, etc., on the colour circle.

motor self. As we proceed clockwise toward the point I, this antagonism may be thought of as becoming continuously less, until at I an alliance relationship appears. But at this same point, I, the inferiority of motor stimulus strength and the corresponding increase of motor self energy reaches its maximum, and begins to change toward the opposite relationship, which first appears decisively at S. At this lowest nodal point, S, the alliance relationship between motor stimulus and motor self has reached its maximum, and begins to fall off as we proceed upward toward C, where alliance has disappeared altogether and antagonism relationship has reappeared. At the point C, again, the decrease of motor self intensity and response to superior stimulus strength has reached its maximal value, changing again to the opposite relationship by the time our starting point, D, is again reached.

Starting at the nodal point, C, which is the point at the extreme left of the diagram, we may summarize the relationships and reactions at the nodal or primary points of the diagram as follows :—

C

Motor stimulus.......	(a)	Antagonistic to motor self.
	(b)	Superior strength to motor self.
Reaction of motor self	(a)	Antagonistic to motor stimulus.
	(b)	Decrease of strength.

D

Motor stimulus.......	(a)	Antagonistic to motor self.
	(b)	Inferior strength to motor self.
.Reaction of motor self	(a)	Antagonistic to motor stimulus.
	(b)	Increase of strength.

I

Motor stimulus.......	(a)	Allied with motor self.
	(b)	Interior strength to motor self.
Reaction of motor self	(a)	Allied with motor stimulus.
	(b)	Increase strength.

S

Motor stimulus.......	(a)	Allied with motor self.
	(b)	Superior strength to motor self.
Reaction of motor self	(a)	Allied with motor stimulus.
	(b)	Decrease strength.

We are now prepared to define the term " primary emotion " with complete objectivity. We must first recall that, according to the psychonic theory of consciousness, all relationships between motor stimuli and motor self represented in the diagram above, constitute *complex units of motor consciousness, or emotion, at the time they occur in the form of psychonic impulses upon the appropriate motor psychons of the central nervous system.* By defining objectively the elements composing these psychonic units of energy, we thereby, *ipsc facto*, define the physical aspect of the different types of emotional consciousness which we are seeking to discover. With this premise in mind, then, we may suggest the following definitions.

An emotion is a complex unit of motor consciousness, composed of psychonic impulses representing the motor self, and of psychonic impulses representing a motor stimulus ; these two psychonic energies being related to one another,

(1) by alliance or antagonism ; and,

(2) by reciprocal superiority and inferiority of strength.

A primary emotion may be designated as an emotion which contains the maximal amount of alliance, antagonism, superiority of strength of the motor self in respect to the motor stimulus, or inferiority of strength of the motor self in respect to the motor stimulus.

Emotions are complex motations, formed by conjunctions of various types between the motor self and transient motor stimuli. It is suggested that the possible types of conjunction constitute a continuous series, wherein each unit represents a quality of emotional consciousness just noticeably different from the emotions most closely resembling it, which lie adjacent to it, on either side, in the total series. At certain nodal points, in this emotion series, there seem to appear definite emotions which represent clear cut types of unit characters of conjunction, between the motor self and the motor stimulus. These nodal emotions are not modified by the admixture of modifying emotional qualities from other adjacent emotions in the series. There seem to be four such nodal points in the entire emotion circle, and the four emotions occurring at these points may conveniently be termed primary emotions.

The names which I have ventured to select for the four primary emotions in the above integrative analysis were chosen to meet two requirements. First, the commonly understood meaning of the word employed must describe, with as great accuracy and completeness as possible, the objective relationship between motor self and motor stimulus which was to be conceived of as the integrative basis for the primary emotion in question. Secondly, the name chosen for each primary emotion must suggest the experience in question, as it is observed introspectively in everyday life. Another minor consideration which entered into the choice of names for primary emotions was the advantage of new terms not already weighted with dissimilar affective meaning of literary origin. No matter how clearly one may define in objective terms words such as " fear ", " rage ", etc., the previous connotation which an individual reader may have attached to these words, as a result of life-long learning, will continue reflexly to come to mind each time the term is used.

(I) *Compliance* is the name suggested for the primary emotion located at " C " in Figure 3. The dictionary defini-tion[1] of the verb " comply " is :

" 1. To act in conformity with.

2. To be complacent, courteous."

Both these meanings of compliance (" the act of complying ") seem rather aptly to characterize the integrative relationship indicated at " C " on the diagram. The motor stimulus, which is antagonistic and of greater intensity than the motor

---

[1] Definitions herein quoted are taken from Funk and Wagnalls, *Desk Standard Dictionary.*

self, evokes a response of diminution of the motor self, designed to readjust the self to the stimulus. The motor stimulus is permitted by this response, to control the organism, in part and for the time being, antagonistically to the motor self. In the course of such a response, the motor self certainly acts " in conformity with " the motor stimulus. In its final adjustment, the self may be said to be " complacent " with respect to control of the organism by its antagonist.

Introspectively, the word " compliance " seems to suggest, to a great majority of the several hundred persons whom I have asked, that the *subject is moving himself at the dictates of a superior force.*

There is no difficulty arising from the use of this word to designate emotion in literature, since " compliance ", in its literary usage customarily signifies a type of action rather than the emotion accompanying the action.

(II) *Dominance* is the name suggested for the primary emotion indicated at " D " on the diagram of integrative relationship. " To dominate ", according to the dictionary means :

" 1. To exercise control over.

2. To prevail ; predominate."

The integrative situation described by dominance (" the act of dominating ") is chiefly characterized by victory of the motor self over an antagonist of inferior intensity. The motor self obviously " prevails." and " predominates " over its phasic antagonist throughout this integrative situation. The motor self " exercises control over " the final common path and hence it " exercises control over " the behaviour of the organism, removing environmental obstacles to the pattern of behaviour dictated by means of its own superior reinforced power. Thus the total objective situation, provided our integrative analysis is correct, is fairly described by the term " dominance ".

Introspectively, dominance suggests to all persons of whom I have inquired, a superiority of self over some sort of antagonist.

The word " dominant " has been used most frequently in literature to describe an " aggressive ", " strong-willed " type of personality or character. This seems rather in accord with the proposed use of the word than otherwise.

(III) *Inducement* is the name suggested for the primary

emotion indicated at " I " on Figure 3   " To induce ",
according to the dictionary is :
   " 1 To influence to act ; prevail upon.
   2. To lead to."
   The integrative situation for which the term " inducement "
is proposed consists primarily of a strengthening of the motor
self in order more effectively to facilitate the passage of a
weaker motor stimulus across the common psychon. The
motor self, in such a relationship to its weaker ally, certainly
" influences " the motor stimulus by facilitation to " the
act " of traversing the final common path. If, as we shall
see later, it frequently happens that the motor stimulus is too
weak to win its way alone to efferent discharge, then the motor
self truly " leads " its weaker ally across the synapse, " prevailing upon " it, meantime, to facilitate the passage of the
stronger motor self impulses.
   Introspectively, inducement ("the act of inducing")
indicates to a majority of the subjects asked, a process of
persuading someone, in a friendly way, to perform an act
suggested by the subject. This meaning, if expressed in
bodily behaviour would be very close to the expected behaviour result of the integrative relationship already described.
The subjects' emphasis upon the " friendliness " of the persuasion is very significant in making clear the nature of inducement as a primary emotion. The nature of the integrative
relationship would necessitate perfect alliance between the
interests of inducer and induced throughout the entire response.
The power of inducement in evoking alliance from the induced
person lies entirely in the extent to which the inducer is able
to serve the other's interest, while initial weakness in the
person " induced " is the element which calls forth increase
of strength from the inducer.
   The word " induce " in literary usage, like the word
" compliance ", has been employed, for the most part, to
describe a certain type of behaviour, in which one individual
persuades another person to do something which the first
individual desires him to do   Little use, if any, has been
made of the term " inducement " in designating emotional
states of consciousness.
   (IV) *Submission* is the name suggested for the primary
emotion represented at " S " in Figure 3. The dictionary
defines the verb " to submit " as meaning :

" 1. To give up to another.
  2. To yield authority or power ; to surrender.
  3. To be submissive."

Submissive is defined as " docile ", " yielding ", " obedient ", " humble ".

The integrative situation to which the term " submission " is applied consists, in essence, of a decrease in the strength of the motor self to balance a corresponding superiority of strength in the motor stimulus.   In assuming this relationship, the motor self might certainly be described as being " humble " and " yielding ".   The motor self, in essence, is " giving up to " its stronger ally a portion of itself.   After the motor self has completed its response as far as decreasing its own volume goes, it continues, as a weaker ally, to be " docile " and " obedient " in rendering facilitation to its stronger ally in their common path.   This continued rendering of alliance to the motor stimulus might well be described as " yielding " to the authority or power of its stronger ally, while the continuance of a motor self to render such facilitation as weaker ally throughout the persistence of the relationship seems aptly characterized as being " submission ".   The bodily behaviour to be expected from this type of integration would be characterized as that of an obedient child toward a loving mother.

Introspective records on the question of what suggestion is conveyed by the word " submit " reveal that the essence of " submission " to nearly all subjects, is *voluntary obedience to the commands of the person in authority*.   With women subjects, *the additional meaning of mutual warmth of feeling between the subject and the person submitted to* is introspectively present when the submission is thought of as rendered to a loved mother, or to lover of the same or opposite sex.   The element of mutual friendliness (represented by alliance in the integrative picture), does not appear in the majority of male reports concerning the introspective suggestion evoked by the word " submission ".   This is unfortunate, but I have not been able to find any other word adequately covering the objective description of this emotion which, at the same time, would also include the introspective meaning of mutual warmth of feeling between the person submitting and the person submitted to.   The word " submit ", as a name for the primary emotion designated, is intended to convey emphatically this

meaning of *pleasantness experienced in the act of " submission "
by the person submitting.*

Literary use of the word " submission " has followed rather
closely the integrative meaning as reported by my subjects.
" Submission ", in literary parlance, customarily indicates
a passive yielding, one to the other, yet not necessarily with
any great amount of pleasantness in the submission exacted.
Perhaps, this limitation found in both introspective and
literary connotations of the word " submission " indicates
that the connection between submitting to a lover and submission to a person of superior power (which is submission
closely akin to compliance) is not found properly developed
in our present civilization and its literary records.

*Outline of Integrative Principles of Primary Emotions and
Feelings*

Concept	Definition
Psychon :	Junctional tissue, at synapses of central nervous system.
Psychonic impulse :	Completed excitation of any psychon from emissive pole of one neuron, to receptive pole of next.
Consciousness :	Psychonic impulses, or psychonic energy.
Environmental stimulus :	Object or force exciting organism's sensory receptors.
Sensation :	Psychonic energy at sensory synapses.
Motation :	Motor consciousness ; affective consciousness ; psychonic energy at motor synapses.
Motor self :	Continuous, tonic, motor discharge across motor psychons ; psychonic impulses of tonic motor origin.
Motor stimuli :	Phasic motor impulses at motor psychons ; psychonic motor impulses of phasic reflex origin.
Integrative principles of reaction of motor self to motor stimuli :	(1) Exerts antagonistic influence towards antagonistic motor stimulus, and facilitating influence toward allied motor stimulus. (2) Increases intensity in response to inferior intensity of motor stimulus, and decreases intensity in response to superior motor stimulus intensity.
Primary feelings :	Simplest recognizable motations ; pleasantness and unpleasantness.
Pleasantness and unpleasantness :	Psychonic motor impulses in relationship, respectively, of mutual facilitation or mutual antagonism.

Emotions :

Next simplest motational compounds to primary feelings ; composed of :

(1) Psychonic motor impulses of motor self and motor stimulus in relationships of mutual alliance or conflict.

(2) Motor self increasing or decreasing its intensity in response to inferior or superior intensity of motor stimulus. Psychonic impulse combinations of these two relationships found in continuous series.

Primary Emotions :

Nodal points of emotion series, where relationships of alliance, conflict, and increase or decrease of motor self reach maximum, and begin to change toward opposite type of relationship.

Primary emotions are termed : compliance, dominance, inducement, and submission.

Compliance :

(1) Motor stimulus : *Antagonistic* and *superior intensity* to motor self, (initially unpleasant).

(2) Response of motor self : *Decrease of intensity*, and *antagonistic compulsion of motor self* (producing indifference and then pleasantness in proportion to volume and inter-faciliations of superior motor stimuli yielded to).

Dominance :

(1) Motor stimulus : *Antagonistic* and *inferior intensity* to motor self, (initially unpleasant).

(2) Response of motor self : *Increase of intensity*, and *antagonistic compulsion of motor stimulus*, (producing pleasantness in proportion to success, co-existing with original unpleasantness).

Inducement :

(1) Motor stimulus : *Allied* and *inferior intensity* to motor self, (pleasant).

(2) Response of motor self : *Increase of intensity*, and *allied compulsion of motor stimulus*, (increasingly pleasant).

Submission :

(1) Motor stimulus : *Allied* and *superior intensity* to motor self, (pleasant).

(2) Response of motor self : *Decrease of intensity*, and *allied compulsion of motor self*, (increasingly pleasant)

CHAPTER VII

DOMINANCE

ALTHOUGH the method pursued in building up an integrative basis for primary emotions may have seemed to consist, up to this time, of making a purely logical analysis of neurological results, I may say that the discovery of the four nodal points of primary emotion was the result, originally, of quite a different type of analytical procedure. I had worked for a number of years with systolic blood pressure and reaction-time deception tests, and other physiological measures of emotion, amassing a considerable quantity of unpublished material. I found it impossible to interpret or understand this data without the aid of some tenable hypothesis of basic psycho-neural mechanisms of emotion.

No such hypothesis existed. The literary names for various emotions popularly used were utterly confusing, overlapping, and misleading. I had found in the deception test results, for example, what seemed to me clear enough indication of two antagonistic emotional influences concerned with the " deceptive " consciousness. To lump these two opposite emotional states, which appeared to manifest observably contrary effects upon bodily behaviour, into a single un-analysed compound, and to label this unknown quantity " fear ", seemed to me scientifically inexcusable. At the same time, systolic blood pressure and reaction-time measurements of emotion, by themselves, do not offer nearly meaningful enough a basis for construction of such a hypothesis as seemed necessary.

It appeared to me that the procedure best adapted for forming a tenable hypothesis of emotional mechanisms would necessarily contain two types of research. First, a series of clinical studies of child and adult behaviour, somewhat after the Watsonian fashion. Second, an objective analysis of the behaviour observed with a view to discovering its common factors and least common denominators, if any such existed.

I have been greatly aided in this process, begun in 1922, by volunteer student assistants, who invariably manifest keen interest in emotional behaviour, and who frequently seem to possess more genuinely scientific attitude in report and analysis of such behaviour than do persons more highly trained in research who are compelled, perhaps, to conform to conventional methods of already established schools of scientific thought.

I was also fortunate in being able to observe a great deal of emotional behaviour " in the raw " during a mental health survey of school children in New York City, and a similar survey of penitentaries in the state of Texas. During the New York survey it was my good fortune to make individual personality studies of approximately two hundred and fifty children who represented school behaviour-problems, of one sort or another, under the able leadership and tutelage of Edith R. Spaulding, M.D., who directed the survey.[1] Doctor Spaulding's keen insight into emotional problems of delinquent behaviour revealed in her report of the Bedford Hills studies,[2] coupled with her clinical work in endocrine diagnosis and treatment, suggested new and constructive points of view in analysis of emotional behaviour.

During the Texas survey, we administered the usual intelligence tests to prisoners in thirteen prison farms scattered throughout the state, and to the prisoners confined in the penitentary proper, at Huntsville. After scoring and classifying the group tests of all the prisoners held at a given place of confinement, I was given the opportunity to interview each convict individually for the purpose of making a separate study of each individual. While interviewing the prisoner I had before me his complete record. This included a brief account of the crime of which he was convicted, his own statement regarding guilt or innocence, his behaviour record while in prison, a special physical examination record, and his intelligence and performance-test records. 3,451 convicts were studied in this way, approximately ninety per cent. of

[1] This survey was conducted under the auspices of the National Committee for Mental Hygiene.
[2] Edith R. Spaulding, *An Experimental Study of Psychopathic Delinquent Women*, New York, 1923.

whom were men. 1,591 of the subjects were negroes, 364 Mexicans, while the balance were American born, or natives of English-speaking European countries. The largest occupational group was that of the farmers, who numbered 656. Fifty-eight per cent. of the prison inmates admitted having been arrested more than once, while forty per cent. claimed that they had never previously been charged with criminal behaviour. Altogether, this group of prison inmates may be taken as fairly typical of prisoners caught in asocial behaviour in the less densely populated regions of the United States. I was able to make rather satisfactory studies of the prisoners' attitudes toward their own conduct, their views of society and its treatment of them, and also of the homo-sexual relationships inevitable in prison life.

During the personality studies of Texas prisoners, the four primary emotions suggested in the last chapter began to take definite shape. I classified the main behaviour trends of the prisoners, so far as these trends could be reduced to emotional common denominators, into four primary classes which I then termed " acquisitiveness ", " dominance ", " creation ", and " submission ".

After conclusion of the prison survey, I applied these four primary emotional behaviour mechanisms, as suggested by the previous work with students, and the survey studies, to clinical subjects during a year's practice as consulting psychologist.

The following year, I conducted a student's clinic at Tufts College, Massachusetts. During this clinical work we used a somewhat amended version of the four primary emotions concepts previously mentioned. The problems which came to us included not only student difficulties of adjustment to college work and environment, but also the students' economic problems, and affairs of the heart, which in some instances, had serious ramifications. Parallel with the student clinic, a course was given in emotional analysis of normal persons. The first half year was devoted to analysis of emotional behaviour concerning remunerative work which the students had done or desired to do. The second half-year was given over to behaviour studies concerning home and love adjustments. A great deal of worth-while material was discovered and reported upon by the students in the course of attempted analysis of themselves and of their fellow students. The four primary emotion mechanisms received further clarification, and revision, the term "adaptation" taking the place of "acquisitiveness".

I spent another half-year in fitting together the various types of results at hand, and in attempting to work out a definite neurological basis upon which the "emotional common denominator", which seemed clearly to appear in the clinical results, might most probably be based. The results of the entire procedure as outlined are being reported in this volume.

One of the most striking aspects of human behaviour throughout the series of observations seemed to me to be a close resemblance between certain human reaction tendencies and the general principles observable in the behaviour of the physical forces of nature.

Dominance in the Behaviour of Forces of Nature

It has become a proverb that a stream of water flows over (i.e. dominates) the course of least resistance. If we compare the gravity-impelled onrush of the water to the tonic motor discharge of the human organism, we find that the reactions of the two toward opposing obstacles follow much the same principles. Opposition which is weaker than the rushing water is dominated by the stream roughly in proportion to the difference between the strength of the current and the weakness of the opposition offered. Moreover, in proportion as the opposition is overcome the stream grows more powerful. When the obstacle offered by a river bed is completely removed, the falling water rushes downward in a cataract of terrific force, like Niagara Falls. Other forces of nature react in the same way toward opposing forces. Electric charges, like streams of water, selectively dominate those conducting materials which present the least opposition. Gases expand into those areas where there is least opposing gaseous pressure. The intensity, or power of all these reacting forces, each in its individual way, increases in proportion as its opponent is overcome. The stimulus to the dominant reaction of any natural force may be defined in the same way that we defined an adequate stimulus to the dominant response of a human being, that is, an opposing force of less power than the reagent.

So far our observation concerning the reaction of one physical force to another merely amounts to defining the relationship between two physical forces, which obtains when one force acts as adequate stimulus evoking dominance from the other. The domination of the weaker force by the stronger one seems so wholly axiomatic that it hardly needs comment. Nevertheless, looking at the weaker or less complex force as a mechanistic-type cause, it is important to observe that by its very element of weakness relative to a stronger or more complex physical force, it is able to control the latter by causing the stronger force to select this particular weaker force to dominate. Granting that the weakness of one force constitutes the selective stimulus evoking dominance response from a stronger physical force, what do we find to be the measure of increase, if any, which the stronger force gains in the process of dominating the weaker one? That is, in so far as interactions between physical forces go, does the dominant reagent increase its power in the course of dominating its weaker opponent? It would seem to be the fact that the stronger reagent does increase its force in the process of dominating its weaker opponent, and that the increase is approximately equal to the strength of the vanquished antagonist.

A river, for instance, when opposed by a dam, piles itself up against the barrier with accumulative increase of water pressure exerted against its opponent. This increase in the river's power, in the form of water pressure, increases in proportion to the increase of the opponent's force. The higher the dam, the more water accumulates behind the dam, and the more total pressure is exerted by the river against its opponent. When, at last, the river rises above the dam and begins to flow over it (or when an opening is offered through or around the barrier) the river's domination of its weaker opponent is consummated. The force then exercised by the water pouring over or through the conquered barrier will be greater than the original force of the undammed river by an increment of increase approximately equal to the opposing force of the dam which the river was obliged to overcome in attaining its dominant end.

We may summarize by the statement that, as far as the physical forces go, it would seem to be the attribute of relative weakness in the inferior force that constitutes the adequate stimulus to dominance reaction by the stronger force. The stronger force increases its power during the process of dominating the weaker by an amount approximately equal to the opposing power of the weaker force which was overcome in the process of domination.

Contrast between Motor Stimuli and Environmental Stimuli

When we apply this dominance equation to dominance reaction of the motor self to motor stimuli of inferior intensity we must first of all distinguish sharply between environmental stimuli and motor stimuli. The amount of dominance emotion which will exist upon the appropriate motor psychons of the central nervous system and the intensity of the dominance behaviour expressive of this dominant psychonic energy will represent not the reaction of the motor self to the observable environmental stimulus, but rather the response of the motor self to the motor stimulus which, as a result of past experiences, may be released by a seemingly trivial environmental stimulus.

For example, homicide is not infrequently committed as a reaction to an environmental stimulus furnished by the gesture of a perfectly harmless person toward his hip pocket. The environmental stimulus in such cases was of negligible intensity and probably not even antagonistic in its relationship to the subject. But upon previous occasions the gesture of reaching toward a hip pocket where a revolver was carried constituted an environmental stimulus requiring prompt and violent dominance response to overcome it. Thus, as a matter of learning or conditioning by past experience, this mild environmental stimulus had become endowed with the power to evoke motor stimuli antagonistic to the subject's motor self. These motor stimuli, though of great intensity, are yet known to be less powerful than the available motor reinforcements at the subject's command. Therefore, these motor stimuli are adequate to evoke a dominance response to maximal violence, and this response is called forth by an environmental stimulus of totally different nature.

In such an instance the great discrepancy between environmental stimulus and motor stimulus is clearly evidenced by the nature of the resulting behaviour. It should also be noted that in such an instance the increase of the intensity or strength of the motor self which reacts dominantly toward the environmental stimulus is measured by the intensity of the antagonistic motor stimuli, and has no relation whatever to the strength of the environmental stimulus which sets off the reaction. Though the case cited is no doubt rather an extreme one, incongruities of the same nature between environmental stimulus and motor stimulus should be looked for in every instance of behaviour analysed.

Dominance in Human and Animal Behaviour

Dominance seems to comprise the most fundamental and primitive type of emotional integration found in animals or human beings. As we have already noted, the decerebrate dog and monkey manifest a typical domination emotion in response to any antagonistic motor stimulus possessing less integrative power or intensity than the reacting motor self of the animal possesses.

Goltz found that a decerebrate dog manifested no emotion except what Goltz described as " rage ".[1] This response as described in the animal's behaviour seems to have constituted a very uninhibited and aggressive type of *dominance emotion*. The difference between this dog and a normal animal, which evidently accounted for the absence of other emotional responses, was the fact that no motor stimulus could be evoked, in the decerebrate animal, which was integratively stronger than the entire motor self.

This effect, of course, was to be expected in the absence of higher integrative centres of the cerebral hemispheres. All motor stimuli, moreover, would effect the motor self as opposition stimuli, for the same reason. Overwhelming of minor units of tonic discharge on the one hand, and alliance with minor units on the other could only occur at motor psychons *below* the level of the tonic centres. Such interruptions or facilitations therefore, would be unable to effect an antagonistic diminution or an allied increase in the motor self, or total tonic discharge. Hence, according to our foregoing integrative analysis, compliance emotion on the one hand, and the higher pleasure emotional elements of love or " sex " (i.e. inducement and submission), on the other hand, could not possibly occur. This was precisely the result reported by Goltz. The only integrative mechanism intact in this animal would apparently be reinforcement of the tonic outflow in response to an integratively weaker opposition motor stimulus. This response would remain so long as the tonic reinforcement mechanisms themselves remained un-

[1] F. Goltz, " Der Hund ohne Grosshirn, *Arch. fur d. gesam. Physiol.* 1892, vol. i, p. 570.

impaired. The behaviour resulting would be an uninhibited aggressive attack upon the environmental stimulus, and the only emotion remaining would be pure dominance.

When we examine the behaviour of human infants, we find, similarly, that this same type of *dominance* emotion is among the first to develop. In fact, Watson reports[1] that this dominant type of behaviour constitutes an inherent or un-learned emotional response. Watson, following the literary precedent, refers to this reaction as " the emotion of rage ". Were it not that the behaviour as described by Watson seems clearly to indicate both pure dominance response and com-plicated factors of a thwarted nature, there would be no especial objection to following the lead of the poets and term-ing the whole response " rage ". There is, however, distinct evidence of a baffled or thwarted element which is not normally present in the infant response of dominance at its inception, both according to my own observations, and to those of Watson. This element creeps into the child's reaction more or less gradually as the emotion proceeds toward its climax.

Watson describes the environmental stimulus to " rage " response as " hampering of bodily movement ". He used the method of holding the infant's head tightly between the hands, pressing the arms to the sides, or holding the legs tightly together. These environmental stimuli, of course, are felt by the child as opposition forces. But the opposing stimuli are *integratively inferior* to the tonic motor self of the infant, for otherwise the pre-existing bodily position or attitude would be altered, and new anti-tonic types of bodily movement would appear. Instead, however, there is a " stiffening of the whole body, free slashing movement of the hands, arms and legs, and the holding of the breath ". All these symptoms constitute enhancement or exaggeration of the previously maintained tonic posture and movement, which the opposition stimulus hampers but does not integrat-ively interrupt. In short, *the motor self of the infant increases in the process of overcoming an opposing or hampering force of less integrative force than itself.*

Up to this point there is no evidence of any integrative phenomenon except that of pure dominance. " There is no crying at first ", says Watson, " then the mouth is opened to the fullest extent and the breath is held until the face

[1] J. B. Watson, *Behaviorism*, 1925, New York, p. 122.

appears blue ". Screaming and crying may also enter the total response after the thwarted or baffled element has begun to manifest itself. The nature of this complicating element of thwartedness will be described at greater length in a succeeding chapter. For the present it is sufficient to distinguish clearly between pure dominance of child behaviour, and dominance plus thwartedness. The latter may accurately enough be termed " rage ", since literary meaning seems to accord fairly well with the psycho-physical fact at this point.

Easily observable dominance emotion, then, is to be found in decerebrate animals and in human infants ten to fifteen days after birth.

Development of Dominance Response in Young Children

In the average child dominance emotion seems to develop unchecked, for the most part, during the first two or three years of infancy. Watson mentions " the never to be forgotten experience " of arousing extreme dominance in his two year old daughter while walking across a crowded street. The child suddenly pulled her father in an opposite direction to that in which she was being led. The father " quickly and sharply jerked her back, and exerted steady pressure upon her arm to keep her straight ". The child then " suddenly stiffened, began to scream at the top of her voice, and lay down stiff as a ram-rod in the middle of the street yelling with wide open mouth until she became blue in the face, and continuing to yell until she could make no further sound ". This bit of behaviour is given by Watson as illustrative of " rage " and there certainly seems to be a definite amount of baffledness or thwartedness in the total response which justifies use of the term " rage " to characterize a part, at least, of the episode.

But the entire reaction seems to me to reveal an underlying basis of maximally intense dominance throughout. Every action, even including the screaming, constituted an increase of the force of the motor self, to overcome the opposition stimulus represented by the father. The child was simply determined to " have her own way ", as the current phrase puts it, and she called on her motor reinforcement mechanism to its utmost possible power to accomplish this result. Moreover, so far as Watson informs us, the child *did* have her own way. The fact that she might have been carried bodily in the direction the father desired need not, and probably did not operate as an integrative defeat to her unchecked dominance. Only an environmental stimulus capable of producing motor stimuli more powerful than the motor self of the child could have operated to turn her dominance emotion into compliance.

According to my own observation, little girls are apt to develop certain emotional elements of inducement and submission about the time the earliest indications of sexual development appear. This may occur from the third year on. Boys, on the other hand, appear to suffer an accession of dominance practically parallel with the appearance of other secondary sex characteristics. I have observed in some cases what seems to be a continuously cumulative development of dominance in male children from birth to adolescence. In a properly trained child this dominant development may be fairly well controlled by a parallel learning of compliance response. But in male children of inadequate home training, dominance may develop, at an extraordinarily early age, to an extreme where it cannot thereafter be checked by environmental restraint, no matter how physically overwhelming the restraining influence may be.

I once had occasion to observe a boy, five and a half years old, who was spending the summer in care of an adoring but incompetent mother. This child seemed to possess no more than a normal male complement of dominance emotion. Yet a total absence of emotional training had brought the boy to the point where no environmental stimulus which could be inflicted upon him evoked motor stimuli more powerful than his own determination to do as he pleased. He paid no attention whatever to his mother's commands to give up other children's toys, or to come home for meals. One day the mother had been searching some time for her small son, when she noticed a group of children playing on the beach.

" Is Edgar there ? " she called.

" No, he is not ", replied Edgar's voice from the midst of the group on the beach.

To Edgar, an excited and physically powerful mother represented an opposition stimulus capable of being brushed aside by the slight increase in his own motor set necessary to speak a few words of reproving denial. This was the sort of thing that went on in Edgar's case throughout the greater part of the summer.

Then the child's father came down to the shore for a two weeks' vacation. The father was of different emotional mould from the mother. During the first week of his vacation he systematically chased Edgar, carrying him off forcibly from his play when called, and taking away forbidden toys with a considerable excess of violence when the child refused to give them up. But a week's treatment of this sort had no observable effect on Edgar. When his father snatched a toy out of his hand, the child attacked the father's leg with both fists, howling the while for the return of his plaything. I saw this occur perhaps twenty times, with no diminution whatever in the boy's dominance. Then Edgar's father decided that it was time for sterner measures. But these likewise had no effect for some time.

Finally, the father actually injured the child by whipping him with what looked like a good sized club. After this, the first evidences of compliance began to appear in the child's behaviour toward his father. Gradually under this method of training, continued by the mother as well as by the father, the boy began visibly to weigh in the balance the strength of the opposition which he would be called upon to face in case he failed to obey. If he decided, on the basis of his new experience, that his parents were within easy reaching distance of himself, and that they were worked up emotionally to an intensity of feeling likely to result in a whipping, Edgar would trot along, unconcernedly, in obedience to their commands. On such occasions he appeared to be the most docile child in the world. If, on the other hand (especially in the case of his mother) the tone of voice or physical pre-occupation of a parent seemed to argue comparative weakness in relation to Edgar's own running ability, the boy would dash off in an opposite direction, defying the parental dictum quite as unconcernedly as he had previously obeyed it. Edgar now invariably manifested, however, a very much greater increase in his own motor energy than he had displayed in resisting commands at the beginning of the summer.

I have given this example of child behaviour at length, not because it is unusual in type but because it seems to illustrate rather completely the natural development of untrained dominance in a perfectly normal male child.. It also illustrates rather well, the difference in emotional meaning between environmental stimuli which are more integratively powerful than the child's motor self and those which are merely more powerful physically than the child's body. In this case of Edgar, actual injury was done to the child's body before the resulting motor stimuli evoked within his central nervous system proved to be more intense than his motor self. Had the parents been wiser, of course, they might have been able to devise environmental stimuli of superior intensity in a more humane and expeditious manner. But this result is not an easy one to accomplish once the dominance response is permitted to develop in excess of the other primary emotions.

Borderline between Normal and Abnormal Dominance

It should again be emphasized that Edgar was, as far as I could determine during a rather careful study of three months, a perfectly normal child. When a child is emotionally abnormal, especially as a result of some continuous internal stimulation like hypersecretion of a glandular substance, control of dominance emotion may be still more difficult. Many of the children who were sent to us as behaviour problems in the public schools undoubtedly fell into this classification.

A boy between ten and eleven years of age, for instance, had developed a singular predeliction for " gang " warfare with boys of his own age and older. This youngster was particularly bright mentally as indicated by the Stanford-Binet test, and also by teachers' reports and school records. He was alert, and attractive in physical appearance. Moreover, he possessed a certain amount of tractibility when asked by a woman teacher, as a personal favour, to behave himself in school ; and when under the influence of older persons whom he liked during outside activities. But his home training had been woefully deficient, and in addition to this lack of emotional training, he was also suffering from endocrine imbalance, according to the medical diagnosis. The emotional appeal which any sort of opposition exercised over this lad's dominance was truly astounding. An opposition stimulus aroused a dominant response no matter how intense or physically powerful the environmental stimulus might be. For example, this boy led his own " gang " into a deliberate attack upon a rival group of youths many years

older than the subject's crowd, and outnumbering the younger
boys almost two to one. When stones, knives, or heavy
sticks were used in a fight it seemed to stimulate the boy Jack
to almost superhuman strength and aggressiveness. In short,
an opposition environmental stimulus was not ever felt as
stronger than the boy's own motor self. The added environmental intensity seemed to register only as an increase in the
opposition or antagonism.

Jack represented a type of boy whose dominance had been
developed, evidently by endocrine abnormalities, to a degree
where no amount of intensity in the environmental stimulus
was capable of evoking motor stimuli more powerful than
the boy's motor self, even though severe physical injury might
be inflicted by the environmental stimulus. This case is
cited here merely to mark the border line between unbalanced
dominance emotion resulting from lack of training, yet susceptible to being turned into compliance merely by intensifying
the environmental stimulus sufficiently ;   and unbalanced
dominance emotion abnormally maintained in a state of
hyper-excitability by continuous intraorganic stimulation.
This type of over-dominance is definitely abnormal because
it is incapable of integrative conversion into compliance by
means of increasing the strength of the environmental stimulation applied, sufficiently to cause bodily injury.

 There are other methods of controlling dominance, besides
this compulsory transition to compliance, which will be discussed later. In the present chapter, however, we are concerned, primarily, not with the methods of emotional education,
but merely with tracing the characteristics and limits of
dominance emotion as it appears in various types of human
behaviour.

Summary and Analysis

Summarizing our analyses of dominant behaviour up to this
point, we may detect in every instance the following elements :

(1) An antagonistic motor stimulus of less intensity than
the motor self.

(2) A dominance type of response evoked by this type of
stimulus, including,

(3) An increase in the strength of the motor self equal to
the intensity of the opposition stimulus dominated.

In the decerebrated animals studied by Sherrington and

Goltz, deprivation of the integrative motor centres possessing ascendency over the tonic centres presumably caused every environmental stimulus to evoke motor stimuli antagonistic to the motor self of the animal, and of inferior integrative potency to the free tonic discharge, enhanced as it was by removal of cortical inhibition. The animals manifested typical domination response to these inferior antagonistic motor stimuli. The increase of the tonic discharge in each case was easily observable and was apparently proportionate to the exaggerated intensity of the intervening motor stimuli.

In Watson's observation of unlearned rage emotion in young babies, we find first of all an antagonistic environmental stimulus consisting of " hampering of the child's movement ". As above noted, the motor stimuli evoked by this type of environmental stimulus must be less intense at all times than the child's motor self since the previously existing motor set or attitude was not altered. The response evoked was purely dominant in type, at least at its inception. The increase in the intensity of the motor self, in this type of reaction, seems to approximate very closely the measurable intensity of the environmnetal stimulus administered. That is, the observed increase in strength of the child's muscular contractions runs closely parallel to the increase in weight or other types of antagonistic pressure which the child is compelled to overcome in trying to carry out his former movements. It may be noted in connection with this type of dominance response that opposition pressure sufficient to stop all movement of the child's arms and legs does not suffice by itself to evoke motor stimuli of superior intensity to the child's motor self.

In the case of the two year old child who lay down in the crowded street rather than yield to guidance which was opposed to her own pre-existing motor set, we find an extraordinary increase of intensity of the child's motor self occurring in the course of her dominant behaviour. It is, of course, possible that this marked increase in intensity of the motor self represents a learned incongruity between environmental stimulus and the motor stimulus which, through previous experience, it had acquired power to evoke. On the other hand, if we assume that the child had not had previous experience with " quick, sharp jerks ", administered by an apprehensive parent, by naughty boys in the course of play, or by experimenting psychologists in the course of testing her

" rage " emotions, we may regard her excessively intense dominance response as approximately equal to the antagonistic motor stimuli which would probably be evoked by the environmental stimulus consisting of a " quick sharp jerk ".

In considering the " rage " emotion of fifteen-day-old babies, we noted that opposing pressure sufficient to prevent all movement did not evoke motor stimuli of superior intensity to the motor self. A " quick sharp jerk " seems to be an environmental stimulus peculiarly well adapted to evoking motor stimuli still more intense than those resulting from mere stopping of the movements. The " quick sharp jerk " then, evidently was felt by the child as more intense opposition to her motor self than a more steady, continuous pressure, sufficient to prevent her from moving as she desired. Yet, this quick, sharp jerk did not suffice, apparently, to evoke motor stimuli more intense than the child's motor self. The dominance response still appeared with an increase in the intensity of the motor self again approximately proportionate to the antagonistic environmental stimulus, even though this time the stimulus quickly and sharply jerked the child's whole body antagonistically to the maximal opposition of the motor self.

With Edgar, the five and a half year old child whose dominance had been allowed to develop unchecked, we may note the intensity threshold of environmental stimulus necessary to evoke motor stimuli more intense than the motor self in a normal organism. In Edgar's case, at least, this threshold was not passed until actual injury had been done to the subject's body. Not only did " quick sharp jerks " and shakings fail to register in Edgar's organism as more powerful than his own motor self, but even a considerable amount of pain stimulation inflicted with a small whip and moderate sized sticks similarly failed to pass what may be called " the compliance stimulus threshold ". The intensity of the motor stimuli evoked by an injury to the child's body may have arisen quite as much from the idea that something very serious had happened to him, as from the actual pain experience accompanying the injury itself. The pain, however, was undoubtedly more severe than that which the child had experienced from previous whippings. At any rate, bodily injury giving rise to considerable pain did succeed, apparently, in making itself felt by the child as a stimulus more intense than his own motor self.

At the point of passing this threshold, Edgar's behaviour became a mixture of dominance and compliance. Evidently part of the environmental stimulus was still felt as of inferior intensity, while the other part had passed the threshold and had ceased to evoke dominance response at all. This case illustrates, in all probability, the limit of normal, naive dominance, pretty much unmodified by admixture of other primary emotions.

In the case of Jack, the youthful gangster, we find an abnormal condition of the dominance mechanism which raises the compliance stimulus threshold to a point where it could not be passed even by environmental stimulation consisting of bodily injuries (of which Jack had received a number). In short, no possible intensity of environmental stimulus seemed capable, in Jack's behaviour, of evoking motor stimuli more intense than the child's motor self. When such a condition of the dominance mechanism is found in a child below the age of adolescence, it almost inevitably indicates that the child has experienced or is experiencing continuously, an amount of dominance stimulation abnormally great in proportion to adequate stimulation of the other primary emotions.

Dominance Behaviour of Less Extreme Character

The instances of dominance emotion so far considered have all shown dominance responses of extreme intensity, with behaviour symptoms the character of which was obvious. When dominance occurs in more ordinary and usual behaviour, its emotional quality is still easily discernible from objective analysis of bodily response, and from its relation to the environmental stimulus. We may note a few such instances.

When the infant grasping reflex develops, almost immediately after birth, the reinforcement of this response is particularly notable. An attempt to pull away from the baby a rod or stick which he has grasped, or about which his fingers have been passively pressed by the experimenter[1] will be felt by the baby's grasping the stick more tightly, to resist the experimenter's attempt to take the stick away. There we have the motor self increasing its own intensity in order to overpower

---

[1] Watson states that he employs this method of evoking the reflex in the first place. J. B. Watson, *Behaviorism*, p. 98.

an antagonistic stimulus of less intensity than itself. This dominance response may continue until the child is actually suspending its own weight by means of his grasp on the rod.

Older infants, in their play, continually manifest dominance emotion. A small boy of three or four years may persist for a quarter of an hour or more in trying to push a velocipede or toy wagon into a space too small for the toy. In one instance of this sort which I happened to observe, the child finally succeeded in this effort at the cost of a broken wagon wheel. The environmental stimulus in this case was clearly antagonistic, and to the child, with his limited experience concerning the strength of environmental opponents, the stimulus seemed weaker than himself. At any rate, the motor stimuli which the wagon evoked actually proved weaker than the child's motor self since he persisted in his action without change of method.

Dominance of the Chase

One type of dominance response common to animals, young children, adult males, and some women, consists of chasing anything that runs away from the subject. Running away is a type of behaviour which makes the fugitive a perfect stimulus to the dominance emotion of the pursuer. On the one hand, it makes the fleeing animal *antagonistic* to the subject, because it diminishes the subject's visual and other sensory perception of the disappearing object, and may also indicate that the running animal is being driven away by the subject's antagonistic influence. On the other hand, it clearly stigmatizes the fugitive as *inferior in strength* to the subject. Once the subject begins pursuit, his dominant purpose is to *stop the flight of the fugitive*. The fleeing animal *opposes* this purpose by continuing to run, while, all the time, he admits himself weaker than the pursuer by his very flight. The subject responds with the purest possible type of dominance response; his motor self increasing, cumulatively, and his antagonism to the fugitive correspondingly increasing at every stride.

This type of dominance response may aptly be called " dominance of the chase ". It has most frequently been regarded as " *hunting instinct* ", or " the instinct to kill ". Nothing more elaborate than the simplest type of dominance integration seems necessary to explain the phenomenon in

k

its entirety. The feature that has led to such striking uniformity in hunting behaviour of men and animals is the peculiar aptitude of this type of stimulus to evoke pure dominance response ; and the existence of a compliance response mechanism also in men and animals, the untrained development of which causes them to run away if the strength and nature of another creature is unknown. Thus the primary emotional response mechanism of one animal inevitably causes it to stimulate another animal to dominance of the chase.

Berry reported that kittens which had been given no opportunity to learn from older cats, made no effort to catch or kill mice when the mice did not run away from the kittens.[1] Yerkes and Bloomfield, upholders of instinct, reported that one kitten out of four (younger than those studied by Berry) chased a mouse spontaneously, and after some practice caught and killed a mouse.[2] But as nearly as one can tell from their report, *the mouse ran away first.* And the other mice did not happen to run away from the other kittens. Once dominance of the chase is evoked by a mouse running away, the bodily structures of the cat, tonically innervated, and dominantly reinforced, seem sufficient to result, inevitably, in catching and killing the fugitive mouse. These same structures, activated by dominance of the chase response, also cause the cat to chase and " kill " a fugitive mechanical mouse, or a wad of paper on a string. It is the integrative mechanism of dominance emotion which is inherited, and which activates, because of its connection with the motor self, all body structures tonically innervated, whatever those structures may be in any animal species. If the structures are adapted as are the muscles, claws, and teeth of a cat, to catching and killing a smaller animal, then the fugitive is caught and killed. A naive human child, without such bodily structures, makes no effort to tear apart or kill a fugitive kitten or dog which he has caught, though he may maul the animal about in the manner to which the tonically innervated muscles of his hands and arms are best adapted.

[1] C. S. Berry, " An Experimental Study of Imitation in Cats," *Journal of Comparative Neurology and Psychology*, 1908, vol. XVIII, p. 1.
[2] R. M. Yerkes and D. Bloomfield, " Do Kittens Instinctively Kill Mice ? " *Psychological Bulletin*, 1910, vol. VII, p. 253.

Cats chase mice, dogs chase cats, young children chase cats and dogs, and adult males chase women and wild animals. In every case, *running away is the stimulus which evokes dominance of the chase.* In several of the cases cited, the fugitive *wants* to be chased, (animals for purposes of play, women for purposes of love), and runs away because experience has taught that dominance of the chase can almost certainly be evoked by flight, and that this response once evoked, nearly always supercedes all others in controlling the subject's emotions.

" Destructive Dominance "

Another form or expression of dominance emotion which frequently appears in the behaviour of boys from the ages of two or three to the end of adolescence, is what might be termed " destructive dominance ". A young child may spend an hour or more erecting a structure of blocks, only to knock it down with great violence and apparently with great satisfaction. The blocks have worked themselves into the position of antagonists to the child by virtue of their refractory behaviour when he tried to place them in unbalanced positions, in the course of his building activities. The completed pile, however, represents an environmental stimulus known to be very much weaker than the child's good right arm. There follows, then, a dominance response peculiarly satisfying to the child because the intensity of the emotion is out of all proportion to the intensity of the environmental stimulus as it then presents itself, which is all the opposition that need be overcome to give the child a dominant triumph over environment. The intensity of the dominance emotion thus expressed is the product of motor stimuli aroused by past building difficulties, and transferred to the blocks by a process of learning, or reflex conditioning.

At a later age, destructive dominance of this same type may reach rather dangerous heights. Vacant houses are pretty sure to have their windows and doors thoroughly smashed if there are any number of male youngsters in the neighbourhood. I have known several instances where deserted barns and outbuildings have been set on fire by boys ten to thirteen years old, apparently as an expression of sheer destructive dominance.[1]   All dominant behaviour of this type manifests, of course, a variety of emotional transfer by which harmless environmental objects acquire the tendency to evoke intense antagonistic motor stimuli.

Competitive Dominance

The dominance response evoked by competition with other youngsters is of great importance, both in the school room and on the play ground.   The essence of competition seems to be an arrangement of the total environment situation in such a way that each child feels every other child engaged in the same task or game to be his antagonist, yet an antagonist of inferior ability or strength.   I have made the experiment of removing this element from a competitive situation by demonstrating conclusively to one of the competitors that his opponent could undoubtedly do better work than himself.   Once the boy became really convinced of this fact he lost all interest in the competition and turned in a result (arithmetical sums) only about fifty per cent. as good as his previous average under former conditions of competition.

I have also observed, in giving mental tests both to adults and to children, that the test scores apparently can be greatly improved by emphasizing the possibility that the group to be tested has an excellent chance of bettering the score made by another rival group.   This result was especially notable in certain convict groups and in the army testing. I have also many times observed the converse situation where unusually poor test scores appear to result from initial knowledge that the individuals tested do not compare well in test passing ability with other persons tested.

In general, moreover, the two elements of the competitive situation, antagonism to rivals and regarding the rival of inferior ability, are very much harder to establish with groups of women than with male subjects of similar qualifications. In one instance, a girl art student of unquestionably superior ability, habitually refused to work if required to do so under conditions of competition.   The explanation of this girl's

---

[1] Of course, it might be more exciting to suppose, as some psychoanalysts do, that all incendiary behaviour is expressive of suppressed " sex desire ".   But we must sometimes sacrifice " mental sex-stimulation " to truth.

behaviour seems to be that the competitive situation immediately imposed upon her the feeling that the work of the other students might be better than her own. This interpretation of the stimulus situation totally eliminated its character as an adequate stimulus to dominance. Again, the explanation of female incompetence in passing a mental test may very frequently lie in the subject's seeming inability to regard fellow students as rivals, or to feel any element of opposition in either the test itself or the examiner. Girls frequently appear just as well satisfied with a poor record as with a good one, and seem willing to submit to any degree of harshness of criticism, or reproof from the teacher or examiner without themselves assuming the least antagonism of attitude.

An illustration of this type of behaviour may be found in the case of two girls whose test scores in both the group tests and individual Stanford-Binet tests placed them in the feeble-minded class. The IQ of one of these girls, figured from total test results, was about sixty-five. The other showed an IQ of less than fifty. In the course of a personality analysis, and not for the purpose of rectifying test results, I induced one of these girls to answer accurately nearly all the Stanford-Binet questions appropriate to her physical age (the child having had no opportunity to learn the correct answers, since the personality interview immediately followed the Binet test). The other girl could not be induced to answer more than half the questions, even under the conditions of the personality conference. Of those she answered, more than eighty-five per cent. were answered correctly. In short, these children responded normally to a friendly, or allied environmental stimulus, but they did not respond at all to the element of antagonism or rivalry in any stimulus presented to them.

Conditioning of Adult Dominance Responses

In adult life dominance is almost always found to be very much modified as a result of two types of emotional learning. First, nearly all normal adults have come to regard a great majority of the environmental stimuli presented to them as more powerful than themselves. The motor stimuli evoked by most environmental situations, therefore, are more intense than the motor self of the adult subject. As a result, the stimulus evokes compliance rather than dominance.

Secondly, nearly all normal adult males have learned to express dominance toward certain special types of environmental stimuli connected with their business or principal occupation. Doctors, especially, exemplify this type of emotional learning. It seems significant in this connection that the central tendency of mental tests scores found among medical officers in the army was notably lower than the central tendency of test scores among most other classes of army officers. The doctors, in other words, had become more highly specialized with regard to the class of environmental stimuli capable of evoking dominance response than men of education in other occupations.

Examples of intense dominance emotion in adults are very easy to find by analysis of crucial situations occurring in the course of the subject's special business, or other occupation. If a business man learns that a rival is getting the best of him in competing for a certain market, he immediately releases his utmost personal energy and financial power to overwhelm the rival and recover the market. It has been frequently stated in the press, for example, that Henry Ford, finding himself in danger of being outdone in the cheap car market, has reorganized and retooled his entire manufacturing plant at a cost estimated at $100,000,000, for the purpose of re-establishing his control over the car market. This seems in point as an example of sheer dominance response. The environmental stimulus represented by General Motors and other rival car interests was unquestionably antagonistic to Ford, and was, moreover, of such intensity that it would have evoked motor stimuli stronger than the motor self in nearly all individuals. Ford, however, the strength of whose motor self may be measured in terms of both his enormous wealth and his extraordinary personal ability, felt his rival to be less powerful than himself, and responded to the challenge with an increase of his own power which may well prove sufficient to overcome the opposition offered. (There is also, of course, in Ford's behaviour, a large element of compliance which we may refer to again in the next chapter).

Adult males manifest dominance emotion to a considerable extent in sports as well as in business. International tennis matches, polo matches, swimming competitions, and

Olympic games are of absorbing interest to a great majority of men in the competing countries, no matter how little inclined these men may be to engage personally in athletics of any kind. The social or vicarious element in this attitude will be dealt with in a later chapter. But at the present moment we may note that the underlying emotional interest which supports international athletic competitions is a dominant one. Such athletic events merely represent highly specialized and selective competitive stimulus situations. In a Davis Cup tennis match, for example, the best player on both sides is necessarily a man who possesses extraordinary reserve reinforcements of tonic energy. His opponent is an environmental stimulus rendered completely antagonistic both by the rules of the game, and by the conflicting personal and national interests involved. Each antagonist must regard his opponent as less powerful than himself, for otherwise, his motor self would comply instead of increasing its intensity at the crucial moment of the game. Each endeavours to reinforce his motor self, then, by an increment of energy sufficient to overcome his rival and reap the honours in store for the winner. In addition to this rather naive dominance response, manifested by the players themselves, the popular press of the rival nations involved in the tournament endows each of these best players with a motor self of enormous proportions, by the systematic alignment of the national dominance, so to speak, behind the individual dominance of the players. Thus, millions of individual motor selves may actually be fluctuating with the changes in the tonic energy experienced by the men on the court. This situation is practically the only one to be found in which the dominance response of enormous numbers of people not only can be combined, but also even synchronized. A large amount of compliance is involved in the athletic competition situation, just as in the business behaviour mentioned. The compliance elements remain to be considered in the next chapter.

Sex Differences in Dominance

Sex differences in adult dominance emotion are perhaps, on the whole, less pronounced than are sex differences in the dominance responses of children and adolescents. Women are now engaging more and more extensively in business and sports. The emotional training which they thus receive tends, apparently, to enhance their dominance emotion and to place it more nearly on a par with that of men. The effect of this development is now beginning to make itself apparent in the emotional training of the younger generation. Adolescent girls and very young women are pre-empting the spot light of publicity in national sports contests to nearly as great a degree as adult murderesses, mistresses of kings, and other notable female characters pre-empted it in former generations.

The mainstay of adult female dominance emotion, however, still remains, to a considerable extent, the same in this generation as it was in the days of Roman intrigue and Alexandrian revelry. That is, the seeking of " social " prestige probably represents the most usual female expression of dominance. Rival matrons and debutantes represent antagonistic stimuli of varying intensity, but always seem incapable of evoking motor stimuli superior in strength to the "society woman's " motor self. The lady in question responds to such a stimulus by increasing her social energy in the form of more lavish display and so-called " entertainment ", or by the purchase of more expensive and fashionable gowns or other possessions. By this increase in her motor self, the seeker for social prestige purposes to sweep all rivals from her path, and to control that extremely intangible but much-talked-of "society ". Since the prize sought is itself based upon other emotions than dominance, we may defer further analysis of this type of dominance response until a later chapter.

Summary

In summary, we may define dominance as an emotional response which is *evoked by an antagonistic motor stimulus of inferior intensity to the motor self of the subject.*

There frequently appears a marked incongruity between the nature and intensity of the environmental stimulus and the resulting intensity of dominance emotion expressed in dominance behaviour. This incongruity simply means that the animal or human being has undergone previous experiences which have endowed an inadequate environmental stimulus with the ability to evoke, in the subject organism, antagonistic motor stimuli of an intensity corresponding to the dominance increase in the strength of the motor self actually manifested in the instance observed. The *dominant character of the emotion* is determined by the inferiority of strength which the motor stimuli are felt to possess in comparison with the motor self. But the amount of intensity increase shown by the motor self in the dominance response approximately equals the intensity of the motor stimulus which the dominance reaction is intended to overcome.

Dominance response possessing the characteristics just defined is to be found as a behaviour principle in the interaction between inanimate forces of nature, in decerebrate animals, in children immediately after birth (suspending self by reinforcement of grasping reflex), in adolescents, especially boys, and in adults of both sexes, principally males.

Dominance emotion may be said to constitute by far the largest and most important element in the emotional influence upon the behaviour of all children for the first three to five years of life, and of a great majority of males from birth to death. Since our civilization is man made, dominance is probably the emotion most universally admired by both sexes.

Dominance is found to be the theme expressed in countless monuments, sculptures, musical compositions and other works of art. Of all these glorifications of dominance, Henley's " Invictus " is perhaps the most succinct and complete.

> Out of the night that covers me,
>   Black as the Pit from pole to pole,
> I thank whatever gods may be
>   For my unconquerable soul.
>
> In the fell clutch of circumstance
>   I have not winced nor cried aloud.
> Under the bludgeonings of chance
>   My head is bloody, but unbowed.
>
> It matters not how strait the gate,
>   How charged with punishments the scroll,
> I am the master of my fate;
>   I am the captain of my soul.

The Pleasantness and Unpleasantness of Dominance

The consciousness experienced during dominant behaviour

of the kind described, varies considerably in its pleasantness or unpleasantness, according to introspective reports of different observers. Jack Dempsey, former heavyweight boxing champion, has stated (to friends, and not for publication), that he "likes" a fight, from beginning to end : but that his "biggest kick" comes at the moment he delivers a knock-out "sock". Sometimes he enjoys the crowd's enthusiasm after a victory, but sometimes he does not. As far as one can judge, the degree of pleasantness that Dempsey says he feels depends rather upon his consciousness of personal dominance over his opponent, than upon the attitude of other people toward him as victor. Another type of pleasant emotional response is no doubt felt upon the receipt of the cash won by the fight in one way and another, but that need not be considered here.

It is hard to say how much of this subsequently reported pleasantness was actually felt prior to the knock-out, and how much of it has been retrospectively injected into experiences which were, at the time, unpleasant. From my own introspection, and from the reports of students (one a professional wrestler) who were more highly trained in self observation than was Dempsey, I should say that the *early portion of an ultimately successful, dominant contest is felt as a mixture of pleasantness and unpleasantness.* There is a certain "grimness", "strain", "over-tension", or "desperation" about any protracted dominant struggle, in its initial stages, that is distinctly unpleasant. At the same time, there is also a distinct pleasantness normally felt by a truly dominant contestant, which seems to spring from the feeling of "my own strength increasing" to meet the danger, and which seems unmistakably to increase in proportion to the subject's success in reducing the strength of his opponent.

Dempsey's report that his greatest pleasantness is felt as he delivers a blow which finally puts his opponent out of the fight is probably accurate. But so long as the issue of ascendancy between the antagonistic environmental stimulus (the opposing contestant) and the subject's own physical powers is undecided, there is apt to exist a parallel struggle, on fairly balanced terms, between the antagonistic motor stimulus and the motor self. This struggle is felt as distinctly unpleasant, according to the concensus of the self-observations of subjects who have no end to serve by pretending otherwise, and who are sufficiently trained in self-observation to make their introspections worth while. Several American football players of note have published articles, within the last few years, setting forth their opinions that the unpleasantness of successful college football greatly exceeds its pleasantness.

It is my own conclusion that *dominance emotion is a mixture of pleasantness and unpleasantness throughout each dominant response.* Even after the " knock-out " of an opponent, there remains a certain tinge of remembered antagonism which gives the final pleasantness its distinctly dominant savour. If the strength of the obstacle to be overcome is markedly inferior to the strength of the subject (like the child's block pile, or the windows of an empty house), the initial unpleasantness of undecided conflict may be comparatively slight, with the nearly unalloyed pleasantness of final success reaching a speedy climax. It must be remembered, however, that the unpleasantness has its origin in the psychonic struggle between motor stimulus and motor self, while the final intense pleasantness has its source in the facilitation due to increased out-pouring of tonic energy (motor self) through the motor centres. If the initial unpleasantness of dominance emotion be slight, because an opponent is weak, the final accession of pleasantness due to increase of the motor self necessary to overcome this obstacle will prove correspondingly inconsiderable. *If the dominance response is successful, it will contain a much larger comparative percentage of pleasantness at the end than it did at the beginning.*

The proportion of unpleasantness may reach a climax, in some instances of dominant response, at the point where self and opponent are most evenly matched, the proportion of pleasantness increasing thereafter, and the proportion of unpleasantness decreasing, in parallel degree with the increase of unhampered outflow of the motor self and the defeat of the antagonist. It is an interesting result of my own clinical researches that I have found many women subjects who repeatedly refuse to dominate business situations to the maximum of benefit to themselves, apparently for no other reason than that the dominance emotion involved is too unpleasant to them. I think that most men devote their lives to dominance not because they actually find it pleasant, but because they can't help it.

Distinctive Conscious Characteristics of Dominance Emotion

What is thought of, introspectively, as the peculiar emotional quality of dominance emotion has been variously characterized in literature, pseudo-psychology, and psychology. It has been named " ego-emotion ", " aggressiveness ", " fury ", " rage ", " self-assertion ", " initiative ", " will ", " determination ", " high spirit ", " self seeking ", " courage ", " nerve ", " boldness ", " dare-deviltry ", " purposiveness ", " persistency ", " unconquerableness ", " stick-to-itiveness ", " go-getiveness ", " force of character ", " force ", " power ", " pioneer spirit ", " strength of character ", " strength ", " stubbornness ", " bulldog character ", " doggedness ", " fighting instinct ", " instinct of self-preservation ", " superiority complex ", " inferiority feeling ", (Alfred Adler), " ego-centricity ", and many other nom-de-plumes. Sometimes the passive aspect of dominant resistance to the antagonist is emphasized, sometimes the active aspect of dominant removal of the opponent from the subject's path is stressed. Sometimes the term used carries the suggestion that dominance is despicable (this is usually when the writer feels himself or his hero to have been dominated), and sometimes the word employed implies a certain sanctification of dominance (as in the press enconiums of Lindbergh, following his flight over the Atlantic, or in the religious praises of the " Almighty "). But whatever attitudinal meanings may be included in the term used, and whatever aspect or behaviour expression of the emotion may be selectively suggested by the word used, the *common denominator of emotional meaning is always dominance emotion, consisting of increase of the self to overcome an opponent,*

Introspectively, there is unanimous agreement among reports obtained from many different types of subjects that the essence of dominance emotion (no matter what name the subject may know it under), is *a feeling of an outrush of energy to remove opposition. This feeling, with an admixture of unpleasantness accompanying the obstruction of the outrushing energy in so far as it is obstructed, and an admixture of pleasantness accompanying the increase of energy outrush in so far as it is increased, constitutes dominance emotion.*

CHAPTER VIII

COMPLIANCE

THE forces of nature comply with one another under appropriate conditions, just as they dominate each other, as we have already noted, under other circumstances. A river may be turned from one channel into another by a wall of rock which chances to crop out across its former course. The stream does not continue to attack an opponent stronger than itself, but complies with such an antagonist by letting the opponent have its own way, and by turning its own energies in another direction. If the path which a stream or other natural force will dominate is determined by the inferior strength of the materials dominated, so in the same way is the course which a river will *not* follow determined by the superiority of strength possessed by an opposed barrier.

It is certainly a part of the fundamental essence of any physical force that it must go on dominating whatever opponent proves weaker than itself. But it is also just as essential a part of the innate nature of the same physical force to comply with any opponent which proves stronger than itself. If unable to dominate any of the forces surrounding it, a physical force must cease to act upon them. In so far as it may continue to exert pressure upon the stronger opponents which hem it in, the force has not yet been completely dominated by those opponents. Complete compliance can always be imposed upon any physical force by a sufficiently strong physical opponent, although the opponent may have to exert its power upon the compliant reagent in such a way as to compel the reagent to change its physical form, (from solid to liquid, or from liquid to gas). But, according to the fundamental law of conservation of energy no physical force can be destroyed. It can only (1) dominate, or (2) comply. If it continues to act in its existing form, it may comply with a hundred stronger opposing forces, but it must also find at least one weaker opponent to dominate. If any physical force is compelled to ultimate compliance, it must change its form in such a way that its new physical expression can find weaker antagonists to dominate.

For example, a river dammed up, as in the instance analysed at the beginning of the last chapter, may be completely dominated by the opposing dam so far as the free flowing of the stream goes. That is, one type of activity or expression of the river is completely dominated by a dam so strong and so high that the river cannot pass it. If, then, the soil of the river bank at one end of the dam proves sufficiently soft to be dominated by the river, the stream may simultaneously comply with the unpassable dam and also dominate its weaker opponent, the river bank. But if such outlet cannot be made around or under the dam then the river still continues to exert increased pressure against the barrier. In this particular, the dam cannot dominate or over-power the river, and the river, therefore, is not compelled to comply with an opponent which is weaker than itself in this particular.

The sun, however, constitutes another type of opponent which is stronger than the river in the matter of reducing its pressure. The action of the sun's rays upon the water is able to compel the water to change its form of physical expression altogether, from a fluid to a gas. The water thus vapourized no longer exerts pressure against the dam. Plants and other vegetable growths upon the bank of the dammed-up river also are able to dominate the water by compelling it to change its form chemically, and to enter into organic molecular structure of a new type, composing the cells of the various plant organisms. The fish and amphibia which make their home in the dammed-up river also possess sufficient dominance over the river to compel a chemical metamorphosis even more radical, by absorbing the river water into the chemical structures of their own body cells. All types of inanimate physical forces must behave in the same way according to the fundamental reaction principle of compliance, whenever they are confronted by antagonistic forces more powerful than themselves.

' If the physical forces faced by an opponent of superior strength comply with that opponent by decreasing the force of their opposition to the stronger antagonist, what is the measure of this decrease which the compliant reagent must undergo ?   In the case where the river, dominated by its opposing dam, was able to find its way around or under the dam, the volume of water which thus escaped evidently would represent the difference between the former total overflow of the river and the value of the opposed holding power of the obstacle to the river's progress. In the same way, the amount of water vaporized under action of the sun's rays represents a total volume of loss to the water pressure power of the dammed up stream equal to the difference between the initial volume of water and the strength of the antagonistic sun's rays acting upon it. The total volume of loss to the river of its molecular chemical structure H_2O, as a result of the superior chemical forces exerted by plants and animals upon it, must approximately equal the difference between the initial quantity of H_2O molecules present in the dammed-up river and the antagonistic forces exerted by plants and animals with which it was necessary for the water of the river to comply.

A rule may be formulated from these examples as follows : *A physical force decreases its power in making a compliance reaction by an amount approximately equal to the difference between its own initial strength and the force of its superior opponent.*

Compliance Response in Human and Animal Behaviour

Compliance response is to be found in the behaviour complement of a decerebrate animal such as those studied by Sherrington and Goltz. Such compliance, however, as is manifest in the reactions of artificially simplified organisms of this type does not carry with it compliance emotion as we have defined it in the integrative analysis of chapter six. Although a physical reflex can be made integratively to supersede a single tonic discharge unit of the motor self, the mechanism by which this conquest is brought about by a motor stimulus is of a nature comparable with the interaction of inanimate physical forces. The motor stimulus appears merely to overpower one specific unit of the motor self at a motor centre leading to the final common path but below the centres through which the intensity of the entire tonic self is regulated. Though the central nervous system interacts between higher and lower levels in such an exceedingly complicated manner that we cannot say with certainty what neural units are involved even in the simplest reflex response, we may yet feel fairly certain that the strength of the motor self is neither increased nor diminished throughout the persistence of the control of the lower motor centre by the intercurrent reflex. That is to say, in this type of conquest of tonic discharge by intercurrent motor stimuli, we apparently find the result accomplished by means of a greatly simplified antagonistic mechanism. One small unit of the motor self seems initially to contest possession of a motor psychon with a stronger antagonistic motor stimulus. When the stronger motor stimulus has won its way through to discharge there seems to be no further integrative action taking place because the higher centres capable of bringing about a further adjustment of the entire tonic discharge in reaction to the supremacy of this motor stimulus have been removed from the animal by operation. If this analysis of results is correct, we may conclude that all primary emotions except dominance require the presence of motor areas of the central nervous system integratively predominant over the tonic centres involved in that particular emotion.

The work of Head and Holmes[1] already mentioned, seems to indicate that both dominant and compliant adjustments of the motor self may be mediated through the thalamic centres alone, after these centres have been freed from the influence of the cerebral cortex. Many of the physical reactions to affective stimuli made by patients suffering from unilateral thalamic lesion described by Head and Holmes were reactions of the so-called adaptive type. That is, many of these responses were of a compliant nature giving free rein to the influence of an antagonistic motor stimulus upon the organism, by diminishing and readjusting tonic motor discharge. Such reactions were clearly compliance responses. They were all over-reactions, and all were unpleasant at their inception so far as one may judge from the reports, with indifference or even marked, contrasting pleasantness accomplished as a result of the adaptive readjustment. Does this behaviour indicate an integrative picture of exaggerated compliance response? It seems to be a justifiable guess that it does.

Compliance in Infant " Fear " Responses

Watson has described a certain type of infant behaviour[2]

---

[1] H. Head and G. Holmes, " Sensory Disturbances from Cerebral Lesions," *Brain*, 1911, vol. 34, p. 109.
[2] J. B. Watson, *Behaviorism*, pp. 121 ff.

which he calls " fear ". Only two situations, according to Watson, are capable of producing this " fear ". One is a removal of all support from an infant's body, and the other is a sudden loud sound near the infant's head. The " fear " response described by Watson consists, first, of " a jump, a start, a respiratory pause followed by more rapid breathing, sudden closure of eyes, clutching of hands, puckering of lips ". Following this initial response occurs an entirely different type of behaviour. This second group of reactions consists of " crying, falling down, crawling, walking, or running away, often defecation and urination." The first group of behaviour symptoms clearly indicate an access of tonic energy calculated to combat and dominate the motor stimuli in various ways. The second group of the behaviour symptoms just as clearly indicates a decrease of the strength of the motor self and a yielding to whatever effect the motor stimulus may have upon the organism. Mixed up in the subsequent symptoms, however, there are behaviour indications of certain thwarted or defeated elements, which perhaps, when present, justify use of the time-worn literary term " fear ". Without the admixture of this defeated element, however, the second group of symptoms described by Watson show only two types of environmental stimulus capable of evoking motor stimuli of sufficient intensity to integratively overpower the motor self. It is probable, of course, that many other types of environmental stimuli too severe to be inflicted upon a human infant experimentally might possess this same power. Watson reports that this compliant type of response was more pronounced in infants without cerebral hemispheres, a result in accord with our interpretation of the findings of Head and Holmes mentioned above.

The Watsons also found that normal human infants grasped all objects with no regard for the nature of the stimulus, even though it might be a furry animal, a noise-making stimulus, such as a pigeon in a paper bag, or even a lighted candle. It was found, however, that the child could be taught not to reach for an object by a varying number of burns inflicted by a candle flame, or by rapping the hand of the child sharply with a ruler when he reached for the object. It is to be noted that compliance response could not be brought about by an environmental stimulus of comparatively mild intensity such as the sight of a candle flame or the combined tactual sensations and visual perceptions of an animal which might be capable of biting and injuring the child. Compliance response could, however, be compelled by an environmental stimulus as intense as the tactual pain administered by contact with the flame, or by the painful sensations following a brisk stroke of the ruler upon the child's knuckles. The compliance response, once learned in this way, was readily transferred to whatever environmental stimulus might be associated with the pain in the child's experience. To put the matter in our own terms, the environmental stimuli of burns and blows administered to the child's hands proved inherently capable of evoking motor stimuli of superior intensity to the motor self. By administering such burns or blows simultaneously with perception of an environmental stimulus which naturally aroused motor stimuli weaker than the motor self, this inadequate environmental stimulus could be endowed with the power of evoking antagonistic motor stimuli more powerful than the motor self.

Compliance in Adult " Fear " Responses

Blatz[1] has performed an experiment with adult subjects which indicates that adults manifest much the same type of compliance response as that reported by Watson in infant behaviour. Blatz constructed a chair in the laboratory in such a way that it could be made to fall backward suddenly by pressing a lever in an adjoining room. Subjects were led into the laboratory blindfolded, and were then seated in the chair and bound securely to it. Electrodes connected to an electrocardiograph were attached to the subject's body together with apparatus for recording the breathing. A majority of the subjects were women. Each subject was told that the purpose of the experiment was only to record the breathing and heart beat during a fifteen minute period of quiet. After several periods of quiet had been given each subject, as promised, the chair was suddenly pulled over, without warning, causing the subject to fall backward.

All subjects reported an experience of fear when they felt themselves falling backward without support. This situa-

[1] W. E. Blatz, " Cardiac, Respiratory, and Electrical Phenomena Involved in the Emotion of Fear," *Journal of Experimental Psychology*, 1925, vol. 8, pp. 109-132.

tion precisely duplicated Watson's experiments during which he pulled the bed clothes from under babies, or suddenly dropped them on pillows while they were in the process of falling asleep. The behaviour symptoms also closely duplicated the infant behaviour reported by Watson. Blatz's subjects first struggled sharply to escape from the chair while it was falling, and after it had come to rest in a horizontal position. When they found that they could not escape the bonds which held them to the chair, they called out to the experimenter, believing that an accident had occurred. When they found that they could not escape, and that the experimenter paid no attention to their cries, the subjects accepted the situation and remained quiet in the chair in its down-tilted position (practically horizontal).

This behaviour indicates that the adults reacted in precisely the same way as did Watson's infants ; first reacting with dominance response, and then with compliance emotion. The initial struggle to escape clearly required increase of the motor self in an effort to overcome the motor stimuli evoked by the loss of bodily support. The cry for help to the experimenter indicated that the subject had realized the superior intensity of the antagonistic motor stimuli, and this call for assistance represented his last dominant effort to escape from the awkward and unusual position imposed upon his body. Thereafter all subjects showed complete compliance response, consisting of acceptance of the environmental stimulus imposed, and a readjustment of their own bodies to meet the new situation without attempting to alter it in any way. This necessitated an initial decrease in the motor self to permit the dominant environmental stimulus to effect the body in any way it pleased.

Bodily measurements of heart and breathing, recorded automatically while the subject was falling and for a period of ten minutes or more thereafter, revealed a double series of alternations between dominance and compliance response.

1, For a period of five seconds following the fall, the pulse rate jumped from 88 to 102, with other bodily symptoms similarly indicating *increase* of the motor self running parallel. This might be termed "*unsuccessful dominance response*".

2, Next followed a ten second period during which the pulse was retarded and tonic energy, expressing itself in strength of heart beat, pulse rate, and breathing, was clearly *decreased* below its initial status. This period might be termed one of " *compulsory compliance* ".

3, Next followed a second period during which the pulse was accelerated, not so high as during the unsuccessful dominance response, but of longer duration. Other bodily symptoms also indicated *increase* of the motor self during this period. This might be called a period of " dominance readjustment " to the superior environmental stimulus.

4, Gradually the pulse rate and other symptoms of bodily tonicity declined. This decline continued until the third minute after the fall. This again may be regarded as a *compliant decrease* of the motor self possibly designed to permit the triumphant motor stimuli to exercise whatever effect they were capable of exerting upon the readjusted balance of energy, in order to insure complete conformity of the decreased motor self in its readjustment condition to the dominant motor stimuli. It might be termed a *compliance testing period.*

5, This final compliance period in turn gave way to a final *increase* in heart rate and other tonic symptoms, to a level slightly higher than the initial one. At this level, the motor self seems to have remained constant throughout the remainder of that particular day's record. This final period represents a continued compliance with the motor stimuli imposed, yet a slightly *increased dominance* exerted toward other stimuli than the one of superior intensity. The compliant element, of course, was evidenced in the bodily symptoms only by way of comparison between the strength of the motor self during the final period and its strength during the first period of unsuccessful dominance response while attempting to overcome the intruding stimulus. This final period might be termed the " *successful dominance period.*"

Basic Dominance and Compliance Response Mechanisms are not Altered by Learning

It is important to observe that the emotional reactions of the adult subjects examined by Blatz showed no important differences from the emotional reactions of infants as described by Watson. This may be taken to indicate that the operation of the dominance and compliance mechanisms remain pretty much unaltered throughout life, provided that environmental stimuli can be found intrinsically adequate to evoke antagonistic stimuli of inferior strength to the motor self of the subject. The similarity of dominance and compliance emotions expressed by infants and adults indicates that *emotional learning does not alter the integrative character-istics of these two primary emotional responses in the least.*

In the case of Edgar, considered in the last chapter, a true compliance response was found to be evoked for the first time by an environmental stimulus, bodily injury, which was intrinsically capable of evoking antagonistic motor stimuli of superior intensity to the motor self. Edgar's first compliance response was evoked in just the same way that similar compliance responses were evoked from infants by loud noises and by falling, and in just the same way compliance response was evoked from Blatz's subjects by falling backward. Physical pain stimuli of severe character were felt, by Edgar, to be superior to his bodily powers of resistance, just as similar pain stimuli, resulting from candle burns or ruler blows, were felt by infants as superior to their own organisms. Edgar, in short, represented a case whose compliance response mechanisms remained normal, though in a completely naive condition so far as the learned conditioning of compliance response upon inadequate environmental stimuli was concerned.

Dangerous Environmental Stimuli are not Necessarily Adequate Stimuli to Compliance Response

Environmental stimuli of the most dangerous character to human or animal organisms may yet be of such a nature as not to possess power to evoke motor stimuli more intense than the motor self and to thus bring about compliance response. This fact, of course, is one of every day experience. But it is also a phenomenon, the mechanism of which is not, apparently, understood. Parents and other educators of children of the newer schools seem prone to assume that first hand experience with the antagonistic forces of the environment is the best form of compliance teaching. Such is far from being the case even if the child survives his first contests with crowded streets, dangerous implements of various kinds, and other children. For, if the dangerous environmental stimulus is incapable in itself of evoking compliance from the child before the full force of its destructive character is directly experienced, the resulting response (inevitably transferred to other environmental stimuli also) is rather sure to be of an exaggerated nature, preventing efficient reaction to this type of stimulus in later life even though no actual " fear " results.

Compliance Response Prevented by Over-Intensity of Motor Self

In the case of the boy Jack, we noted, in the last chapter, that he responded with dominance reaction even to environmental stimuli that should have the intrinsic capacity of evoking compliance response in child or adult. Working against' these environmental compliance stimuli in Jack's case, however, there probably existed endocrine stimuli in his blood stream. These endocrines had the effect, perhaps, of raising the compliance threshold. This result may have been accomplished in several ways, notably : (1) by stimulating the motor self continuously to greater than normal intensity ; or (2) by interfering in some inhibitory way with the connective units in the central nervous system by means of which environmental stimuli such as pain, normally evoke motor stimuli of superior intensity to the motor self. In Jack's case it seemed fairly clear that the endocrine stimulus evoked a result of the first type, that is, it seemed to be producing a continuous over-intensity of tonic discharge. Although Jack failed to respond compliantly to physical pain inflicted in the course of his gangster activities, he showed some compliance reaction when reasoned with. Once, in fact, according to a report which we received from the teacher, the child had genuinely given up his marauding activities after being convinced by the principal of the school that he could enjoy life better in other ways. But the boy's incessant restlessness and physical over-intensity seemed to make it impossible for him to continue for a long period in a compliant manner of living. After a couple of months of compliance, his motor self evidently became so intense that it could no longer be dominated by argument (a connective type of cause in the total integrative picture, i.e. (d) in the causal analysis, Chapter IV).

Suddenness of Stimulation Tends to Evoke Compliance

I was also able to evoke brief compliance responses from Jack during my interview with him by sudden startling remarks and movements. *Suddenness of stimulation* by an environmental stimulus of superior intensity often produces compliance response, in cases where no amount of sheer intensity of stimulation is able to bring about this result if the increase of stimulation intensity is applied gradually rather than suddenly. The explanation of this phenomenon is a simple one. So long as the motor stimulus remains inferior to the motor self, dominance emotion will persist. If, then, the intensity of the environmental stimulus be increased gradually enough, time will be allowed for the motor self to increase its own strength prior to attack of the motor stimulus upon it. But if a great intensity of environmental stimulation be suddenly applied, motor stimuli of superior intensity to the motor self in its initial state of strength may be evoked before the reinforcement mechanism can operate to make the motor self superior once more to the motor stimulus. It is an every day experience with nearly all of us to be " startled " by some sudden, loud noise, or perhaps by a jovial friend's clapping us on the shoulder suddenly from behind.

No matter how exaggerated the continuous motor self intensity may be it is easy to produce an environmental stimulus capable of evoking a motor stimulus more intense than the motor self, if the latter is not given time to reinforce itself. As far as my observations to date can be depended upon, it seems the fact that a motor self which remains continuously more intense than that of the average individual tends to be rather more susceptible to suddenly applied motor stimuli of superior intensity, than is the motor self of lower intensity level. The reason for this seems to be that the greater the continuous intensity of tonic motor discharge, or motor self, the more quickly does it react to any motor stimulus which may be applied to it (i.e. the latent period is shorter). Such an intense motor self, therefore, tends to react to a motor stimulus of superior intensity before the self has had time to be reinforced sufficiently to dominate the stimulus. There is, therefore, very frequently, a momentary flash of compliance emotion before the reinforcement mechanism is able to re-establish the normal dominant balance. The fact that Jack could be thus startled or compelled to momentary compliance by application of a sudden intense stimulus seems to indicate that his abnormality of dominance response was attributable to continuous over-intensity of the motor self, rather than to any interference with the connector mechanism necessary to the evoking of superior motor stimuli by an intense environmental stimulus.

In studying convicts, I found many of the prison incorrigibles to be men whose compliance response was exceedingly difficult to arouse because of this same, constant, over-intensity of the motor self. One prison farm camp was given over to confinement of younger criminals; that is, boys between eighteen and twenty-five. Among these prisoners the percentage of incorrigibles of the type mentioned was very high. Many of these youths appeared to me to be over-sexed. The male sexual hormone produces, according to my own observations, increase of dominance as a secondary sex characteristic, quite as definitely as it produces hair on the face and a deeper toned voice. The over-intensity of motor self from which many of these boys suffered might very probably be attributable to a surplus male sexual endocrine. These cases might prove almost exactly comparable to that of the child Jack. Other cases, where the continuous motor self seemed even stronger could not be accounted for on the same basis. In fact, the physiological causes underlying such over-intensity of the motor self are at best extremely speculative in the present state of our medical knowledge. Some of the youths at the prison farm in question seemed to suffer principally from lack of early compliance training, which had led them into various types of activity tending to intensify the continuous tonic discharge or dominant set. A few cases of war veterans seemed to fall into this category.

Prolongation and Frequent Repetition of Stimulation Tend to Evoke Compliance

In addition to suddenness as a condition tending to produce compliance response, we may also list *duration or repetition at frequent intervals of* an over-intense environmental stimulus, as a second condition sometimes capable of producing compliance emotion, when a single application of an environmental stimulus, no matter how intense, will have no effect.

A physician who had been connected with army work at the federal prison at Fort Leavenworth told me that incorrigible prisoners at that institution, who refused to go out to work with the other men, and who could not be shaken in their rebellious attitude by any extreme of rough treatment, were frequently compelled to work by *prolongation* of a comparatively mild punishment. They were handcuffed to the door of their cells, in a normal standing position, with their hands at no higher level than their shoulders, during the time that the other men were at work. These incorrigible prisoners were evidently able to resist environmental stimuli of any intensity whatever without manifesting compliance response. But they yielded compliance to an environmental stimulus of comparatively mild intensity, when that stimulus was applied for seven or eight hours a day three or four days in succession.

On the other hand, one instance which came to the personal attention of the survey staff during examination of the Texas prisoners indicated that repetition of environmental stimulus of great intensity might be expected to overwhelm a prisoner who showed an almost abnormal lack of compliance response. A young and exceedingly incorrigible prisoner, possessed, apparently, of a motor self so intense that his condition of restless tenseness was evident even to guards totally inexperienced in personality analysis, finally refused to go to work in the fields with the other convicts. This refusal was the result of a punishment which had been given him for a comparatively slight breach of prison rules. The manager of the prison farm tried in various ways to compel the prisoner to go to work, but without result. Finally, he made application, as provided by the Texas penal code, for permission to whip this prisoner. The Texas law provided that a warden or farm manager might administer a maximum of twenty strokes of a leather strap, of prescribed size and weight, to an incorrigible prisoner, upon permission being granted by the prison commissioners. This punishment was used fairly frequently, and was of such severity that mere threat to apply for permission to whip a prisoner was usually sufficient to compel the most incorrigible convict to comply with the manager's orders.

The young prisoner in question, however, knowing that twenty strokes was the maximum allowed by law, defied the "captain", and received his whipping in due course. Although the man's suffering was undoubtedly severe, he still refused to comply. Now the Texas law did not limit the number or frequency of whippings to which the prisoner might be subjected, provided only that permission be granted by the commissioners. The prison manager, therefore, immediately put in another application, and received a second permission to give the prisoner twenty strokes. This time, however, instead of delivering all the blows at one time, he decided to give the prisoner four or five strokes every day until this second permission was exhausted. He told the convict what he proposed to do, and added a statement that he intended to apply for further permission to whip the prisoner as soon as this present permit was exhausted. The man still refused to comply, and the " captain " administered several strokes that day, as he promised. Next day he came back again with the strap, and began to deliver another instalment of blows. After two strokes had been administered, however, the prisoner yielded, and complied with the order to go to work. This convict told me, when I interviewed him, that he could not endure the strain of taking a whipping every day because " *fear lasted over from one whipping to the next.*" He said that no matter how much pain one punishment might cause he " knew that he could stand it if it was going to be over all in one ' lick ' ".

The potency of persistent, or frequently repeated antagonistic environmental stimuli in evoking compliance emotion seems to depend upon the inability of the motor self to sustain itself at a greatly increased intensity level for any considerable length of time. If, therefore, antagonistic motor stimuli of considerable intensity can be made to persist for a period longer than that during which the reinforcement mechanism can be operated, defeat of the motor self will result and compliance response must necessarily follow.

High Connector Threshold to Compliance Response

There is another type of insufficiency of compliance which seems to be due to the second type of integrative cause mentioned above, that is, to a lack of adequate connector mechanisms enabling environmental stimuli of overwhelming intensity to evoke motor stimuli superior in strength to the motor self. In other words, individuals suffering from this type of compliance difficulty exhibit extraordinary resistance to physical pain and other similar types of over-intense environmental stimulation. This sort of person manifests many symptoms of chronically low motor self intensity, though when aroused to action such an individual's motor self may be increased to a point of unusual strength.

One subject of this type whose behaviour I was able to observe, was a college youth of considerable athletic ability. He played football, basketball, and other sports successfully, being a member of the varsity teams for several successive years. In basketball his game was peculiar and erratic. On certain occasions, he played extraordinarily well, while on other occasions he seemed completely phlegmatic and failed to respond aggressively to any amount of rough handling by an opponent. The basketball coach told me that on several such occasions he had " given him hell " in every way he could possibly think of. He had taken him out of the game several times, had threatened to drop him from the varsity squad, and had insulted him personally in every way that he knew. All to no avail. The boy only looked at the coach apathetically, and in a pitying sort of way, sometimes saying that he didn't feel like playing, and sometimes making no reply whatever. I asked the boy himself what he thought of the coach, and he told me, " Blank if alright, a very good fellow, but I can't say he ever taught me any basketball. I don't think he can teach anybody. I just have to go on and play my own way "

This boy was a student in one of my courses where a great deal of discussion was required. He seemed to follow the lectures rather well, but consistently refused to incorporate the material given him into his own methods of thought. Occasionally he would utter a surprisingly keen criticism or comment, but once his own idea was expressed he could never be induced to comply with the general discussion of the other students. His speech was excessively slow, and so low one could hardly hear it at times. Frequently he seemed actually to fall asleep in the middle of a sentence, his eyes closing, and his whole body slumping somnolently into his chair. This was in appearance only, however, for he never failed to complete the thought which he was expressing. The whole picture presented by the behaviour of this youth was one of a motor self of very low intensity, able to reinforce itself almost without limit upon the rare occasions when an antagonistic motor stimulus could be evoked. The difficulty, however, of evoking such motor stimuli by means of environmental stimulation was extreme.

Moreover, never once, during my study of the boy, did I see any evidence that a motor stimulus of superior intensity to his reinforced motor self had been evoked.

In one instance, at least, environmental stimuli of an intensity adequate to evoke compliance from any ordinary subject were administered to this youth without avail. It was a college custom for a certain sophomore society to " rag " or haze the freshmen systematically. The most popular method of compelling the freshmen to obey their tormentors was to " paddle " the disobedient ones with considerable energy, using an instrument very similar to a short-handled canoe paddle. I was informed by the sophomore who had charge of ragging a group of freshmen, including the youth under discussion, that he had hit this boy more than twenty times with all his strength, finally breaking the paddle over the subject's buttocks without compelling the boy to comply in the slightest degree with the commands which the sophomores were attempting to impose. I asked the boy himself, some time after the punishment had been inflicted, how he was able to endure such a severe beating.

" Oh ", he replied with an interested expression on his face, as if he were describing an event that had happened to somebody else, " there was nothing to that. I didn't mind it."

" Didn't you feel like hitting the fellow who did that to you ? " I asked.

" No ", he answered thoughtfully, " it didn't make any difference to me especially, so long as he couldn't make me do anything I didn't want to do."

In subjects of this type it seems safe to assume that whatever antagonistic motor stimuli are evoked by an intense environmental stimulus must be exceedingly feeble in comparison to the strength of the subject's motor self. That this comparative weakness of motor stimuli is not due to lack of acuity or high threshold in the sensory mechanisms is indicated by the fact that the college boy whose behaviour has just been reported showed unusually keen sensory perception, with very low auditory and visual thresholds. It will be remembered also that he was able to follow the subject matter of lectures rather well and to reproduce it if he chose.

This sort of integrative situation may be characterized by the statement that the *connector threshold between en-*

vironmental stimulus and motor stimulus is unusually high.

" Passive " Dominance is Resistance to Compliance Response

Cases of high connector threshold like that of the college student just mentioned illustrate very well an aspect of dominance response which may be called " passive " dominance. The motor self fails to take the initiative, in such cases, because it is sensible of no threat to its supremacy. It is able, therefore, to manifest a high degree of what is ordinarily called " resistance ". Resistant behaviour when attributable to passive dominance emotion, is a type of response during which the reagent remains satisfied with resisting any change in the motor set maintained by tonic discharge. Active dominance in contrast to passive would be defined as a condition where the motor self, becoming sensible of a motor stimulus obstructing its path, actively hurls its increased energy, as it were, against the obstacle. Although no very hard and fast line can be drawn between active and passive dominance, the contrast between these two phases of dominance behaviour, in the conduct of subjects analysed, is often sufficiently extreme to make the use of specific terms representing the two extremes convenient and justifiable. In literary and psycho-literary terminology we find the distinction between active and passive dominance fairly well marked. " Aggressiveness ", " initiative ", " self-assertion ", and similar terms emphasize clearly enough the active aspect of dominance, while " stubbornness ", " doggedness ", and " resistance " refer particularly to passive dominance expressed in various different ways.

" Passive " and " Active " Compliance

It may prove advisable to emphasize, at this point, similarly contrasting active and passive aspects of compliance emotion. First the contrast may be taken with respect to the behaviour of interacting of physical forces. In the case of a river whose flow is completely stopped by an opposing dam, the emphasis is upon the passive aspect of compliance emotion. The dam, as we noted at the beginning of this chapter, is unable actively to remove the river from its present bed and, is similarly incapable of compelling the water of the river to change its form physically or chemically. Thus no new motion, or active response is required of the dammed-up stream. When, however, the sun begins to heat the river water, additional energization of the water occurs, and it undergoes a form of active physical change from liquid water to water vapour. Thus the sun, acting dominantly upon the river water, compels the latter to comply actively by undergoing physical change. In a similar way plants, fish, amphibia, or an electric current might compel *active* compliance from the river water by forcing its atoms to move in new ways conducive to chemical changes imposed.

Simple illustrations of active compliance may be found also, in the case of stones rolled down a mountain side by the impact of sliding earth, or other debris from above. The stone is not only compelled to move in active compliance with the force applied to it during the length of time that it is being acted upon by the force in question, but also must continue to move in that same direction until gravity ceases to control it, and the momentum imparted to it is exhausted.

In the integrative mechanisms of animals and human beings the existence of mechanisms for active compliance response have already been noted. The phasic reflexes, whenever able to supplant the tonic motor discharge in the control of a final common path, may contrast the opposing or anti-tonic muscle. The total effect of such a procedure is to enable a victorious or dominant motor stimulus to compel active compliance from the organism by injecting new energy into it initially just as the sun compelled active physical compliance by causing the river to vapourize, and the electric current compelled still more active compliance by causing the water to manifest new chemical behaviour.

Whenever a compliant motor stimulus succeeds in compelling a subject organism to comply actively in the manner suggested, the principal influence upon the subject's behaviour will cease with the removal or cessation of the motor stimulus. There will, however, be a certain persistence of the active compliance movement after the motor stimulus itself has actually ceased, due to the integrative phenomena of after discharge, central spread of phasic excitations, etc. This continuation of active compliance may aptly be compared to the law of momentum in the behaviour of inanimate physical objects.

Difficulty of Compelling Active Compliance Response by Imposing Intense Environmental Stimuli

We have previously considered the threshold of compliance response as this threshold was affected by increased intensity of an environmental stimulus. We have had occasion several times to note, however, that over-intensity of nerve impulse is not a condition especially conducive to smooth and maximally effective integration. Bearing this fact in mind, we should not expect to find that over intense environmental stimuli, such as those furnished by physical pain or bodily injury, would be by any means maximally efficient in producing the active aspect of compliance response. In other words, we might expect to train an infant not to grasp the lighted candle by rapping his knuckles sharply each time the candle is presented, but this would be *passive* compliance. Similarly, we might expect that it would be comparatively easy to train an older child, or even an adult person to refrain from being impertinent to his mother, or "talking back to" a prison guard or warden by administering a comparatively light whipping. Again, such responses would represent an extremely passive type of compliance.

If, on the other hand, the attempt is made to compel positive action on the part of the infant, child or prisoner, a problem of much greater difficulty is faced. An environmental stimulus must be administered of such a nature that it will be able to evoke motor stimuli more powerful than the motor self of the subject, yet at the same time not intense enough to jeopardize the smooth and efficient functioning of the compliant integrations which it is desired to produce. This is, so to speak, the problem of the ages. It has been faced by all tyrants of every imaginable type and degree who have attempted to control the behaviour of other human beings by sheer force. The mechanisms by which atoms and molecules can be compelled actively to comply with the dominant individual's desire are extremely simple compared to the integrative mechanism which must be used forcefully to control a human being. The human body may be forcibly confined or kept from certain activities by barriers of superior physical force. It may also be compelled to cease from selected activities or from all activity, if desired, by administering to it sufficiently intense physical stimulation to produce integrative inhibition or central stasis. But neither of these types of environmental stimulus is capable of compelling active compliance of a maximally efficient variety.

Maximally Pleasant Environmental Stimuli Evoke Active Compliance

How, then, can active compliance be evoked ? Sherrington[1] states that reflexes tend to be prepotent which provoke strongly affective consciousness. He further cites two opposite types of prepotent active reflexes, the nociceptive, painful reflexes, on the one hand, and the sex reflexes, accompanied by maximal pleasantness, on the other hand. Defining unpleasantness as motor conflict, and pleasantness as motor alliance, we should then interpret Sherrington's statement as meaning that there are two maximally prepotent types of reflexes : (1) Those producing the most motor conflict possible, and (2) those producing the most alliance possible. Since compliance response depends by definition upon the prepotency of motor stimulus evoked, we should anticipate, according to Sherrington's result, that those motor stimuli producing greatest integrative conflict, and those producing a maximum of motor alliance, would constitute the maximally effective stimuli to compliance. There seems little doubt but that environmental stimuli capable of producing severe physical pain are those causing greatest unpleasantness. Therefore, we may say, according to our own pre-suppositions, that painful environmental stimuli evoke motor stimuli causing a maximum of motor conflict. This motor conflict is precisely the factor which results in extreme passive compliance. That is to say, a pain stimulus ultimately producing a maximum amount of central conflict and inhibition, thereby is able to produce a maximum amount of blockage to integrations which it is desired to break up. But, as we have seen, this process, by very definition, is incapable of originating new integrations of the type which it is desired to dictate to the organism. If, then, the purpose is to originate and carry forward successfully such new integrations, a different sort of prepotent reflex must be resorted to. This second type of prepotent reflex is, according to Sherrington, the class of reflexes which are accompanied by a maximum amount of pleasantness, or motor alliance.

[1] C. S. Sherrington, *Integrative Action of the Nervous System*, p. 230.

It should be possible, then, to evoke compliance response by means of any environmental stimulus which, though antagonistic to the motor self, is nevertheless capable of producing, *intra se*, an amount of pleasantness of motor alliance superior to that accompanying the tonic discharge at the moment of stimulation. In short, a motor stimulus, though antagonistic to the motor self, might nevertheless prove of greater strength than the motor self, provided the motor stimulus were of greater total volume, and provided this total volume, in its assemblage from various sensory connector sources, produced a greater total amount of motor alliances. If these conditions were fulfilled the motor stimulus need not be of greater intensity than the motor self at any time.

Over-Intense Motor Self Must be Taught to Comply with Volume

It might well prove true, however, that a motor self of too great intensity might fail to yield to, and comply with a motor stimulus depending for its victory upon greater harmonious volume of motor discharge. The very intense motor self might, however, be taught to comply with an antagonistic motor stimulus of greater harmonious volume.

Such teaching might follow one of two methods. First, a motor self of great intensity might be initially **defeated** by a motor stimulus of great intensity and might, while in such a state of defeat, be stimulated with a motor stimulus of superior harmonious volume only. In the second place, a motor self of great intensity might be taught, initially, to *submit* to an allied stimulus of greater volume, and transfer of the yielding element in this submissive response might then be made to an antagonistic motor stimulus of greater volume.

Summary

In summary, then, we are able to predict, on neurological grounds, that a stimulus of greater harmonious volume than the motor self may be able to evoke compliance response from a motor self of moderate or low intensity, even though the motor stimulus be antagonistic to and of less intensity than the motor self. We may further predict that a motor self of great intensity will not yield spontaneously to a motor stimulus whose superiority consists only of greater harmonious volume than the motor self possesses. Such a motor self of great intensity might, however, be taught to comply with a motor stimulus of this type in two ways. (1) By transferring defeat of the motor self brought about by an *antagonistic* motor stimulus of superior intensity, or (2) by transferring surrender brought about in the course of submissive response to an *allied* motor stimulus of greater volume.

Environmental Stimuli Evoking Compliance With Volume Response

In examining human behaviour for the purpose of verifying or refuting the foregoing suggestions, what types of environmental stimuli should be sought for as likely to evoke motor stimuli of greater volume than the motor self though antagonistic to it ? In the instances of compliance enforced by bodily pain which we have already considered, we discovered a certain rough correspondence between intensity of environmental stimulus and intensity of motor stimulus correspondingly evoked. This correspondence of intensities between environmental and motor stimuli, though by no means infallibly present, is in a one to one ratio and furnishes the only rough basis upon which parents, prison officials, or college students could proceed in their attempts mechanically to control the bodies of their subjects. Following this analogy, then, we might seek, first, *environmental stimuli of large volume as probably productive of motor stimuli of correspondingly large volume.* In a similar way, we might expect to find *environmental stimuli which are objectively ordered in a definitely harmonious pattern producing correspondingly harmonious pattern of the connector-motor integrations* which must contribute the element of harmony to a given group of motor stimuli. Environmental stimuli of large volume and harmonious interrelationship in respect to the manner in which they stimulate the sense organs of the body, might be expected to evoke, correspondingly, motor stimuli of large volume and harmonious interrelationship of constituent elements.

"Nature" is the Environmental Stimulus of Greatest Volume and Most Harmonious Pattern

The greatest possible volume of environmental stimulation of moderate intensity which can be simultaneously administered to a given subject may probably be found in "nature".

That is, if a human being is placed all alone in an unbroken pine forest, for instance, or upon the top of a mountain from which no human habitation is visible, the element making the greatest impression upon the consciousness of the individual so situated is usually found to be the *immensity* of his surroundings. This appears to be especially true of persons who have spent a major portion of their lives in large cities. Country residents, and especially mountain guides, and frontiersmen, seem to have acquired, to a considerable extent, the habit of limiting their sensory attention to particular objects which it is necessary for them to manipulate in some way, in order to adjust themselves efficiently to the outdoor environment. But even persons of this sort, I have found, when they return to their previous habitat after spending some time in the city are again impressed by the immensity and openness of the country landscape. This consciousness of immensity (which is evidently in itself a connector or ideational element) appears to have its origin in the tremendous volume of sensory stimulation of moderate intensity simultaneously received by the subject's organism.

There also appears to be a certain amount of naturally ordered regularity and harmoniousness of pattern in this type of sensory stimulation. Neither the tinkling, gurgling noises of the brook, nor the sighing, rustling sounds made in the trees by wind of moderate intensity are loud enough to drown each other out or to prevent the twittering of birds from being perceived simultaneously. The sun's rays produce a mild temperature stimulus of warmth upon the face and body while the breeze brushing across the cheek gives a co-existant sensation of coolness and also various light touch or pressure sensations. If the landscape viewed by the subject contains woods or forests, the colour stimuli are balanced in such a way as to permit simultaneous perception of light yellow-green foliage, dark blue-green masses of shrubs or leaves chancing to be seen against a darker background together with browns, reds, grays, and purples visible in tree-trunk shadows, rocks, and other natural objects usually to be seen. The shapes of a thousand trees, perhaps all following roughly the same pattern, may stimulate the retinæ simultaneously. The turning of leaves in the wind, and the tossing, and rise and fall, of tree branches, give kaleidoscopic change and variety to the stimuli of both colour and form without ever completely disarranging their basically symmetrical pattern. One might go on with such an analysis of stimuli almost endlessly without exhausting the possibilities of harmonious arrangement and tremendous simultaneous volume of sensory stimulation to be obtained from a country landscape. But the brief suggestions given above may suffice to indicate that nature constitutes a total stimulus situation satisfying both requirements of large volume and harmonious interrelation of constituent stimulating units.

Country Environment Evokes Compliance from a Cat

I once made the experiment of taking a cat to the seashore after it had been living in a city apartment for some time. Just prior to its residence in the city, this animal had spent three months in the same shore house to which I took it. When placed on the sand near the house, and some distance from the shore, the cat gave every appearance of being desperately frightened. It shrank close to the ground and looked around apprehensively for some moments. It then dashed toward the house and made its way immediately to the second floor, where it cowered under a bed in a far corner of the room. The cat was later brought down forcibly and was given milk and other food. It showed evidence of remembering the house, and also the premises outside. So long as the animal remained indoors it was only troubled, apparently, by the dull rhythmic pounding of the surf on the beach. But when it was again brought out and placed in the sand with large open spaces on every side, and the open water not more than two hundred yards distant, it behaved exactly as it had before. I repeated this procedure four or five times with identical results. The cat was clearly overwhelmed by the large volume of sensory stimulation administered to it simultaneoulsy. There was no single environmental stimulus or any combination of environmental stimuli nearly as intense as the sound of traffic in New York City to which the cat had been adapted during the preceding months. I concluded that it was not the " strangeness " (what is strangeness ?) of the stimulus situation which affected the cat in the manner described, since the animal showed familiarity with the house and surroundings. It seemed to me possible that the *cat was compelled to compliance response by the greatness of harmonious volume of environmental stimuli simultaneously received.*

Country Environment Evokes Compliance from Children

Children who have been born in the city and have remained there continuously up to the age of seven or eight years, frequently manifest a similar type of response when taken to the country for the first time. Such children have been accustomed, it is true, to great volume of simultaneous stimulation, caused by city traffic and by enormous numbers of people in the city tenement districts. But all these city stimuli are not harmoniously arranged in such a way that they produce the type of stimulus under discussion. City sights and sounds are of extreme intensity, and probably to a certain extent the intensities of various sights and sounds may be summed together to produce greater total intensity than any one alone. The child's sensory receptors, therefore, must become accustomed to this high intensity of stimulation and the child's motor self must clearly become adjusted to a constant level of rather great intensity, in order to meet the almost continuous stream of disconnected antagonistic motor stimuli evoked by the city stimulus situation. In short, the city child is one whose motor self has become adjusted to combat disconnected stimuli of considerable intensity and comply with separate stimuli of extreme intensity. A country stimulus situation, by way of contrast, presents a total stimulus of low intensity but very great volume. Any one unit in this country stimulus can easily be combated and overcome by the child's dominance reaction toward it. But the overcoming of one unit in the total stimulus has no appreciable effect in diminishing the volume of the total stimulation. This volume is overwhelmingly greater than the volume of the motor self adapted to meet disconnected, though intense, opposition. The reaction of the city child to the country stimulus situation is one frequently described as " awe ". The child seems temporarily overwhelmed and unable for the time to select appropriate reactions to meet the situation. When responses are finally selected, perhaps after a period of hours or days, these responses seem to correspond, compliantly, with the environmental stimulus. That is, the child's activity decreases somewhat in intensity but increases greatly in volume. All the numerous units composing the complex environmental stimulus produce individual units of behaviour many of which can occur simultaneously and all of which together constitute a very large volume of compliant response. The child, for instance, breathes more deeply and perhaps less quickly. His heart, after a time, begins to beat more strongly and probably with less rapidity. His vision becomes adjusted to focussing over long distances. All the child's physical movements, while less intense and sudden, perhaps, than were his jumps and short dashes to avoid traffic in the city, are, on the other hand, much more continuous and extensive. He covers three or four miles in the country to every mile traversed in the city. He climbs trees, wades in brooks, walks up hill and down, and perhaps wanders many miles over pasture and hillside looking for berries, etc., all of which activity could never be called forth by a single disconnected environmental stimulus no matter how intense such a stimulus might be.

In summary we may say that when the city child is transported into the country, the overwhelming volume of environmental stimulation of moderate intensity, tends to evoke a totality of behaviour preponderantly compliant in nature, and much greater in volume than that previously occurring.

Dominance Is Evoked by Single Objects, Compliance by the Country as a Unit Stimulus

Not all city children react in this manner when placed in the country stimulus situation. I once had occasion to observe a boy of about eleven years, who was spending a summer with his mother in the country for the first time. This lad possessed a motor self of apparently great intensity. He was restless, tense, self-centred, and very dominant. He seemed never to perceive the country or rural surroundings as a single unit stimulus, but rather appeared to react separately to each object with which he was confronted. This child's chief purpose in regard to each separate object seemed to be to get that object out of his way as quickly and as destructively as possible. For instance, he would not accompany the farmer's boy on his search for the cows in the pasture, but if he happened to find one or two of these animals drinking out of the trough in the farmyard he would take a big stick, or a handful of stones, and start the cows running at full speed. His mother tried upon one occasion to make him turn the handle of a churn with which the farmer's wife and daughter were accustomed to make butter. The boy, however, managed to break the handle of this churn in some way, and thereafter paid no attention to it. Similar incidents multiplied to such an extent that the farmer asked the mother to leave. This she did, moving to an hotel at a near-by resort, where there were many other city children, with games and amusements much like the average summer resort. In these surroundings, the boy behaved acceptably, and no further difficulty was experienced according to the mother's report. It was evident that the child responded separately to the various units in the total " country " situation, finding each one of these units antagonistic to his motor self, and of inferior strength. This would seem, perhaps, to illustrate the situation suggested in our foregoing analysis, wherein mere superiority of volume of the total stimulus might fail to be felt as of superior strength by a motor self of high intensity.

Child May Comply with Superior Volume but not with Superior Intensity of Stimulus

In direct contrast to the last case cited, I have found at least one case of a child whose compliance could not be evoked by extreme intensity of environmental stimulus, but who yielded compliance very readily to environmental stimuli of superior volume, harmoniously arranged. This child, M, showed a marked liking for flowers and for the woods, and fields at the age of six to seven. In " telling fortunes " by enumerating the petals of a daisy, M was unwilling to pluck the petals from the flower as the other children did. Instead, she would touch the petals with her finger, reciting the appropriate " fortune " rhyme with each petal as she did so. When asked why she did not pluck the petals out and throw them away, she replied that she " couldn't bear to hurt the flowers ". She also said that she hated to step on any sort of flower. Several years later, when entering early adolescence, this same child would gaze at sunsets until the last light had faded. At this time also, she would seat herself on a hill side and stay for hours apparently absorbed in the shifting lights and colours of the rustic panorama spread below her. She said that she felt herself " drinking it all in " and also that she felt that she " understood nature " and " seemed to be one with it ".

On the other hand, when M's mother commanded her to do things that the child did not wish to do, M would defy the utmost parental penalty rather than comply with

the command. When M. was six to seven years old, the
mother, who was a strict disciplinarian, sometimes used up
half a dozen beech switches in whipping the child without
exacting obedience.   M's father was still less successful
in eliciting compliance. After numerous unsuccessful attempts, he seems to have given up the effort to discipline
M altogether. M, at a later age (i.e., at about the beginning
of adolescence), developed a very great fondness for her
mother, and submitted to her commands thereafter quite
readily. From this submissive behaviour, an additional
increment of compliance developed.   Nevertheless, the young
girl still showed and continues to show a very high compliance
threshold toward environmental stimuli of great' intensity.
She has continued to show also, an extremely low compliance
threshold toward harmoniously arranged environmental
stimuli of large volume.

Compliance with Volume is Pleasant, Compliance with Intensity is Unpleasant

The contrast between what might be termed *compliance
with intensity* and *compliance with volume* is a contrast, primarily, between unpleasant and pleasant compliance   A
compliance with stimuli of overwhelming intensity is not
only unpleasant at the beginning, before the conflict has
been resolved in favour of the stimulus, but it attains 'indifference, at best, after the compliant adjustment has been
accomplished. Compliance with superior volume, on the
other hand, is certainly pleasant throughout a major portion
of the entire experience. The initial period during which
the stimulus is overwhelming the motor self, may contain a
considerable tinge of unpleasantness : though to subjects
like the girl M., even this initial period seems altogether
pleasant. The degree of unpleasantness, if any, at the beginning of the response appears to depend upon the readiness
with which the motor self yields to the environmental stimulus
of superior volume. If the initial surrender is made virtually
without even a momentary struggle, then the response contains no observable unpleasantness. If on the other hand,
the subject is intensely active, a brief initial period of unpleasantness may occur before an harmoniously arranged
environmental stimulus of great volume can evoke complete
compliance. In either case, however, once the motor self

has diminished its intensity and volume sufficiently to permit the organism to comply freely with the stimulus, the compliance response is wholly pleasant.

The pleasantness is a product of the alliance between the different motor stimuli units evoked by different constituent units of the environmental stimulus. The more units the environmental stimulus contains, therefore, harmoniously arranged as far as their stimulus function goes, the more harmonious motor stimuli will be evoked, and the greater total pleasantness the entire compliance response will contain.

Human Beings Can Be Controlled by Offering a Stimulus of Superior Volume

Compliance with volume is not only a primarily pleasant response, but also, when properly combined with dominance (a full description of which will be taken up in a latter chapter) constitutes the only method by which one human being can efficiently control another. That is to say, compliance with intensity, while most effective for the enforcement of passive compliance, is as we have seen, extremely inefficient in evoking active compliance. When compelled to comply with an overwhelmingly intense stimulus, a human or animal subject invariably minimizes the amount of active compliance given. Moreover, if the stimulus is too intense, causing bodily pain and injury, the subject no longer possesses capacity for maximally efficient active compliance. When compliance is evoked by a superior volume, however, as in the case of city children transported to the country, the response of active compliance corresponds in volume very closely with the volume of the environmental stimulus. Since compliance with volume is a fundamentally pleasant experience, there is no tendency on the part of the subject organism to minimize the quantity of active compliance rendered. *Really efficient work in any line of commerce, industry, or intellectual or artistic endeavour can only be obtained from workers who have learned compliance with volume.* Prison labour or other services exacted under threat of punishment (overwhelmingly intense environmental stimulus) can never be maximally efficient, unless the prisoners or other subordinates can be taught compliance with volume, after their motor selves have been initially conquered by environmental stimuli of superior intensity. If a prison or other disciplinary pro-

gramme were arranged with this in view (which, in my experience, it seldom is) incalculable benefit could be done to
the subjects by thus training them to a pleasant compliance
with volume as a substitute for unpleasant compliance with
intensity.

Compliance with Volume is a Learned Response

Whether compliance with volume can ever properly be
termed an unlearned reaction is extremely doubtful. We
have already noted that compliance with intensity is a response which the child must learn, apparently by either
painful or submissive experiences. Watson has shown
that babies grasp lighted candles, and other potentially
injurious objects, quite as readily as they grasp a rattle
or stick. We will have occasion to note in a following chapter
that the hunger-pang mechanism, which seems to be inherent,
is capable of administering over-intense stimulation which
ultimately evokes compliance response. But hunger-pangs
are a stimulus mechanism and not an integrative mechanism.
Therefore, we may still regard compliance with intensity
as a *learned* emotional response. Similarly, compliance
with volume is probably a learned emotional response
also.

It is true that, as in the case of M, we may find an inherent,
integrative balance, making possible a very low threshold
for compliance with volume. But even in the case of M,
a close analysis of the child's history showed that M.'s mother
had trained the child very efficiently, along lines calculated
to teach the child the pleasantness to be experienced in
complying with flowers, trees, and other objects of nature.
M, at the age of five, had believed that fairies lived in flowers
and that, therefore, to destroy a flower was to deprive the
fairy of her home. Other similar evidences of the mother's
teaching made it apparent that the compliance threshold
had been considerably lowered, at least, by a line of teaching
ingeniously adapted to what amounted to an individual
peculiarity in the child's inherent integrative balance. Thus,
M's marked response of compliance with volume, though no
doubt made possible by neural mechanisms especially susceptible to this response, was none the less learned as far
as the compliance itself was concerned. One of my students,
experimenting with a baby three weeks old, was unable to

evoke the slightest compliance behaviour as a reaction to flowers presented to the child in various ways, including olfactory and visual stimulation. Preyer[1] maintained that a child is able to distinguish disagreeable smells from agreeable ones a few days after birth. Preyer based this conclusion upon the expression of the child's face. The examples cited by Preyer have to do with the smell of milk and the mother's breast. It is possible that the hunger-pang mechanism, to be considered shortly, which teaches compliance with volume following compliance with intensity, has begun to make evident its effect within a few days after birth. But this would not detract from the character of resulting compliance emotion as a learned reaction. It seems safe to conclude that compliance with volume, like compliance with intensity, as an emotional response wherein the integrative patterns of emotional consciousness must be learned. (This may be contrasted to dominance emotion, wherein both integrative mechanism and integrative pattern are apparently present at birth, since the motor self may very probably have been reinforcing itself to overcome stimuli of less intensity during spontaneous movement of the embryo for some time before birth.)

Aesthetic Emotion is Compliance with Volume

The emotion of compliance with volume finds its greatest pleasantness and subtlest expression in the so-called " aesthetic attitude ". Certain adult subjects, who are probably endowed with an inherently low threshold for this response, and who have developed it extensively to the exclusion of dominant pursuits, regard aesthetic attitude as the highest development of human emotion. The aesthete is a person who enjoys to the full the experience of permitting his motor self to be overwhelmed by the harmonious volume of motor stimuli, evoked by an environmental stimulus of moderate or low intensity but of large volume. The greatness of the volume of the stimulus, however, need be only relative to the compliance threshold of the aesthetically developed individual. We have every reason to believe that a beautiful flower, for instance, would not succeed in evoking compliance from the most aesthetically inclined infant ever born. But

[1] W. Preyer, *Mental Development in the Child*, pp. 3 ff.

we may be equally sure that the average adult has developed compliance with volume response to the point where the balance of his motor self may be overturned by the harmoniously arranged stimulus units of a single rose or violet.

Aesthetes Possess Delicate Balance of the Motor Self

Aesthetes, as a rule, possess motor selves which are to be described as delicately balanced, rather than as weak or of low intensity. The aesthete's attitude seems to be a matter of elaborate training of the motor self, to respond selectively to motor stimuli whose constituent units possess a high degree of alliance or harmony, *inter se*. In the process of learning this aesthetic attitude, environmental stimuli are first selected which possess large volume as well as harmonious arrangement. The girl M, for instance, had the beginnings of an unusually well developed aesthetic attitude. A landscape or rural scene, containing flowers and trees, evoked such complete compliance from M that even a " temper fit " (overintense dominance emotion) could be overwhelmed and superceded by a few moments spent in viewing such a scene of rural beauty. As his aesthetic development is continued, the subject learns to respond in the same way to any environmental stimulus, the stimulating elements of which are harmoniously arranged in relation to the subject's organism ; regardless of how great or how small a total volume of motor stimuli may be evoked. That is to say, aesthetic training consists, for the most part, in learning to obtain the pleasantness of compliance with volume emotion from any environmental stimulus whose units are harmoniously arranged, no matter how little the total volume of stimulation may be. This development is sometimes carried to an extreme where non-aesthetic persons regard the aesthetic pleasure gained as exceedingly anaemic. In fact, any person of balanced emotional development continues to feel the need of considerable volume of aesthetic stimulus in order to yield compliantly to it. If such an emotionally balanced individual is induced by training or example to comply with (take an aesthetic interest in) an harmonious environmental stimulus of inconsiderable volume, the resultant emotional tone is apt to carry very little pleasantness, and is apt to be characterized as " formal " or " artificial ".

Motor Discharge to the Viscera Gives the Greatest Unit Motor Pattern for Aesthetic Compliance Response

Aesthetic attitude is a form of compliance with volume which excludes all dominance, because the aesthetic or harmonious environmental stimulus is always reacted to as a unit. Breaking up this unit response into particular reactions of the skeletal muscles to different parts of the unit stimulus, would mean that a certain amount of the harmonious volume must necessarily be sacrificed in the interest of a smaller, though more energetic group of reactions. Such a reduction of the total possible harmony or alliance of motor stimuli would be wholly opposed to the aesthetic principle of seeking always the maximum volume of compliance emotion in response to the aesthetic stimulus. If, then, the purpose is deliberately to keep the harmonious response volume at its maximum, the only method of doing this is to condition the organism in such a way that only visceral reactions will be evoked by aesthetic environmental stimuli. Visceral reactions, because of the nerve-net principle of the autonomic ganglia, offer much greater possibilities for a large, simultaneous, unit pattern of motor discharge. Therefore it becomes part of the aesthetic attitude to learn to respond viscerally, and not with the skeletal muscles, to environmental stimuli selected with reference to their aesthetic value, that is, with reference to the large volume of harmoniously interrelated motor stimuli which the environmental stimulus is able to evoke.

Many aesthetes who also possess very well developed dominance, and who can be induced to make introspective reports in language more explicit than gasps and fragmentary phrases which are frequently considered to be necessary parts of the aesthetic expression, report that along with the more vague and general " aesthetic one-ness with the object ", they are also aware of subliminal " feelings of movement " in various skeletal muscles, " as though dancing " or " gliding through the air ". It is interesting to note in these reported subliminal or " imaginary " movements which take place during the typical aesthetic experience, that there is almost always a notable absence of the dominant phase of each movement described.

For instance, one young man whom I had occasion to study, and who appeared to possess an unusually complete aesthetic development, frequently felt himself swinging on a high trapeze. He had the feeling, he said, of making graceful curves and loops, as his body swung passively over the bar of the trapeze, and sometimes passed from one trapeze to the next. I had half a dozen clinical conferences with this young aesthete, cross-examined him closely in regard to the muscular sensations accompanying his trapeze imaginings, and analysed the neural components of the movements he said he felt. The notable feature in all these trapeze movements seemed to be the *absence of all voluntary or dominant effort.* For example, there was no feeling whatever of clinging to the trapeze bar with his hands, which would be practically the only portion of the swing requiring any muscular support or tension. In all the movements reported *gravity did the work, not the subject. He felt his body passively moved by a force larger in volume than his own but not as intense.* He also felt *all the movements enforced upon his body to be graceful harmonious movements devoid of purpose to himself yet perfectly co-ordinated one with the other.* This case seems to typify aesthetic compliance with volume emotion, in an instance where the motor stimuli are permitted some outlet to the skeletal muscles as well as unlimited outlet to the viscera.

Work Contains Both Dominance and Compliance ; Aesthetic Attitude in Pure Compliance

In the instance cited above wherein the city children transported to the country were first overwhelmed by the superior volume of the country stimulus, and thereafter reacted to the various component parts of the country stimulus one unit at a time, dominance was injected into the total response each time that a specific reaction was undertaken. If, for example, a child complied with the brook by beginning to move toward it, the initial movement might be a purely compliant one, antagonistic to the customary position of the foot as maintained by the motor self. But the moment the body was swung out of balance by this compliant movement, the motor self must compensate by dominating the motor stimuli once more in bringing the body back into a proper state of equilibrium. Thus every specific group of compliant responses must be compensated by a correspondingly strong, antagonistic group of dominance responses. The child's wanderings over hill and dale, therefore, would consist, roughly, of a mixture of half compliance and half dominance. In the same way all useful work which has its origin, as we have seen, in compliance with volume response, must contain, nevertheless, an admixture of fifty per cent. or more dominance. Some types of very strenuous work, though they may be initiated as compliance with volume responses, necessarily require a much larger proportion of dominance than of compliance before the task can be successfully completed. The contrast, therefore, between such behaviour and aesthetic response is a contrast between a mixture containing the two ingredients of compliance and dominance, and a pure primary emotional consciousness, containing only the ingredient of compliance. The actual quantitative amount of compliance in the activity of work or exploration may exceed by far the total quantity of compliance in an aesthetic response. But the latter, in so far as it is aesthetic, contains only compliance emotion and nothing else. When Buddha held up the lotus flower before his pupils, he did not wish them to diagram it, or otherwise express dominance over it. He was delighted when a disciple *utterly complied* with the flower, i.e. aesthetically appreciated it.

Summary

We may summarize compliance response, then, as follows. Inanimate physical forces comply with antagonistic forces stronger than themselves by decreasing their own strength in the particular wherein it is opposed. This may be termed *passive compliance.* If the stronger force, by injecting fresh energy into the reagent, compels the latter to move actively in a new direction, or to change its form or physical expression this may be termed *active compliance.* In either case, the measure of the decrease in the original force or form of activity will be the difference between the initial strength of the reagent and the superior strength of its successful opponent.

The work of the physiologists in attempting to evoke emotional responses from decerebrate animals seems to lead to the conclusion that compliance response does not occur unless there remains some motor area of the central nervous system integratively predominant over that portion of the motor self which is compelled to comply by a motor stimulus of superior intensity. There is some evidence from cases of thalamic lesion in human adults, and from studies made upon infants born without cerebral hemispheres, that thalamic motor centres free from cortical inhibition may produce an exaggerated type of compliance.

Compliance response in human beings seems to be entirely of a learned variety. While the integrative mechanism of compliance is, of course, inherent, the individual compliance pattern appears to be formed only as a result of experience wherein the infant's motor self is overwhelmed by a motor stimulus of superior intensity. The compliance which follows consists of :

(1) Decrease of the motor self sufficiently to permit the motor stimulus to obtain complete control of the disputed motor centres, and

(2) Unhampered discharge by the triumphant motor stimulus through the conquered motor centres. By means of the synaptic principle of after discharge, the compliant movement may be continued for some time after the cessation of the environmental stimulus which evoked compliance, just as, by the principle of momentum, a physical force or object may continue to move compliantly after its opponent of superior strength has ceased to exert its force upon it.

The normal compliance threshold in infants seems to be reached at the point where an environmental stimulus is sufficiently intense to evoke physical pain (burning of hand by candle), or where the environmental stimulus is of sufficient intensity, combined with suddenness of presentation, to over-whelm tonic motor discharge by evoking motor stimuli of paralysing intensity, though without previous occurrence of physical pain (sudden loud noise near infant's head, throwing body wholly off balance at mercy of unopposed gravity). Compliance emotion thus can be transferred to, or conditioned upon inadequate environmental stimuli of comparatively slight intensity, which serve to give warning of the approach of any destructively intense stimulus. In laboratory experiments upon normal adults, it has been shown that compliance response in every way similar to that of the infant, can be evoked by the same environmental stimuli of overwhelming intensity, without physical pain.

The compliance threshold may be raised above the usual level in various ways.

(1) A child can be protected from environmental stimuli of overwhelming intensity until his dominance response has

developed out of all proportion to compliance (cases of Edgar and youthful criminals).

(2) Constant dominant stimulation may occur due to bodily abnormality, or other cause, rendering the motor self over intense, and practically undefeatable by antagonistic motor stimuli, no matter how great their intensity (cases of endocrine imbalance, precocious sex development in young convicts).

(3) High connector threshold between environmental stimulus and motor stimulus due to integrative cause inherent or unknown.

Two factors of environmental stimulation are effective in producing response over and above sheer intensity of the environmental stimulus.

(1) Suddenness of presentation of the stimulus may evoke motor stimulus which overwhelms the motor self before it has opportunity to reinforce itself.

(2) Long duration of over intense environmental stimulus or repetition of same at sufficiently brief intervals, may maintain motor stimuli of great intensity in a state of antagonism to the motor self for a period longer than that during which the motor self is able to keep itself reinforced to the unnaturally high intensity level necessary to overwhelm these motor stimuli (case of incorrigible prisoner whipped on successive days).

Sherrington has shown that reflexes of high affective tone tend to be prepotent. Environmental stimuli of overwhelming intensity such as those just considered, evoke reflexes of maximum unpleasantness, causing a maximum of conflict between motor stimulus and motor self. An environmental unit stimulus composed of a large volume of stimuli of moderate intensity harmoniously arranged with respect to their sensory effect upon the subject, may evoke motor stimuli harmoniously interrelated and sufficiently great in volume to surpass the volume of the motor self. Such a total motor stimulus should contain within itself a high degree of pleasantness, while at the same time possessing the ability to overwhelm the motor self and evoke compliance response. This type of compliance emotion may be termed *compliance with volume*, as contrasted with *compliance with intensity* evoked by over intense stimuli.

Compliance with volume is a pleasant response after the initial yielding of the motor self to the motor stimulus has been evoked. Since there is no prolongation of the central antagonism or conflict throughout the persistence of compliance with volume response, this type of integration constitutes the only mechanism by which the subject may be made to comply actively with an environmental stimulus. Compliance with volume is the only primary emotional response whereby any consistently large volume of efficient work can be performed.

Compliance with volume may readily be evoked from some other types of subjects, especially those whose motor selves have been trained to yield only to environmental stimuli of superior intensity. Such subjects may be retrained, however, by conditioning or transfer of response to compliance with volume. This training can be done

(1) By initially overwhelming the motor self with an over-intense stimulus (prisoners injuriously punished).

(2) By evoking submission emotion toward a loved one (*allied* stimulus of superior volume, and subsequently transferring surrender of dominance to respond to *antagonistic* stimulus of superior volume).

While compliance with volume which takes the form of activity of the skeletal muscles must involve an equal or greater volume of compensatory dominance response, in order to restore balance to the body after each compliant movement, it is possible to respond viscerally with complete compliance to an harmonious environmental stimulus of superior volume without any admixture of dominance. Such a response of compliance with volume without any admixture of dominance is customarily termed " aesthetic response " or " aesthetic attitude ". Development of the aesthetic attitude by self training or conditioning leads to a response of pure compliance with any environmental stimulus, all the constituent elements of which are harmoniously interrelated, even though the total volume of motor stimuli evoked is less in volume than the motor self.

Compliance May Be Unpleasant, Indifferent, and Pleasant

When compliance response is completely learned, so that the integrative decrease in the motor self to make room for the superior stimulus opponent is accomplished without struggle, compliance emotion may be freed wholly from unpleasantness. Compliance then becomes either predominantly indifferent in feeling tone, or positively pleasant, depending upon the volume of the motor stimulus which is being complied with, and upon the degree of alliance between the constituent elements in the total motor stimulus.

Compliance with intensity may contain an admixture of "fear" throughout, and this "fear" element is probably the most thoroughly unpleasant of all emotional states. But 'fear," as we shall note at length in a subsequent chapter, results not from successful compliance with a stimulus, but rather from integrative *failure* to comply completely. Compliance with a stimulus of superior intensity contains, at best, little pleasantness, because over-intensity of any neural excitement, as we have several times noted, tends to interfere with alliance relationship between the different groups of impulses composing the total excitation. Unpleasantness can be wholly removed, however, and a rather complete indifference established (as in the case of affective adaptation to hydrogen sulphide, mentioned in Chapter IV, above).

The reason that voluntary compliance may always avoid unpleasantness seems to be that the motor self is physically under control of the organism (that is, under control of higher centres of the central nervous system), so that the motor self can be retired at any time from conflict with a motor stimulus. The moment one integrative opponent is completely eliminated from the battle, no matter which antagonist it may be, unpleasantness ceases, and indifference reigns. In the emotion of dominance, on the other hand, the purpose is to eliminate the motor stimulus, and to keep the motor self's energy discharge intact. The motor stimulus, in so far as it can be mechanistically forced upon the organism by an environmental stimulus, is not under control of the subject. Therefore, during dominance emotion, some degree of unpleasantness inevitably persists until after complete success of the dominance reaction in physically removing its environmental opponent. When that has been done, the typical dominance quality of emotional consciousness ceases, unless the unpleasantness removed is voluntarily remembered in order to experience the dominant emotional "thrill", known as "triumph". Compliance emotion, on the other hand, measures its success not by removal of the opponent, but by the completeness of readjustment of the motor self to that opponent. *When complete retirement of the motor self from conflict has been accomplished, indifference of feeling tone always announces that accomplishment.*

This initial indifference may persist throughout compliance response, or it may give way to positive pleasantness, depending upon the nature of the motor stimulus complied with. The subject organism is powerless to produce this element of positive pleasantness. It is always able, however, if the motor self be under sufficiently complete control, to maintain indifference of feeling tone, by keeping the tonic motor discharge from all conflict with the motor stimulus, no matter how antagonistic or intense the latter may be. *The difficulty with establishing and maintaining such indifference seems to consist solely of a difficulty in establishing control over the tonic innervations of so-called " involuntary " type.* Could these innervations be suspended at will, no stimulation need ever be felt as unpleasant provided the subject elected to comply with it completely.

There appear to be fairly well authenticated cases of Oriental " adepts " who can endure, with seeming indifference, the thrusting of needles and knives through their flesh, and other stimuli of even more severe nature. Systolic blood pressure and pulse rate are both found to decrease considerably during such stimulation, though the subject may continue to converse equably, with no evidence of central inhibitions or conflicts. Lowering of cardiac energy indicates decrease of tonic discharge, integrated reciprocally with the antagonistic motor discharge ultimately flowing from 'the environmental stimuli (knife thrusts, etc.). Perhaps many of the seeming miracles of this particular variety, performed by " occultists " may be attributed, after all, not to hypnotism of the audience, but to hard work in learning compliance response.

My own experiments in self-training along this line have given positive results, though upon a few occasions only, when other bodily and environmental conditions were most favourable. One must be willing to accept the pain as one's sole occupation during whatever time it may continue, just as any work dictated by environmental stimulation may be accepted as all absorbing. Any slightest attempt to engage in any motor activity preventing full discharge of the motor impulses set up by the painful stimulus brings back unpleasantness to its full initial extent. For instance, announcement of a visitor, followed by turning my attention to the subject-matter to be discussed with him, made an ulcerated tooth pain unbearably unpleasant, though previously I had reduced it to indifference by complete compliance with it. After more extended compliance training, such secondary activities might also be adjusted in such a way as not to interfere with the motor discharge from the pain stimulus; but I have only been working on this type of compliance learning intermittently for ten years. " Adepts " devote their entire lives to it.

Another condition of motor set that I have found necessary to remove unpleasantness from pain experience is acceptance of whatever weakness of the motor self may be imposed by the necessity of making room, as it were, for the entire volume of antagonistic pain-excitement motor discharge. Environmental pain stimuli are, by definition, over-intense. As long as over-intensity of psychonic energy persists in the motor centres, there necessarily will be some conflict of impulses and some corresponding unpleasantness. To remove this over-intensity, a sufficient number of efferent paths must be opened, free of all obstruction, to drain off the centrally dammed up excitement, thus keeping its intensity level within the normal conduction capacity of the motor psychons involved. In order to do this, if the pain is extreme, a reduction must be made in the tonic outflow which results in marked symptoms of faintness, collapse, and general physical weakness. This condition also might be minimized, after long compliance learning, by more selective reduction of the motor self ; but, in any case, the subject must accept, without reserve, whatever weakness may result from complete compliance, since reservations bring back unpleasantness.

Positive pleasantness of compliance response seems only to occur when the compliance is a reaction to a motor stimulus of superior volume and moderate intensity, and when the constituent elements of such a motor stimulus are intrinsically harmonious. Compliant pleasantness, then, depends ultimately, upon the nature of the environmental stimulus. Compliance with volume response becomes indifferent, as we have already noted, when artificially conditioned upon an environmental stimulus of inadequate, or inferior volume. The pleasantness of compliance, in short, may be gained only by seeking an adequate environmental stimulus—never by learning to respond compliantly to whatever stimulus happens to present itself. The heroine of " Main Street " was represented quite accurately, as a woman whose emotional nature insatiably craved this sort of stimulus (aesthetic stimuli), and who could find no substitute among the disharmonious surroundings of Main Street. In the same way, we frequently find that a one-sidedly developed aesthete's life consists of little else than a never-ending search for new objects possessing the power of harmonious stimulation evoking compliance with volume, or aesthetic emotion.

Distinctive Conscious Characteristics of Compliance Emotion

The quality of emotional consciousness peculiar to compliance is somewhat more difficult to discover adequate terminology for than is the corresponding quality of dominance emotion. Compliance has been identified frequently with fear, on the one hand, and with religious and aesthetic attitude on the other. Some of the more common literary, pseudo-psychological, and psychological terms for emotional states consisting chiefly of compliance emotion when compliance is with superior intensity, are: "fear", "being afraid to do" some dominant act, "being afraid of" some stronger force, person or object, "timidity", "caution", "weak will", "conforming", "trimming one's sails to fit the gale", "swimming with the stream", "open mindedness", "candour", "getting down to brass tacks", "being a realist", "fall in with" a stronger force or person, "adapting", "yielding to", "resignation", "resigning one's self to fate", "doing God's will", "fear of God", "being well disciplined", "bearing one's burdens", "bearing one's cross", "taking what is coming to you without whining", "humility", "respect" for the strength of the antagonist, "awe", and "tolerance".

Terms especially relating to pleasant compliance with volume are: "Oneness with nature", "joys of nature", "looking to the hills from whence cometh my strength", "tuning to the infinite", "mystical experience", "nirvana", "Buddha", "oneness with God", "harmony", "peace", "receptivity", "feeling of beauty", "aesthetic feeling", "fineness of feeling", "empathy", "aesthetic attitude", "susceptibility to beauty", "rapture", and "aesthetic appreciation".

It is easy to observe a marked difference in affective tone between terms popularly expressive of compliance with intensity, and literary or religious terms employed in the description of aesthetic or religious compliance with volume, the former indicating associated unpleasantness of varying degrees, and the latter implying pleasant associations, for the most part. ' Fear ", or at best, suffering stoically endured, seem to be thought of as inevitable accompaniments of compliance with intensity in a great majority of occidental writings. There seems to exist, in short, little or no understanding of compliance with intensity as a voluntarily accepted emotional response. Compliance with volume, on the other hand, is evidently regarded in literary circles as one of the highest possible forms of emotional development. But there appears, in most of the terms mentioned above, a curious personification, or anthropomorphic idealization of the inanimate stimuli capable of evoking this response. Does this mean, perhaps, that compliance with volume, also, is not clearly accepted as an emotional primary by itself, but always tends to be thought of in mixture with *submission* to a being possessing glorified human love qualities ?

Nearly all the popular emotional terms included in both groups above, however, seem to *contain as a common denominator of emotional meaning, compliance consisting of decrease of the motor self to let an opponent move the organism as it will ; either passively, by making the self give up some dominant activity, or actively, by compelling the organism to move in some anti-dominant way.*

Introspection upon compliance emotion, elicited with difficulty because persons possessing most compliance development tend to be most incoherent and least explicit, generally suggest the essence of compliance consciousness to be a *feeling of acceptance of an object or force as inevitably just what it is, followed by self-yielding sufficient to bring about harmonious readjustment of self to object. This feeling, unpleasant if the stimulus is too intense to be completely adjusted to, indifferent if the stimulus is of small volume or is composed of inharmonious elements, and pleasant if the stimulus is of moderate intensity, large volume, and is composed of units cumulatively harmonious, constitutes compliance emotion.*

CHAPTER IX

DOMINANCE AND COMPLIANCE

We have considered in the last chapter the integrative mechanisms which are responsible for the emotional responses of dominance and compliance, and we have analysed a few simple illustrations of actual human behaviour exemplifying the occurrence of these emotions in as isolated a form as possible. We have still to consider the normal inter-relationship between dominance and compliance when the two emotional responses occur successively. We have also to consider, thereafter, the normal integrative combinations of dominance and compliance when these two emotional responses occur simultaneously.

Passive Dominance Prevents Compliance From Being Evoked

The response of passive dominance may be evoked by an adequate dominance stimulus without previous intervention of any compliance response. If, for example, an infant is holding tightly to its rattle, and if the mother tries to pull the toy from the child, exerting less force upon the rattle than the infant is able to exert in holding it, the child's motor self may simply reinforce itself so promptly and efficiently that the infant's actual grip upon the rattle is never loosened. This result may be carried to the point where the infant actually suspends his own weight from a rod or stick, which he was grasping firmly at the time the experimenter started to pull it away. Such a response represents almost pure *passive* dominance because the motor self was in control of the disputed efferent channels of motor discharge before the motor stimulus began its contest for these paths, and throughout the response the motor self similarly continued to *resist* all encroachments upon its occupied territory. In short, passive dominance consists of simple resistance to the attack of an antagonistic motor stimulus upon the motor self. No compliance whatever enters into this type of emotional response, and the general motor set of the organism is not changed in any way by reaction to the environmental stimulus except that more effort, or energy, has been released to preserve the pre-existing set.

Dominance Represents the Natural Equilibrium of the Organism

If compliance response actually succeeds, even momentarily, in supplanting the dominant control exercised by the motor self over the final motor paths of the organism, then two integrative possibilities appear. First, the compliance emotion may continue undisturbed until the environmental stimulus has ceased to evoke a motor stimulus of superior intensity or volume. In this case, which might consist, for example, of an aesthetic response, the emotion experienced is one of compliance without the admixture of dominance. This corresponds, it would seem, to the situation just considered where pure dominance emotion of passive type remained uninterrupted. There is one important difference. The compliance emotion which persists without any admixture of dominance is an *active* compliance response whereas the uninterrupted dominance just considered was of passive type only. In short, compliance can continue to rule the subject organism only for so long as it keeps the organism actively moving in an anti-dominant way. *The moment the organism ceases to comply actively with a given stimulus, the natural reflex equilibrium automatically re-establishes itself, and dominance emotion inevitably supplants compliance.*

For example, a beautiful picture may control the attention and main avenues of involuntary motor discharge to the viscera so long as the harmonious volume of motor stimulus evoked by the art object is sufficiently superior to the volume of the motor self. But if the studio light begins to wane, or if the individual sense organs become fatigued in gazing at the picture, the environmental stimulus at once ceases to evoke a motor stimulus of superior volume. The immediate result of this change in the motor stimulus is to bring about a cessation of active compliance motor discharge of an anti-tonic sort. This, of course, frees the tonic impulses from their previous restraint and the motor self automatically re-establishes its control of the efferent centres. This process of re-establishing control constitutes a response of *active dominance*. It will be felt by the subject himself in most instances of the type cited as a feeling of active criticism of, or boredom with, the picture (this of course assumes that no other stimulus intrudes to claim the subject's attention). Another type of reassertion of dominance after aesthetic compliance with an art object might consist of a sudden determination to possess the admired object, followed immediately by behaviour appropriately directed toward its purchase or acquisition.

Active Compliance may Oppose More and More of the Motor Self Until it Evokes Dominance

If, then, compliance is permitted to continue without interruption to the point where the stimulus ceases to be effective, it must necessarily be followed immediately by dominance emotion accompanying the mere automatic return of the organism's natural integrative balance. A second type of termination of compliance appears in the case last mentioned, where continued aesthetic compliance with a beautiful picture was superseded by dominant attempt to possess the picture itself. It seems clear that the compliance response did not merely run itself out but rather brought about the dominance emotion which superseded it. The mechanism for this type of integrative causation would seem to be a sort of passing of the quantitative limit beyond which the motor self cannot comply with the motor stimulus because a large enough proportion of the motor self has become involved in the reaction to make it superior in strength to opposed motor stimuli. That is to say, if the motor stimulus opposes only a comparatively small portion of the motor self the stimulus may be more powerful than the self ; but, *when the same stimulus opposes more and more of the self a point is sooner or later reached where the increment of motor self involved in the conflict has become more powerful than the motor stimulus.* At that point the stimulus becomes an adequate dominance stimulus instead of an adequate compliance stimulus, and the subject's response similarly transforms itself from compliance into dominance.

In the instance where the subject first feels aesthetic compliance emotion toward a picture, and later, as the response progresses, suddenly assumes a dominant attitude toward the picture in trying to acquire it for himself, it seems reasonable to assume that the original compliance with volume response was able to control the organism for only so long a time as a comparatively small portion of the motor self was engaged in compliance. When the reaction to the picture had spread sufficiently in the higher motor centres of the central nervous system and a larger portion of the motor self consequently became involved, this total increment of the motor self was no longer of suitable size for compliance response, but rather proved sufficient for dominance over the picture.

In instances like this, where the intensity of the environmental stimulus, and consequently the intensity of the motor stimulus is comparatively slight, there would be an ever present likelihood throughout the response that the strength of the stimulus might be felt at any moment as inferior to the strength of the motor self. The aesthetic attitude, in other words, is an extremely unstable one and difficult to maintain over any considerable length of time of response. That is, there seems to come a point in any compliance response where the environmental stimulus ceases to be felt as an adequate compliance stimulus, and in the type of instance now under examination, its effect upon the organism in evoking compliance response appears to endow it subsequently with positive potency as an adequate dominance stimulus. In persons of extreme aesthetic training, it is true, this change from aesthetic reaction to dominance response might be long deferred or might, in fact, never occur. But with the ordinary individual there seems to be a certain piling up, or summation of the motor self during an extended compliance response, which, when the point of overflow is reached, transforms the compliance emotion into dominance of equal or greater strength.

The Shift from Compliance to Dominance When the Whole Motor Self is Opposed is " Instinct of Self-Preservation "

The fact that rats will fight when cornered has become proverbial. I would suggest that this response is probably expressive of the same mechanism as that underlying the change from aesthetic to dominance response just considered. The rat complies with the antagonist of superior strength by running away from his opponent. This continues for as long a period as the proportion of the rat's motor self which is overwhelmed by his superior enemy is a comparatively small one. When, however, every avenue of escape is cut off, the animal's entire motor self is brought to bay, as it were. The full intensity of this animal's motor self when increased by its reinforcement mechanism to maximum strength, and when the entire motor self is involved in the conflict, evidently proves stronger than the sum total of motor stimuli which can be evoked by the most dangerous foe. This is the so-called "instinct of self-preservation". It is a type of behaviour shown frequently by the most timid of human beings when suddenly confronted by an extreme danger from which there is no possible escape by flight. In fact the *" instinct of self-preservation " might be defined as a change from compliance response to dominance response at the point where a sufficient proportion of the motor self becomes involved in conflict with the stimulus to render motor self more powerful than motor stimulus.* The state of emotional consciousness involved in this shift is frequently termed "desperation".

Dominance Always Replaces Compliance

If, then, active compliance is followed in any event by a dominant re-establishment of control of the organism by the motor self, it might be permissible to formulate the rule in some such way as follows : *Active compliance is normally followed by active dominance.*

The same rule evidently holds also with respect to passive compliance. That is, if the motor self is compelled by a stimulus of greater intensity to give up control of certain disputed paths, the tonic discharge will automatically re-assume control of these paths as soon as the prohibitory barrier has been removed, even though the contest has been a mutual stand-off, as it were, and the motor stimulus has not succeeded in itself moving the organism actively. There seems, however, this qualification to be made concerning the reversion to dominance following compliance of passive aspect only. If the subject's motor self happened, in the first place, to be in a condition of marked reinforcement, or increased intensity for the purpose of dominating object A, and if the motor self were compelled passively to comply with stimulus B by giving up its dominance over object A then should stimulus B cease to operate, the motor self would not necessarily return to its previous condition of increased intensity, but only to its normal strength when no antagonistic motor stimulus was operating upon it. Nor would the motor self necessarily return to the process of dominating object A, which might by that time have passed entirely out of the subject's environment. Passive compliance, therefore, might be followed by a state of dominance more passive than active, though there must always be some active dominance in the process of re-establishing reflex equilibrium after the compliance stimulus has ceased to operate. It seems, in short, to follow from the very nature of dominance response as an enforcement of the integrative system's normal equilibrium that *dominance must always eventually supersede active or passive compliance.*

Compliance Protects the Organism Against Superior Foes

Such an arrangement obviously makes for maximal efficiency in adapting the organism successfully to its environment. If an animal or human being is already well enough adapted to his surroundings to be able to maintain his existing posture and position despite the utmost antagonistic influence which can be brought to bear against him at any given moment, the mechanism of passive dominance provides a means for counteracting minor fluctuations of posture and position which could serve no useful purpose, and which would result only in disturbing the progress of the organism's vital functions. On the other hand, if any antagonistic factor in the subject's immediate physical environment be sufficiently powerful to destroy or seriously injure the subject's organism, the compliance mechanism permits the *stronger antagonist to expend its force in moving the subject rather than in destroying part of the motor self which must serve throughout life as the dynamic source and main-stay of the subject's entire behaviour.*

Were it not for this possibility of integrative compliance, an antagonistic motor stimulus of superior intensity, operating through a centre of the central nervous system above the tonic centre, might eventually succeed in inhibiting the entire mass of tonic discharge *in toto*, with extremely serious consequences to the organism.

Compliance Responses Have Selective Value in Evoking
Maximally Efficient Dominance Responses

The tendency of the dominant balance of the organism always to re-establish itself following compliance response gives to the intervening compliance reaction another important value. The separate compliance emotions enforced by an antagonistic environmental stimulus *act as selective agents arousing to special activity the specific tonic reflexes recriprocally opposed to the intervening compliance reflexes.* That is to say, in the response of passive dominance there appears a general blanket type of reinforcement of the motor self, not specifically directed against the environmental stimulus which is being responded to. But, if the environmental stimulus in question is permitted first to effect a compliance response, then selective reinforcement of those portions of the motor self best adapted to oppose and remove the antagonistic stimulus can be made, with resultant conservation of energy and increasing efficiency of the dominance response. Examples of this selective value of initial compliance with a stimulus which is later to be dominated are to be found in all the rudimentary behaviour patterns of the human organism in which tonic and phasic reflexes alternate to bring about progressive movement of the body or limbs.

The fingers of the hand, for instance, if extended in compliance with the object to be grasped, automatically bring about the reinforcement of the particular tonic grasping reflexes best adapted to seize and handle that particular environmental object. The more completely extension of the hand is permitted to comply with the size, shape, and position of the object to be grasped, the more efficiently will that object subsequently be mastered or dominated. The difference in this respect between infant and adult behaviour is well marked. When an infant naively extends his fingers to grasp a proffered object of very small size, he opens his hand wide, extending all the fingers equally regardless of the shape and small size of the thing to be grasped. In other instances infants may fail to extend the fingers sufficiently to surround the object to be grasped. In either case, the extending of the hand would seem to be more in nature of general, unselective reaction to the object, than a compliance response closely controlled by the object itself.

We have noted several times previously that compliance is a learned response, and so when we compare the behaviour of infant subjects with the reactions of adults we should expect to find compliance response much more highly developed in the latter as, in fact, it is, in nearly all types of reaction. The interesting point for the purpose of our present discussion is that such increase in delicacy and completeness of compliant response to any given object automatically produces corresponding increase in the strength and effectiveness of the dominance response which follows. Any number of examples of this increase of dominant efficiency following increased learning of compliance might be cited. All the finer and more powerful movements of attack upon an opponent, whether in mortal combat, or in some ultra-civilized sport like tennis or baseball, depend for their accuracy and power upon the completeness of the preceding compliance responses.

In savage combat, the spear must be directed toward a vital spot in the antagonist's body by a careful and accurate compliance response, evoked by the antagonist's body itself. The power of the dominant driving home of the attacker's weapon bears a fixed and constant relationship of dependence upon the extent and intensity of the preceding compliance response of withdrawing the arm and hand holding the spear in an initial direction *away from the individual to be attacked*. In tennis a never-ending series of very subtle compliance reactions must be performed in order to bring the body, arm, and racquet into postures which themselves determine maximally effective dominance reactions to follow. All preparedness, in short, consists of compliance reactions, whose principal function is to serve as selective agents within the integrative centres of the subject's organism, to pick out the dominance reactions most effectively antagonistic to the compliance responses themselves. The normal relationship, then, between compliance and dominance emotion is a relationship in which compliance is used for the success of the dominance responses. We may say that *active dominance is effective in reaching its antagonist directly in proportion as it is immediately preceded by compliance with the opponent.*

Compliance Must Not Be Carried Beyond Its Usefulness to Dominance

It is necessary to qualify this statement in two particulars. First, compliance response may be carried to such an extreme that it postpones the ultimate dominant reaction too long for maximum efficiency, or lowers the strength of the motor self to such a degree that it is unable to cope with the antagonist. Secondly, the organism may comply with an antagonist which it has not the strength to dominate, even when the motor self is at its maximum intensity. An illustration of the first qualification to the usefulness of compliance as a servant of dominance may be found in over-careful adjustment of bodily position, in baseball or tennis, before the actual swing of the bat or tennis racquet toward the ball is begun. The timing of the stroke has been delayed too long for success, by an over extensive preparatory compliance response. In wrestling or boxing, it frequently happens that one contestant withdraws an arm or leg too far, so that the tonic muscles, which otherwise would have brought the limb back with maximum force, are no longer able to exert maximally efficient leverage upon the limb in question. Or, in terms of nerve impulses, the same result may occur when an aesthete permits such volume of compliant motor discharge to control his organism that he subsequently finds himself lacking in strength to arrange his art collection in a manner most effective for his own aesthetic enjoyment.

Illustrating the second qualification placed upon the value of compliance to dominance, we may cite the very common instance of an individual who allows himself, while swimming, to be carried too far from the shore by the current. Such a person has complied with a force stronger than his own physical power at its best. He finds himself, therefore, shut off from shore by a barrier of water which it is beyond his physical strength to conquer or dominate. In both types of instances cited, compliance, though undertaken in the service of dominance, was carried to such an extreme that the compliance response had the effect of rendering subsequent dominance less effective, or altogether impossible.

Compliance Normally Precedes and Is Adapted to Dominance

It seems clear from the foregoing analysis, that if dominance is to maintain maximal efficiency, it must be preceded by compliance response. But the compliance must not be carried too far or continued for too long a period. In short, *the simplest normal combination between dominance and compliance responses beneficial to the organism consists of initial compliance response adapted to dominance emotion to follow.* This relationship between these two primary emotional responses may conveniently be expressed by the simple formula $C + D$. When this formula is used, it should be understood that the order of the letters represents the temporal order in which the emotinal responses occur, and the plus sign represents the relationship of adaptation of the, response indicated by the first letter to the response symbolized by the following initial. Thus, in the formula $C + D$, C,, compliance is *adapted to* D, dominance, as well as occurring prior to the beginning of D, the dominance response.

CHAPTER X

APPETITE

IN the preceding discussion we have attempted to discover the normal relationship between dominance and compliance when these responses occur successively. We have now to discover the normal relationship between compliance and dominance when these emotions occur simultaneously. In the first place, there are certain logically conceivable simultaneous combinations of dominance and compliance which may be eliminated by brief consideration of the behaviour elements involved. Active compliance and active dominance, for example, may occur simultaneously as an emotional mixture but not as an emotional compound. When active dominance and active compliance, evoked by the same stimulus, take place simultaneously, they tend to cancel each other out, or at least, mutually to modify one another in such a way that the integrative description of the resultant emotional state would consist of a relationship between the motor self and the motor stimulus which would be half way between the nodal points, C and D as indicated on the emotion circle diagram (see Chapter IV).

Dominance and Compliance Responses Toward the Same Object Blend or Inhibit One Another

For instance, a person when confronted by a dangerous animal several yards distant, would undoubtedly feel the environmental stimulus to be an antagonistic one and would assume in response, an attitude of antagonism. This element of antagonism, would, however, be common to both dominant and compliant types of response. If it was perfectly clear to the subject that the animal was a fox, or other prey distinctly weaker than himself, his response would tend to be a dominant advance upon the animal with the purpose of attacking it, that is, a dominance of the chase. On the other hand, if the subject were equally sure that the animal was a mountain cat or tiger, distinctly stronger than himself, this response would, no doubt, be the compliant one of moving away from the animal cautiously, and as rapidly as possible. In the instance supposed, the animal is at such a distance from the subject that he cannot be sure whether the environmental stimulus is weaker or stronger than himself. In such a case, or in an instance where the animal is actually recognized, and is known to be stronger than the subject in some particular, and weaker in others, both active dominance and active compliance may tend to be evoked simultaneously. If these reaction tendencies are equal and perfectly simultaneous, they will counterbalance one another and the subject will go on about his previous business without either attacking or running away from the animal.

Dominance and Compliance May Exist Simultaneously in Different Centres

If different parts of the same environmental stimulus evoke different primary emotional responses, these two may well occur simultaneously in comparatively unrelated motor centres, without forming integrative relationships one with the other. This may be called an emotional mixture rather than an emotional compound. Dominance and compliance might thus occur in an emotional mixture. For example, while fleeing on horse-back from a pursuing enemy, a man might turn in his saddle and shoot at the pursuer. His compliance flight need not be broken, or altered in any way by this simultaneous attack upon his enemy. Yet, the emotional consciousness evoked does not constitute any new, compound, emotional quality, or characteristic. Dominance and compliance may alternate in the fugitive's consciousness ; they may modify one another to the point of eliminating one or both for a brief interval ; or they may co-exist in consciousness simultaneously as responses to different portions of the same stimulus. The pursuer's superior physical strength may evoke compliance response, while his lack of firearms and conspicuous position against the sky line might evoke dominance in the form of a rifle shot. Simultaneous feeling of being overpowered by an opponent in one particular, while attacking the antagonist with intent to dominate him in some other respect, are not at all unusual or difficult to account for. But, they do not constitute a truly compound emotional quality or integrative picture, because the two primary emotional elements are integratively unrelated.

Active Dominance and Compliance Toward Different Objects Cannot Co-exist In Same Centres

One more set of logical possibilities of simultaneous combination of dominance and compliance responses may also be eliminated by examination of the integrations involved. Such an examination leads to the discovery that active dominance and active compliance with different objects cannot occur simultaneously in the same, or closely related motor centres. If we suppose that the tonic motor discharge innervates extensor muscle A^1, then any dominance reaction, no matter what object it may be directed toward, must utilize the final common efferent path to contract the muscle A^1, while any compliant response involving the same motor mechanism must use the final common path to contract the reciprocally opposed flexor muscle B^1. If, then, the organism attempts simultaneously to dominate environmental stimulus A by contracting the extensor A^1, and to comply with the environmental stimulus B by permitting it to contract the flexor muscle B^1, there will result a conflict in the entrant motor psychons, which must be resolved definitely in favour of one or the other opponent before either the dominant, or the compliant response can occur. In cases where final common paths or closely related motor centres are involved, therefore, it would seem impossible to form an integrative compound from active dominance and active compliance reactions no matter how diverse the environmental stimuli evoking these responses may be.

Similarly, it will be found impossible, integratively, to combine passive compliance and passive dominance even though these responses be directed toward different environmental stimuli. If, for example, environmental stimulus A evokes a reaction of passive dominance with respect to the muscle A^1, it simply means that the tonic innervation of muscle A^1 is increased sufficiently to resist any attempt of stimuli evoked by object A to utilize the final common path to contract muscle B^1. If, then, object B tends to evoke a reaction of passive compliance in this same motor centre, it will be seen that the stimulus B tends to prevent any dominant reinforcement of the tonic contraction of muscle A^1. We should, then, have the same conflict in the common motor centres in the case of a passive dominance response and a passive compliance response, evoked simultaneously in this common centre, by different environmental stimuli, that we had in the case of active dominance and compliance response simultaneously evoked by different objects. The passive dominance response to object A would be attempting to prevent the passive compliance evoked by object B from utilizing the common efferent path, and the passive compliance response would similarly be acting to inhibit reinforcement of the path to muscle A^1 called for by the compliance response before mentioned. It would not seem possible, therefore, for passive compliance to co-exist in the same or closely related motor centres with passive dominance response, even though opposing reactions were evoked by different objects.

Illustrations in human behaviour of the incompatability between simultaneous dominance and compliance responses are not far to seek. If a metal container full of some attractive food or drink is set to heat upon the stove, then the food, when heated, will tend to evoke dominance response consisting of grasping the pan, and moving it toward the lips. The stove's heat, however, and the heat from the metal pan itself will bring about the compliance response of withdrawing the hand from the pan. In this case active compliance triumphs over active dominance, when both are simultaneously aroused. In the case where a baby has grasped one of its playthings and the mother raps the child's hand with a ruler, to compel it to release its grip upon the toy, we have a contrast between passive dominance and passive compliance. The mother's antagonistic pull upon the toy in trying to remove it from the child's hand evokes simple resistence or passive dominance on the part of the infant. The rap on its knuckles, however, tends to make the child comply passively by giving up its grip upon the toy. In many instances of this sort which I have observed the passive dominance response is successful in the contest with its passive compliant antagonist. The child retains its grip upon the toy.

Possible Combinations

What possibilities remain for simultaneous combinations of dominance and compliance responses? Two further possibilities of such combination may be considered. First, we may examine the possible compounding of passive compliance with one object and active dominance toward another object. Secondly, we may consider the compounding of active compliance with one object while simultaneously reacting with passive dominance toward another object.

Active Dominance and Passive Compliance May Form an Emotional Compound

Any situation in which we are confronted by an antagonistic force stronger than ourselves, and to escape from which we are obliged to seek the aid of another opposite force of our environment, weaker than ourselves, is based upon the mingling or compounding of passive compliance and active dominance for just so long as we are seeking and obtaining the weaker environmental object. Let us cite a concrete example. A man is walking through the forest toward some important objective, such as a settlement where he plans to obtain supplies. He comes out upon the bank of a swift stream, and finds himself confronted with a barrier which it is beyond his own unaided strength to pass. The strength of the current and the jagged rocks over which the stream is rushing make it absolutely impossible for him to swim the river and come out alive upon the other bank. Here is an antagonist stronger than the subject, yet one that does not compel the subject to perform any positive action, but only *to give up a type of dominance behaviour in which he was previously engaged.* The subject must, for the time being, comply passively with the impassable river by giving up his journey toward the settlement.

But the man sees a tree on the bank of the stream which, if felled, would stretch from bank to bank. The tree in question is growing out at a precarious angle from the river bank over the stream, its roots clinging insecurely to the shallow soil. The tree in this unstable position seems to represent an antagonist *stronger than the river but weaker than the man.* If, then, the subject can dominate this weaker antagonist by pushing it down, across the river, he will immediately be in a position to cross the hitherto unconquerable barrier. In pushing or dominating the tree, the subject, of course, must continue to comply passively with the river by refraining from all actions incompatible with the force exerted by the stream upon his organism, throughout his dominance response directed against the tree. In short, this subject complies passively with a stronger antagonist, the river, simultaneously with his attempted dominance over the weaker antagonist, the tree.

Integratively, there is no difficulty in the simultaneous occurrence of passive compliance response to one stimulus and active dominance response to another within the same or closely allied motor centres, provided only that the motor stimulus to be dominated is not one of those which the passive compliance response requires the motor self to give up dominating. There might be, conceivably, a large number of motor stimuli which might be dominated by the motor self without running counter to the superior motor stimulus simultaneously influencing the same motor centres. Or, as in the case mentioned, there might exist but a single motor stimulus (evoked by the one available environmental stimulus, the over-hanging tree) which the superior motor stimulus enforcing passive compliance permitted the motor self to dominate. The psychonic picture might be thought of as an inhibitory control of the crucial group of psychons by the compliance stimulus excitation of great intensity which, however, was not capable of exercising its inhibitory influence upon one or more selected types of motor stimuli. These motor stimuli, therefore, might be conceived of as energizing the motor psychons simultaneously with the compliance stimulus. Undoubtedly the actually existing integrative picture is a far more complicated one, involving different levels of the central nervous system and a multitude of cross connective nerve paths and psychons. But with this complex picture reduced to diagrammatic form it might be represented in some such way as suggested.

pCaD is Desire

A compound emotional quality of consciousness comes into existence as a result of the integrative compounding of passive compliance and active dominance. This compound emotion is popularly termed " desire ". " Desire " (the integrative formula for which may be written pCaD) contains two types of conscious elements so intricately intermingled and inter-dependent that it becomes exceedingly difficult to analyse them with introspective clearness.

From the self observations of many subjects, I have found

that two types of consciousness are nearly always recognized in the emotional state of " desire ". First, there seems to be a feeling of restless seeking, dissatisfaction with the existing state of dominance activity, and a feeling of *necessity to satisfy some arbitrarily prescribed inner requirement*. This somewhat laboriously expressed aspect of desire seems to comprise the *passive compliance* element altered somewhat, and carrying new emotional qualities as a result of its integrative compounding with active dominance. Secondly, self-observations indicate the existence of a somewhat more definite and active aspect of desire consciousness. Introspective reports upon this element may be boiled down to " wanting to dominate " a particular environmental stimulus. This active determination to possess or to change a given object in some way seems attributable to the active dominance emotion modified and given new qualities by its integrative compounding with compliance.

Desire, as a unit emotional response, may *be characterized, because* of its prevailing active dominance, *as the active aspect of the entire emotional consciousness connected with the using of an environmental object of inferior strength to overcome an environmental antagonist superior in strength to the subject.* That is to say, of the two possible combinations between dominance and compliance, the combination of passive compliance with active dominance produces a compound emotion in which the motor self is more active than in the compounding of active compliance and passive dominance.

Passive Dominance and Active Compliance May Form an Emotional Compound

Let us continue, then, to analyse the compounds of dominance and compliance contained in the incident discussed above. As soon as the man who had been stopped, on his journey, by a river too swift to cross, has succeeded in pushing the over-hanging tree across the river, a complete shift of emotional responses occurs. The strength of the tree trunk lying across the river from bank to bank may now be added to the strength of the subject in his struggle with the swift-flowing stream. In order to increase his own strength, however, the subject must comply with the fallen tree. The tree trunk, instead of representing an antagonist of inferior intensity, now represents an environmental stimulus of superior volume to the subject's motor self, because its strength is measured by its ability to overcome the river which the subject himself did not previously possess. In short, the superiority of volume of the fallen tree over the motor self of the subject has been transferred, like most superiorities of volume, from the superior intensity of the antagonistic river. The entire volume of fallen tree stimulus is superior to and, therefore, takes the place of the superior intensity of the river. This effect is exactly the same as that previously considered in the cases of children or prisoners whose motor selves might be initially over-powered with the whip, and might thereafter learn to regard as of superior volume the environmental stimulus of useful work to be performed. Compliance with this work, once it is learned, would be a pleasant compliance with volume, and not an unpleasant, or at best indifferent compliance with intensity. So in the situation of the traveller who has pushed a tree across the hitherto impassable river compliance with the volume of the fallen tree represents a learned or transferred response, acquired in the course of this single emotional experience.

Integratively, we may think of the motor stimuli aroused by the river and thereafter taking the position of integrative control as the motor centres formerly occupied by the merely inhibitory excitations constituting the original passive compliance. The motor stimuli representing the fallen tree or bridge would then find the way clear to free, efferent discharge ; and the behaviour result of such discharge would be active compliance with the tree in place of the previous passive compliance with the river. This active compliance would, at the same time, remove the over-intense motor stimuli evoked by the river and permit the motor self to go on dominating its original avenues of discharge (that is, the interrupted journey for supplies). In short, *active compliance with the tree* reduces the strength of the opposing river to that of an antagonistic inferior to the motor self in intensity. The motor self then immediately is enabled to *resist the influence of the motor stimuli evoked by the river*, which constitutes the emotional response of *passive dominance*.

The traveller then complies actively with this tree-bridge, by walking across it to the opposite bank of the river. Throughout this activity he is passively dominating the river by resisting its antagonistic influences upon the conduct of the journey on which he had been initially engaged. Here, then, we find a *simultaneous combination of active compliance and passive dominance*. Neither of these responses need interfere with the other, even though both occur through the mediation of the same or allied motor centres. The active compliance, though superseding active dominance directed toward the accomplishment of the journey, is nevertheless of such a nature that it performs the passive part of the motor self's task by successfully resisting the river's intensity. The motor stimuli evoking active compliance may be thought of, schematically, as permitting the motor self to resist certain selected antagonists just as the motor stimuli to passive compliance, in the last instance, permitted the motor self actively to dominate certain selected stimuli. Reducing this type of integration to diagrammatic simplicity, we might think of the motor stimuli evoked by the tree-bridge as controlling the psychon for the same purposes of conduction into their own paths of discharge ; while, at the same time, this controlling excitation did not exert any antagonistic influence upon the increase of the motor self impulses necessary to check antagonistic excitations which had previously inhibited them together.

aCpD is Satisfaction

The integrative compounding of active compliance and passive dominance gives rise to distinctive emotional consciousness customarily called " satisfaction ". Just as in the case of desire, introspective analysis of satisfaction is usually difficult because the two compounded primary emotions each give and receive new qualities in the process of integrative compounding. Consensus of self observations, however, indicates, as before, a certain possible separation of two aspects of satisfaction, the first attributable to active compliance and the second resulting from passive dominance. The first aspect of satisfaction is variously reported as " quiet pervasive pleasantness ", " acquisitiveness ", " enjoyment of gifts ", " acceptance of assistance ", and " aesthetic pleasantness ". Perhaps the phrase most expressive of this aspect of satisfaction according to my own observations is " pleasant active acquisitiveness ". This phase of satisfaction emotion seems attributable to active compliance modified and given special qualities by its integrative compounding with passive dominance.

The remaining aspect of satisfaction is a more easily distinguishable one to most subjects. It has been regarded as " relief ", " triumphant self expansion ", " pleasant self-enlargement ", " owning the world ", " being on top of the world ", and " elation ". These introspective characterizations seem to refer especially to the aspect of satisfaction attributable to passive dominance, which consists, it must be remembered, of the motor self enlarged and made able to resist successfully its previous victorious antagonist. " Triumphant self enlargement " seems to me to characterize this aspect of satisfaction acceptably.

The compound emotion, satisfaction (the integrative formula for which can be expressed by aCpD) is distinctly a passive type of response with respect to the motor self as contrasted to *desire*, in which the motor self is the active agent.

Desire and Satisfaction Compose Appetite

In proportion as satisfaction is attained, it replaces and supersedes desire. Desire is related to satisfaction, integratively, in a way not hitherto considered. We noted, in the last chapter, that compliance normally precedes dominance (when in successive combination with it), is adapted to dominance and finally is superseded by dominance. This same relationship appears to exist between the active dominance of desire, expressed toward the object needed (a tree-bridge, in the illustration used), and the active compliance of satisfaction, expressed toward this same object. An identical relationship, moreover, seems to appear between the passive compliance of desire expressed toward the river-barrier, and the passive dominance of satisfaction expressed toward this same stimulus, now no longer an obstacle to progress.

There is a sort of kaleidoscopic shifting of emotional pattern, from desire to satisfaction, wherein the controlling element, dominance, becomes passive instead of active, and the subsidiary response, compliance, changes from a passive to an active type of emotion. The active compliance, also, is compliance with volume (object of desire) which is very pleasant, as contrasted to the replaced passive compliance with the intensity of a superior antagonist, which is distinctly unpleasant throughout a major portion of its duration. This change gives *a gradual elimination of sharp, decisive unpleasant-*

ness, and a gradual gaining of deep pervasive pleasantness. The change from active to passive dominance gives a *gradual elimination of restless, active, craving, and a gradual gaining of restful passive, self-sufficiency.*

Still another series of changes may be noted in the succession of satisfaction to desire. Desire is an emotion wherein there is felt a continuous demand upon the external environment, and a forced harmony with the demands and requirements of the organism's own, inner purpose (completing the interrupted journey). Satisfaction gradually reverses this situation, until, when it has wholly supplanted desire, *there is felt a grateful harmony with the external environment (helpful tree bridge), and a stabilized successful dominance over the subject's own inner purpose (completing journey).*

The blending of desire in satisfaction, as thus analysed begins at the very moment when the possibility of conquering the river with the tree is first perceived ; and the blending continues until the river is actually crossed, and the traveller looks back at it safely, from the other side. Only at the very first of the whole proceeding, when the subject is balked by the river and has not yet realized the possibilities of the leaning tree, is *desire alone* experienced. Only after crossing the river and looking back at it is *satisfaction alone* felt. During all the time in between, *desire is being gradually adapted to satisfaction and supplanted by it. This complex inter-relationship of the two compound emotions, desire and satisfaction, may aptly be termed the emotion of appetite.* Appetite emotion, because of the blending and ordered transition of its compound elements, attains a certain new, characteristic emotional quality of consciousness, not discoverable in either of its elements when experienced separately. A formula conveniently symbolizing appetite emotion may be devised, using the formula for desire pCaD, and the formula for satisfaction aCpD, with a plus sign (+) between signifying that desire precedes and is adapted to satisfaction. Appetite would then be represented by the complex formula pCaD+aCpD. Since the *active* element of appetite, is desire, it might be written aA ; and since satisfaction is the passive appetitive emotion unit, it might be written pA. Appetite would not, then, be symbolized by the formula aApA but by the formula aA+pA.

The term " appetite " receives dictionary definition as

follows : " A physical craving, as for food—a mental craving
—longing ". This definition suggests at least two limitations,
which must be eliminated in the use of "appetite " as an
emotional term in the way proposed. First, appetite as
defined and customarily used, refers principally to a series
of bodily hunger mechanisms. While the *emotional compounds evoked during the satisfaction of bodily hunger conform
precisely to the emotion of appetite as above analysed and defined,*
it is by no means possible or desirable to limit the use of the
emotional term appetite to physical ingestion of food.
Appetite, as we shall hereafter use it, is to be taken as the
name of an emotion made up of the compound emotion
desire and satisfaction whether these emotions be aroused
by physical hunger stimulation, or by other stimuli of vastly
different type such, for instance, as the river and tree in the
instance analysed, or desire for money and property, and the
acquisition of such objects.

The second difficulty suggested by the dictionary definition
of appetite is to be found in its disproportionate stressing of
the desire aspect of appetite, rather than its satisfaction
aspect. This difficulty, however, is not serious, and needs no
corrective comment beyond the statement that appetite
as a unit emotion is not to be taken as terminating at the
beginning of satisfaction, but must rather be considered as
persisting until satisfaction is finally completed. As already
noted, desire may predominate throughout the early stages
of appetitive behaviour, and satisfaction may predominate
throughout the later period. But both must be present in
proper inter-relationship to give the characteristic emotional
quality recognized as appetite emotion. Neither desire
alone, nor satisfaction alone constitutes appetite emotion.

What literary usage has been made of the term appetite
as designating a definite emotional state has been based,
for the most part, upon introspective recognition of the
typical emotional experience connected with physical hunger
and its satisfaction. This use of the term appetite is quite
in accord with its meaning as defined above, provided only
that physical hunger be considered as only one among many
conditions giving rise to appetite emotion.

Summary

In summary, then, we may define dominance and compliance

as primary emotions, expressed conveniently by the letters D and C. Each of these primary emotions possesses an active and passive aspect. Active aspects may be expressed by the small letter a, and passive aspects, by the small letter p, immediately preceeding the emotion symbol to which the a or p is intended to attach. Thus " aD " indicates active dominance, and " pC " passive compliance.

pCaD indicates a simultaneous combination of passive compliance and active dominance. The emotion thus integratively compounded may be called " desire ". aCpD represents an emotion integratively compounded in the same way, which may be called " satisfaction ".

When the symbol for one emotion is placed immediately before that for another emotion, with a plus sign between, the relationship between the two thus indicated is a successive occurrence, or combination of the emotions, in the order in which the letters occur, and the plus sign placed between signifies that the first emotion is adapted to its immediate successor. Thus, C + D indicates compliance followed by dominance, with the compliance adapted to the dominance. Such a successive combination and relationship between desire and satisfaction may be indicated by the formula pCaD + aCpD. According to this formula desire precedes and is adapted to satisfaction.

This successive combination of compound emotions may be termed appetite, " A ". Desire constitutes the active aspect of appetite and satisfaction its passive aspect. Thus the formula pCaD might be written instead aA, and the formula aCpD might be written pA. Activity and passivity, when used as descriptive of the emotion A, refer to the relative activity and passivity of the motor self in the particular aspect of the total emotional response indicated.

There seems to be little doubt but that the emotion of appetite is an acquired, or learned response in the same sense that compliance emotion must be learned. I have emphasized elsewhere, the fact that all the mechanisms of physical appetite were inherent in the organism,[1] including the adequate, intra-organic stimuli causing hunger pangs. This inherency of stimulating mechanism is quite a different

[1] W. M. Marston, " A Theory of Emotions and Affection Based Upon Systolic Blood Pressure Studies," *American Journal of Psychology*, 1924, vol. XXXV, pp. 469-506.

matter from the conceivable inheritance of neural patterns, upon which many physiologists have based their theories of emotion. It is against the inherent existence of any such predetermined neural pattern, in the case of any emotion save dominance, that I wish particularly to inveigh. The pattern of dominance, depending as it does upon the tonic discharge pattern, must be truly inherited ; or at least, the neural structures upon which it is based must be energized by environmental stimuli prior to the birth of the child. With regard to the other emotional patterns, it would be my own suggestion that the structures of the integrative mechanisms alone are inherited, while the actual integrative patterns constituting the emotions themselves are actually formed after birth, by the reactions of the organism to environmental stimuli.

Hunger as Teacher of Appetite Emotion and Behaviour

The rôle of the bodily hunger mechanisms by which human beings and animals are compelled to seek and eat food at regular intervals throughout life, is to be thought of as that of *a teacher of appetite emotion.* Even though the organism comes ready equipped with integrative mechanisms capable of producing dominance emotion, compliance emotion and the two simultaneous compounds of dominance and compliance already designated as active and passive appetite, the actual initiation and development of all these emotional responses would be a very haphazard matter nevertheless, if the new born human being or animal were dependent upon chance stimulation from the environment to evoke the various emotional patterns in adequate sequence and degree. Such is not the case, however. Not only are animals and human beings equipped, at birth, with integrative mechanisms capable of manufacturing D, C, and A, but also their organisms are equipped with chemico-physiological stimulating mechanisms which automatically compel the formation of the emotional patterns pCaD and aCpD. The stimulus mechanism of hunger continues to evoke appetite emotion with its constituent primary emotional patterns, at regular intervals of two to five hours throughout the life of the organism. It would seem, then, that the natural, or normal pattern of appetite emotion is properly to be learned only from a study of the integrative patterns imposed by this inherent hunger mechanism of the organism itself. In studying adult appetitive behaviour we must recognize the possibility that chance environmental stimulations, rather than the bodily hunger mechanism, may have determined the appetitive emotional pattern in whole or in part. The results of these environmental influences, in so far as they differ from the hunger-model are to be regarded rather as perversions or variations imposed upon the natural pattern, than as norms on which description of appetite emotion should be shaped. It is my own suggestion, therefore, that our understanding of the natural or normal appetitive pattern be based upon examination of inherent integrative emotional mechanisms, already considered, and upon physiological accounts of how these integrative patterns are arranged by the equally inherent organic mechanisms of hunger stimulation.

Physiology of the Hunger Stimulus

Carlson and Ginsburg have shown that hunger pangs occur in infants two hours after birth and in pups born eight to ten days before term.[1] Contractions of the infants' stomachs resembled those of adults except that the infant hunger contractions showed relatively greater vigour and frequency. Carlson and Luckhardt have shown that these hunger contractions may be started up in the full stomach of a dog just after feeding, by injection of blood taken from an animal kept in a state of hunger for several days.[2] These results indicate that the hunger contractions of the stomach may be set up, at least partially by a " hunger hormone ", generated by body tissues in need of nourishment. The authors cited state their belief, however, that the origin of hunger pangs is also to be attributed in part to a specific nervous automatism, both central and peripheral, independent of afferent impulses. Cannon and Washburn[3] first showed that these contractions

---

[1] A. J. Carlson and H. Ginsburg, " The Tonus and Hunger Contractions of the Stomach of the New Born," *American Journal of Physiology*, 1915, vol. 38, p. 29.

[2] A. J. Carlson and A. B. Luckhardt, " On the Chemical Control of the Gastric Hunger Mechanism," *American Journal of Physiology*, 1914, vol. 36, p. 37.

[3] W. B. Cannon and A. L. Washburn, *American Journal of Physiology*, 1912, vol. XXIX, p. 441.

of the stomach were felt by the human subject as hunger pangs, followed by a desire for food. Carlson and Ginsburg showed that such hunger pangs occurred in the stomach of both human infants and animals before any food had been taken into the stomach.

As a result of the researches mentioned, therefore, we may summarize the inherent, appetitive, stimulating mechanism of the body as follows : A hunger hormone, together with an inherent nervous automatism, initiate stomach contractions, in both animals and human beings. Such contractions may occur immediately after birth and before any food has been taken into the stomach. These hunger contractions begin as a constriction in the cardiac end of the stomach, and sweep rapidly toward the pyloric end, increasing in strength as they proceed.[1] These automatically initiated hunger contractions are the organic sensations which are felt by the normal adult as hunger pangs, followed by desire for food.

Motor Self Discharge Predominantly Sympathetic

Bearing in mind, then, these automatic hunger contractions as an environmental stimulus, we must next determine the nature of the motor stimuli evoked by hunger contractions. In order to discover whether the motor discharge from hunger contractions is antagonistic to the motor self, we must also examine the natural tonic condition of efferent discharge over final paths common to the motor self and to the motor stimuli evoked by hunger. In other words, it is necessary, first, to discover the discharge paths of the motor self ; and then to examine the effect of the motor stimuli of hunger upon the tonic discharge.

Cannon has shown[2] that wherever the viscera are innervated by both sympathetic and vagus impulses the sympathetic impulses prevail. That is, the tonic balance maintained by the motor self distinctly favours sympathetic motor discharge as against vagus innervations. The esophagus, stomach, and intestines are, in general, contracted by vagus impulses, and inhibited by sympathetic motor discharge. Both these influences are probably exerted upon the digestive tract

[1] A. J. Carlson, *Control of Hunger in Health and Disease*, Chicago, 1919, p. 60.
[2] W. B. Cannon, *Bodily Changes in Pain, Hunger, Fear, and Rage*, Chapter I, " The Effect of the Emotions on Digestion."

continually to a certain extent as shown by Patterson.[1] But Cannon has shown that emotions which are followed by sympathetic discharge tend to inhibit the vagus contractions of the stomach, slowing up digestion or abolishing it altogether. All these effects seem to be results of the simple fact that *sympathetic impulses to the viscera naturally dominate vagus or cranial impulses.* We might express this fact, in our own terms, by saying that the *motor self tends to energize the blood vessels and other viscera contributing to activity of the skeletal muscles predominantly at the expense of the blood vessels and smooth muscles used in the process of digestion.*

Motor Stimuli Discharging Through Cranial Channels Would be Antagonistic to the Motor Self

Thus, reinforcement of the motor self would be expected to lead to increased supply of blood to the skeletal muscles, increase of adrenalin in the blood, and other visceral preparation for activity of the skeletal muscles. Reinforcement of the motor self would be expected, similarly, to inhibit the movements of the esophagus, stomach and intestines, to slow up or stop altogether the secretion of gastric juice, and to interfere with the normal output of saliva into the mouth and throat. Any motor stimulus which had the effect of increasing the flow of saliva and gastric juice, and of enhancing the digestive movements of the stomach and intestines would be described, in our own terminology, as a motor stimulus antagonistic to the motor self.

Such an antagonistic motor stimulus would throw the reflex balance over to the vagus side, as opposed to the natural reflex equilibrium where sympathetic impulses predominate. If a motor stimulus could be shown to tend toward this vagus outlet of discharge, but only resulted in an increased sympathetic motor discharge, we might assume that the motor stimulus though antagonistic to the motor self, was of *inferior intensity.* The increased energy in skeletal muscles and sympathetically innervated viscera might be taken as evidence of a dominance response, wherein the motor self had reinforced itself in order to maintain its natural reflex balance despite the attempted upsetting of this balance by the weaker antagon-

[1] L. L. Patterson, " Vagus and Splanchnic Influence on Gastric Hunger Movements of the Frog," *American Journal of Physiology,* vol. 53, p. 239.

istic motor stimulus. If, however, we found an initial reinforcement of motor discharge through sympathetic channels,
followed by a marked decrease in this sympathetic outflow
together with a sudden appearance of vagus motor discharge,
evidenced by increased secretion of saliva and similar symptoms, we might assume that the antagonistic motor stimulus
had proved of *superior intensity* to the motor self. As a consequence of its superior strength, such a motor stimulus might
force its way through the barrier which the motor self sought
to set up, the superior, antagonistic motor stimulus finally
expressing itself through its own vagus channels. Such an
occurrence, in short, would constitute an emotional response
of *compliance with intensity.*

Autonomic Channels of Motor Self and Motor Stimuli Summary

We may summarize as follows : the natural reflex balance
maintained by the motor self seems to call for a predominance
of sympathetic motor discharge over vagus discharge. Sympathetic motor impulses inhibit digestive movements and
gastric secretions, while at the same time increasing blood
supply to the muscles and release of adrenin into the blood
stream. Sympathetic visceral impulses of this sort have also
been shown to run parallel, usually, to tonic impulses increasing
the tonus of the skeletal muscles.

Vagus impulses increase the digestive processes, and tend
to inhibit blood supply and tonic impulses to the skeletal
muscles. A motor stimulus, therefore, which sought vagus
channels of discharge would be antagonistic to the motor self.
Such a motor stimulus would tend to upset the natural reflex
equilibrium maintained by the motor self in which sympathetic
impulses predominated. If an antagonistic motor stimulus
were weaker than the motor self, we should expect to find
exaggeration of the natural reflex equilibrium ; that is,
increased nervous energy sent through sympathetic channels.
If, on the other hand, an antagonistic motor stimulus were
stronger than the motor self, we should expect to find, first,
an attempted reinforcement of sympathetic resistance by the
motor self ; and secondly, a marked decrease in sympathetic
motor discharge accompanied by a corresponding increase
of vagus discharge, swinging the reflex balance over to the
vagus side, and signalizing a defeat of the motor self by the
antagonistic motor stimulus.

Increase of sympathetic discharge would, in short, indicate a successful dominance response of the motor self; while initial increase of sympathetic discharge followed by decrease of sympathetic discharge and corresponding ascendency of vagus discharge would constitute a compulsory response of compliance with intensity.

Hunger Pangs Evoke Motor Stimuli Antagonistic and Superior to the Motor Self

With the situation thus outlined, we may hope to discover whether ·the motor stimuli evoked by hunger pangs are antagonistic to the motor self ; and, if they are, whether they are stronger or weaker than the tonic motor discharge. Carlson, of Chicago, with his collaborators, has made a series of studies of the effect of hunger pangs upon various other functions of the body.[1] Carlson was fortunate in obtaining a subject, Mr. F. V., who had a complete closure of the esophagus and a permanent gastric fistula. When eleven years old, this subject accidentally drank a strong solution of caustic soda, and ever since that time, for more than twenty years, has fed himself through the gastric fistula. Carlson reports that F.V. has enjoyed good health through this period and is in every respect, with the exception of the closed esophagus, a normal individual. Stomach balloons and other recording devices could be inserted very easily into the stomach through the gastric fistula, which opened into the fundic end of the stomach, without producing the somewhat abnormal condition of consciousness necessarily caused by swallowing a stomach balloon with connecting tubes. In this way Carlson and his associates have been able to make studies of extraordinary accuracy and reliability, and they have given us a rather complete picture of the different types of motor stimuli, or motor discharge resulting from hunger contractions of all degrees of intensity.

In the first place, Carlson has shown that no marked hunger is felt unless the stomach contractions are very strong. Accompanying strong hunger contractions the following phenomena have been found :

[1] The results of these studies are found in A. J. Carlson's *Control of Hunger in Health and Disease*, Chicago, 1919, which is cited as authority for the account of Carlson's findings here rendered.

(1) Increased knee jerk,

(2) increased heart rate,

(3) increased blood volume of the arm,

(4) a brief gush of saliva at the maximum point of each strong contraction,

(5) marked irritability, restlessness, and inability to retain fixed attention.

The blood volume of the arm increases up to a point near the height of the stomach contractions, and then begins to diminish before the contraction is complete. The knee jerk has been found by Lombard to be less during hunger than after satisfaction of hunger (although Carlson holds that it is greater during hunger than when neither hunger nor satiety is present). All these physical symptoms, taken together, present a clear picture symptomatic of *antagonistic motor stimuli, superior in intensity to the motor self.* The gush of saliva, and irritability and restlessness (evidently representing an interference with energy to the skeletal muscles) appear only at the height of strong hunger contractions. Salivary secretion is produced by vagus innervation only, and interruption of sympathetic impulses by vagus discharge might also account adequately for the interruption of previous dominant activities in which the subject had been engaged, as evidenced by restlessness and irritability. The blood volume of the arm also increased by sympathetic innervations during the early part of each hunger contraction, begins to shrink before the contraction reaches its maximum height indicating once more a triumph of vagus over sympathetic innervations. The results of Lombard, if verified, might indicate that the knee jerk, though enhanced by hunger contractions, was reduced below its possible maximum by partially successful vagus opposition. Measurement of the knee jerk, however, is scarcely fine enough a determination to make comparison of this sort absolutely accurate. The heart rate is frequently found to increase *pari passu* with a decrease in strength of the heart beat, as evidenced by dimunition of blood volume in an arm or leg, or by systolic blood pressure measure at the brachial artery.

The only dependable measurements of bodily changes caused by hunger pangs indicate exaggeration of the tonic balance (dominance response) up to a point close to the maximal intensity of the stimulus. At this point, the antagonistic motor stimuli evoked by the pangs seem to break through the barrier set up against them by the motor self, just sufficiently to compel the motor self to give up its previous dominance response, and to seek some form of dominant activity which will be compatible with the hunger pang stimulus. This analysis indicates that *hunger pangs constitute a stimulus antagonistic to the motor self and of superior intensity nicely calculated to compel a response of passive compliance with intensity.* (Passive because only sufficient victory is attained by vagus impulses to compel the motor self to give up its previous dominance).

Subject Passively Complies with Hunger Pangs and Actively Dominates Food (Desire)

This analysis seems to be confirmed by examination of certain subjects with very strong stomach contractions, who experienced only nausea, weakness, and faintness during the contractions. Boring[1] and Carlson have both reported subjects of this type. I myself studied a woman subject of this type for about a year and a half. During stomach contractions she felt nausea and marked bodily weakness. At such times systolic blood pressure measurements showed marked drops apparently parallel with the stomach contractions. Because of the absence of conscious hunger, and the presence of nausea during hunger contractions, this subject could eat very little food, and was in an under-nourished physical condition. She had consulted a number of medical specialists, and had tried various diets without result. After analysing her emotional responses, I came to the conclusion that the case was a psychological rather than a medical one. It seemed to me that she had developed compliance to a point where compliance response was controlling the visceral functions which normally are not under voluntary control. The case seemed not unlike that of the Hindu adept, with the additional complication that her excessive bodily compliance was not suited to an active strenuous life, and was not, in fact, physically possible under conditions of dominant occidental civilization. Treating the case on this theory, I induced the subject to take an active, aggressive attitude toward her stomach pangs, regarding them as opponents which she must destroy

---

[1] E. G. Boring, " Processes Referred to the Alimentary and Urinary Tracts : A qualitative Analysis," *Psychological Review*, 1915, vol. XXII, p. 320.

by forcing food into her stomach, even though nausea made this very difficult (the esophagus also seemed to be in a hypertonic condition). At first the subject experienced great difficulty, and frequently could not retain the food swallowed. Eventually, however, under repeated suggestion, she began to regard the stomach pangs with aggressive antagonism. Soon after this she was able to swallow food with no great difficulty, her hunger pangs coming at two hour intervals. Within six months, feelings of nausea and faintness which had formerly accompanied the pangs had turned into feelings of ravenous hunger and appetite for food. Upon several occasions, I observed this subject in such an aggressive condition of hunger that she seized a loaf of bread and bit into it savagely, without being able to wait for the bread to be cut and buttered. At this point in the case, the subject began to put on weight ; and about three and a half months later she had gained fifty-one pounds.

My own analysis of this case just described was that the element of active dominance had been eliminated from the subject's emotional response to the hunger pang stimulus. As we have noted above, active appetite consists of simultaneously compounded passive compliance (in this case with the hunger pangs) and active dominance (directed toward seizing and biting food). The woman subject in question had so trained herself in schools of occultism and esoteric religion that she was able to comply actively with any antagonistic motor stimulus, no matter how intense this stimulus might be. But her compliance training had been carried too far, and had not included a proper combination of dominance with compliance in the compound emotion of appetite. This additional training I was able to supply, and the result seemed to justify my analysis.

We may summarize then, as follows : Hunger pangs, consisting of sudden stomach contractions beginning at the fundic end of the stomach, constitute an inherent stimulating mechanism. This inherent, automatic stimulus evokes in the normal individual motor stimuli antagonistic and of superior intensity to the motor self. The resulting emotional response is one of compliance with intensity. The superiority of strength in the motor stimuli, however, is nicely adjusted to produce passive compliance only, permitting the motor self to react dominantly toward a single type of environmental stimulus, food. Thus in the total response of active physical appetite, *the individual is reacting simultaneously with passive compliance toward the hunger pangs and active dominance toward the food.*

Subject Actively Complies with Food and Passively Dominates Hunger Pangs

Selection of food as an object toward which dominant activity can be directed evidently depends primarily upon the power of the chemical stimuli of smell and taste to inhibit the hunger pangs. It will be recalled that the hunger pangs themselves are not attributable to motor discharge into the central nervous system since it has been proved that hunger pangs may occur normally in a stomach which has been completely disconnected from all nerve connection with the central nervous system. We find, therefore, a situation wherein antagonistic stimuli of superior intensity evoked by hunger pangs cause motor discharge through vagus channels ; while a second antagonistic stimulus, food, while causing motor discharge through these same channels inhibits or removes the first antagonistic stimulus, hunger pangs. For the sight and smell of food have been proved by Cannon, Carlson, and others to result in (1) inhibition of hunger contractions of the stomach and (2) in vagusly innervated secretion of saliva and gastric juice, with decrease of blood supply to the skeletal muscles, and increase of blood to the digestive viscera. Chewing of food, and swallowing of saliva and food have also been shown to inhibit hunger pangs by means of vagus discharge. *The motor stimuli evoked by food are thus superior in integrative strength to the motor stimuli arising from hunger pangs.*

The food when thoroughly smelled, chewed, and tasted evokes motor stimuli which are superior in volume to the motor self, and for this reason may be pleasantly complied with. Thus, we have a total picture of food stimulation evoking antagonistic motor stimuli of superior volume but inferior intensity to the motor self. At the same time, these motor stimuli evoked by food are enabled to gain an initial victory over the motor self by virtue of the fact that they utilize the identical motor channels followed by efferent discharge from hunger pang stimuli, which were of sufficient intensity originally to overcome the motor self.

Finally, we find that, in proportion as the motor stimuli

evoked by food inhibit and reduce in intensity the hunger pangs themselves, the motor self is enabled to re-establish its successful resistance to the motor stimuli from hunger pangs. In this situation we find *active compliance of the motor self with the food stimuli simultaneously compounded with passive domin-ance directed toward the antagonistic motor stimuli evoked by hunger pangs.* The activity of the response of compliance with food is made up of unchecked vagus discharge, resulting in tremendously increased secretion of saliva and gastric juice, and digestive movements of the stomach and intestines accom-panied by transfer of the major blood supply from the skeletal muscles to the digestive viscera. In short, the active com-pliance with food consists of an entire shift in the natural reflex balance of the organism from sympathetic preponderance to vagus preponderance. Yet this shift of reflex balance is accomplished by a large *volume* of antagonistic motor stimuli which are of moderate intensity only, permitting the motor self to continue to control its own normal motor channels, with even some increase in its own volume (as indicated by a slight increase in systolic blood pressure level of six to eight mm, on the average, after a full meal has been eaten.) Thus a *response of compliance with volume toward food is compounded with a response of passive dominance toward hunger pangs.*

Spread of Active Compliance, During Satisfaction to Other Environmental Stimuli Besides Food

My own studies of satisfaction of physical appetite have shown that passive appetite (that is, satisfied hunger as above described), carries with it an emotional attitude of active compliance toward nearly all environmental stimuli, besides food itself ; and also an emotional attitude to expansive self-satisfaction frequently expressed in talkativeness, mild boasts of the subject's accomplishments, and friendly condescension toward table companions. It is not by accident, apparently, that business men follow the custom of inviting to luncheon an important business connection from whom they hope to obtain a large order, or business contract favourable to themselves. I have studied at least a score of instances where a business man who, during the forenoon, rejected with great firmness the proposals of salesmen or business associates, yielded to these same proposals of salesmen with hearty good will after eating to the point of satiety at lunch (no liquor having been taken). Following a satisfactory meal, the active compliance with which the subject responds to his food seems nearly always to extend itself toward other stimuli of appetitive nature, such as business deals and joint undertakings, conviviality, and amusements of various sorts. If precautions are taken by the salesman, or business man desirous of having his proposition accepted, not to increase the intensity of his proposals too greatly (that is not emphasizing his own ego or business strength unduly) this extended active compliance may be utilized to great financial advantage.

Passive dominance also plays its part in rendering the average male susceptible to appetitive stimuli after the satisfaction of physical appetite. The subject feels much more sure of himself and nearly always possesses a distinct consciousness of having mastered all threatening or dangerous antagonists. While this element of passive dominance is really felt toward the physical hunger pangs, it nevertheless tends to extend itself toward elements in the business situation under discussion, which had seemed, before luncheon, formidable and dangerous to the subject's own business security. While the state of physical satisfaction persists, however, the man is apt to feel much more secure, and able to undertake hazardous enterprises.

Summary of Physical Appetite

We may summarize, then, as follows. Food is, the only environmental stimulus toward which the subject is able to react dominantly while hunger pangs are enforcing passive compliance with themselves upon the organism.

Once the food has been dominated, however, and placed within stimulating distance of the nose or mouth, it evokes motor stimuli antagonistic to the motor self and superior to it in volume, though of only moderate intensity. This superior volume of motor stimuli evoked by food is able to control its vagus channels of discharge freely because the over-intense motor stimuli from hunger pangs have already opened these vagus channels, in spite of the resistance of the motor self. The food stimuli, moreover, reduce by inhibition the strength of the hunger pangs themselves, to a point where the hunger pangs motor stimuli can be successfully resisted by the motor self. This simultaneous combination of active compliance with food and passive dominance toward hunger pangs constitutes passive appetite emotion, or satisfaction.

Both the active compliance and passive dominance elements of this emotional compound tend to respond to many other appropriate types of environmental stimuli besides food, during the persistence of satisfaction emotion which was actually brought about by removal of hunger pangs by food.

Characteristics of Dominance and Compliance Revealed in Eating Behaviour

I have had occasion to study some cases showing interesting personality traits easily detectable by analysis of behaviour during eating. For instance, many male subjects, both adolescent and adult, possess personalities in which active dominance is very highly developed at the expense of active compliance. Several subjects of this type were college students whose eating behaviour I was able to observe at a college cafeteria five or six days a week. Out of seven subjects thus studied, five invariably "bolted" their meals, attacking the food much as they would attack an opponent of the athletic field. They almost always swallowed the food very hurriedly and with unnecessary energy, by the process popularly known as "gulping it down". Two, at least, of these subjects had serious digestive difficulties apparently due to insufficient secretion of saliva and gastric juice, and also to inadequate chewing of the food before swallowing. One other subject, out of the seven, ate in a similar way whenever he was in a hurry to get to some class or engagement ; while on other occasions he ate more rapidly than the average person. This type of behaviour in eating seems clearly to reveal an imperfect, or altogether lacking active compliance with food, coupled to an excess of active dominance which the subject continued to express toward the food even after he had it completely captured on the table in front of him. The spread of this over-dominance and under-active compliance through the personalities of these college students was very striking.

Adult males, especially business men, sometimes carry active dominance toward business to such an extreme that their food, even when thoroughly chewed, is reported as tasteless and "like sawdust". In two such cases I have been able to restore pleasurable taste in eating to the subjects by inducing them to learn active compliance with food. Flow of saliva generally increases in response to sight, smell, and taste of food, and " taste " and enjoyment of the food increases correspondingly. Various other types of business men, and especially " white collar " employees whom I have studied, experience considerable pain and discomfort in digestion of their food, apparently because they will not give up physical activity of the skeletal muscles after eating. In other words, they may actively comply with their food during the meal itself, but immediately rush away to make the most of their noon hour in some physically active way. Or, in the case of business men of this type, they return to business calculations and planning immediately after eating. Active compliance with food, to be successful, must be continued for twenty minutes to three quarters of an hour after finishing the meal, if a proper pattern of passive appetite emotion is to be built up in the natural way, by full satisfaction of the physical hunger mechanism.

Hunger Pangs Can Build Up Model Integrative Pattern for Appetite Emotion

In concluding our initial study of appetite emotion the nature of the rôle played by the bodily hunger pang mechanism should again be emphasized. Countless other environmental stimulus situations besides physical hunger are perfectly adequate to evoke simultaneous passive compliance and active dominance which constitute the active element of appetite emotion. Many stimulus situations other than satisfaction of physical hunger pangs are adequate to evoke the simultaneous combination of active compliance and passive dominance which together comprise passive appetite emotion. *The hunger pang mechanism*, however, *represents an inherent adequate stimulating mechanism*, which if intelligently studied and permitted to control the organism *is capable of building up a perfectly normal and well balanced integrative pattern for the emotion of appetite, in both its active and passive phases.*

Active and passive appetite, moreover, are brought together and fitted into one another by the physical hunger mechanism, in a maximally well ordered manner. Active appetite gradually gives way to, and is supplanted by passive appetite, as the food is taken into the alimentary canal for ingestion. Moreover, this inherent emotional stimulating mechanism, hunger pangs, repeats its stimulation at periods three to five hours apart throughout the waking life of a normal human being, from birth to death. Such continually repeated enforcement of the entire, evenly balanced, integrative pattern of appetite emotion furnishes a condition for the proper learning of appetite that could scarcely be found in any other series of experimental stimuli which could be devised for purposes of appetitive training. Surely, the average person would scarcely be expected to experience such a series of perfectly arranged stimuli in the more or less casual and haphazard environment met with in ordinary life. The hunger pang mechanism, therefore, should be accepted as the teacher of appetitive emotion, and environmental stimuli devised for teaching appetite emotion either to children or to adults should be patterned upon it.

CHAPTER XI

SUBMISSION

COHESIVE forces of nature may be said to submit to one another. Those relatively stable forms of energy known physically as " matter " each possess attractive force toward all material bodies, and this force of mutual attraction is known as " gravitation ". The largest material body with which we come into daily contact is the earth itself. The attractive power of the earth operates in alliance with the attractive force which each of these smaller bodies exerts toward the earth. This alliance of attractive forces, with that of the larger body, the earth, predominating, results in a tendency of each smaller body to move towards the centre of the earth, its motion being accelerated continuously as it moves. This law of the behaviour of smaller physical bodies toward the earth is called " gravity ". Gravity, then, represents an alliance of attractive forces wherein the *weaker attractive force progressively weakens itself by facilitating the compulsion exercised upon itself by the stronger attractive force.* Such behaviour presents a perfect objective picture of *submission.* The lesser ally submits to the greater by decreasing itself to make the alliance closer.

Submission Response Requires Thalamic Motor Centres

It seems an interesting fact, at least, that constant tonic motor discharge constituting the motor self is largely composed of reflex responses of the organism to gravity. The bodies of human beings and of animals, like all other material objects on this planet, tend to submit physically to the pull of gravity. The tonic energization of skeletal muscles counteracts this gravitational pull, and holds the body erect. Thus physical submission must be opposed and counterbalanced by psychoneural dominance, throughout the life of the organism.

We have already noted, in the results obtained by Goltz and Sherrington, and others upon decerebrate animals, that the dominant, or tonic opposition to gravity is greatly exaggerated when all cortical influence has been removed. The condition of enhanced tonic posture called decerebrate rigidity results ; and this tonic outflow, in the absence of the cerebrum, responds to all intercurrent motor stimuli dominantly, that is, with increase of itself to overcome the increased opposition. Compliance response is abolished ; and submission response, which must occur in sex emotion, and which represents the exact integrative antithesis of the prevailing dominance reaction of a decerebrate animal likewise fails to appear. Goltz found, in fact, that no aspect of sex emotion could be evoked. We may be reasonably sure, therefore, that submission response, like compliance, requires the mediation of some motor centre integratively superior to the tonic centres. On the other hand, it was established more than a century ago[1] that only thalamic connections are necessary to spontaneous movements, and to centrally innervated sex response. Since the latter depends primarily, as we shall have occasion shortly to note, upon a submission type of integration, we may conclude that the primary emotional response of submission may be mediated by thalamic motor centres, in the absence of the cerebral hemispheres.

ı True Submission Appears in Infant Behaviour

Watson lists " love " response as an unlearned type of emotional reaction.[2] " The stimulus to ' love ' response," he says, " may be stroking of the skin, tickling, gentle rocking, or patting." The response is also elicited by stimulation of the so-called erogenous zones, including the nipples, lips, and sex organs. If the infant is crying when thus stimulated, its crying will cease and a smile will take its place. Gurgling and cooing appear and the infant may extend its hand or foot to be tickled or stroked. Erection of the penis, changes in circulation and respiration, are also included by Watson in his list of love responses. *All the reactions thus listed appear to depend upon a lessening of the tonic resistance to environment for the purpose of enhancing the effect which an allied motor stimulus is having upon the organism.*

---

[1] A. Desmoulins and F. Magendie, *Des Systemes Nerveux*, 1825, vol. II, p. 626.
[2] J. B. Watson, *Behaviorism*, p. 123.

In some of the reactions listed, such as erection of the penis, we know that cortical inhibitions antagonistic to the motor self and love reactions alike must have been removed by the motor stimulus, prior to its passage down the spinal cord to the sacral ganglia innervating the external genitals. Removal of this cortical inhibition could not be accomplished by the motor self under ordinary conditions and we know, therefore, *that the motor stimulus must have proved itself to possess greater integrative strength than that possessed by the motor self.* The same conclusion may be drawn from the effect of submission stimulation in successfully overcoming the over-dominant type of response probably expressed in crying. Whether the motor stimuli adequate to submission response gain their integrative power through superior allied volume or through innate prepotency of the nerve channels employed, need not be discussed. If the motor stimulus possesses superior strength to that of the motor self and is in alliance with the motor self, the stimulus falls within the definition of an adequate submission stimulus suggested in chapter five.

Though parts of the sympathetic and sacral branches of the autonomic nervous system, innervating respectively the internal and external genital organs, seem to be antagonistic to one another, it is nevertheless a fact that internal and external genitals are excited simultaneously throughout the sexual act until this condition is terminated by the sexual orgasm. To bring about this simultaneous excitement in both sets of genital organs, however, the sympathetic or tonic motor discharge must apparently be reduced in intensity. Thus the final integrative condition during erection of the penis following environmental stimulus described by Watson, would seem to be a *decrease of motor self for the purpose of increasing alliance with the stronger motor stimulus. This constitutes the nodal type of integration designated as submission response.* The infant, during "love behaviour" described by Watson, decreases its motor self for the purpose of surrendering more completely to the direction of an allied motor stimulus.

Similar Submission in Behaviour of Older Children

Behaviour of older children in response to the hugs and caresses of a mother, or other loved adult, follow the same general trend of reaction discovered by Watson in very young infants. The child, when caressed, responds by yielding its body freely to the embrace or other stimulation imposed by the adult. If the child is in a state of " being naughty " (that is, overdominant), caresses and similar love stimuli will very frequently abolish the naughtiness or temper fit. Spontaneous caresses may be given by the child to the parent, and a general tendency to *draw near* to the parent may always be observed. Responses of so-called obedience to the loved one's commands soon become an important part of the submission behaviour pattern. Such obedience to command is rendered spontaneously and gladly with an apparent accompaniment of extreme pleasantness. •

Learning of Submission is Pleasant, Learning of Compliance Is Unpleasant

It is necessary to emphasize the distinction between submission and compliance. Both are learned responses in the sense that there seems to be no submissive lowering of the strength or volume of the tonic discharge prior to birth, or at least none brought about by the transitory type of environmental stimulus which induces submission response in infants describd by Watson. Submission, however, is a response which appears to be learned much more readily and by altogether pleasant means. Whereas compliance, as we have seen, often requires very harsh and even destructive stimulation to evoke it directly.

This initial point of contrast between submission and compliance response is brought out in the many cases of little boys, from three to seven years old, who respond obediently and affectionately to their mothers, or, sometimes to nursemaids and girls older than themselves, while they may react dominantly toward their fathers and toward older boys with whom they play. I have had occasion to study three or four cases of this type for short periods of time. One boy, aged four, in the public kindergarten obeyed the commands of an older sister, a girl between twelve and thirteen years old, without protest and apparently with considerable pleasure derived from the obedience itself. This same child, however, was reported as extremely rebellious toward his father's authority, and also caused some difficulty at school because of disobedience to a woman teacher whose manner was rather

Q

harsh, and whose attitude was that of a strict disciplinarian.

Another case in point was that of the boy Jack, already mentioned in chapter seven. Jack, it will be remembered, suffered from some glandular disturbance, which seemed to over stimulate his dominance to the point where he could not be compelled to comply, even by physical injury. Yet, Jack responded *submissively* to his " class teacher ", who was a very gentle-mannered girl of twenty-three or twenty-four. Despite her soft and pleasing approach, however, Miss B. was very firm in her commands, and had a reputation for keeping excellent order among the children in her charge. Jack responded to this treatment more readily, even, than did some of the other children. Jack and Miss B. were " great friends ". As we have already observed, Miss B. succeeded in obtaining Jack's promise to forego his youthful gangster activities, and this promise was kept for as long a time as the child's physical abnormality permitted. Jack's promise to Miss B., and his marked obedience to her commands in the school room, were clearly expressions of submission and not of compliance. Jack admitted to me with some reluctance that he "liked to mind Miss B." Submission, apparently, was even more pleasant to Jack than was dominance, though submission occupied a much smaller proportion of Jack's life than dominance, because he was stimulated to dominance much more continuously than to submission response.

Stimulus Evoking Submission Must Be Allied to Subject ;
Stimulus Evoking Compliance is Antagonistic

These cases suffice to illustrate the fact that submission response is naturally, and always pleasantly learned, when it is learned at all ; whereas in compliance, if the attempt is made to evoke it directly, it is extremely difficult to arouse, and requires great harshness and unpleasantness of stimulation. The same cases also illustrate the fundamental difference between an adequate stimulus to submission and an adequate stimulus to compliance. The sister who was able to evoke complete submission from her little brother, Paul, first evoked this response from the child by caressing and petting him. During the year preceding my examination of the children, E, the older sister, had been given almost complete charge of little Paul during his play hours. She had never, so far as I could learn, treated the child harshly or unjustly in any way. She had allowed Paul to play with children his own age, but had always insisted on prompt obedience whenever she decided it was time for him to stop playing. The mother stated that E. always brought Paul home in time for meals, and that he let E. wash his face and hands without protest. In short, E. had consistently acted for Paul's benefit rather than for her own. This fact, strangely enough, seems to have impressed itself upon the consciousness of the child much more effectively than did the severe whippings which he had received from his father, from time to time. *Paul submitted to E. because he felt E. to be an ally of superior strength.* It is this *allied* quality of the stimulus which gives it the power to arouse submission. And it is the manner and general attitude, including vocal inflection and gestures, which seem to convey to a child the allied aspect of the older person's behaviour toward him.

Submission Not Dependent Upon Erogenous Zone Stimulation

In the case just cited, the sister E. had, of course, kissed, caressed, and otherwise petted the child Paul, and it might be supposed, perhaps, that these caresses were the most important element in evoking the child's submission. In the case of Jack, however, so far as I was able to learn from the teacher, and also from other persons who had observed Miss B's relations with Jack, there had been no physical contact whatever between the two. The girl had not, so far as she could remember, even placed a friendly arm about the boy's shoulder, nor had she taken him by the hand while talking to him. Yet Jack's submissive behaviour toward Miss B. was pronounced and consistent. Jack was impressed, among other things, with the justness of Miss B.'s decisions and especially with the fact that she was "looking after the kids'" interests rather than her own. Again it seemed to me that the manner and attitude of the teacher were the aspects of her behaviour which made the greatest impression upon the children who submitted to her, including Jack. This teacher, by the way, spent her hours outside of school in further collegiate studies for her own advancement, so she had no contacts with the children except those in the school room. *The effectiveness of an adequate stimulus to*

*submission does not seem to depend upon stimulation of the
" erogenous zone " directly or indirectly, nor does it appear
to depend upon the duration of the stimulus.*

Stimulus Evoking Submission Must Be Stronger Than the Boy But Not Too Intense

When children, especially boys, reach adolescence, a somewhat more intense type of stimulation seems to be necessary
in order to evoke submission response. A very nice adjustment of this intensity must be made, oftentimes, for if the
intensity is not sufficient, a dominant boy is apt not to perceive the stimulus as stronger than himself, even though he
recognizes its allied quality. Whereas, if the intensity of
stimulation is too great, a dominant boy almost invariably
regards it as antagonistic rather than allied. One example
illustrating the former situation, where stimulation was of
insufficient intensity, may be taken from the case of a high
school teacher, Miss R., who " loved " all the youngsters in
her various classes, the word " love " being Miss R.'s own
description of her attitude. Miss R. was, in fact, an excellent
teacher, but a complete failure as a disciplinarian. In one
case which I actually observed, a large, dominant football-
playing youth rose calmly at the back of one of the school
rooms, and threw a book at another football player who
happened to be reciting at that moment.

" Now, now, Edward," protested Miss R., in a voice of
deep concern, " is that a fair thing to do ? I didn't think
that of you, Edward ; I am *surprised*."

Edward agreed : " That's right, Miss R., I'll wait till Ben
is looking next time. It's not fair to hit a fellow when he
isn't looking, I know."

The class broke into a roar of unsuppressed merriment,
and that was the end of the incident. Miss R., though she
flushed deeply, and seemed for the time undecided whether
or not to send Edward to the principal for discipline, finally
ignored the action altogether and went on with her teaching.
Miss R.'s conduct is not to be interpreted, I believe, as over
compliance or " fear ", for she had performed many acts
during her teaching career which expressed both moral and
physical courage. She was herself over-submissive and could
not, therefore, evoke submission from others. Edward, and
nearly all the boys under Miss R.'s tutelage, however, were

extremely fond of her. Edward, in fact, took her to one of the school dances after the incident narrated above. He explained his action by stating that "he was afraid he had hurt Miss R.'s feelings" in the book-throwing occurrence. But this regard for Miss R.'s feelings did not make Edward or any of the other boys obedient to her at that time, or at any other subsequent period. *Miss R. impressed herself upon the boys as an allied stimulus weaker than themselves.* Such a stimulus fails to evoke submission.

In the same school was an assistant head master who was regarded by the boys as a strict disciplinarian. The more intelligent of the youths under his charge did not question the man's sincerity, or the fairness of his decisions as to where the guilt for any misdemeanour should be placed. The less intelligent boys concocted traditions supposed to reveal the injustice and egotism of Mr. Y. Both the intelligent and the less intelligent youths, however, agreed that Mr. Y. was a "hellion", and not only did they fail to obey him, but also it had seemingly become a matter of principle with them to find ingenious and subtle methods of "beating" Mr. Y.'s commands. One example of the harshness, or over-intensity of stimulation with which Mr. Y. sought to evoke submission will suffice to reveal the emotional cause for the boys' disobedience.

'It' was a school custom to give as punishment for minor offences one or two hours extra work in some appropriate school subject, to be performed in the afternoon after the other pupils had been dismissed for the day. One boy had quite inadvertently knocked an eraser off the rack. In picking it up from the floor, this youth drew it across the back of another boy, who was at the board working with his back to the room. The children, of course, laughed, and the class teacher reported the culprit to the assistant head master for the usual minor disciplinary measures. Instead of sentencing the boy to the customary one or two hours extra work, however, Mr. Y. delivered a terrific lecture to this youth, calling him everything but a murderer, and concluded his tirade by giving the boy forty hours extra work to be performed in the afternoons. From my own studies of Mr. Y. and his methods, I am convinced that he acted sincerely, and, as he thought, for the boy's own good. This particular youth had been doing poorly in his school work, and Mr. Y.'s idea was that he should bring him back to a submissive frame of mind by sheer severity of punishment. Not only, however, did Mr. Y. fail to evoke the desired submission but the boy actually left school with the approval of his parents (who sent him to another, more fashionable school), rather than comply with the punishment sentence meted out. *Even though a stimulus is actually allied in nature, it will be regarded as antagonistic if it is too intense, and in such case will not evoke submission.*

Allied Stimulus of Superior Volume Effectively Evokes Submission

Mr. H., principal of a continuation school in New York City, may be cited as an example of a person using an effective degree of intensity in evoking submission from boys twelve to seventeen years of age. A continuation school is designed to give instruction to those children who have gone to work before completing the grades of school required by law. The pupils in such a school are apt to be much more dominant than those in the ordinary day school. For example, while we were engaged in surveying Mr. H.'s continuation school, one pupil was discovered to be a full-fledged boot-legger, and another was intercepted by Mr. H. in the act of manufacturing a black-jack in the carpenter shop, " for sale to a friend " as the boy said. Mr. H.'s method of handling these youths was first of all to impress upon them in every way possible the fact that he was ready to act in their interests at all times, whatever the inconvenience to himself. He obtained positions for his pupils, appeared for them in juvenile court whenever he could legitimately do so, and undertook to assume a sort of paternal guardianship over boys of notoriously bad character. As a result of these activities there were no doubts in the boys' minds that Mr. H. was their best friend. On the other hand, Mr. H. insisted upon strict obedience to the rules which he laid down, not only as to conduct in the school itself, but also in regard to the boys' behaviour while working at the jobs Mr. H. obtained for them, and in the home and local community.

Mr. H. was continually alert in obtaining information as to the boys' conduct, and very prompt and emphatic in calling the boy to task for any misdemeanours which might be discovered. Mr. H., however, used a method of discipline quite the opposite from that employed by Mr. Y. in the case last cited. Mr. H. restrained the boys, by force, if necessary, from doing something they wanted to do, as punishment for misdemeanours. But never, so far as my observation went, did Mr. H. impose positive punishment upon an offender which required active compliance or which gave the boy punished actual pain or suffering. Mr. H. might require a boy to remain in a certain recitation room instead of going to do the shop work which that boy especially liked. Again Mr. H. might withhold certification which would enable the boy to take a desired position. Or Mr. H. might refuse to allow the boy to come to his school for a time (one youngster kept coming every day for several months before Mr. H. took him back). In extreme cases, Mr. H. might withdraw his endorsement of a boy who had misbehaved very badly, thus causing the youth to be discharged from a lucrative position, or exposing him unprotected to some juvenile court penalty.

These punishments, which were all of a restraining or withdrawing nature, were actually more severe in many cases than a sharp physical whipping would have been. *But here severity was felt as one of volume rather than intensity.* The effect of superior volume seemed to be that the allied aspect of the stimulation remained unchanged, while the stimulus, Mr. H., assumed the rôle of superior strength. Of course, there were individual instances in which the punished boy would react dominantly for the time being. But in all the cases I studied, with a single exception, such initial dominance later turned into submission with increased affectionate obedience to Mr. H. after this final submission had been evoked. We may summarize Mr. H.'s method by the statement that *an allied stimulus capable of impressing both its allied character and its superior strength of volume upon the subject is maximally efficient in evoking submission, especially from dominant subjects.*

Woman's Strength Seldom Felt as Superior by Adolescent Males

Under our current social conventions and existing social attitudes, it is decidedly more difficult for a woman teacher or disciplinarian to impress her superiority of strength upon adolescent boys and girls than for a male teacher of corresponding ability. One young woman who acted as principal of the major portion of a combined grammar and high school which we studied, succeeded in evoking submission by the sheer strength of her physical alertness and intensity of manner. Most women preceptors who attempt this method succeed only in making themselves felt as antagonistic to their pupils. This particular woman, however, was young and good looking, and, like Mr. H , took a personal interest in the welfare of her charges outside of school activities. She helped them in many ways, and impressed upon them her regard for their interests even more strongly than she impressed upon them the tenseness and vigour of her physical attitude. Some of the older and more dominant boys, however, failed to be impressed with her superior strength ; and although they expressed a liking for her, they did not submit to the extent that might have been brought about by a male teacher possessing only a small part of the acting principal's regard for her pupils.

Allied, Intellectual Superiority May Evoke Submission

I have discovered only one woman teacher of pupils of high school age (thirteen to eighteen years) who was able to impress her superior strength upon the most dominant of the youths under her charge. One of these youths, after he had become a college professor, told me that he considered this teacher to have exerted over him one of the strongest and most beneficial influences that he had ever felt. He described her as an " inspiration, and a wonderful woman ". Miss C. M. seems to have devoted herself, without stint, to helping her students with their own personal problems, in every way possible. So far as I could determine, this woman teacher not only studied her pupils individually, giving each the treatment best suited to his or her needs, but also proved herself so resourceful in quelling the rising dominance of an obstreperous youth before it broke out into open rebellion, that the pupils felt her influence over them to be mysterious or magical. This teacher's method might be called the intellectual technique of making one's superiority of strength felt by those from whom submission is to be evoked   It requires not only intellect in its ordinary sense, on the part of the teacher, but also a subtle understanding of the emotions of the pupils whose obedience is to be exacted. By means of this superior insight, dominance can be met at its inception and transferred to objects other than the teacher. The result of such ingenious handling of a pupil's own emotional responses impresses the youth strongly, it seems, with the irresistibleness of the teacher's influence, while her power is felt to be one of volume rather than intensity. In the ability of Miss C. M. we find exemplified, therefore, another very effective type of submission stimulation. *An allied stimulus may be applied so skilfully to the individual emotional mechanisms of dominant subjects that dominance is never evoked toward the stimulus person, and the stimulus is felt to be of superior strength at all times, thus evoking submission successfully.*

Stimulus Person Must Resemble Subject to Evoke Submission

A common factor to be found in all the adequate stimuli to submission response so far examined, is a close resemblance in species, race, and habits of behaviour and speech between the person who evokes submission response and the subject from whom submission is elicited. I have been informed by a Chinese professor of psychology that he and his fellow students, when first attending school, expressed very little submission toward English and American teachers. In Chinese schools taught by " foreigners ", the Chinese boys, while feeling genuine submission toward learned men of their own nationality, were not impressed with the genuineness of the friendship for them which the mission teachers expressed. The Chinese boys, as a means of obtaining the instruction which they desired, complied very skilfully and subtly with the exactions of their foreign teachers. Their response, however, was one of passive appetite emotion combining active compliance with the teacher and passive dominance over the student's own scholastic needs. Though the behaviour of the young Chinese had the appearance of submission, it did not, in fact, contain any submission response at all. The reason for the failure of the foreign teacher to evoke submission seemed to be the outstanding difference in dress, colour of skin, and eyes, facial features, language, vocal inflection, mannerisms and social standards of conduct. These so obvious differences between stimulus and subject prevented the Chinese students from feeling the foreigner as an allied stimulus, no matter how much the teacher might actually do for the student, or how friendly an attitude the teacher might express in the class room. Of course, the general attitude of Chinese toward foreigners may be advanced as the conditioned cause of their behaviour. But whence arises the general failure to submit to foreigners in friendly intercourse, if not in their dissimilarity to the subjects ?

The first requisite, therefore, which must be possessed by an adequate stimulus to submission in order to impress upon the subject its allied quality would seem to be the requirement that the stimulus should be a human being of a race and civilization possessing general characteristics similar to those of the race and civilization of the subject. Normal human beings seldom, if ever, submit to animals, and never, save by perverted transfer of a response first evoked by some fellow human, do they submit to inanimate objects. The reason for this fact seems to lie in the dissimilarity between a human subject and the animal or material stimulus which, therefore, fails to impress its allied quality upon the subject's organism. It is a well recognized social phenomenon that foreigners are seldom, if ever, accepted on the same social basis as natives of the social community in question. " Foreigners are not understood ". They are regarded as " queer " and probably antagonistic, in secret at least, to the interests of the natives. Social opposition to a foreigner occurs frequently.

On the other hand, foreign mannerisms of a supposedly cultured or distinguished type frequently serve to impress certain types of persons, notably women, with the supposed superior ability of the foreigner. This effect of foreign mannerisms is enhanced by popular stereotypes, attaching glamour or romance to certain types of foreigners. Thus in America, mannerisms suggesting those of the British nobleman, or the French, or Italian diplomat are often sufficient to lend temporary social superiority to the person of some very ordinary European, who may very possibly, also, be a fortune seeking imposter. On the other hand, members of the Asiatic races, no matter how clever or socially superior they may actually be seldom succeed in evoking personal submission response from Americans of either sex, the difference of skin colour, facial features, and bodily mannerisms and customs being too marked.

In summary, then, we may say that only human beings are normally felt to be sufficiently allied to other human beings to evoke submission responses. Skin colour, and general racial types of body and social customs, must also be similar within comparatively narrow limits to be felt as sufficiently *allied* to evoke submission response. If, however, this requirement of general similarity of species and race be met, minor differences in language and social mannerisms may serve to add the necessary impression of superior strength to a given individual to furnish the second necessary attribute, superiority, rendering that individual an adequate stimulus to submission response.

Female Behaviour Contains More Submission Than Male Behaviour

Finally, my own emotional studies have shown that girls between the ages of five and twenty-five manifest a much larger proportion of submission response in their total behaviour than do males of ages corresponding. It must be remembered that this comparison does not refer to the amount of submission response in comparison with inducement reactions, but simply refers to the relative importance of submission in the total behaviour pattern. A large proportion of the submission responses of those girls within the ages mentioned whose behaviour I have been able to study in clinics appears to be directed toward the girls' mothers, or in some few cases, toward an especially beloved woman teacher or girl friend, usually older or more mature in some way than the girl herself. The usual feminine attitude toward males or toward male parent and lovers, though containing a great deal of submission response, is nevertheless more markedly characterized by inducement, as we shall have occasion to observe in a subsequent chapter. It is the girl's attitude toward her mother, or especially toward her girl friend which, according to my own observations, contains the greatest proportion of true submission.

Many adolescent girls whom I have talked with during a personality interview seem never to have questioned the advisability of rendering complete submission to the mother, even in the matter of rejection of friendships with members of both sexes which the girl dearly longed for. Italian girls fourteen to sixteen years old, though far from submissive to some of the school authorities, their brothers, and their fathers, nevertheless submitted to their mothers' commands to the extent of working six to eight hours a day at weaving in the home, besides attending public school. Several of these girls told me that they " were crazy to go to dances and movies ", but, as a matter of fact, they were not allowed to go more often than three or four times a year. Work was done at the mother's command, however, without the slightest feeling of rebellion, so far as I could discover ; and the personal part of the submission response to the mother appeared to give these girls very great pleasure. In such instances the mother, of course, was acting for her own interests rather than for those of her daughter. But the relationship and early training of the children had been such that the possibility of selfishness on the mother's part had never occurred to the girls. The mother who had always cared for and clothed them ever since their earliest recollections, was accepted as a completely allied stimulus, and by virtue of the same earliest experiences and training, was endowed with the attribute of superior strength. So far as I could discover, physical caresses played only a minor part in the relationship between mother and daughter.

In other instances, girls whose families were of various racial stocks including English, Irish, German, and French, had gone to work outside the home, yet gave their full pay regularly to their mothers without question. Many of these girls' brothers at a much younger age had refused to bring home their pay envelopes, and some of these boys, when threatened by the father with a beating, had left home altogether. I found two instances, moreover, where girls had similarly left home when the father had attempted to compel the girl to further obedience by threat of punishment. These same girls had frequently been whipped by their mothers without rebellion. It was the custom, however, in these particular families for the children to give over their earnings to the father rather than to the mother, and it was this situation which resulted in the breach of relationships reported.

In clinical work with college girls, I found that the most effective influence could frequently be brought to bear upon an over-dominant girl through the help of another girl whom she especially admired or cared for. In one instance a girl was easily persuaded by her friend to engage in certain social activities which proved most beneficial to the subject, though she had previously failed to respond to attempted persuasions by relatives and male admirers. In several other instances girls responded submissively to their older sorority sisters, attaining marked improvement in college grades as a result.

These submissive responses were seemingly more easily evoked and enduring in character than any submissive reactions evoked from male subjects under similar conditions, in my experience. In all instances of submissive response cited in this chapter, especial attention should be given to the fact that we are dealing, as far as possible, with simple submission, and not with the compounds of submission and inducement which form the love response. Emphasis has been laid purposely upon relationships of the subject and stimulus person which do not involve strong love attachments of complicating nature. Some of the results herein cited will undoubtedly be seen to vary considerably when a complete emotional response of love is involved, especially those relating to influence exerted by one sex upon the other.

Active and Passive Submission •

In all the instances of submission response thus far cited we have found the stimulus to be a human being whose behaviour is closely allied with the subject's own, but who manifests at the same time superior strength to that of the subject. In technical terms adopted for purposes of describing emotional mechanisms, an environmental stimulus closely allied and superior in volume to the portion of the subject's organism stimulated, tends to evoke motor stimuli allied to the motor self and possessed of superior volume to the motor self. The response of submission, in each instance considered above, consists of a voluntary weakening of the subject organism's resistance to the environmental stimulus, and an allied movement of the self thus weakened tending to establish still closer alliance between the subject and the person to whom the subject is submitting. In more precise terms, we may describe this situation by saying that the *motor self, responding to adequate submission stimulus, decreases its own strength in order to move itself as directed by the stimulus.*

Passive submission may now be defined as a decrease in the strength of the motor self sufficient to permit the motor self of the organism to be moved by the motor stimulus, but with no active movement on the part of the motor self destined to further the purposes of the motor stimulus. The baby, when it ceased crying and permitted itself to be stroked or caressed without resistance, or the woman lying passive in her lover's arms, constitute examples of passive submission.

Active submission requires a decrease in the motor self to whatever point is necessary for the motor self to move as directed by the motor stimulus, and also an active movement of the self to bring about the accomplishment of those ends toward which the motor stimulus is tending to move the subject organism. Examples of active submission may be found in infant behaviour, when the child under its mother's caresses pushes itself closer to the mother's body, or, when older, presses its lips actively against hers when kissed. Active submission may be evidenced in the conduct of adults, when, for example, a male lover changes his residence or occupation at the behest of the woman whom he loves.

Motor Self Decreases Its Strength Sufficiently to be Controlled

The measure of the decrease of strength of the motor self which occurs during submission seems to differ somewhat from a similar measure of change in motor self strength during dominance and compliance. During submission response the motor self may frequently increase its strength toward objects other than the submissive stimulus, for the very purpose of carrying out the commands of the person to whom submission is being rendered. Yet, the motor self must be kept in a sufficiently weakened state in its relationship with the submission stimulus to permit the stimulus to direct the reaction of the self toward other objects. The measure of this decrease in the motor self, therefore, will be equal, approximately, to the difference between the original strength of the motor self and the strength at which it can be wholly controlled by the motor stimulus to submission. Thus if the motor stimulus were a very strong one, and the motor self of comparatively low intensity, only a slight decrease of strength might enable the stimulus to direct the self to the fullest extent. On the other hand, if there were very little difference in strength at the inception of the submissive response, between motor stimulus and motor self, the motor self might be compelled to reduce itself by a very large proportion of its initial strength before coming under full control of the motor stimulus.

Examples of these two extremes may be cited as follows. A little girl five years of age, who is trained to submit promptly to her mother's commands, only needs to reduce her existing outflow of energy sufficiently to fix her attention upon the mother's words in order to become fully controlled by the instructions of the mother. The superiority of the strength of the motor stimulus evoked by the mother is naturally very great because of the habitual relationship between mother and daughter, the great difference in physical size and strength between adult and young child, and the integrative influence of systematic training in this same type of response.

As an example of the opposite extreme of required reduction in the strength of the motor self in order to submit to an appropriate motor stimulus, the case of a tired business man who is required to submit to being " the horse " for his small son, might be cited. In this instance the father's physical size and strength is very much greater than that of the child. The thresholds of all the responses of his entire organism are raised by fatigue, and his habitual emotional attitude toward the child is one of inducement or command rather than submission. Yet such a man's emotional responses toward the child may have been organized in such a way (perhaps through the wife's influence) that submission has been learned as a response to the child's demand to " play horse ". Tremendous reduction in the strength of the father's motor self must occur if it is to be put under the control of the motor stimuli evoked by the child's lisped commands and tiny tugs at the reins. That such tremendous reduction in the motor self may be made successfully, however, is a matter of everyday experience.

Summary

Submission is found as a principle of reaction between inanimate objects, in the behaviour of a smaller unit of matter which is drawn toward a larger unit by the attractive force of gravitation. Both objects are allied in the mutual force of attraction which they exert over each other. The smaller material object decreases its own force by moving itself in such a way as to increase the force exerted upon it by the larger object, and thereafter the smaller object's attractive power is entirely directed by the larger object.

It seems to be an interesting fact that the motor self, or continuous tonic discharge is produced by reflex opposition to the body's physical submission or the force of gravity exerted upon it by the earth. Psycho-neural submission, therefore must consist of lessening the motor self's opposition to gravity sufficiently to permit control of the motor self by an allied motor stimulus of superior volume. Experiments upon decerebrate animals indicate that the primary emotional response of submission requires the mediation of some motor centre integratively superior to the tonic centre. It further appears from the work of the physiologists that thalamic motor centres suffice for the appearance of the submission response.

Submission has been shown to occur as a spontaneous and apparently pleasant response of very young infants. Though submission, like compliance, is probably a learned response, it may be distinguished from compliance by the ease and pleasantness with which submission response is acquired. The comparatively great efficiency with which the submissive response is learned seems to be due to the allied character of the stimulus, since positive pleasantness is experienced in yielding of the motor self to allied motor stimuli. Submission response is found well established even in overdominant children from whom the response of compliance can not be directly evoked even by environmental stimuli so intense as to be physically injurious.

If submission is to be evoked from dominant subjects, the environmental stimulus in addition to being capable of impressing its allied character upon the subject must also be capable of evoking motor stimuli of perceptibly greater strength than the motor self of the subject. Increasing the alliance characteristic of the environmental stimulus is found not to compensate for insufficient strength of the allied stimulus. Too great intensity of the environmental stimulus, even though it be actually completely allied with the subjects' interests is found to evoke antagonistic motor stimuli within the subject's organism.

If the subject from whom submission response is to be evoked is a human being, the environmental stimulus must also be a human being, in order to possess the *alliance characteristic* of an adequate submission stimulus. In most cases, also, an adequate degree of alliance in the stimulus is obtained only when the individual submitted to belongs to the same race as the subject and possesses the same or similar bodily and social characteristics. Within these limits, however, national differences in social culture may serve to imbue the person submitted to with a certain spurious superiority of strength to the person from whom submission is evoked.

As far as my own studies of emotional response have progressed to date, girls between the ages of five and twenty-five appear to express a greater absolute amount of true submission response than do males' of corresponding ages. Girls show lower thresholds to the submissive type of reaction. Submission response seems to be evoked from these girls most readily and most extensively by women older or more mature than themselves, notably their mothers, teachers, and especially selected girl friends.

Active submission consists of spontaneous readjustments and movements of the motor self at the dictation of the motor stimulus to submission. Passive submission consists of decrease of the strength of the motor self to a sufficient degree to permit passive movement of the organism and passive readjustment of the motor self by the submission stimulus.

The measure of decrease of the motor self during submission response consists of the difference between the initial motor self intensity and volume, and the intensity and volume at which the motor self can be completely controlled by motor stimuli of the strength actually evoked by the adequate environmental stimulus to submission response.

Pleasantness of Submission

Submission response, according to unanimous introspective agreement, is pleasant from beginning to end. Since the environmental stimulus is, by definition, in complete alliance with the total interests of the subject organism, the adequate motor stimulus to submission, once it is aroused, must be correspondingly in complete alliance with the motor self.

There may be an intermediate period, however, before the allied character of the environmental stimulus impresses itself fully upon the organism, when preliminary, transient motor stimuli are aroused, antagonistic to the motor self. These preliminary stimuli may cause temporary conflict, with consequent unpleasantness, before the motor stimulus adequate to submission is evoked and the submission type of integration is initiated. A child, for instance, may first reply, " I won't do it ! " to the mother's command ; then, dominance giving way to submission, the child may add, " Oh, yes I will, mammy ", in repentant tone of voice. The momentary, initial flare-up of dominance may be unpleasant, and its memory may give a tinge of unpleasantness to the beginning of the subsequent submission response, in the form of regret for initial disobedience. But once the submission behaviour

R

is fully under way, without admixtures of dominance or compliance, the reaction becomes extremely pleasant.

Again, it is always necessary to determine whether the response is one of true submission, or only one of compliance. In the latter case, as when children are required to perform various household tasks before being permitted to play, the affective tone at its best is one of indifference, and usually contains positive unpleasantness. The differential criterion, of course, by which one may judge whether submission or compliance is being expressed, is the motor attitude of the subject toward the task imposed. If the work is regarded as " something that *has* to be done ", even though the subject does not " want " to do it, then the motor stimuli controlling the situation are antagonistic to the motor self and the re-action is one of compliance. This is true, also, if the necessity compelling the action is one of hoped-for reward only. In such case, there is dominance also in the compound, making the total response one of appetite emotion. But if the subject " wants " to do the task imposed, " because mother wants me to do it ", then the response is one of submission. If the act is performed " to please mother ", there is probably present some inducement emotion, and possibly an admixture of submission and inducement, making the compound emotion, love. But in this case, just as in the case where the response is one of fairly unmixed submission, the affective tone is strongly and continuously pleasant.　　　.1

The pleasantness of true submission response, (as exemplified in love passion, for instance) may increase continuously from its inception to its consummation. Even when the submission is not compounded with inducement to form any aspect of love emotion, but appears as a unit response by itself, increase of pleasantness seems to accompany increase of alliance between subject and stimulus. That is to say, pleasantness increases *pari passu* with successful accomplishment of the submissive task undertaken at the command of the person to whom the subject chooses to submit. The pleasantness decreases toward indifference only if the task imposed tends to separate the subject from the person submitted to ; in which case, of course, the true submission response itself diminishes, or changes its emotional character to that of compliance simply because actual perception of the submission stimulus is necessary to maintain a pure submission response at full strength. So long as any memory or stimulus intimately associated with the person originally submitted to remains, however, some vestige of pleasantness and of the initial submission reaction also remain. And *under no possible conditions can true submission be unpleasant.*

Distinctive Conscious Characteristics of Submission Emotion

Various inexact terms applied to submission emotion, or to some complex emotional pattern based principally upon submission, may be listed as follows : " willingness ", " docility ", " sweetness ", " good nature ", " a good child ", " kindness ", " tender-heartedness ", " soft-heartedness ", " benevolence ", " generosity ", " being obliging ", " being accommodating ", " being considerate ", " gentleness ", " meekness ", " obedience ", " slavishness ", " admiration ", " being tractable ", " being manageable ", " being an easy mark ", " altruism ", " unselfishness ", " willing service ", " servility ", " slavery ", " being a willing slave ".

An interesting characteristic of a majority of the terms listed is the objectivity with which they describe submission behaviour, no matter whether the submission referred to is regarded as a character trait or as a type of relationship to other people. In cases of both dominance and compliance, introspectively derived words like " will " and " rage ", or " timidity " and " fear ", seem to be prevalent in popular parlance. But submission is a type of conduct which writers appear quite willing to describe as an attractive sort of behaviour when performed by someone else, but which they rather shrink from acknowledging as a conscious element of their own emotional life. When submission is given unreserved endorsement, as by the terms " obliging ", " considerate ", and " accommodating ", the spontaneous emotional enjoyment of submitting to another person is tacitly justified or excused by adding a tinge of compliance, or appetite. There is a certain suggestion contained in the words " obliging " and " accommodating " that the submissive favour is done as a habit of action found efficient in procuring appetitive reward. Among fifty male subjects recently questioned, only two expressed unqualified pleasure in the possibility of being a " happy slave " ; that is only two admitted without disguise that pure submission emotion was pleasant to them *per se.* (Perhaps the " happy slave " emotion is a compound, constituting passion, as we shall have occasion to note in the next chapter ; but, even so, its controlling element is active submission).

There is little equivocation, however, in the emotional implications of the submission behaviour jointly referred to by the popular terms listed above. By *submission, in every case, is meant a decrease of the self to permit an allied person to direct at will, not only the organism apart from the motor self, but the motor self, also.* Active submission would consist of positive selections from among its activities which the motor self might be compelled by the submission stimulus to make. *Passive submission* would occur when the motor self voluntarily refrained from one or more of its natural activities under compulsion of the submission stimulus.

Introspective descriptions of submission emotion, mostly obtained from girls, though some were male reports, dealing with the experiencing of submission during passion, suggest the definitive characteristic of submission to be : *wanting to give the self helplessly, without question, to the dictation of another person. This feeling, increasingly pleasant in proportion as the self is increasingly controlled by the person submitted to, constitutes submission emotion.*

CHAPTER XII

INDUCEMENT

DURING the action known as gravitation between large and smaller units of matter, it has been suggested that the behaviour of the smaller body might aptly be described as a submission to the larger one. It remains to suggest that the behaviour of the more massive object, in attracting to itself the smaller body, might be characterized as inducement. The forces of mutual attraction exerted by each object upon the other are, as we have seen, closely allied one with the other. The force exerted by the larger body, however, as by the earth itself during exercise of its gravitational influence, is superior in strength to the attractive force exerted by the smaller body, and consequently compels the smaller body's own force to move it towards the earth, or larger material body. This attraction exercised upon the smaller matter unit may be described as inducement since *the stronger attractive force progressively strengthens itself by compelling the weaker attractive force to obey its dictates, while all the time the stronger force remains in alliance with the weaker.* Inducement, as a suggested principle of behaviour of inanimate objects, bears exactly the same relationship to submission, as a similar principle of mutual attraction between physical objects, that human or animal inducement bears to human or animal submission. Inducement in both cases may be thought of as exercising the initiative in that movement of the weaker allied body which actually results from the simultaneous, allied action of both stronger and weaker re-agents.

Inducement Emotion Requires Thalamic Motor Centres

Like compliance and submission, the inducement response probably cannot occur as a primary emotional response in animal or human subjects except through the mediation of some motor centre integratively superior to the tonic centres. Inducement reaction, like compliance or submission responses failed to appear in the decerebrate animals studied by the physiologists. All environmental stimuli, as we have already noted, appear to evoke antagonistic stimuli only, in animal subjects thus prepared.

Moreover, it seemed impossible to discover an environmental stimulus that could evoke motor stimuli of superior strength to the motor self within the experimental animal's depleted central nervous system. Since inducement response depends both upon the allied character of the motor stimuli evoked, and upon its superiority of strength over the motor self, inducement response may be regarded as impossible to evoke in animals prepared in the manner described by Goltz and Sherrington. As in the case of submission response, however, inducement will be found to be a necessary constituent of centrally mediated sex response since spontaneous sex response of this type can occur, as we have already noted, by way of thalamic motor mechanisms. It would seem probable that inducement, like the other primary emotions may occur in thalamic motor centres.

Inducement Appears in Infant Behaviour

In the love responses listed by Watson as found in the behaviour of infants, we discover a number of naive or unlearned reactions which may possibly be termed inducement. Inducement may consist, at an early age, of spontaneous holding out of hands or feet to be tickled. At a somewhat later period, apparently, the baby may embrace mother or nurse. Holding out of arms toward the person to whom the child has been submitting, and certain infant vocal sounds which might be interpreted as invitations to continue previous petting, may also be listed in this more active category of love behaviour. The result of all these infant invitations or inducements, if successful, is to cause the mother or attendant to move as directed by the infant. No antagonistic compulsion can, however, be exercised over the adult by the infant inducer. The mother in submitting to her child is reacting with learned submission, which permits the allied motor stimuli evoked by perception of the infant organism to be of superior strength to the mother's motor self. The infant's earliest inducement responses, therefore, are frequently more successful than those attempted at a later age.

Inducement Is Important Element In Girls' Behaviour

Inducement response seems often to appear as a spontaneous type of reaction, in the behaviour of girls from three to five years old. In boys of similar age, the reaction may also appear spontaneously, according to my own observation, in the form of aggressive teasing of attractive little girls, or smaller and younger boys. In the case of male children, however, initial inducement exercised toward a weaker child is minimized, an attempted antagonistic compulsion of the other's compliance is far more pronounced and the whole response is apt to become mixed with and controlled by dominance very soon after its initiation, often taking the form of torturing weaker children and animals. Males, even at a tender age, appear to place little confidence in the efficacy of *inducement*. They lapse readily into attempted *compulsion* or *domination* of other humans, evidently failing to distinguish fellow humans, to any great extent, from inanimate objects.

" Playing (at) school " and " playing (at) house ", usually with one of the older girls as " teacher " or " mother ", has been described in psychological literature as "imitative instinct ", or as " play instinct ", expressing itself in imitation of the adults whom the children see most frequently. Were " imitation " or " play " (whatever that may be) the sole explanation of such activities, however, there is no particular reason why mother and teacher should be the chosen rôles to be impersonated rather than nursemaid, cook, kitchen maid, gardener or janitor. In many households the servants named are with the children much more frequently than are the parents. But in practically all parts of the globe where the play of children has been observed, little girls will be found enacting the part of mother, or of some sort of preceptress toward all those younger children whom she can persuade to join in this type of game. It seems fairly clear that inducement, in a singularly unmixed form, is the response expressed in this type of behaviour. I have noted during my own observations of children at play that other girls, younger than the " mother " or " teacher " child, appear to enjoy this sort of activity much more than do little boys of corresponding age, who may also be in the group.

The boys are frequently persuaded to play " house "

or " school " only with the utmost reluctance. Their choice of games usually calls for some sort of contest or more violent physical activity expressive primarily of dominance. While the " tomboy " type of little girl shares this dominant predilection in choice of play activities, to a considerable extent, with the boys of her particular group, there exists, also, even in her contests with the male children, a considerable element of active inducement directed toward winning the admiration and esteem of the boys in question. " Tomboys " evidently possess more dominance than the average girl, with perhaps a normal assignment of female inducement. Dominance in such cases is found to be a more efficient method of stimulation for the purpose of evoking submission from the boys of the group than is inducement exerted directly upon male children, under guise of playing house or school.

The true inducement character of the controlling emotional response in many " tomboys " reveals itself clearly in their leadership of other children during adolescence. In one case which I had occasion to observe, a girl, who when young chose to play boys' games, and engage competitively with them in juvenile athletics, became, during adolescence, the undisputed leader of the girls in her group at her preparatory school, and later in college. Her leadership expressed itself in various types of appetitive, or dominant, and compliant activities, not limited by any means to athletics. ,.She was editor of her school paper, president of her class, leading lady in school dramatics, and later president of her class in college. She became one of a very small number of undergraduates representing the student body in the governing council of the college. So far as I know, A.B. never turned any of her successes into financial or other appetitive advantage for herself, as many American students do even though blessed with parents of high social and financial standing. A.B., according to my own observations, obtained, first of all, a dominant satisfaction from her success in competitive activities of all sorts, physical and social. But this dominance response appeared always to be controlled by inducement, since the ultimate accomplishment almost invariably took the form of gaining leadership or directorship over other persons of less strength who were at the same time willing and desirous of being thus directed.

Males' Inducement Is Controlled by Dominance and Appetite

Male inducement which often begins, as already noted, in a mildly sadistic attitude toward weaker children, seems to become subordinated during later adolescence to the outright control of dominance. The element of submission, as we shall have occasion to observe in the next chapter, is essential to the compound emotion captivation. And captivation is an essential constituent of sadistic teasing or torturing of weaker human beings or animals. During later male adolescence it would appear that a certain separation occurs, in most cases, between active inducement and passive submission, with inducement tending to become transferred out of the love compound altogether, taking its place under control of appetite emotion. Captivation, of course, may continue as a separate type of sex behaviour, but this does not prevent inducement, also, being used to assist dominance and appetite.

Behaviour indicating this gradual male transfer of inducement under appetitive control may be reviewed briefly as follows : The so-called " cruelty " which young boys express toward one another has been commented upon repeatedly both in psychological and literary writings. A boy who has any outstanding peculiarity or weakness almost invariably becomes a butt for the jokes and attacks of his companions. One instance which was brought to my attention by the principal of a school in which we were making a mental health survey, concerned a boy with a deformity of the right leg which rendered this limb some three of four inches shorter than the left. The child had recently undergone an operation which was unsuccessful. After the operation he wore a shoe on the right foot with an extra thick sole sufficient to compensate for the shortening of his right leg.

The other boys of the school (eight to twelve years old) immediately began to call him " club foot ". The deformed boy, Harry, who had undergone considerable suffering, physical and emotional, in connection with the operation, was peculiarly sensitive to the taunts of his former friends. He could no longer run away from them successfully, and when he failed to escape after trying to run away, the older boys chased him and formed a daily habit of gathering around him and teasing him in various ways not physically injurious

but ingeniously devised to give Harry as much emotional
unpleasantness as possible. I was able to question three or
four of the boys who had just teased Harry. I discovered
that they had not the slightest attitude of ill will toward
the child. In fact, one or two of the boys appeared to like
Harry better than most of their other play fellows, and all
the boys questioned except one, expressed pity and regret
for Harry's deformity. When asked why, when they felt
this way toward Harry, they should consistently make life
miserable for him by tormenting him, one or two of the boys
replied : " I don't know. I can't help it. It's fun to chase
him and make him cry, but after that you don't feel so good.
Feel kind of sorry for him." Another boy said that he
thought Harry was " yellow " for running away, and that
it was his own fault if the boys " picked on him ". A third
boy said it was " sort of exciting to tease Harry ". But he
pointed out that they teased other boys just as much at
other times, only " the other boys don't take it so hard ".

This rather ordinary instance of a group of young males
teasing and tormenting a weaker companion may very readily
be seen to depend, primarily, upon inducement, partially
compounded with submission into captivation emotion (see
next chapter), but controlled by dominance. Harry represented, at first, an allied or friendly environmental stimulus,
weaker than the other boys. This made Harry, under our
suggested definition, an adequate environmental stimulus
for evoking active inducement response from his stronger
companions. When, however, Harry began to cry and to
run away, his alliance with the other boys was to a considerable extent severed, in their minds. He then represented a weaker boy than themselves who would not submit
to their mixed dominance and inducement. This made
Harry an antagonistic stimulus, weaker than the boys who
were reacting toward him. Immediately the antagonism
of the stronger boys was increased to the extent where dominance completely controlled their conduct toward Harry
Yet they still felt an undercurrent of friendliness and interest
in him, evoking from them some continuance of the inducement purpose of making him submit to them. In this situation, inducement was adapted to and controlled by dominance.
And Harry suffered accordingly.

Another instance of boys' behaviour which came to my

attention may be cited to show the difference in the responses evoked from the stronger group of boys when the boy being teased elects to submit to his tormentors. In this case it was the school custom to " initiate " any new boy by subjecting him to such physical punishments and torments as the older boys of the school might devise to suit the occasion. Several boys, new to the school, had received cuts, bruises, and other minor injuries, as well as having had their clothes badly torn and soiled, in the process of this " initiation ". All the boys thus hurt had resisted to a greater or lesser extent the treatment meted out to them. However, during the initiation, which I was able to observe without my presence in any way interfering with the behaviour of the boys, the new boy showed a remarkable willingness to undergo whatever was meted out to him. I learned, afterward, that he had been informed by a friend at the school of the treatment he might expect, and had been advised " not to run away from it ". This boy, therefore, showed no desire to get away, nor did he try to evade the commands of the leaders among his " initiators ". As a result, apparently, of this attitude, I heard several of the older boys remark to each other " He's not afraid of anything ", " He's a good kid ", " He is all right, let him off ", " That's enough for him ". After putting this boy through only two comparatively mild stunts, he was released and welcomed with enthusiasm as a fully initiated member of the school.

The point seemed to be that the dominance of the older boys out-weighed their inducement emotion at the very beginning of the affair. When, therefore, the object of their attack failed to show the slightest resistance or antagonism in return, a good part of this initial dominance died out for lack of stimulus. Only the inducement increment remained in their subjection of the new boy, and this inducement (compounded, it must be remembered with submission, into a dilute captivation emotion) was not sufficiently extensive to carry on the initiation very long after dominance had subsided. One or two successfully evoked submission responses on the part of the new boy were sufficient to satisfy the inducement emotion of this entire group of young males. In short, we might conclude that inducement is not a sufficiently well developed emotion in the average adolescent male to control any considerable portion of his behaviour when it is completely divorced from dominance.

Male Organism Not Suited to induce Other Males

It is frequently reported that homosexual relations are prevalent in that type of boys' school called a " public school " in England, and a " private school " in the United States. I have had occasion to observe one or two such relationships. In the cases which have come to my attention an older, stronger boy has compelled a young and much weaker boy to give him erotic pleasure, as well as to perform many other services of an appetitive nature for the benefit of the older youth. In such cases as these, the emotional response of inducement on the part of the older boy wins for him a greater total amount of pleasantness, both appetitive and erotic, than that which can be obtained from mere teasing and torturing of younger boys. Moreover, the younger boy's combined submission and inducement attain for him a certain amount of freedom from being made the object of dominance response. The older boy in these affairs usually protects and favours, in various ways, the boy who submits to him. Frequently he not only refrains from hazing or tormenting the younger boy, but also prevents other boys from doing so. In this type of behaviour, therefore, we may see a certain amount of inducement expressed by a male subject free from control of dominance.

The limitation to such relationships seems to be a physiological one. Since neither the body nor the emotional development of the younger boy is suited to act as an effective stimulus to the passion of the stronger youth, the dominance of the younger boy yielding to dominance of the older boy becomes a matter of compliance by the weaker one rather than submission. The older boy as environmental stimulus, in short, evokes motor stimuli stronger than the motor self of his companion, but, for the most part, antagonistic to it. Thus, the stronger youth becomes an adequate stimulus to compliance but not to submission. The younger boy yields, not because he enjoys the relationship as such, but because it seems to be to his appetitive advantage. The compliance of the weaker boy, in turn, makes itself felt by the would-be inducer, and the inducement fails to produce sufficient pleasantness to be long continued.

From this sort of relationship, however, both boys frequently emerge with an unusually complete appetitive development, and with a transfer of inducement into adaptation to, and control by appetite. In other words, the older boy has learned that he can use inducement to obtain services and pleasures which would otherwise be beyond his reach. The younger boy, also, has been taught that by a compound response made up of inducement and submission expressed toward a stronger companion, he can obtain protection, gifts, and perhaps advancement in school activities of various sorts. In the cases I have studied, at least, both boys entering into such a relationship, tend thereafter to use the primary emotional response of inducement not for its own sake nor for the completion of a true love response, but rather as first aid in furthering the ends of active and passive appetite or both. This use of inducement, as we shall have occasion later to observe, constitutes one of the most unfortunate of personality developments.

Normal Adult Male Transfers Inducement From Sadism to Business

The element of inducement in males who have not had experiences of homosexual type, nevertheless, tends to follow a somewhat similar course of development. The behaviour called " cruelty " toward other males continues to be expressed in some degree throughout adult life. Business men, as well as men engaged in professional and academic life, appear to obtain a certain emotional pleasure by means of imposing hardships and minor torments upon other males who come under their authority. And this same type of pleasure is still more obviously manifested when failure of another man is reported, even though this individual is in no sense a rival. Criticisms or attacks made upon another male appear to be enjoyed without restraint by most men, and it would appear that the dominant or appetitive satisfaction in disposing of a rival fails to account satisfactorily for the entire response. There exists, in addition, a certain emotional gratification (captivation emotion) in the thought that the person attacked is thereby subjected to the subject himself as well as to all other persons who witness the attack.

With the normal and fairly successful business man, however, these occasional enjoyments of perverted inducement response must be strictly limited to those occasions when the subject's own appetitive interests can not be injured by indulging in enjoyment of the other person's enforced subjec-

254 EMOTIONS OF NORMAL PEOPLE

tion. During late adolescence there is indication that dominance, compliance and their appetitive combinations develop very rapidly with male subjects, until appetite may be said to exercise undisputed control over the average male's emotional responses. With this maturing appetite comes the suppression and limitation of inducement expressed in forcefully bullying and injuring other males. The youth begins to discover that he cannot afford to alienate other males who may later serve his interests in one way or another, no matter how insignificant these persons may seem at the time when he has an opportunity to subject them injuriously in some way.

For instance, one boy may successfully dominate another lad of the same group during athletic competition or competitive seeking of the same class office or scholastic prize. The natural tendency of the male following such successes seems to consist of an expression of open triumph over the rival, with perhaps a certain patronizing condescension expressive of the defeated one's subjection to the superior strength of the more successful boy. The triumphant boy does not regard this defeated rival as an enemy or antagonist. In fact, the whole pleasure of the inducement response would be turned to indifference were the other boy regarded as a real antagonist. To enjoy this type of victory to the full, the defeated male must still be thought of as a friend, though a friend of inferior strength and position. It soon transpires, however, that the defeated boy has reacted to the openly expressed superiority of the successful youth by becoming a real enemy. Perhaps, at a subsequent election of class officers or in the course of academic relationships, if the two boys are taking the same courses, an occasion arises where the formerly successful youth needs the support of the boy whom he has been treating as an inferior. He finds this support is not forthcoming. The formerly defeated youth now responds with dominance to the previously controlling dominance in the other boy's behaviour and the formerly triumphant youth suffers accordingly. I studied several instances of this type, and found that in these instances only a few such experiences were necessary to lead to a splitting off of inducement from open dominance, and the initiation of a new pattern of behaviour in which inducement was used to further the ends of appetite instead of thwarting them. In other words, instead of giving free rein to the pleasantness of injurious subjection of other boys, the subject quickly learned to use inducement to acquire and regain their appetitive assistance and service.

Inducement in Business

This system of emotional organization, wherein inducement is used as first assistant to active appetite, forms what may be called the extensor muscle of modern business. Selling goods is a clear cut example of this type of composite emotional response. The salesman not only stimulates the appetitive mechanisms of his prospective customers by impressing upon the buyer the financial advantage which these particular goods hold for him, but he also uses a considerable amount of " personal appeal " to the buyer. That is to say, the salesman endeavours to impress the buyer with his own qualities as a good fellow and reliable person. And if the prospective customer allows himself to become sympathetic the salesman may even make an open statement of his own personal needs and desires in winning the patronage of the merchant to whom he is talking. All this consists of rather clear-cut, active inducement behaviour, on the part of the salesman. In itself such behaviour has no connection whatever with the intrinsic merit or usefulness of the goods to be sold. Yet, no business man to-day doubts the importance of such inducement technique in effecting sales.

Even printed advertisements which do not, of course, enable the seller to appear personally before the buyer, contain as large an element of inducement as it is possible to convey with the help of words, pictures and suggestions of both form and colour. Pretty girls are depicted extending the article to be sold invitingly toward the reader of the advertisement. The concern manufacturing the product advertised is symbolized as the family's best friend, or as the generous saviour of humanity in distress. Another form of what might be called substituted inducement, commonly found in advertisements, is the attempted identification of the advertiser with some member of the prospective customer's family, who is represented as inducing the reader of the advertisement to buy the product advertised. For instance, a picture of a baby may be shown with the heading : " Bring happiness to your child, buy this cuddly, dimpled baby doll ! " Or a picture of two attractive children sharing a bottle of soft drink, may be displayed with the legend : " Let your children enjoy these taste-tempting drinks ".

In nearly all selling methods of modern business some element of inducement can be found directly or indirectly expressed, over and above the appetitive appeal contained in descriptions of the intrinsic values and delights of the goods themselves. This use of inducement response as a servant of appetite emotion tends to be learned by the average male about the time of sexual maturity. Thereafter, he limits more and more the use of inducement in enjoyment of the captivation of other males, and extends its use further and further for the purpose of procuring appetitive benefits from other people of both sexes.

Confusions Between Inducement and Dominance

The behaviour just considered, which might aptly be styled the evolution of male inducement, serves only to illustrate the tendency which all males exhibit, at times, to confuse and intermingle dominance and inducement responses. *The integrative element which is identical in dominance and inducement is the superiority of the motor self over the strength of the motor stimulus. The integrative difference between the two responses consists in the fact that an adequate stimulus to dominance emotion is antagonistic to the motor self while adequate motor stimulus to inducement must remain in alliance with the motor self.*

If there appears to be the slightest doubt as to whether the person who constitutes the environmental stimulus is willing to accept the rôle of inferiority to the subject, then the average male organism immediately tends to react to the individual in question as to an antagonistic stimulus. The " boot-licking," or utterly servile attitude which male underlings of great men so frequently find it necessary to adopt, in order to retain their positions, furnishes dependable evidence of the tendency just referred to. If the assistant or employee inadvertently manifested, at any time, behaviour which impressed his chief with a possible superiority of strength on the part of the supposedly inferior male, the employer would feel immediate necessity for reducing his employee's strength to a level obviously lower than his own. This emotional purpose, again, is a common one both to dominance and to inducement responses ; but since dominance is the prevailing male emotion, the employer almost invariably seeks to reduce his subordinate's strength by action antagonistic to the other man's interests. He may reprimand him before others, decrease his pay, or discharge him. I have observed many instances of each of these methods used by males in authority to reduce the strength of a subordinate.

Nor are such methods limited to business or other appetitive relationships where there may be, in most cases, some actual opposition of interests between chief and subordinate. In the home, a wife or son may be " put in their place " by this method. Deliberately cutting and insulting remarks may be addressed to the wife. A son who shows any tendency to dispute the superiority of a " successful " father is likely to receive more definitely injurious treatment. Physical abuse, cutting off a son's allowance or privileges, or even (in one actual case) causing the son's arrest and sentence in juvenile court, may be used as methods of reducing the " uppishness " of the boy. All these courses of action are dominant and not inductive methods of reducing the strength of the person regarded as inferior to the subject, since all these methods of treatment disregard utterly the interests and well being of the person thus treated.

Were inducement the prevailing response, the actions of the father, or person in authority must have been kept in complete alliance with the welfare and happiness of the persons subjected. Had this been done, and true inducement actually exercised, the inferior persons must have been induced voluntarily to reduce their own strength to a required degree, in order to accept completely the control of the inducer. Most males, who appear to possess very meagre development of inducement emotion in pure form, would regard such a task as utterly impossible. An average male is prone to remark " the only way to show the boy his place is to beat him within an inch of his life ". Often the sentiment expressed is more violent than the action which follows, but the two are usually similar in nature. Whenever another person's strength is to be reduced to a level inferior to a man's own, the person is treated as an opponent and dominance takes the place of inducement in nine cases out of ten.

Girls Express Inducement Not Mixed With Appetite

The development of inducement response in girls and women

is quite different from that of males. All girls from three to five years of age not infrequently manifest a startlingly sophisticated inducement technique. In one case, at least, which I had occasion to study, males were unmistakably preferred to women as objects of inducement. Yet the little girl, Patricia, also exercised inducement toward her mother, aunt, and also toward girls younger than herself. For a period of about three years, inducement appeared, in fact, to be the controlling response in this child's behaviour pattern. Patricia sought systematically to induce people to watch her antics and to think highly of her. This inducement did not seem to be coupled with overt eroticism, nor on the other hand, did inducement appear to be complicated by appetitive cravings or desires. The child seemed solely intent upon establishing her superiority over those people who attracted her, while simultaneously seeking a more intimate and friendly relationship with them.

In other cases studied, female children of similar age showed marked inducement response coupled with and apparently springing from sexual precocity. In girls of this age, and girls between this age and adolescence, inducement seems frequently compounded into an admirably organized love response, expressed in taking care of babies and younger children. Detailed consideration of this love behaviour may be reserved until a later chapter. Our attention may be called to it at this point as an indubitable expression of active inducement in a pure or natural form, not perverted by admixture with appetite.

Forced Use of Inducement for Appetite by Women

Women have been regarded conventionally, for thousands of years, as the weaker sex. This almost universally recognized concept of woman's weakness has included not only physical inferiority, but also a weakness in emotional power in relationships with males. No concept of woman's emotional status could be more completely erroneous. Woman actually is inferior to man at the present time, on the average, in her dominance development ; but since real relationships, other than those of business, depend upon inducement and love responses and technique, rather than upon dominant and appetitive reactions, there seems little reason to doubt that women, as a sex, are many times better equipped to assume emotional leadership than are males. As a matter of fact, women have always exercised this emotional leadership by controlling, to a considerable extent, the home life and the education of children. But they have been controlled, in turn, in exercising these functions by the dominant and appetitive compulsions exerted upon them by a predominantly male civilization.

The situation in which women have found themselves, while being kept in a status of dominantly enforced weakness, has had the effect of compelling them to use inducement (and submission, also) as a means of obtaining appetitive benefits and protections. Men, by controlling social customs and usages, have forced their own perverted use of inducement as a servant of appetite upon the females of the race, whose native emotional equipment does not appear to tend toward such a development if, and when, the female herself is freed from appetitive compulsion. If the source of food and appetitive supply of all sorts is in the hands of persons possessing superior strength and reacting with prevailing dominance, two options only are open to weaker members of the race. The weak ones may obtain supplies by using their love responses to serve their appetite, or they may perish from appetitive weakness. A majority of women have learned to follow the first of these two courses of conduct. The most optimistic emotional feature of modern civilization seems to be that women are now beginning to escape both horns of this dilemma by increasing their own appetitive powers. They are nearing the point where they will be able to provide for themselves quite as well as men can provide for them. When the female sex, as a whole, has arrived at this appetitive equality, it would seem probable that their inducement responses will be pretty much freed from appetitive control.

Women's Inducement Conditioned on Males by Appetitive Compulsion

An interesting line of demarcation has grown up in the behaviour of women compelled to depend upon inducement for appetitive reward. The inducement responses of such women have become conditioned, apparently, upon men, to a very much greater extent than upon other women. Since it has been a male or males toward whom women subjects must exercise inducement in order to be fed and clothed, and since

the men from whom appetitive supplies are to be obtained
have not been subject, in the main, to dominant conquest by
women, the woman's inducement responses toward males
have not been mingled or confused to any great extent by
admixture of dominance. In short, if money or sustenance
must be obtained from a physically stronger male, pure inducement response must be expressed by the woman who seeks
his assistance, free from all suggestion of dominance. If
dominance is allowed to creep into the woman's attitude
toward such a male, at any point, the reward will not be
forthcoming. This seems to have had the effect of making
the inducement technique which women employ in attaining
support from men much more clear-cut inducement behaviour
than men are able to express toward other males.

Women Inducing Males for Appetitive Supply are Business Rivals

On the other hand, women who depend solely for their
supply upon success of inducements directed toward males
inevitably regard all other women similarly engaged as actual
or prospective rivals. If the other woman succeeds in per-
sauding Mr. Z. to support her, then Mr. Z is not likely to
support the rival female inducer. Even if Mr. Z. were willing
to yield to the inducements of both women, he is likely to
spend less money upon both than he would spend upon
either one alone. Women inducers find themselves in the
same relationship to other women inducers that one automobile salesman occupies with respect to another automobile
salesman who is after the same customer of moderate means.

The result of this situation seems to have been the growth
of " society ", or " social " competition between women,
wherein each woman treats her rivals with very much the
same mixture of inducement and dominance that men exercise
toward one another. Women's taboo upon " fallen women ",
or women of inferior social standing, seems to represent the
same prevailing dominance response that a male employer
or bureau chief exerts over his male employees. Moreover,
the outcast or socially snubbed female is supposed to retain
the same friendly attitude toward the more dominant member
of her sex that the humiliated male underling is required to
maintain toward his appetitive superior. This expected
attitude of submission is not, of course, evoked in either

case. Dominance may compel an unpleasant type of compliance response, but true submission responds only to inducement. Social dominance between women, with its thin, transparent disguise of inducement, is the less excusable because the dominance power expressed is borrowed power, originally obtained from males by the use of real inducement.

Except in Social Rivalry, Girls Express Pure Inducement Toward Other Girls

In contrast to the " society " type of situation, however, I have found that nearly all girls and women who are not engaged too extremely in social rivalry express genuine inducement and love toward their girl friends, women' relatives, or, very frequently, toward destitute or otherwise unfortunate persons of both sexes. These female responses may be discussed more fully after we have considered the combining of inducement and submission into completed love response.

I have recently observed one instance, however, worth mentioning at this point. A college girl, about twenty years of age, listed as her chief emotional interest her companionship with a girl friend. I had occasion to observe this young woman for a period of several months, and could discover no indication that a complete love or sex relationship existed between Miss D. and her friend. Miss D., however, devoted a great deal of time and attention to pleasing Miss F. Miss D., for instance, threw away a hat which Miss F. disliked. She also joined a group of young people whom she did not care for, in order to be with Miss F. Yet Miss D. was unmistakably the leader in her relationship with the other girl. Miss F. submitted to requests of Miss D. which were virtually commands, and even chose her courses in college under Miss D.'s direction (although Miss F. was the better student). There seemed to be an absence of passion between the girls, in this case, which deprived the relationship of a mature love character, and likewise prevented it from resulting in any physical union. As nearly as I could determine, Miss D.'s one desire was to exercise affectionate leadership over Miss F. ; while Miss F. accepted this leadership by responding with very evident active submission. (It is possible that Miss F. experienced some passion in this rôle, but if so it apparently had no counter effect upon Miss D.)

Miss D.'s conduct seems to constitute a clear cut example

of inducement for its own sake, and illustrates rather well the difference between the pure inducement response, which seems to be a natural product of the female organism, and the mixture of inducement and dominance customarily expressed by males. When Miss F.'s tasks or interests lay in a direction divergent from those of Miss D., for the moment, Miss D. found nothing more pleasant than keeping her own behaviour in alliance with her friend's. Miss D. did not comply, for she felt herself to be the leader over Miss F. at all times, so far as I could discover; nor did it occur to Miss D. to treat the other girl as an antagonist, or opponent, and to attempt to compel her to change her existing tendencies and interests. Miss D. simply maintained her previous close personal alliance with Miss F., while at the same time she expressed in this alliance her own superior strength. A hat, or a group of indifferent people, were not weighed in the balance against the pleasure Miss D. derived from Miss F.'s society. These obstacles were swept aside, or were used merely as methods of allying herself with the friend whom she wished to induce. As a result, the friend, Miss F., accepted Miss D.'s companionable relationship even more completely than before; eventually voluntarily adopting Miss D.'s opinion regarding the social group of whose activities Miss D. did not approve. This example of the behaviour of a sexually mature young woman toward a girl friend seems to consist of nearly pure inducement, with very little admixture of other primary emotional responses.

Characteristics of Adequate Stimulus to Inducement

Nearly all the examples already mentioned serve to point the necessity for the reagent to remain in close alliance with the stimulus, if the response is to be one of inducement rather than dominance. But what of the stimulus to inducement? We have noted that an environmental stimulus in order to evoke inducement response must be considered by male subjects to be of markedly inferior strength to the subject, as well as allied in nature. In the case of submission response the emphasis, so far as adequacy of stimulus was concerned, seemed to be upon the allied characteristic. Varying degrees of stimulus strength served, for the most part, to determine whether the response would be of submission or of inducement. In the present chapter, we have noted that males appear to substitute dominance for inducement whenever a stimulus person whom they consider less powerful than themselves shows any tendency to increase his strength toward an equality with that of the subject. If we analyse this behaviour with a view to determining the nature of an adequate environmental stimulus to inducement, we discover that in the case of males, at least, the margin of difference between the strength of the inferior stimulus and the strength of the subject himself must be a wide one if inducement is to be evoked. So far as I have been able to observe, there is no minimal threshold of strength or intensity beneath which an allied stimulus will cease to evoke inducement. That is to say, though an allied stimulus must impress itself upon a male subject as being very much weaker than himself in order to evoke inducement response, it is not likely to cease to evoke inducement no matter how weak it may become, provided it has once secured the attention of the subject.

Male Inducement Threshold Varies With State of Appetitive Responses

The margin of inferiority which an environmental stimulus must maintain in order to evoke motor stimuli of inferior intensity to the male's motor self will depend more upon the subject's own condition of appetite, desire, or satisfaction, than upon the intrinsic strength which the stimulus person exhibits. Since dominance is the prevailing primary emotion in males, a comparison is likely to be made by the subject between himself and the entire stimulus situation of which the inferior person is a part, rather than between the subject and the inferior person *per se*. If a man has been appetitively successful, and is in what is known as a " good humour ", then he is already in a state of consciousness where he feels that he has demonstrated the superiority of his strength over that of his environment. In such a mood, a lesser degree of servility is usually required from his underlings in order to satisfy him that the employees are less powerful than himself.

Men, as a rule, appear to make very little distinction between persons and things. The employees, or underlings, therefore, tend to be lumped in with the inanimate units of environment, and the subject's attitude toward these inanimate elements tends to be inclusive of the human beings who regularly form part of that environment. On the other hand, whenever a man has met defeat, or is in a state of unsatisfied desire, he usually tries to satisfy the dominant element in his unsatisfied desire by dominating all persons as well as inanimate objects weaker than himself, unless their inferiority and alliance with his own interests are overwhelmingly apparent. It is in states of unsatisfied desire that men kick the dog, meet their wife's advances with scathing rejections, order the children sharply to bed, and berate the servants and other employees without other excuse than the subject's own ill temper. Extreme servility (that is, exaggerated inferiority of strength) together with unusually successful service in supplying articles most pleasing to the man at that moment, may possibly succeed in eliciting a brief and rather perfunctory inducement response. He may be led to remark to his wife : " Very good cigars, Alice. I wish you'd buy some more for me ". Or, to an employee : " Well done, Jones, if you can do that again, I think it would be good business ". Beyond such fragmentary inducement responses, however, no stimulus, no matter how closely allied, or no matter how obviously inferior it may be to the subject himself, has the power to evoke further inducement.

When Inducement Serves Appetite, Inducement Threshold is Low

When appetite emotion is the initial and basic response, with inducement playing the minor rôle of a mechanism whereby the appetitive need is to be accomplished, the adequacy of the environmental stimulus to evoke the total response pattern depends not upon the integrative mechanism of inducement, but rather upon the adequacy of the environmental stimulus to evoke appetitive emotion. Inducement, in such cases, is initiated as a form of compliance ; yet inducement response must follow its own proper course if it is to be successful in accomplishing the appetitive result. Whatever aspect or attribute of the stimulus person, therefore, can possibly be interpreted as allied with and weaker than the subject tends to evoke motor stimuli appropriate to inducement. This situation represents an opposite extreme of inducement stimulus to that just considered. In the former instance, a man in a state of unsatisfied desire requires for an inducement stimulus extreme subservience, and perfect alliance with his own interests. In the case now under consideration, the slightest suggestion of possible alliance of interests, together with a mere possibility of inferiority of strength at one point only, will be sufficient to evoke an extremely active and prolonged inducement response.

For example, a woman may be dependent for her own living and for that of their children upon a husband whose parsimony is well known and frequently demonstrated. Yet under the irresistible drive of appetitive desire, such a wife may exercise inducement toward her husband for days, or even weeks, in order to obtain the desired supply. In thus exerting inducement toward an obviously inadequate environmental stimulus, the wife is compelled to select, and to dwell upon whatever interests and tastes she and her husband may have in common, and to select the few responsive points which experience has shown to exist in his submission response mechanism. Attention must be focussed continuously upon these slight stimuli to inducement in order to prolong the wife's inducement response sufficiently to offer any hope of success in obtaining her desire. These inducement stimuli, slight as they are, however, are absolutely essential to the evoking of true inducement response, which alone is able to serve the woman's appetitive desire. If no such stimuli are to be found, or if the wife's attention is not kept continuously upon the more or less inadequate stimuli mentioned, her behaviour will at once lose its inducement character, and will impress itself upon the niggardly husband as a dominant drive against his money. The man's response to this stimulus will render him more than ever antagonistic to her dearest interests. The mere form of inducement will not do, if the wife's purpose is to be accomplished. For this reason, the use of inducement as a servant of appetite produces a situation wherein environmental stimuli only slightly allied with the subject and slightly, if at all, inferior to the strength of the subject, become adequate to inducement response.

The situation outlined leads to a consideration of a sort of border-line group of stimuli, where it is difficult to tell whether the initial appeal to which the subject is responding is that of antagonism or alliance. With subjects of both sexes, there is a tendency to regard a member of the opposite sex who appears difficult to subdue by inducement as an opponent to the supremacy of the subject as an expert inducer. Thus the stimulus person may arouse a response of inducement for the very reason that he constitutes an obstacle or opponent, to the subject from whom the inducement is evoked. This means that the stimulus person originally evokes dominance response from the subject, and that dominance response is immediately compelled to utilize inducement behaviour, as the subject organism has learned to do, in order to accomplish its dominant purpose.

Thus a college youth frequently employed excellently devised inducement behaviour toward girls who were popular with other men, solely for the purpose of proving that the girl in question was no exception to the alleged rule that all women became easy victims to his charm. The inducement emotion seemed to be pure inducement during the time that he was attempting to captivate the young woman selected. He exerted no dominance toward her so far as I could observe, nor, on the other hand, was his inducement mingled to any extent with submission to produce real love emotion. Yet once the object of the inducement behaviour was accomplished, and the girl was willing to accept A.'s attentions, the boy's emotional attitude became an obviously dominant one. This consciousness of success contained, frequently, alternate and mingled elements of inducement, with dominance prevailing. I have also observed many instances of unusually love aggressive girls who sought to induce popular young men to bestow favourable regard upon them, seemingly for the purpose of removing the youth in question as an obstacle to the girl's complete supremacy over the opposite sex.

Resistance May Evoke Pure Inducement

On just the other side of the line, however, I have observed instances of feminine inducement evoked directly by a stimulus person who was not regarded as an antagonist at any time during the relationship. In one case, at least, attractive males always seemed to evoke real inducement response from a girl subject, pretty much in proportion to the indifference which they expressed toward her. So far as I could discover, this girl did not regard an indifferent man as antagonistic, but rather as an allied stimulus person whose strength she felt to be inferior to her own. The fact that the man himself expressed indifference toward her impressed itself upon her apparently as an adequate stimulus to reduce his inferior power to a level where it should be easily manageable by her own. The line of demarcation at this point, between pure inducement response and mingled inducement and dominance, is very fine, but can usually be drawn clearly enough by a detailed study of the case.

With subjects, especially girls, whose inducement emotion is highly developed, true inducement may nearly always be evoked by an attractive person of the opposite sex who manifests complete indifference toward the subject. The subject's strong inducement development, in such cases, evidently consists of an unusually low threshold of motor self reinforcement in response to allied motor stimuli. The indifference of the environmental stimulus person serves to evoke a volume of allied motor stimuli corresponding in strength to the indifference expressed toward the subject by the stimulus person. The motor self, with its low reinforcement threshold to stimuli of this type, is thereupon stimulated to rapid and extensive reinforcement, thus producing an inducement response of corresponding strength. *The indifference of the stimulus person, therefore, is seen as determining the volume or quantity of the inducement response which it evokes*, rather than exercising *any peculiar potency in evoking inducement in the first place.*

The type of subject just analysed, who responds with true inducement to an attractive though indifferent stimulus person, tends to respond with inducement to any person who is sufficiently attractive, that is, closely allied to the subject's standards and tastes. Such a subject is always susceptible to inducement stimuli, in short ; only in cases where the stimulus person is very easily induced to submit, the strength of inducement response evoked is not so great and, therefore, the whole response is less noticeable.

Measure of Motor Self Inducement Increase

Incidentally, we might draw the conclusion, from this type of inducement response, that the *measure of increase of the motor self during inducement response is the difference between the existing strength of the motor self and that strength which is required to replace the stimulus person completely under the control of the subject.*

Girls More Closely Allied to Other Girls than to Males

Girls like Miss D., who possess normally developed female inducement emotion, respond more readily with inducement, on the whole, to other girls than to men.   This seems to be accounted for by the fact that other girls impress themselves upon the subject as more closely allied to her than males. Also, if the subject herself possesses a motor self of no great strength, and has only an ordinarily sensitive reinforcement mechanism, other girls are more apt to be felt as being of inferior strength to the girl herself than are men.   In the case of Miss D., however, the emphasis was clearly upon the increased closeness of alliance which she perceived in other girls, since Miss D. responded toward men, for the most part, with unconcealed dominance.   She seemed to regard males, in short, as of inferior strength to herself, but antagonistic rather than allied.

Another feature of this close alliance, in one or two cases of the same type which I have observed, seemed to be a camaraderie of supremacy over males.   The girls like Miss F., who evoked inducement response from other girls most readily, did not yield to men.   Love affairs with the male in control seemed to alienate the girl thus offending to the extent that the inducement response of her girl friend was not evoked. *Submission* to a male appeared to be the alienating behaviour element objected to.   If the girl who evoked inducement response, like Miss R., expressed a great deal of *inducement* toward men, however, this behaviour seemed not to interfere in the least with her efficacy as an inducement stimulus to inducer girls like Miss D.   In fact, successful inducement of men, provided the men were made to submit and the girl herself did not submit to their desires, seemed to contribute an added element of alliance between stimulus girl and inducer girl.

Alliance Requirement of Stimulus Inversely Proportional to Its Strength

If the stimulus person who evokes inducement from another is so much and so obviously inferior in strength to the subject that only slight reinforcement of the motor self is required to bring about inducement, then it would appear that a lesser degree of alliance with the subject is necessary in order to evoke inducement.   Children of another race and colour may evoke inducement response (though less probably love) from the average woman, almost as readily as her own children do. Small boys and weak or injured persons of both sexes may evoke inducement responses of fairly pure variety from adult males of normal strength, even though the boys or feeble adults are especially alien to the standards and tastes of the male from whom inducement is being evoked. Animals even, may frequently evoke inducement from human beings, even though the animal's behaviour is annoying and repulsive to the subject. It would seem that, in all cases, the greater the inferiority of strength, the less close the alliance of the stimulus need be in order to evoke inducement.

If we compare the degree of alliance always required in an environmental stimulus in order to evoke submission with the requisite degree of alliance necessary in an adequate environmental inducement stimulus, we find that submission stimuli must possess, on the whole, much closer alliance to the subject than is required of inducement stimuli. The reason for this would seem to be that most normal human beings have learned that reducing their own strength in order to be controlled by another person is apt to prove a dangerous undertaking, since the person submitted to, though closely allied at the moment of submission, may become antagonistic at any time, if the appetitive interests of the person submitted to dictate such a change of attitude.

A girl, for example, may submit very completely to her mother during her childhood, at which time the mother's attitude is one of complete alliance with the child's welfare and interests. At a later period, however, it may be very much to the mother's appetitive interests in every way to keep the girl at home, rather than permitting her to attend school or college in some distant part of the country. Or the mother's appetitive interests may dictate marriage of the daughter to a wealthy man of accepted standing, whom the girl does not love, and who will never be able to evoke her love responses. In such cases, mothers frequently employ the response of submission which they are still able to evoke from their daughters, for the purpose of furthering their own appetitive satisfactions. Thus it is that emotionally mature adults usually have learned to yield submission only to stimulus persons whose degree of alliance with themselves is indubitably close.

Inducement response, on the other hand, may be expressed toward persons weaker than the subject, even though such persons later turn out to be distinctly antagonistic to the subject's interests, without serious injury accruing to the subject as a result of such attempted inducement responses. Through learning, therefore, a much closer degree of alliance is required to evoke submission than is necessary to evoke induced. It is this same type of learning, probably, which leads to a still further lowering of the alliance requirement in an inducement person or animal, when the latter is tremendously inferior in strength to the subject.

Summary

We may summarize the findings of this chapter as follows. Inducement, like dominance, compliance, and submission, may be found as a principle of the behaviour of inanimate objects. When two physical objects exercise attractive, or gravitational force upon one another, the smaller body is drawn toward the larger. During this movement, the stronger, allied body controls and directs the attractive force of the smaller object, increasing its own correspondingly. Both forces remain in progressively increased alliance with one another throughout the reaction. Human and animal inducement behaviour follows the same rules, with the sole difference that human inducement behaviour is brought about by means of integrative mechanisms, and so attains consciousness.

Inducement response cannot be evoked from decerebrate animals, and probably depends upon the mediation of motor centres integratively superior to the tonic centres in control at the time inducement is evoked. Inducement, as an important response element in spontaneous love behaviour, evidently can be mediated successfully by thalamic centres.

Inducement response is found in infant behaviour described by Watson and others, where it frequently follows submission to petting, when the petting is discontinued. Pure inducement response forms an important part of the behaviour of girls, from the age of three on. " Playing (at) house ", " playing (at) school ", and similar games may be cited as very commonly reported types of inducement emotion in female children, the " mother ", or " teacher " girl inducing the others to submit to her.

Cases are reported in which girls of adolescent age, and older, appear to manifest pure inducement response toward other girls, slightly younger or less mature than themselves ; this behaviour being free from the erotic or so-called " sex " element. The suggestion is made that inducement response tends to develop in pure form, or as a constituent part of properly organized love emotion (compounded of inducement and submission), in normal girl and women subjects whose inducement is not constrained by appetitive compulsion to become the emotional tool of dominance or appetite. In such normal, female, inducement responses, the subject allies herself, throughout the response, with the interests and welfare of the person induced, impressing the superiority of her own strength upon the consciousness of the person induced until voluntary submission is evoked. In male subjects, however, the development of inducement emotion is quite different. Inducement is confused with dominance, and tends to be controlled by it. During late adolescence, the average male learns not to use inducement-dominance in tormenting or triumphing over other males, since such behaviour is not expedient. He learns to use inducement response, rather, as an appetitive tool, whereby he can obtain assistance and benefits from other males.

Women's enforced use of inducement as an emotional tool for appetite has made every woman the business rival of every other in inducing males to supply her needs. Now that women are increasing their dominance sufficiently to supply their own needs, they are becoming free to express pure inducement and love toward one another, which their organisms tend to compel them to do.

In general, a lesser degree of alliance is required to evoke inducement response than is required to evoke submission.

The measure of increase of the subject's motor self during inducement emotion, is the difference between its initial strength and the volume necessary effectively to control the stimulus person.

Pleasantness of Inducement

Introspective reports are more frank in declaring inducement behaviour to be pleasant from beginning to end than are reports concerning submission. Since true inducement necessitates complete alliance between the motor self and

motor stimulus, there is no possible source of unpleasantness
in this response, provided neither dominance nor appetite
emotion are permitted to intrude.

Many subjects report that inducement becomes very
unpleasant if unsuccessful, or when its success remains in
doubt. Use of the word " success " in such reports evidences
the true dominant nature of the behaviour characterized as
" unpleasant ". When one strives for " success " as a conscious end, then one is expressing dominance and not inducement. The purpose sought in such responses is to compel an
antagonist into allegiance with the self, and *not* to *lead* or
induce an ally into conduct favourable to both persons. True
inducement is positively pleasant at all times, whether successful or not, because the other person is regarded as a friend,
or ally, throughout. Should a wish be entertained to compel
the stimulus person to do something against his will, then
dominance must have replaced inducement response, and
unpleasantness will accompany the failure of the dominance
reaction to accomplish its purpose.

*The pleasantness of inducement emotion undoubtedly increases
pari passu with increase in the closeness of alliance brought about
by the inducement response itself, between stimulus person and
subject.* Inducement is a type of reaction that does not
represent a resting balance of the organism. Inducement
seeks rather to draw the stimulus person into such close alliance
that the subject can submit to the other without further
striving, or effort. In proportion as this ultimate resting
balance of the organism is secured, therefore, the pleasantness
of inducement is observed to increase. Many subjects report
this self observation in the belief that the added pleasantness
is a dominant satisfaction, and without being in the least
aware that the culminating pleasantness occurs when induce-
ment-striving is able to merge in the resting-balance response
of submission, which is undoubtedly most pleasant of all when
thus arrived at.

Distinctive Conscious Characteristics of Inducement Emotion

Some popular terms for emotional behaviour characterized
principally by inducement are : " persuasion ", " attraction ",
" captivation ", " seduction ", " vamping " (i.e. acting the
vampire), " convincing ", " making an impression on "
another person, " alluring ", " luring ", " attractive per-

sonality ", " personal ˌcharm ", " personal magnetism ", " appealing ", " leading " a person, " convincing " a person, " converting " a person, " charming " a person, " selling " an idea or oneself, " showing a person it is to his iɾterest " to do something proposed, " inducing a person " to do something, " winning a person's confidence ", and " winning a person's friendship ".

The chief differences in meaning between these and similar terms for inducement behaviour lie in the varying degrees of appetitive purpose or technique, suggested as constituent parts of the total action indicated. Like submission, these popular descriptions of inducement are objective, for the most part, giving little clue to the emotion which the inducer observed in his own consciousness, while his inducement response was in progress.

Even a casual analysis of the terms descriptive of inducement as a type of action toward another person reveals a substantial unanimity of meaning as to the actual nature of the response itself. In every case *inducement consists of an increase of the self, and making of the self more completely allied with the stimulus person, for the purpose of establishing control over that person's behaviour.*

Self-observations of inducement emotion, reported by subjects of both sexes (though male reports concerned inducement responses used for business or other appetitive purposes) suggest 'he definitive characteristic of inducement to be : *a feeling that it is utterly necessary to win the voluntary submission of another person to do what the subject says. This feeling, increasingly pleasant in proportion as the other person submits, constitutes inducement emotion.*

CHAPTER XIII

INDUCEMENT AND SUBMISSION

IT is evident that a child, in actively submitting to its mother's commands, must place its motor self under the integrative control of motor stimuli evoked by the mother. This control consists, in the first place, of dictation by the mother as to which parts of the motor self shall be reinforced. That is to say, the determining cause which influences the child to reinforce the motor discharge innervating his grasping muscles will consist of the mother's command rather than the object which is grasped. If the infant is grasping a rod and the rod is pulled in a direction opposite to the child's grasp upon it, his motor self reinforces itself as a response to motor stimuli evoked by the antagonistic moving of the rod. Let us suppose, on the other hand, that the child is holding one end of a steamer rug, which he is helping his mother to fold after a picnic on the beach. The rug is heavy, and the mother must exert a considerable pull on her end of the rug in order to straighten it out. The child, having no dominant set, or primary emotional response toward the rug, allows it to slip a little way through his fingers, as the weight of the rug and the mother's pull upon it move it in a direction antagonistic to his grasp.

"Hold it tight, Teddy," commands the mother. And Teddy immediately reinforces his grasp upon the rug until he supports its entire weight in the manner required. In this case the child responds almost exclusively with a submission response to the mother, rather than with a dominance response toward the rug. Later, of course, Teddy may learn to use his dominant responses to carry out submission reactions (D + S), in which case Teddy would express a true dominance response toward the rug adapted to his submission response to the mother.

274

D + S Gives Organism a Resting Balance

We might suppose in this instance, that the motor stimuli evoked by the mother's command, being in every respect allied with the motor self of the child, were able to gain motor discharge simultaneously with the child's own tonic impulses over the efferent paths leading to the grasping muscles which held the rug. The increased tension of these muscles which follows, would reflexly reinforce the particular portion of the tonic motor discharge leading back to the rug-grasping muscles, both through the operation of the muscular proprioceptors giving additional stimulation when the tension of the muscles increases, and also through corresponding central reinforcement mechanisms. This would account adequately, it seems, for *active submission responses which would thus appear to be the natural ally of, and complement to dominance reactions.*

The motor self of the subject would not, at any time during submission response, be thrown out of its natural reflex balance in control of the organism. Yet within itself, the total tonic discharge might be redistributed with appropriate partial reinforcement and diminution according to the dictates of the submission stimulus. This stimulus, in turn, in order to remain in complete alliance with the motor self would be compelled to dictate to the motor self the most harmonious and efficient adjustment possible to the total environment. Thus the submission stimulus would simply supplant the environmental stimuli to dominance, and compliance, in evoking perfect adjustment of the motor self to the total environmental stimulus situation, the motor self remaining in its natural or normal balance more effectively by virtue of its submissive relationship to the submission stimulus. This integrative condition would represent, then, a resting balance of the motor self, supplemented and made secure by the directing presence of its superior ally.

Inducement Response Requires an Unstable State of Reflex Equilibrium

With regard to inducement response, the integrative picture must be quite different. Inducement is a type of reaction which seems to procure the presence of an ally within certain selected portions of the total discharge pattern of the motor self. Inducement is not, primarily, a resting adjustment of the motor self to total environment. The motor self must bring about its own adaptation to surrounding dominance and compliance stimuli. It must also maintain itself at an increased level of strength, in order to secure the continued presence of the weaker, allied impulses in those portions of the tonic motor discharge pattern where the allied impulses are to be captured and controlled.

Let us attempt to reconstruct the integrative situation which must obtain within the organism of the mother, who in the submission incident just analysed, induced submission successfully from her small son with respect to the folding up of a rug. The mother in that instance first observed that her weaker ally, Teddy, was growing too weak to maintain his alliance with her in their joint project. Her problem, then, was one of increasing and rearranging her own motor self in such a way that the ally might be strengthened. This increase and rearrangement of strength took place when the mother commanded her child to strengthen his grip on the rug. Throughout the remainder of the process of folding the rug, the mother must similarly have continued to exert herself on Teddy's behalf, to the extent of issuing instructions as to the movements she wished the child to make, together with a continuous supervising attitude, making sure that Teddy was performing the appropriate movement at the proper time.

The mother must, moreover, exert her power upon Teddy in accordance with Teddy's organism, as well as her own. A command, for example, directing the child to hold the rug with his teeth or with his feet would be futile. Again, any relaxation of the influence exerted upon Teddy would bring his assistance to an end, since he was responding to the mother and not to the rug itself. First then, within the mother's own organism, her motor self must permit the allied, weaker, motor stimuli representing Teddy, to select those parts of her own total motor discharge pattern wherein motor stimuli and motor self may continuously reinforce one another. Secondly, the parts of the mother's motor self already occupying these paths must be strengthened, in order to reduce the resistance in the common paths sufficiently for the weaker allied motor stimuli to enter them. While this condition persists, the weaker motor stimuli would be kept as allies in the common paths ; but only so long as the motor self keeps itself selectively reinforced in the requisite pattern.

This integrative condition of inducement response must be an unstable one due to the constant tendency on the part of the motor self to return to its natural resting state or equilibrium, thus lapsing from its temporarily assumed, selective increase, which alone holds the weaker allied impulses in a state of captivation. The only way in which the mother's integrative adjustment could be made permanent, or stable, would be through the strengthening of the allied motor stimuli to a level where they would not only remain in their present state of alliance without assistance, but also would be able actively to select the paths of alliance wherein the mother's motor self should be decreased or diminished.

In other words, the mother's natural reflex equilibrium could not be restored to a completely resting, or balanced condition, until Teddy had learned to perform his part of the rug-folding process perfectly, and was further able to take the initiative in directing his mother's movements so that they would co-operate completely with his own. This, of course, would constitute a reversal of the initial relationship between mother and child, with the mother submitting and the child inducing. Looked at from the point of view of the mother, this termination of inducement response by supplanting it with submission would not only restore her integrative equilibrium to its natural, or resting state, but it would also accomplish in a permanent way the need for which the inducement response was striving ; namely, the acquiring of a permanent ally in that particular undertaking.

I is to S as C is to D

If the suggested mechanisms by which inducement and submission responses are brought about are approximately accurate, then *inducement bears the same relationship to submission, when the two occur successively, that compliance bears to dominance response.* Inducement can persist as the controlling primary emotional response of the organism only so long as the environmental inducement stimulus keeps the organism actively engaged in holding the stimulus in allied relationship. When this inducement reaction stops, the motor self, if it continues to react to the same environmental stimulus, which is allied, though weaker than itself, will automatically assume the state of adjustment most closely allied with the environmental stimulus as it then is, without any effort to bring the stimulus into closer alliance with itself. This condition would constitute a state of passive submission response. The allied stimulus, in such a case, would possess sufficient power to attract the motor self into a pattern determined by the stimulus ; but it would not exert sufficient power over the motor self to compel it to perform actively within that pattern. Active inducement response, therefore, tends to be followed automatically by submission.

If, on the other hand, inducement is successful, as in the instance of the mother directing her child in folding the rug, the *complete success of the inducement response itself would tend to bring about an attitude of active submission immediately following the successful inducement.* Inducement response contemplates, as its ultimate purpose, the increasing of the strength of the allied stimulus to such a degree that it will become superior in strength to the motor self, rather than inferior to it. Consider, for example, the unlearned child behaviour reported by Watson wherein the infant extends its feet or hands to invite stimulation, or spontaneously hugs its mother as an inducement to her to continue petting the child. In such cases the inducement response is designed to increase the strength of the allied stimulus to a point where the child may submit once more to the stimulus thus increased.

Teaching is I + S

Any teaching which has for its purpose the increasing of a student's own knowledge or ability to deal successfully with a certain type of subject matter tends to bring about the ultimate result that the student, when he has increased his knowledge sufficiently, will be able to call upon the teacher for such further instruction as may be best suited to the student's principal needs and abilities. *The skilful teacher exercises only sufficient initial inducement to raise the pupil to an intellectual strength where the teacher can submit to him effectively.* Thus, we find the elementary college course, in America at least, consisting largely of lectures and arbitrary instructions to the student as to required procedures necessary to master the elementary technique of a given subject. The most advanced courses in this same field will be found to consist largely of seminars and research work, in which the student undertakes original investigations or theoretical expositions of his own devising, calling upon the professor and upon his fellow students for help and criticism at the points where such assistance is needed.

Again, if we consider the student's controlling emotional responses in the behaviour mentioned, we discover that the seeker after knowledge has been obliged to offer inducement of some sort to the teacher, before the latter agreed to undertake the instruction of the student at all. This first inducement response on the part of the prospective student was a comparatively brief one, possibly consisting of paying the requisite fee to the college, arranging the proper application and registration for the course in question, and perhaps, asking the professor's personal consent to the student's enrolment in that course. This brief inducement behaviour, however, if successful, resulted immediately in an increase in the strength of the professor as compared to the student, which enabled the instructor to induce and the student to submit throughout the academic period set for the study in question. Thus the total series of prevailing responses, in this type of behaviour, might be listed thus :

(1) Student induces professor to accept student's enrolment in the professor's course.

(2) Professor submits to student's inducement by accepting him as requested.

(3) Professor induces student to follow certain mental behaviour prescribed as work in the course.

(4) Student submits by performing this work.

(5) Student, in advanced courses following, induces professor to give special assistance in student's own problems.

(6) Professor submits by giving help required.

(7) Student submits by altering his methods accordingly.

In the above series of inducement-submission responses, as also in the series of infantile inducement responses before mentioned, two aspects of the relationship between inducement and submission might be noted. First, submission in all cases eventually supercedes inducement. Secondly, inducement responses act as selective agents determining the nature and strength of the submission responses which follow.

Learning by I + S is Pleasant ; Learning by Trial and Error (C + D) is Painful

The proper relationship between the primary emotional responses of inducement and submission, as analysed above, is a most important and beneficial one to the organism as a whole. By this method, the organism is permitted to seek guidance and help from persons more developed in some particular than the subject. The subject, thereafter, is enabled to submit to the instruction imposed, or assistance given, as soon as the more highly developed person has been induced to give all the leadership required by the subject. It is by this emotional mechanism, combining in proper relationship the responses of submission and inducement that human beings and animals, to a lesser extent, are enabled to accomplish without suffering the same or better results than those attained by the harsh method of compulsory compliance, followed by compensatory dominance. The latter method of learning is known as " experience ", or " the trial and error method ".

Without inducement and submission responses, the pain and suffering of human and animal life, great as it already is, would be inconceivably increased. Every acquired response of compliance with intensity entails a certain amount of inevitable unpleasantness or suffering while it is in the process of being learned. The dominance response, moreover, which must follow and counteract this enforced compliance, is often more intensely unpleasant than was the original compliance. *In contrast to this double dose of unpleasantness, experienced in learning by the C + D method, we find, in the inducement-submission mechanism, a possible method for acquiring the requisite action ability even more effectively, so far as end result goes, with a double dose of pleasantness attached to the process of learning.*

Both inducement and submission responses, when in the proper relationship one to the other as analysed above, are capable of rendering sustained pleasantness of motation as a background to the entire learning process. Compliance with intensity responses acquired by animals and human males in the course of the " struggle for existence ", and under the rule of " survival of the fittest ", usually entail positive destruction of important portions of the learner's body and consciousness. Nearly all the unpleasant, abnormal feelings of childhood, and the perverted and exaggerated reactions of over compliance and needless dominance which eventually lead to the office of a physician or psychiatrist in adult life, may be classed as injuries received in the process of learning by the compulsory compliance method. Learning by the inducement submission method, on the other hand, never entails injury or loss of function to body or consciousness, provided only that inducement and submission responses are kept in proper relationship one to the other. If the teacher selected for learning by inducement-submission method possesses an erroneous or inadequate knowledge of his subject, the student, after learning the teacher's faulty technique, may suffer injury in attempted application of his false knowledge, that is, in trying to manipulate the environment with inadequate tools. But in that case, though a wrong choice of inducer was originally at fault, the actual injury is suffered as before, in the course of compliance and dominance behaviour which attempts to utilize the supposed knowledge.

Anglo-American Law Forbids Use of Dominance Toward Human Beings

It is possible to differentiate sharply between the normal reactions of human subjects to other human beings, and the normal reactions of human subjects to the inanimate objects of nature, by discovering the difference between environmental stimuli adequate to compliance-dominance responses, and environmental stimuli adequate to submission-inducement reactions.[1] It can be shown that the basis of civilization, including its laws and all its social institutions, rests upon a prohibition of the use of compliance-dominance behaviour toward human beings, and compulsory use of inducement-submission behaviour in all social relationships. The common law, which has been the source of English and American jurisprudence, attempts, by its law of crime and punishment, to prevent the use of dominant compulsion in business and economic relationships between human beings. Unrestrained dominance can only be exercised over human beings, according to common law principles, by the state itself ; and the state in thus compelling its citizens to comply with its intensity is acting, at least theoretically, in submission to the highest needs of the greatest possible proportion of those human beings who constitute its citizenry.

The constitution of the United States, embodying this principle, contains the well known provision that no citizen

---

[1] The author has in preparation a volume dealing with problems of social psychology, based upon this differentiation between responses to people and reactions to things.

shall be deprived of life, liberty, or the pursuit of happiness " without due process of law ". In terms of primary emotional responses, this protects from compliance with intensity, not only when their fellow citizens might attempt to exercise such dominance over them, but also in case the agents of the state itself should attempt to do so. The individual human being is conceived of as possessing an inherent right not to be made to comply with dominant intensity imposed upon him by any other human being, except as a punishment for having committed a similar act against some other citizen. Confessions obtained by torture and physical violence are not admissible, theoretically at least, in court proceedings. Police are not permitted by law to compel obedience to their commands by direct imposition of physical attack of sufficient intensity to compel compliance, unless they themselves or some other citizens are threatened with similar violence by an offender against the peace of the community.

Parents and teachers are not allowed by law to compel compliance from unruly children by whippings of sufficient intensity to enforce compliance upon a stubborn child. The child must be brought to court, and the court may restrain, but cannot whip the child. If the parent does impose physical punishment of intensity sufficient to compel compliance from the child, it is frequently the parent who is brought to court on criminal charges of cruelty to the child. This provision against compulsion by dominance is ever carried to the point of forbidding the use of this method in the training or treatment of animals. Statutes in nearly all American states provide criminal penalties for " cruelty to animals ".

Not only is man, under the common law, prohibited from responding to his fellow man with the same dominance response that he is encouraged to use against inanimate objects, but also, in matters of commerce and trade, he is forbidden to take full advantage of certain dominant compulsions which forces of nature may exert upon other human beings. The United States' statute called the Sherman Anti-Trust Act, forbids certain " combinations in restraint of trade ". This federal statute recognizes that dominance may be exerted upon the public indirectly, by a group of people who have obtained a monopoly of a certain commodity which has become necessary to the comfort and well-being of the community. If some " trust " is able to corner this commodity and fix the price upon it at an exhorbitant figure highly profitable to itself, the psycho-physiological laws of the human organism may compel large numbers of people to pay the extortionate price demanded.

Maximum price fixing on food, rentals, and clothing, by government regulation, became a well accepted legal principle during the world war. There, again, we find recognized the principle of protecting human beings against physical compulsion, even when such compulsion is actually exercised by their own bodies, by the climate, and by other antagonistic forces of the environment, and is subsequently taken advantage of by profiteering fellow humans. Even the extent to which the state can go in exercising dominant compulsion upon an offender against its laws is now being limited by humane public opinion and legislative enactment. Capital punishment, the theory of which is that threat of complete destruction will exercise the maximum possible dominant compulsion upon prospective killers, is being abolished in the United States. Tortures, and "cruel and unusual punishments" have long been abolished by American law, as methods which the state may not employ to compel compliance, either before or after conviction for a crime.

Common Law Enforces the I + S Relationship in Business

Following our analysis of common law principles into the field of commercial law, including the law of contracts, and the law of sales, we find that the basis of business law appears to rest upon tacit recognition of the proper and normal relationship between successive inducement and submission responses. Common law, in general, requires that delivery of goods, or payment of money must follow either a contractual agreement to make such delivery or payment, or an actual enrichment of one party to the proceeding at the expense of the other party, if such enrichment is accepted by the person enriched. In terms of primary emotions, the legal principle of contract and sale reveals itself as follows : The seller A, induces the buyer B, to submit to A by paying over a certain sum of money for goods which A is to deliver to B at a subsequent date. The law does not, of course, require that A shall induce B, or that B must respond by submitting to A's inducement. But once B has responded by submitting to A, *the law requires that A must regard B's payment as an inducement stimulus, to which A must respond by submission consisting of delivering over the goods in question.* We have already noted that this legally enforced succession of inducement-submission responses is the integratively correct one. *A's inducement having been successful, he must follow his inducement by a submission response to the individual whom he himself has made into an adequate submission stimulus to himself.* It is curious indeed that the integrative principles of primary emotions should be found thus deftly formulated into the principles of jurisprudence, hundreds of years before the primary emotion mechanisms themselves were suggested.

If the subject, A, fails completely to submit to the person B, whom A has indeed induced into becoming an adequate submission stimulus to himself, and if it can be demonstrated that subject A never intended to submit to B even before he had induced B to submit to him, then both English and American law would probably hold A guilty of a crime called " obtaining goods under false pretences ". If, on the other hand, A intended in good faith to submit to B after B had submitted to him, but was prevented from doing so by circumstances outside A's control, then it is clear that B would be able only to bring a civil action against A's *property*, and not a criminal action against A's person. In this distinction we may trace another recognition of the proper distinction between primary emotional responses to things and persons. *If A has not offended against B by treating B as a thing, B is not aided by the state to punish A by similar treatment.* But A is considered to have forfeited his preferential rights over the thing, or property, in his own possession by having failed to control this property properly in B's behalf. B is thereupon permitted, through the submission relationship which A has incurred toward him, to compel the things possessed by A to conform to the relationship to B which A had undertaken to enforce upon the property in question, but had failed to carry out.

There are strict legal limits, moreover, to the completeness with which A's submission must correspond with his inducement. The maxim, " *Caveat Emptor* ", arose from the situation wherein B, the person induced, volunteers a certain amount of submission to A, over and above the amount which should reasonably be attributed to A's original inducement. That is, A says, " I have for sale the most marvellous watch in the world ". He then shows B the watch, making the while, certain exaggerated statements concerning the merits of the time piece. This type of inducement, the law says, is not capable, *per se*, of evoking the submission response of paying an exhorbitant price for the watch corresponding in amount to the selling talk of A ; *because B is presumed to be acting with mixed emotional responses of dominance and submission.* B is not expected to yield to the full strength of A's inducement unless the article put up for sale itself stimulates B to a response of *dominance toward the watch*, which, by the degree of desire it evokes, justifies payment of the price demanded. Thus the law again recognizes that appetitive dominance is a proper and commendable response toward *things*, which are the ultimate objects of trade ; while, at the same time, requiring that an integratively proper sequence of inducement-submission responses must be employed in the human relationships arising during the course of mutual dealings with the inanimate object.

Law Recognizes I + S as Proper Learning Method

Finally, in this connection, it is interesting to note that the law recognizes, to a considerable extent, the merits of inducement-submission relationships between certain classes of persons, of supposedly mature development, and other classes of less developed individuals. It will be remembered that, by virtue of the inducement-submission relationship, learning of diverse sorts can be obtained without the suffering inevitable in the " school of experience ", where dominance-compliance learning methods prevail. The common law, seemingly basing itself upon this integrative principle of the primary emotions, provides for the existence of various relationships, designed to require this type of training and protection by the inducement-submission method of learning. Such a relationship is legally known as a " status ". The legal rights pertaining to a certain status do not arise from particular agreements, consisting of isolated inducement and submission responses between the persons concerned. The legal rights and duties pertaining to a given status arise from the status itself, and are of comparatively fixed and constant nature, until the status is dissolved.

A child below " legal age " is regarded by the common law as occupying the status of a " minor ." Toward a minor, the parents or guardians are required by law to respond with various types of inducement and submission reactions. They are required, for instance, to induce the child to attend school, to obey the law of state and community, to eat proper food in sufficient quantity, to sustain health, and to behave, in general, in such a way as not to offend the currently accepted proprieties and conventions of the community in which the child and his parents reside. All these reactions toward the child which are required of the parents by law are simple inducement responses. The child, on the other hand, is also required by law to submit to his parents' commands in respect to all the points of behaviour mentioned. He is also required to submit to various other persons who are placed in relationships where they express inducement toward him, such as his teachers in school, the city doctor, health authorities, and others. When the minor passes the legal age of sixteen, eighteen, or twenty-one as the case may be, his submission status to his parents and other persons ceases as does their status of required inducement toward the child.

Other instances in which an inducement-submission status is established by law are police and private citizens ; a country and its citizens ; husband and wife (though in this status, at the present time, practically identical inducements and submissions are required mutually of both parties) ; and prison authorities and prisoners.

It seems an extremely interesting fact that the principles of jurisprudence, which have evolved practically unaided by science, should reflect thus accurately the fundamental principles of inducement-submission relationships between human beings. These legally devised relationships are able, if rightly utilized, to bring about the teaching and training of both adult and juvenile individuals by the I + S method, the only normal method for human learning. Persons inferior in some particular are thus related by law to persons of presumably superior development, in such a way as to avoid, or at least to mitigate, the inevitable suffering entailed in the dominance-compliance " survival of the fittest ".

CHAPTER XIV

LOVE

LOVE must be differentiated from " sex ". " Sex ", according to the dictionary, means " the physical difference between male and female ; the character of being male or female ". Accepting this meaning for the word " sex ", " sex emotion " must mean that emotion which one has by virtue of being either male or female. The contention has never. seriously been advanced that love is an emotion experienced by one sex only. Undoubtedly, both men and women love, and women, at least, love one another in exactly the same way as they love males. Therefore, love emotion cannot be regarded as a " physical difference between male and female ", nor can it be supposed to depend for its existence upon the existence of sex differences. The identification of love emotion with sex is responsible, in a large degree, for the social taboos which occidental civilizations place on love. To regard love as an emotion the expression of which is facilitated by sex differences of body structure is wholesome. But to identify love emotion with sex characteristics in general, especially those of the male, leads to a most unfortunate lack of understanding of love, since the male sex is characterized chiefly by a preponderance of appetite. It also leads to a confusion of sex differences in love, with sex differences in appetite. Each sex possesses certain secondary appetitive characteristics, just as each sex possesses secondary love characteristics. The sex differences in bodily love structures are localized on the outside of the body ; while the sex differences in appetitive bodily structures are less obvious, manifesting their presence by different glandular balance, differences in hunger mechanism, and differences in bodily shape and musculature. There is no more reason for identifying love with sex under the name " sex emotion " than there is for identifying appetite with sex under a similar title.

Infants Manifest Active and Passive Love Behaviour
Infant behaviour reveals, apparently, simultaneous com-

binations of certain aspects of inducement and submission, just as we have seen that it reveals integrative compounds of dominance and compliance. As already noted, the infants observed by Watson, Jones, and others, are reported as manifesting two types of love behaviour. In the first type of love behaviour wherein the infant ceased other activities and gave himself up completely to the control and direction of the stimulus, we have already noted that active submission to the stimulating person constituted the explicit response. This might be termed, tentatively, *passive love response*, and its other constituent element besides submission will be considered presently. The other type of love behaviour manifested by infants, wherein the child pressed itself against the parent, hugged its mother or nurse, and sought in various ways to control the actions of the loved person, contains active inducement as its most explicit emotional response element. This aspect of love behaviour may conveniently be termed *active love*, and its additional emotional constituent also must be analysed.

Passive Love Is a Compound of pI and aS

In passive love, the obviously controlling element is active submission. Infants, during the responses analysed, reacted both explicitly and implicitly according to the dictates of the person stimulating their sensitive zones. After an initial diminution of the motor self sufficient to put the allied stimulus completely in control, (as evidenced by giving up of dominance response, crying, etc.) the motor self increased those parts of its total motor discharge required by the motor stimulus. That is to say, the stimulus person tickled, stroked, and petted the infant, thus selecting certain tonically innervated parts of the child's body, both skeletal muscles and viscera, which responded actively, with tonic reinforcements, to the stimulation imposed. The active responses, moreover, were not of antagonistic nature, but indicated that the tonic discharge paths were being freely opened to the impulses evoked by the stimulation. Erection of the penis, for example, we know to be a tonic end effect ordinarily held in check by cortical inhibition.[1] When this response occurs, therefore, it is

[1] E. G. Martin and M. L. Tainter, "The Inhibition of Erection by Decerebration," *American Journal of Physiology*, 1923, vol. 65, pp. 139-147.

apparent that the motor self has not been further inhibited by the motor stimuli evoked, but rather that it has responded positively and submissively to the allied impulses set up by sensitive zone stimulation. This is active submission.

Passive love, moreover, contains a second element, evidently conditioned, in the first place, by the active submission responses just referred to. This second element consists of the holding out of hands and feet to be tickled, already cited in Chapter XII, as expressions of inducement. The child, one might believe, enjoys the active submission experience so intensely that he offers himself conveniently to the stimulator for its continuance. This behaviour, though properly characterized as inducement, is yet of a somewhat more passive nature than the spontaneous hugging, and pressing against the mother's body which may come later. The stimulated parts are tendered suggestively for further stimulation but no attempt is made to take the initiative in bringing such further stimulation about. The motor self may be thought of as reinforcing itself in respect to the tonic innervations of hands, feet, and other parts presented for stimulation in order to invite attention to those parts. But the motor self does not reinforce itself with sufficient strength and positiveness to press the parts offered against the body of the stimulator, thereby actively evoking corresponding pressures of overwhelming strength, to which the child may submit. *This partial reinforcement of the motor self then, for the purpose of inviting whatever stimulation the stimulus person may choose to administer, may be termed passive inducement.*

It seems quite apparent that passive inducement can coexist effectively with active submission, as actually occurs in the infant behaviour under discussion. Both responses, moreover, being mutually allied with the subject's motor self and with each other, are evoked by and expressed toward the same stimulus person. *Such simultaneous compounding of passive inducement and active submission may be termed passive love.* \

Active Love is a Compound of aI and pS

Analysis of active love as evidenced in child behaviour similarly reveals a pair of primary emotional response elements simultaneously occurring. There must be, of course, some predisposing or determining reaction within the child's own organism, prior to his sudden hugging or pressing against the mother. That is to say, the mother or nurse may frequently hold the child, or remain within reach of it, without any appearance of active love behaviour. On other occasions, the child spontaneously manifests a love initiative. What is the nature of the preparatory response within the infant organism, upon those occasions when active love spontaneously appears toward the mother ?

A clue to the implicit predetermining reaction within the child's organism may be obtained from the frequency with which active love responses follow immediately upon the cessation of previous petting and caressing which the mother has been bestowing upon the child. Upon practically every occasion when I have observed active love responses of the type described in the behaviour of male children, the active love response has appeared immediately after a mother or nurse had ceased petting or stroking the infant. On one occasion the mother had been bathing a male infant three months old. The temperature stimulation from the water and the stroking of the child's skin by the mother had evoked what appeared to be passive love responses. When the bath was over and the stroking stopped the infant extended its arms spontaneously and without crying. When the mother's hand was brought within the child's reach he pressed it between his hands and hugged it against his body.

I have noted similar active love behaviour on the part of girl children of a somewhat older age which did not follow so closely a petting or caressing of the child. But in these cases the active love behaviour was always expressed toward a person who had frequently caressed the child upon previous occasions, or after an interval of unusual length, during which the mother had *not* petted the child.

These instances seem to indicate, in the case of the male children, that active love behaviour tends to occur while the stimulus to active submission is still acting upon the organism, but after it has ceased to possess sufficient strength actively to direct the child's motor self. In the case of girl children the suggestion arises that a love hormone may exist which accumulates sufficiently after an interval to act in a similar manner upon the organism ; that is, by administering an allied stimulus to submission not quite strong enough to produce active submission.

If a submission stimulus which is not powerful enough actively to direct the motor self of the child, is acting upon the organism, *such a stimulus may still prove sufficient in strength to enforce passive submission upon the motor self.* This stimulus, in the cases cited, was applied from within the organism either in the form of after discharge from centres recently stimulated as in the case of the male child, or in the possible form of a love hormone in appropriate regions of the female organism. Passive submission response in either case would seem to consist of a simple passive giving up of every sort of activity of the motor self which was not compatible with the motor stimuli to passive submission evoked within the organism. •

This situation seems to be the predisposing cause of the active inducement response, which is evoked by environmental stimuli consisting of mother of loved one. Just as in the case of passive compliance with hunger pangs, where food was the only environmental stimulus stronger than hunger pangs, so in the case of intra-organic passive submission stimulus, a love stimulating person would seem to be the only possible environmental stimulus weaker than the subject (because subject has learned that this person yields to her inducement), yet stronger than the passive submission stimuli at present controlling the motor self. *This integrative situation predisposes the infant organism to inducement response toward the mother just as hunger pangs predispose both infant and adult organisms toward food.* If the mother were not present to evoke the inducement response, the organism would be incapable of concerted emotional response toward other environmental stimuli for as long a time as the passive submission response to the intra-organic stimuli persisted. Only this one type of active inducement response would seem to be capable of controlling any considerable part of the child's behaviour at this time, just as food alone is capable of controlling behaviour during the persistence of hunger pangs. In children who thus overtly manifest active inducement response while implicitly reacting with passive submission to some intra-organic stimulus, *we find in existence a new emotional compound, composed of simultaneously occurring active inducement and passive submission, and this compound emotion may be named active love.*

Captivation ,

The conscious emotional qualities of active and passive love do not appear with sufficient certainty in the case of infant responses such as those analysed to characterize or name the compound emotions thus discovered. We have already mentioned instances, however, taken from the behaviour of older children, where the characteristics of active and passive love responses are clearly manifest. While discussing inducement, a series of male responses was analysed consisting of cruelty or torments imposed upon weaker males. We noted, at that time, that the underlying love responses which were adapted to and controlled by dominance consisted of a mixture of inducement and submission which cause a type of response designed to *captivate* the weaker male. This *captivation* emotion seems identical in respect to its primary emotional elements and their simultaneous compounding, with the active love response found in the behaviour of infants. When we abstract dominance and appetitive emotion completely from the compound, we find that there remains an active inducement response designed to evoke submission from the boy tormented plus a passive submission reaction, which may be evoked by one of a number of environmental stimuli, depending upon the circumstances. In the case where a group of boys (known in social psychology as " the crowd ") unite to haze or torture a boy weaker than the rest, it would seem that each individual member of the crowd, is submitting passively to the crowd as a whole. A " crowd ", or group, does not possess, of course, a united " will " or " mind ", with which it can actively direct or compel an individual member of the group. But the situation wherein eight, or ten, or twenty other boys are engaged in the same play, may act very efficiently to induce each member of the group to give up all personal desires and activities other than those in which the group is engaged. This response of each individual boy to the group constitutes a clear-cut passive submission reaction.

It is an often reported fact that a few members of a crowd which is engaged in tormenting a single individual, privately demur, and would not continue with the project in hand, were it not for the powerful influence which they feel from the group as a whole. It is this influence which compels them to go on with it. The crowd's influence, of course, to some extent, may be a dominant one, with a corresponding admixture of compliance in the behaviour of the over-influenced group member. *Yet the influence of the crowd upon its individual members is predominantly one of inducement,* for each individual is apt to be much more influenced by his wish to retain the good will of his fellows, and not to be thought of by them as a " quitter ", than by a likelihood of physical violence in case he separates himself from the crowd's activities. In short, regard for the esteem of his fellows causes each boy to submit to the whole group to the extent of staying with them and participating in the bullying of another boy, which they had jointly undertaken.

If to his passive submission response be added an active inducement reaction toward the boy hazed, then we have the compound emotion already designated as active love. In the emotional consciousness of males engaged in tormenting another, this active love element clearly assumes the characteristic of *pleasure in enslaving (making captive) the stimulus person.*

It must be remembered that the male emotion, just considered, contains a controlling admixture of dominance. The violence, and antagonistic quality of its delight in forcing another person into captivity and subjection, therefore, must be discounted before the true quality of active love emotion can be disclosed. When the dominance is abstracted, and pure active love alone remains, we find still the delight in capturing the weaker, stimulus person. But pure active love requires, for its pleasure, the pleasure of its captive. *Active love requires that the person captured must be a willing, wholly submissive captive.* The result can be accomplished only when the captor (or captress) makes himself or herself so utterly attractive to the stimulus person that the captured one submits voluntarily to the attraction exercised over him. Active love, according to this analysis, must be defined as *capturing a loved person by the power of personal attraction.*

The term which most nearly conveys this meaning seems to be " captivation ". Captivation means . " *Making captive by charm* ", which offers a very fair characterization of pure active love emotion. *We may, therefore, adopt the term captivation as a verbal symbol for active love emotion.*

Mutual Captivation Emotion is Evoked by Struggles Between the Sexes

Captivation emotion most frequently occurs in every day

life between members of opposite sexes. Nearly all normal girls or boys experience a considerable amount of captivation emotion during a playful physical struggle with an attractive member of the opposite sex. Still more frequently captivation emotion is experienced in emotional or even in intellectual struggles of the same sort. Such contests are not for the purpose of dominating the opponent as one desires to dominate an inanimate object. The issue of the struggle is intended to decide only who shall induce and who shall submit.

In this type of behaviour, there is no crowd or group to evoke passive submission from either individual. The passive submission, in these inter-sex struggles, consists of passive submission evoked by each individual from the other. That is to say, there exists a learned alliance between the bodies and emotions of males and females. During the struggle each attempts to increase the motor self to induce the other to be captured. Each of these attempts to induce is partially successful, evoking some submission from the person of opposite sex, but this submission response is only sufficient to prevent the other individual from responding to another stimulus than the inducer. This constitutes passive submission response on the part of both.

Each individual, at the same time, continues to attempt to prove his physical or emotional strength superior to that of the other person. This constitutes active inducement. We find, therefore, the same combination of implicit passive submission and explicit active inducement that occurred in the active love responses formerly analysed. In this case of struggles between the sexes, however, there is a cumulatively increasing stimulation of both primary emotional elements, *pari passu* with the increase of the struggle. This situation evokes, therefore, a maximally pleasant type of captivation emotion from both parties to the struggle. Mutual captivation responses between the sexes are of very common occurrence in everyday life. At the seashore, where the bodies are much more completely exposed than upon most other occasions, men frequently seize girl companions and attempt to carry them into the surf. Girls on the beach throw pebbles at their male companions. Both activities are calculated to evoke mutual captivation struggles of the type analysed.

During social relationships which are initiated in a con-

ventional type of meeting between the sexes, the girl is more
frequently the aggressor in provoking captivation contests
than is the male. One case of this sort which came to my
attention in clinic will serve to illustrate the type of behaviour
suggested. A girl twenty years old complained, with apparent
sincerity, that she "simply could not prevent men from
mauling her ". She came to me to ask for help in methods
of preventing what she described as " male bestiality " which
was roused beyond control, as she believed, by her " sex
charm ". This young person, Z, related an incident which I
afterwards verified in part.

A boy, X, meeting Z at a dance, had invited her for the
usual motor ride. Just what happened in the machine is
problematical, since the stories of Z and X differed substantially. Z's appearance, however, on her return from the
ride, was described by several girl friends of Z whom I questioned concerning the affair. " She was a mess " as one girl
described it. Her upper arms were badly bruised, her mouth
was cut and considerably swollen. Her clothes were torn,
and her hair, which was long, was hanging about her shoulders
in complete disorder. There was evidence that the bodily
relationship had not been established by X. Z, when first
seen by her friends after returning in X's motor, was crying
hysterically.

The initial inference from these facts would be that X was,
to say the least, a " cave man " in his treatment of the opposite
sex. Careful inquiries failed to reveal, however, that X had
ever treated any other girl with any rudeness or violence
whatsoever. Several girls had gone for motor rides with X
under circumstances almost identical with Z's case. In one
instance, I was able to verify the fact that X had made love
to a girl who was his guest at a dance, with no untoward
results. " Yes ", this girl told me, " X was perfectly all
right. I had no difficulty in showing him that I did not care
for him ". The evidence is conclusive that this girl did reject
X in the manner reported.

The explanation of X's response to Miss Z undoubtedly lay
in Miss Z's " technique with men ". Z customarily approached
all males, including myself, in a manner effectively calculated
to display and impress upon their attention her own bodily
charms. Her approach was boldly stimulating but challeng-
ing. She flaunted in a man's face, as it were, her irreproach-

able virtue in abstaining from the intimacies of love, but offered an unmistakeable challenge to the male to prove his superior emotional strength by inducing her to change this attitude of self-restraint. In short, Miss Z submitted her person rather freely to a man's inspection, thus evoking from him submission to the extent of fixing the man's attention inescapably upon her charms. At the same time, she bluntly and obviously asserted her superior strength in matters inter-sexual, thus evoking combined active inducement and domin-ance. The simultaneous occurrence of passive submission and active inducement constituted captivation emotion on the part of the male (mixed, of course, with the usual male dominance).

Z challenged all males to inter-sexual combat, not realizing that the captivation response of the average male is inextricably mixed with dominance. When the superior dominance power of society, upon which Z initially relied to quell X's dominance, was removed, in the motor ride situation, Z suffered accord-ingly from X's released dominance. This is a world-old variety of inter-sex emotional response, which women habitu-ally refuse to understand. Their resistance to comprehending its true nature appears to lie in their reluctance to accept the fact already commented upon above, that *women's dominance, under the inducement-for-appetite regime, is a borrowed power, attained from males* who protect her from other males and from females stronger than herself. If she gives up this protection of second-hand strength attained by inducement, her own strength by itself is quickly overwhelmed by the male's superior dominance, physical and emotional. And it is difficult to find a male whose captivation emotion can be aroused to any considerable extent without an admixture of controlling dominance response.

Such was the situation, it seems, in the case of Z and X. The nature of the stimulus furnished by Miss Z's behaviour is made even clearer by its contrast to the behaviour of Miss Y, who evoked neither dominance nor captivation response from X in the process of rejecting his advances, although Miss Y was fully as attractive, physically, as was Miss Z. Miss Y was a girl possessing a very unusual combination of dominance and love development. Her dominance was probably approxi-mately equal to that of X, with strong body development corresponding. Miss Y's response to persons of both sexes was predominately submissive, unless her dominance was aroused by selfish antagonism. Miss Y's treatment of X contained, apparently, little or no inducement. She submitted to his tastes and interests in conversation and companionship, yet when X showed a tendency toward the typical dominant captivation behaviour of a male, Miss Y responded to the antagonistic element in his behaviour with clear-cut, unyielding dominance response, and, aided by X's social training, evoked compliance from X rather than further captivation. In other words, Miss Y's quiet, decisive rejection of X impressed itself upon X as an environmental stimulus both antagonistic and stronger than himself, when coupled with social conventions, at least. At the same time Miss Y's submission to X's tastes and interests evoked a rather pure type of inducement behaviour on X's part consisting of an evident desire to remain friends and enjoy Miss Y's companionship under conditions most agreeable to her. The contrast, in fact, between X's emotional reaction to Miss Z and to Miss Y produced almost a Jekyll and Hyde effect in X's personality, whenever these two divergent types of emotional response could be observed in sequence in X's behaviour. The contrast in emotional response, however, was not attributable to any peculiarity possessed by X, but rather to the extreme contrast between the two types of stimulus, each evoking its own predictable emotion.

Males Capturing Males Experience Dominance-Captivation

Studies of college hazing and inter-class struggles between students were made by F. S. Keller[1] and myself in 1925-26. We found that nearly all the upper classmen gave a high rating of emotional pleasantness to dominance-captivation responses exercised toward freshmen. When a physical struggle between the upper class boy and a freshman preceded the capture of the latter, the strength and enjoyability of the dominance-captivation emotion experienced by the upper classman was greatly enhanced, in nearly all cases reported. The college traditions called for a series of physical struggles between sophomores and freshmen, during which each class attempted to keep their opponents from holding a class dinner. Upon any occasion when the boys of one class had reason

[1] These studies were made at Tufts College, Mass., where Mr. Keller is an instructor in Psychology.

to suspect that their rivals planned to hold their dinner, the method of procedure was to capture as many of the other class as possible, tie them up, and keep them thus bound or otherwise confined until after it was determined that no banquet could be held that day. If a member of the rival class captured wished to escape confinement, he could "sign off" by pledging, on his word of honour, not to attend his class banquet if any was held that day.

A very small percentage, probably only one or two of the boys captured, submitted to confinement for any considerable period. They reported that they experienced no pleasure whatever once they were overcome and bound by their opponents. After that it become a question of complying, either with the discomfort of their bonds, or with the humiliation of surrender involved in signing off. A large majority of both the victors and vanquished, however, reported that they experienced intensely pleasant dominance-captivation emotion during the struggle, up to the point where the issue of superiority was finally decided.

The victors reported that their pleasure in captivation response increased even more during the process of binding and confining their opponents. They experienced much less pleasant captivation emotion on the whole, if an opponent signed off. There were a few boys whose dominance or compliance, depending upon the rôle played in the struggle, was so pronounced that no emotional element recognized as captivation (or "subjection emotion") could be introspectively observed. The behaviour of these boys, however, evidenced a considerable element of captivation response in the total emotional pattern. In this series of struggles it would seem that *passive submission and active inducement were mutually evoked from one another by two males engaged in a bodily struggle, the object of which was not to injure the other boy or to remove him as an obstacle to success, but rather to capture his body by binding and confining it.*

This type of situation seems to present one of the strongest possible varieties of stimulus to captivation emotion. The fact that the dominance responses of male subjects failed wholly to suppress or inhibit captivation emotion in a majority of these subjects seems evidence that the stimulus situation was one operating selectively to evoke captivation emotion. The fact, also, that captivation response was evoked in rather pure form from a male subject by *another male*, who acted as stimulus person, is evidence that captivation emotion is by no means limited to inter-sex relationships.

Girls Punishing Girls Experience Captivation Emotion

Studies of the emotions reported by sophomores and upper class girls during their annual punishment of the freshmen girls were made by Miss Olive Byrne and myself, during the academic year 1925-1926.[1] It was the college custom for upper class girls to draw up a set of rules which freshmen girls were required to follow. These rules called for the usual restrictions of behaviour, wearing freshman buttons, and general yielding to the direction of the older girls. In the spring of the freshmen year, the sophomore girls held what was called " The Baby Party ", which all freshmen girls were compelled to attend. At this affair, the freshmen girls were duly questioned as to their misdemeanors and punished for their disobediences and rebellions. The baby party was so named because the freshmen girls were required to dress like babies.

At the party, the freshmen girls were put through various stunts under command of the sophomores. Upon one occasion, for instance, the freshmen girls were led into a dark corridor where their eyes were blindfolded, and their arms were bound behind them. Only one freshman at a time was taken through this corridor along which sophomore guards were stationed at intervals. This arrangement was designed to impress the girls punished with the impossibility of escape from their captresses. After a series of harmless punishments, each girl was led into a large room where all the Junior and Senior girls were assembled. There she was sentenced to go through various exhibitions, supposed to be especially suitable to punish each particular girl's failures to submit to discipline imposed by the upper class girls. The sophomore girls carried long sticks with which to enforce, if necessary, the stunts which the freshmen were required to perform. While this programme did not call for a series of pre-arranged physical struggles between individual girls, as did the class banquet contest of the boys previously reported, frequent rebellion of the freshmen against the commands of their captresses and

[1] These studies were made at Jackson College, Mass., when Miss Byrne was a student there.

guards furnished the most exciting portion of the entertainment according to the report of a majority of the upper class girls.

Nearly all the sophomores reported excited pleasantness of captivation emotion throughout the party. The pleasantness of their captivation responses appeared to increase when they were obliged to overcome rebellious freshmen physically, or to induce them by repeated commands and added punishments to perform the actions from which the captive girls strove to escape. On the other hand, when a freshman occasionally cried, or showed signs of fear, her sophomore guards, in every instance, reported a feeling of unpleasantness, with emotions of " sympathy " and " feeling sorry for her ". They nearly always told the freshmen thus affected " not to be afraid ", and *persuaded her to go on rather than compelling her to do so*. (This behaviour is in marked contrast to male college hazers, who frequently treated with injurious violence a boy who weakened or " turned yellow ").

From these studies of girls' reactions, it seemed evident that the strongest and most pleasant captivation emotion was experienced during a struggle with girls who were trying to escape from their captivity. A totally different type of love response was invariably evoked by indication of suffering or unpleasantness experienced by the captive.

In the latter case, or when a girl submitted with complete docility, an almost pure inducement response was evoked from the older girl, with considerable admixture of active submission to the needs of the girl who was being punished. It seems probable that the costumes worn by the freshmen girls enhanced, considerably, both the passive submission and the active inducement emotions of the upper class girls although great reticence of introspective description, due to conventional suppressions, prevented this type of response from appearing with complete frankness in the reports received.

On the whole, it would seem that the upper class girls experienced pure captivation emotion of great pleasantness. Little, if any, admixture of dominance could be detected in the reports, or in the observed behaviour of the girls toward their younger charges. While the struggle of the girl punished to escape her punishment by physically overcoming her captress apparently gave the strongest and most pleasant captivation response to both girls, there were many indications

that captivation emotion was present at all times during the
behaviour reported, and even before and after the Baby
Party, in nearly as strong and pleasant a form as during the
struggle situation. Perhaps a love hormone is operative in
the female organism from early childhood, predisposing girls
and women to captivation emotion by evoking passive submission by intra-organic stimulation. Certainly this response
appears in the behaviour and in the naive introspection of
the girls studied in very much purer and more consistent
form than in male responses to corresponding environmental
stimulus situations. Female behaviour also contains still
more evidence than male behaviour that *captivation emotion
is not limited to inter-sex relationships*. The person of another
girl seems to evoke from female subjects, under appropriate
circumstances, fully as strong captivation response as does
that of a male.

Passion

In using the term passion to characterize passive love
emotion, a word of caution is necessary. The term " passion ",
in popular literature, is used indiscriminately to indicate
captivation emotion, true passive love emotion, or a mixture
of both. After obtaining introspection from several hundred
subjects, I have discovered that " flaming passion " or " red
passion ", or " crimson passion " are identifiable, for the most
part, as descriptions of captivation rather than passive love.
Despite the pre-determined active emotional tone in the
emotional states thus designated, however, there is always
a considerable admixture of active submission in yielding to
the lover. Since this emotional element is the principal
characteristic of passive love, it justifies the conclusion that
*active and passive aspects of love in inter-sex relationships of
the sort described are inextricably interwoven.*

Passion, then, in popular parlance, signifies a physical love
emotion containing both active and passive elements but
with the active element predominating. In this particular
it seemed impossible to follow literary terminology. Captivation emotion far more accurately characterizes active
love than does the word " passion " ; *whereas passion, when
properly understood, suggests active submission of self to the
lover.*

With the terms thus defined, nine subjects out of ten find

their introspective ability to observe and analyse their own love emotions greatly clarified. The fact must be remembered, however, that *the term passion as herein used does not indicate love aggression or initiative.* Nor is the emotion herein characterized as passion associated customarily with the colour red.

Passion in Behaviour of Young Children

In a preceding section we have noted that passive love emotion combines, simultaneously, an explicit response of active submission to an inducer with implicit reaction of passive inducement toward the same person. The behaviour previously analysed, however, was infant behaviour, consequently no introspection was available to enable us to characterize the emotional consciousness containing these two compounded primary emotional elements. We must now consider, therefore, responses of both sexes at more mature ages, in order to determine the conscious aspect of passive love.

Children of both sexes, between the ages of two and five, give evidence of a mild degree of passion as a natural response to the mother or nurse. Children of this age are usually able to indicate, by short words and by inarticulate vocal expressions, the general trend of their consciousness. Upon being caressed physically by the mother, in the various ways already mentioned, children frequently cling tightly to the mother, emitting slight gasps, or sometimes panting, gently, in a manner by no means dissimilar to adult passion in intersex relationships. Adoration of the mother is frequently expressed in monosyllabic words, smiles, apparently indicative of marked absorption in the mother as a controlling stimulus, and in gently rhythmic movements of hands and forearms.

At a somewhat older age, when the vocabulary is increased, the child may say " Mama is pretty ", or " I love mama ", and other phrases seemingly expressive of spontaneous and wholly submissive type of love response for the mother. Clearly there exists active submission response to the mother as a determining emotional factor, compounded with the passive inducement attitude already described. These passive love responses are recognized by many psycho-analysts as possessing the conscious characteristic of passion, and are, accordingly, consigned to that limbo of abnormality in which dominantly perverted males are wont to besmudge normal

love emotions with appetitive excreta. While acknowledging
the accuracy of this particular psycho-analytical finding,
I cannot too strongly state my own finding that *passion felt
by children of both sexes toward the mother is a natural and
wholly desirable type of love response.* In fact, if passion in
some degree is not evoked by the mother from her children,
prior to the age of five or six years, the children's development
is initiated under a very serious handicap. It is extremely
unlikely under conditions prescribed by our present civilization,
that opportunity for development of pure passion in a male
child will again be obtained during the entire subsequent life
of the individual.

*Captivation Is Spontaneous Element in Girls' Behaviour, Not
Passion*

Girls of five or six years, or older, are quite likely to experience passive love for other girls of similar age, with or
without mutual stimulation of the genital organs, as the case
may be. This type of passion experience does not appear
to be attributable so much to the existence of intra-organic
stimulation to passion on the part of either child, as to the
spontaneous expression of captivation behaviour by one or
the other girl, with subsequent yielding on the part of the
girl captivated. At least two completed love affairs of this
type between girls five to seven years old have been brought
to my attention. In both cases the children were wholly
normal so far as could be determined by medical and psychological examination.

Though I have not had the opportunity, thus far, to make
an extensive compilation of cases on this point, it seems to
be current opinion among workers having physical charge of
children whom I have been able to consult, that relationships
of this sort between girls, are the rule rather than the exception in the absence of prior teaching of prohibitive variety.
Passion thus aroused in little girls by other little girls clearly
possesses the typical emotional tone of passive love, with
ardent submission to the inducer girl, and complete absorption in the charms of her companionship. Frequently groups
of three or more girls, five to seven years old, become love
associated, spontaneously, in such relationships. Two aspects
of such responses seem deleterious. First, the secrecy enforced upon this type of conduct by prohibitive attitudes on

the part of parents or teachers. Secondly, the ignorance and crudity of the inducement stimulation (whether genital organs are stimulated or not) which the inducer girl is likely to administer. I have not discovered anything but normal female emotional development in this spontaneous arising of the captivation-passion relationship.

Passion Easily Evoked by One Girl From Other Girls

The " crush ", normally experienced by girls of adolescent age and older, for other girls, or for teachers and older women, is too well recognized a phenomenon to require especial description. The girl who " has a crush on another girl " exhibits a singularly intense and absorbing passion emotion toward her *inamorata*. In one instance a number of young girls between the ages of fourteen and seventeen " had crushes on " another girl in the same school.

The girl stimulus to passion was eighteen years old. She was pale, thin, wore her hair in a curiously distinctive fashion, and habitually " toed-in " while walking. " She isn't exactly pretty ", as one of the girl admirers told me, " but she is just charming ". " She seems to *want* people, and to draw everybody right to her ", an apt description of the older girl's captivation influence as felt by one of her " captives ". The active submission responses of the latter were interestingly complete. The girls who had " crushes " on Yvette all began to " toe-in ". They arranged their hair as nearly like Yvette's as possible, and began to practice drawing assiduously, since Yvette had unmistakable artistic talent. Not satisfied with these submissions, Yvette's admirers sat up late at night in order to make themselves as pale as the girl who captivated them.

Yvette did not limit her captivations by any means to members of her own sex, but was accustomed to slip out at night to meet boys who were also in love with her. Much as the younger girls vied with each other for the attentions of the very youths whom Yvette attached to herself, they did not show the slightest jealousy of Yvette's conquests. They helped her in every way to meet these boys illicitly, and " thought it was so brave of her " to carry on these clandestine affairs. In the case of Yvette and her girl lovers there seems little doubt that passion emotion of unusually intense and enduring type was evoked by one girl from many other girls only slightly younger than herself, without any bodily contact or genital organ stimulation.

Study of Passion in Inter-Class Relationships of College Girls

In order to examine the possible existence of passion emotion in the Baby Party situation, Miss L. F. Glidden, of Jackson College, made a study under my direction of the attitudes of her class mates toward the treatment they had received from the older girls. At the time this study was made, the girls questioned were sophomores. They had completed their own period of submission to the sophomores at the Baby Party the preceding spring, and had been actively engaged in disciplining girls of the incoming freshman class for about two months. The girls questioned, however, had never been present at a Baby Party where they were captresses, so that there could have been no transfer of feeling, retrospectively, from one Baby Party to the other. The attempt was made to determine each girl's attitude toward the submission training of freshmen by sophomores when she herself was a sophomore, as well as her remembered attitude toward the sophomores while she was under their control the preceding year. Miss Glidden was instructed to approach her classmates with whom, of course, she was on intimate terms, without allowing them to discover that she was making a psychological study. This instruction was carried out rather successfully.

The girls were asked, (1) Whether they had enjoyed the Baby Party when they were freshmen. They were then asked to rate the degree of pleasantness which they experienced during their own captivity on a scale where ten represented the greatest possible pleasantness, and zero indicated indifference. (2) The girls were asked what their attitude had been toward the sophomores whom they had been required to serve and to obey in various ways during the preceding year. (3) The girls were asked whether they approved and enjoyed the submission training of freshmen which they as sophomores were then engaged in. (4) Each girl was asked whether she submitted voluntarily to men or to women. (5) Each girl was asked to state whether, if she had her choice, she would elect to be an unhappy master or a happy slave. The answers to these questions together with any pertinent introspections were duly recorded by Miss Glidden. The tabulated results are presented in Figure 4, which follows.

Fig. 4.—INTER-CLASS COLLEGE GIRL STUDIES.

Subject	Pleasantness rating of Baby Party	Enjoyed being subjected by Sophomores?	Enjoys subjecting Freshmen?	Submits to man or woman
1.	10	Yes.	Thoroughly.	Both.
2.	1	No.	Decidedly not.	Neither.
3.	1	Yes.	Silly thing, but fun.	Both.
4.		Yes, if the Sophomores are friends.	Yes.	Men.
5.	9	Yes.	Yes.	Women.
6.		No.	Nuisance. Necessary evil.	Neither.
7.	6	Didn't mind	Yes.	
8.		Paid no attention to them.	No.	All men. Two girls.
9.		Recognized their superiority.	Yes.	Neither.
10.	9	Didn't mind	Yes.	Both (at her selection).
11.	4	Hated it.	Yes.	Men.
12.	6	Liked it.	" The bunk."	
13.	5	Yes.	Yes.	Women, and men if they prove they're right.
14.	9	Didn't mind.	Necessary.	Neither.
15.		Willing to do things to please	Necessary evil.	Both, if older.

Fig. 4.- INTER-CLASS COLLEGE GIRL STUDIES.

Subject	Choice of unhappy master (M), or happy slave (S).	Introspection
1.	M	" Big kick " from b.p.[1] Dislikes intensely idea of subjection.
2.	M.	B p. was terrible. Dislikes Sophomores. Likes power.
3.	S.	No fun at b p. because not subjected. Likes to serve whom she loves.
4.		Hated b.p. because made ridiculous.
5.		" Big kick " out of obeying Sophomores.
6.	M.	Watched b.p. from side-lines. Got a " thrill " out of seeing others subjected.
7.	S.	Prefers happiness at any cost. Had wonderful time at b.p., but not pleasantest thing imaginable since engaged at the time.
8.	M.	Took no notice of Sophomores. No " kick " out of b.p. because could see under blindfold. Big joke.
9.	M.	Liked to tell friends about her subjection. Hated making speech at b.p. Can't stand subjection.
10.	S.	
11.	S.	B.p. too " tame ". Burnt her arm on radiator pipe. Must have happiness, and can get it by serving others.
12.	S.	Likes to boss the freshmen. Likes being bossed. Can conceive of being a slave.
13.	S.	No thrill out of doing stunts. Wanted to appear indifferent.
14.	S.	As an upperclassman, loves to subject freshmen. Enjoyed showing off at b.p. Hates submission. Hates unhappiness.
15.	S.	There is happiness in service.

[1] Baby Party.

Fig. 4.—INTER-CLASS COLLEGE GIRL STUDIES—*cont.*

Subject	Pleasantness rating of Baby Party	Enjoyed being subjected by Sophomores ?	Enjoys subjecting Freshmen ?	Submits to man or woman
16.	10	No.	Yes.	Both.
17.	10	No.	Yes.	Neither.
18.		As a matter of course.	Yes, in moderation.	Neither.
19.	5		No.	Men.
20.		Hated it.		Neither.
21.	2	Willing.	Yes.	Both.
22.			" Bunk."	Neither.
23.	5		Silly.	All men and a few girls.
24.		Indifferent.	Yes.	Neither.
25.	8	Yes, with reservations.	Yes.	Both.
26.		Hated it.	Indifferent.	One man and One woman.
27.		Didn't like it.	Yes.	Men.
28.		Didn't like it.	Indifferent.	Men.
29.	8	Hated it.	Fine.	
30.		Hated to be nagged.	Great.	Men.
Totals	Median.. 7 Modes ... 91,0	Yes .. 14 No ... 11	Yes.... 20 No 7	Men ... 17 Women 12

Fig. 4.—INTER-CLASS COLLEGE GIRL STUDIES—*cont.*

Subject	Choice of unhappy master (M), or happy slave (S).	Introspection
16.	M.	Hates to submit to anybody.
17.	S.	Liked b.p. Enjoyed being ordered around. As upper classman, wants freshmen to submit to her. Chooses between happy and unhappy.
18.	S.	B.p. pretty good. Do not allow subjection by anyone.
19.	S.	As upper classman, indifferent to freshmen
20.	M.	Will do things for friend as great favour. Wants no favours done for her.
21.	S.	B.p. silly and childish.
22.	M.	Made to do reducing exercises at b.p. Felt she was being ridiculed.
23.	S.	Will willingly do things for girls on whom she has " crushes."
24.	M.	Doesn't require much of freshmen as upperclassman.
25.	S.	B p. was great. Liked being ordered around. Hates idea of subjection.
26.	M.	Would be unhappy as slave so why not have power.
27.	S.	Likes own way.
28.	S.	As upper classman likes to " wield a high hand " over freshmen.
29.	S.	Likes to subject others to her " will ". Had good time at b.p. Put something over on sophs. Likes power but happiness more.
30.	S.	Enjoyed b.p. immensely. Likes to " boss " freshmen. Conscience would trouble her if she were an unhappy master.

Totals 18 .. S.
10 .. M.

The reliability of this study depends rather upon the intimacy of contact by which the self-observations were obtained, than upon statistical analysis of the results. Not only was Miss Glidden able to win confidence, as a friend, in obtaining Her classmates' reports, but the girls questioned also knew that their questioner had considerable knowledge of their behaviour and general attitudes in the matters under discussion. It is my own opinion, in light of this factor, that less deception, conscious, or "subconscious", was practised in reporting these self observations to Miss Glidden, than is to be found in the usual study of this type.

The central tendency in pleasantness rating or emotion experienced during captivity at the Baby Party appears to be about 7. Several girls refused to give a pleasantness rating, evidencing a good deal of supression in regard to their emotions while captives. It is interesting to note that more girls gave their enjoyment of captivity at 9 and 10, than any other value, indicating greatest pleasantness. It is also interesting to observe that whereas only fourteen girls frankly acknowledged their enjoyment of submission to the sophomores throughout the year, twenty girls asserted their pleasure in making the freshmen submissive to them. Though seventeen girls acknowledged a general attitude of submission to men as against twelve who willingly submitted to women, it seems rather probable that *what is thought of as " submission to men ", in many cases at least, is not submission at all, but inducement.* It seems to be true, however, as we have already suggested, that women are trained systematically under the existing social regime, to use both inducement and submission responses as methods of obtaining appetitive benefits from males.

The significance of the " happy slave—unhappy master " choice is somewhat doubtful. The query was intended to bring out suppressed willingness to be a slave, which might not be elicited in reported self-observations of actual experiences (at Baby Party, etc.). The enjoyment of being made captive seemed to be acknowledged much more frankly, on the whole, than was anticipated. It is a curious result that of the girls who rated their enjoyment of captivity at 10, two also elected to be an unhappy master rather than a happy slave. Does this indicate, perhaps, that these girls frankly admitted maximal enjoyment of being made captive, when their captivity was not labelled, or characterized in such a way that they became conscious of its real nature, while their social inhibitions immediately became operative upon hearing the word "slave"? Some verification of this suggestion may be obtained from the introspection of subject number 1, who rated her enjoyment of the Baby Party at 10, and reported that she got a "big kick," emotionally, from the punishment she received from the sophomores, yet stated that she disliked intensely the *idea* of subjection.

Another distinction which appears in some of the detailed introspections which there is not room for in the table above, is the possible difference of interpretation in the word "master" and "slave". Were it not for the fact that the word "mistress" has acquired a definite tabooed social connotation, it would probably be preferable to the word "master" in studies of this sort, since "master" is interpreted by many subjects to mean a person who uses dominance to compel others to serve his own selfish appetitive purposes. The word "slave" by itself would tend to be interpreted more frequently, by girls at least, as meaning "love slave" rather than appetitive slave. But when "slave" is used in contrast to "master", it may assume a more appetitive interpretation. Some girls who thus understood the meaning of slave insisted, quite rightly, that there could be no such thing as a "happy slave" to another person's selfish dominance. In general, a marked divergence of attitude was found as between a girl's submitting to a person because she loved her, and enjoyed doing it, and submitting to a person (like certain types of house matron and disciplinary official) who were felt to be subjecting the girl to further their own dominance or appetitive convenience. This distinction corresponds precisely to the difference between true submission-passion response, and unpleasant or indifferent compliance reaction.

Conclusions From Study

Our conclusions from the study reported above, were, first, that about three-fourths of the girls physically made captive to other girls at the Baby Party experienced pure, pleasant passion emotion, consisting of active submission to the older girls who were subjecting them compounded with passive inducement toward these same girls. The passive inducement response appeared in such actions as a girl's holding out her hands to show that her bonds had become loose. The lessening of enjoyment when a girl submitted without calling her guard's attention to her lack of sufficient bonds may be noted in the introspection of subject 8, who said she " got no kick out of the Baby Party because I could see under my blindfold ". This girl's inhibition of passive inducement, essential to passion emotion, is further evidenced by her statement that she " took no notice of the sophomores ".

Secondly, we concluded that a much more dilute type of passion response, if any, was evoked, in a majority of the girls, throughout the freshmen year, when they were required to run personal errands, and otherwise appetitively serve their sophomore " superiors ". Dominance response, under these circumstances, was evoked from the freshmen at least as frequently as was submission ; and the actual service was frequently performed with a consciousness of compliance.

Thirdly, we concluded that passion emotion could be evoked from one girl by another girl whom she was compelled to obey, when, and if, the subjecting girl made her commands felt as inducement rather than as dominance, and revealed no possibility of ultimate self-seeking in what she required the other girl to do. In other words, the captivating girl in order to be an adequate stimulus to passion emotion, must ally herself with her captive completely, yet at the same time constantly increase the submissive one's captivity. A freshman girl reported herself as feeling pleasant passion emotion when compelled to kiss the feet of a girl whom she liked. But this same girl took a large amount of extra punishment rather than shine the shoes of an older girl whom she thought selfish.

Summary.

In summary, we may say that passion or passive love emotion consists of simultaneous compounding of the primary emotional response of active submission, evoked by an inducer person, and passive inducement evoked by the same person as a corollary to active submission.

The conscious emotional characteristic of passion emotion appears to be an extremely pleasant feeling of *being subjected and being made more and more helpless in the hands of an allied stimulus person of superior strength.*

It seems undoubtedly to be the fact that girls, acting as inducers, can evoke intense and very pleasant passion emotion from all normal and well-balanced girls who are in appropriate strength relationship to themselves without administering genital organ stimulation directly or indirectly.

Development of Passion Emotion In Males

The situation with respect to the passion emotion of boys and young men is quite different from that obtaining among girls, so far as my own studies indicate. If we waive discussion of the " Oedipus complex " and " mother fixations " there is little to indicate, so far as the literature or my own studies reveal, that true passion response is evoked from a majority of normal males up to the time when inter-sex relationships occur, with consequent stimulation of the external genitals (discussed in next chapter).

There is little doubt but that captivation response occurs frequently in the behaviour of young males, largely mixed with and controlled by dominance. It is probably this dominance element in the older and stronger boys which makes the younger boy suffer physical pain, and emotional unpleasantness, rather than evoking from him the extremely pleasant passion emotion experienced by normal girls five years of age or older, in response to the captivation behaviour of other girls.

The boy's mother, of course, while she remains stronger than himself physically, is able to evoke this passion, as already noted, without stimulation of the genital organs. It is probably because no other substitute stimulus to passion is apt to appear in the average boy's life between the time for normal waning of this mother-child relationship, and the normal period for assuming genital organ relationships with the other sex, that the so-called mother fixation frequently occurs. The really detrimental aspect of such fixations, in the few instances I have been able to observe, seems to be the marked dissociation between the passion evoked by the mother, and the passion evoked by stimulation of the external genitals later in life, by a woman to whom the male normally submits after sexual maturity. The real " resistance " appears to me to consist of a failure to associate the pleasant passion originally experienced with the so-called erotic stimulation later received. A positive inhibitory barrier between these two psychical elements seems frequently to develop in the central nervous system.

This might, of course, be prevented by social sanction of genital organ stimulation by the mother. In the few cases which have come to my attention wherein early passion for the mother appeared to act as a barrier to subsequent passionate surrender to wife or mistress, the youth concerned had never received genital organ stimulation from a nurse-maid, or other female with whom he had come into contact during his boyhood. In one case of a youth who suffered from inability to reinstate, by way of genital organ stimulation, the passion experienced in early life toward his mother, the boy had been stimulated forcibly by older boys, and had suffered physical pain and emotional shame (really a conflict between thwarted dominance and submission) in consequence. Intensely unpleasant emotional experiences of this type serve further to reinforce the inhibitory barrier already existing between passion emotion and " erotic " sensations.

Women's Strength Insufficient to Evoke Passion from Some Males

There is a certain type of youth who, during later adolescence, appears spontaneously to develop emotional longing to be captivated. This type of male frequently fails to find any female who possesses sufficient strength, physical or emotional, to subject him adequately. Under such circumstances, this type of male may gain considerable passion experience from subjections imposed upon him by males superior to himself, despite the dominance which these males inevitably express toward him, along with their captivation emotion.

One boy of this type who was severely bullied as a freshman, reported to me frankly that he enjoyed the experience very greatly. This youth was quite naive in his report, introspecting an almost pure passion response toward his sophomore subjectors. For some reason this boy had transferred to the college where I was teaching at that time, at the beginning of his second year, and was obliged to accept freshman standing again because of insufficient credits for studies previously completed. When he discovered that the hazing to which he was subjected was not nearly as severe as that previously experienced, he expressed very strong disappointment, and criticized the college administration with evident bitterness for their regulations minimizing discipline of freshmen by sophomores. Other boys of this same type have been largely influenced, I believe, in choosing to attend military academy rather than college, by expectation of enjoyment in being subjected to rigid discipline throughout the entire four years' course.

Study of Passion In Inter-Class Relationships of College Men

Emotional studies indicate, however, that this type of male youth, who is able to experience pleasant passion emotion toward superior males despite injuries and suffering of various sorts which he must endure, incidently, at their hands, represents a comparatively small proportion of the male youth of this country. F. S. Keller made a study of the attitude of freshmen boys toward their sophomore subjectors, corresponding exactly in form and subject matter to the study made by Miss Glidden. The results, however, were largely negative. Only one or two boys gave reliable evidence of pleasant passion emotion evoked by sophomores either during enforcement of freshmen " traditions ", throughout the year, or at the special parties where the freshmen boys were " paddled " and otherwise painfully punished. All but one or two expressed decided preference for being an " unhappy master " rather than a " happy slave ", and none of the boys questioned expressed a spontaneous wish to submit either to men or women. Nearly all, on the other hand, expressed their belief in the necessity of *compliance* with their superiors.

In one especial type of situation imposed by the sophomores upon the freshmen boys more evidence of passion emotion was found than in other situations. This occurred when the boys were compelled by the sophomores to march in their pyjamas before one of the girls' dormitories, where they were put through various exhibitions and stunts, to the great excitement of the girls, who watched the performance from dormitory windows. In this situation, marked conflicts seemed to appear in the consciousness of the boys hazed, between passion emotion seemingly evoked by the girl spectators, and thwarted dominance felt toward their male oppressors, the sophomores. The latter unmistakably prevailed, however, and several of the freshmen violently broke away from the sophomore guards. It seemed quite predictable, from the self observations of the freshmen boys, that they would have greatly enjoyed a fairly pure type of passion emotion had the actual captors who exerted the superior force over them been girls rather than other males. The normal boy seems to have learned to regard other males as fundamentally inimical to his interests, while girls, though they may be treated with pretended scorn and disfavour, are fundamentally regarded as friendly and loving.

Conclusions From Study

Our general conclusions in the study cited were :

(1) That pure passion emotion could seldom, if ever, be elicited from one normal male by another, within the group of college boys studied.

(2) That strong passion emotion could be evoked from a majority of the boys studied by girls who made the boys captive in the same way they treated the freshman girls, provided that girls could be found of sufficient strength, emotional or physical, to impress themselves upon the male subjects, by inducement as superior to the males, without evoking their dominance.

Summary

In general, it seems fair to summarize the passion emotion of the male sex as not evokable by other males, in the absence of genital organ stimulation. This conclusion may be qualified by reference to the type of males previously alluded to, whose passion emotion development is sufficiently strong to permit passion to persist under military, or other subjections by superior males, despite the preponderance of dominance behaviour indulged in by such male subjectors.

CHAPTER XV

Love Mechanisms

In view of the foregoing analysis showing the occurrence of both captivation and passion responses without environmental stimulation of the genital organs, it seems hardly necessary to emphasize the fact that these organs are not to be regarded as the sole source of the love responses. Captivation and passion are compound types of integrations which may be evoked by various types of adequate stimuli. The genital organs, however, seem especially designed to bring about love integrations, just as the digestive organs are especially designed to bring about the proper integrative pattern of appetite emotion. The genital organs also serve, very probably, as circular reinforcing mechanisms for love excitement having its origin in receptors totally different from those located in the genital organs themselves. It is possible that motor discharge from the compound emotions of captivation and passion may find its way toward internal and external genitals in certain fixed proportions, just as it is possible that motor discharge from desire and satisfaction may always find its way to the alimentary canal and skeletal muscles of appetite, in certain fixed proportions of volume of discharge. But these possibilities both require experimental proof before formulation even of tentative hypotheses. In any event, *the genital organs, like the digestive mechanisms, are to be regarded as natural, automatic teachers of the compound emotional responses which they are suited to initiate.* That the genital organs are equipped automatically to evoke captivation and submission emotions can be made clear by a brief consideration of the structures and functions of these mechanisms after sexual maturity of the individual. Both sexes possess two sets of genital organs, internal and external.

Genital Organ Mechanisms

The penis is the only strictly external genital organ of the male, the testes, and their appurtenant structures being

317

classified as internal genitals, though actually outside the sexually mature male body. The internal genital organs of the female begin, properly speaking, at the mouth of the vagina. There seems to be a great deal of ignorance, especially among women, concerning the nature and functioning of the female clitoris, which nevertheless corresponds precisely in psychical function to the penis of the male. Some speculative theories of biological evolution have assumed that the female clitoris is a relic of a bisexual condition of the race, which the present human body structure has developed away from. Whatever the historical aspect of the matter may be, psycho-neural results of clitoral stimulation seem to be identical with those produced by stimulation of the external genital organ of the male. Furthermore, though the fact seems little known, the clitoris of one woman may be stimulated nearly as effectively by the vulva of another woman, as can the penis of a male with the vagina of the female. The female emotion resulting from stimulation of the clitoris by another woman (as apparent in the behaviour of women prisoners) seems fully as extensive as the male emotion resulting from stimulation of the penis. In this type of physical relationship, both women most frequently experience simultaneous stimulation of the clitoris with appropriate emotional states following. Neither woman, of course, receives stimulation of the mouth of the vagina.

Langley and Anderson arrived at an apparently accurate description of the innervations of the internal and external genital organs as early as 1895.[1]   In both male and female the external genital organs are innervated mainly through the nervi erigentes while the internal genitals are innervated through sympathetic rather than sacral fibres. Though Cannon and others have emphasized the reciprocal antagonism existing between the sympathetic branch of the autonomic nervous system and the sacral division of the same system, Langley stated in one of his most comprehensive articles defending the concept of the autonomic nervous system, which was originated by himself, that absolute or complete reciprocal antagonisms between the innervations of the central and end branches of the autonomic did not in fact exist.[2]

[1] J. N. Langley and H. K. Anderson, " The Innervation of the Pelvic and Adjoining Viscera," *Journal of Physiology*, 1895, vol. 19, p. 85.
[2] J. N. Langley, " Sympathetic and Other Related Systems of Nerves," Schafer's *Textbook of Physiology*, 1900, vol. 2, pp. 616-697.

*Motor Self Simultaneously Energizes Internal and External
• Genitals*

The most casual observations of so-called sexual behaviour
in animals shows that an extraordinary amount of activity
of the skeletal muscles may be indulged in by the male animal
in seeking the female, and in getting himself accepted by her,
with complete erection of the penis persisting throughout this
period of marked skeletal muscular activity. Since the skeletal
muscles, to be active, must be supplied with an added amount
of blood through the mediation of the sympathetic impulses,
we know that portions, at least, of the sympathetic system
must be co-active with similarly increased discharge through
the sacral nervi erigentes. Moreover, blood pressure and pulse
measurements taken upon human subjects throughout sexual
intercourse reveal that a rise of systolic blood pressure, indicating increased strength of the heart beat produced by
sympathetic impulses, proceeds, during certain phases of love
behaviour, *pari passu* with increased determination of blood
to the external genital organs brought about by sacral innervations.

This simultaneous increase of both sympathetic and sacral
motor discharge is to be contrasted with the decrease of the
sympathetic impulses to the blood vessels of the arm at the
height of hunger pangs apparently simultaneously with the
successful cranial discharge to the salivary glands and through
vagus channels to the heart. From this we may conclude
that, whereas the normal tonic balance of the organism
maintained by the *motor self calls for a marked preponderance
of sympathetic over cranial motor discharge of tonic nature, this
same reflex balance maintained by the motor self calls for a
simultaneous and allied discharge through sympathetic channels
to the internal genitals and through the sacral efferent paths to
the external genital organs.* The usual tonic condition of the
organism, aside from inhibitory influences of the cortex,
probably would maintain a slight preponderance of motor
discharge to the internal genital organs as contrasted with the
motor discharge to the external genital organs, since the latter
are not found in a state of erection except as a result of special
stimulation.

All Motor Stimuli Activating Genitals Are Allied

If this analysis of the balance maintained by the motor self between internal and external genitals is correct, any motor stimulus which tended to seek outlet either in the internal or external genital organs would be allied to the motor self. Motor stimuli which tended to enhance motor discharge to the internal genital organs however, would be in a relationship of submission to the usual balance maintained within the motor self. *If the motor self increased for the purpose of compelling these motor stimuli to follow efferent paths to the internal genital organs, this reaction would coincide with the proposed definition of the primary emotional response of inducement.*

If, on the other hand, a motor stimulus tended to find a path of efferent discharge toward the external genital organs, it would be regarded as in a relationship of inducement to the motor self. *If the motor self decreased to permit additional external genital excitement by the motor stimulus then the reaction would be described as a primary emotional response of submission.*

No Cyclic Love Stimulus in Male Organism

With the meaning of motor stimuli in relation to the motor self thus analysed, we may proceed to discover, if possible, the sequence of integrations between motor self and motor stimuli which occur in the course of inter-sex love behaviour. A number of physiological researchers have endeavoured, in vain, to discover the symptoms of a spontaneous cycle of intra-organic love stimulation in the male, comparable in any way to the menstrual cycle of woman. Males seem to possess no such automatic stimulatory mechanism for initiation of love behaviour as the menses in human females, or periods of heat in females of various higher animal species. It seems to be true that during adolescence boys may experience uncontrolled excitement especially in the external genital organs, with erection of the latter not attributable to any external stimulation. After sexual maturity, however, such occurences seem very rare with the normal male.

Attempts have been made by various authors to establish intra-organic causes for the initiation of love excitement in males such as distention of the seminal vesicles, or even urination. But during my own studies I have found not the slightest evidence of the cyclic operation of any such stimuli inducing spontaneous male excitement. Instances of this sort, when they do occur, seem to me possibly traceable (as I have actually traced them in several cases) to previous sensory stimulation with erotic environmental stimuli. The love excitement which occurs normally in many men during sleep, also seems attributable to previous erotic stimulation, motor discharge from which has been inhibited during waking hours. Such nocturnal periods of love excitement occur just as frequently with young women subjects as with males, and cannot, therefore, be attributed to any secondary sexual hormone peculiar to the male sex. What these occasional spontaneous erections of the external genital organs do show, I believe, is that the tonic balance normally maintained by the motor self is so evenly distributed between internal and external genitals, that a slight diminution of inhibitory influence from the cortex (as during sleep) may bring about a shifting of the balance, if there is only a slight amount of dammed up motor energy, previously evoked by erotic stimuli, which has not been completely discharged during the preceding waking period. My own conclusion is that adult males do not possess any automatic intra-organic stimulus mechanism, appearing without any connection with erotic environmental stimuli previously experienced. So far as I have been able to determine, the normal male, after sexual maturity, at least, must depend upon external stimulation which includes, of course, ideas and remembered sensations or "images", to evoke from him either captivation or passion emotions.

Love Stimulus Cycle in Women

With girls and women, however, we find an entirely different situation. Reports from at least fifty female subjects reveal marked accession of love excitement before the menstrual period, or just following it, or at both times. A small number of cases, studied carefully, reveal a certain difference between the love excitement in the period just before the menstrual period, and the love emotion during the interval following it. (During the period itself there may also be love excitement but since this usually finds no expression in effecting inter-sex relationships, it may be disregarded for the moment.) The stimulation which must be going on in the internal genital organs just prior to the menstrual period, due to the growth and maturation of the Graafian follicle, and also to the tissue changes in the uterus, and determination of blood to the entire internal genital organ tract, appears to result in a more

Y

restless and intensely aggressive type of love seeking than that immediately following the period.

pIaS Evoked During Menses (?)

Immediately following the menstrual period, the love seeking behaviour of the female seems, in the cases mentioned, to contain a larger element of submission. Love excitement at this time is introspectively reported as more pervasive and voluminous than before the period. The evidence indicates that at both times (as well as throughout the period in many cases) motor stimuli are evoked which tend to follow efferent paths toward both internal and external genitals. The presence of the latter can easily be detected by observing the condition of the clitoris, vulva, and sometimes marked alteration in the output of the vulvo-vaginal glands. Following the period, the general nature of the love excitement, in some cases, at least, indicates that there is a greater proportion of external genital excitement than exists prior to the period. The indications seem to be that this external genital excitement following the period is in the nature of an after discharge from still greater external genital excitement during the period itself. In some cases, careful self observations clearly revealed the fact that this excitement of the external genitals was noticably increased, during the menstrual period itself by the wearing of a pad which stimulates the clitoris mechanically. External excitement seems, then, normally, to be in preponderance over motor discharge to the internal genitals during the period itself. The menstrual period, on this analysis, would be a period of passive love (pIaS).

aIpS Follows Menstrual Period

Assuming, then, that the total menstrual stimulation results in enhancement of motor discharge to both internal and external genitals, but preponderantly to the latter, we may analyse the primary emotional responses evoked without difficulty. Motor stimuli of both submissive (to internal genitals) and inductive (to external genitals) types appear to be evoked. The overt response of the organism, consisting of obviously increased love restlessness, motor energy, and excitement, evidences a marked increase in the strength of the motor self. Since this increase of the motor self appears to represent the total algebraic sum of its reaction to the stimuli imposed, we may assume that *a response of active inducement predominates.*

Yet this active inducement cannot restore the initial reflex balance of the organism, since it is evident that a considerable mass of motor discharge is still winning its way to the external genital organs. Toward the stimuli responsible for this discharge, therefore, the motor self is in a state of *passive submission response.*

Female Seeks Male

It will be remembered that hunger pangs evoke motor stimuli rendering the organism incapable of response to any type of environmental stimulus save food. Food, in this case, represented an environmental stimulus stronger than the hunger pangs but weaker than the organism. The subject could, therefore, dominate food at the same time that he complied passively with the hunger pangs. The love response situation brought about by motor stimuli evoked by the menstrual period is identical with this appetitive stimulus situation with respect to the general method by which it compels the organism to react in a prescribed manner to one type of stimulus only. Following her menstrual period, a woman is forced to seek a male, since the body structure of a male enables the woman to respond to him with active inducement ; while at the same time she is responding with passive submission to a portion of the menstrual period stimuli. Just as the food could be dominated by the hungry subject, because the food would in turn dominate the hunger pangs which had proved stronger than the subject, so in the love stimulus situation the woman is able actively to induce a male, because the male is a stimulus weaker than the woman, but stronger than the motor stimuli exciting the woman's external genitals, which had proved stronger than the woman's own motor self.

A moment's consideration of the type of love stimulation which the male's body is designed to give the female, will make this point clear. The penis, extending within the mouth of the vagina, stimulates directly the internal genital organs of the female. Assuming that the motor discharge from this stimulation tends to return to the internal genitals via the sympathetic ganglia, just as motor discharge from stomach stimulation tends to return again through cranial efferents to the stomach, we find that stimuli furnished by the male to the female during physical love contact possesses two characteristics. First, the motor stimuli evoked are completely submissive to the female's own motor self balance. Second, these submissive motor stimuli follow the prescribed path to the internal genital organs, and so tend to increase the discharge to the internal genitals until the motor discharge to the external genitals, set up by menstrual period stimulation, is completely counteracted and the motor self's balance is restored.

This restoration of balance may thus be accomplished by the motor stimuli resulting from male stimulation, whereas restoration of balance could not be accomplished by the female's own motor self, prior to stimulation by the male. This means, as previously shown, that *the woman is simultaneously feeling active inducement emotion toward the male and passive submission emotion toward the menstrual period stimuli, still active within her body.*

When the motor stimuli evoked in a woman's organism by the male finally completely counterbalance the stimuli sending motor discharge to the external genitals, an overwhelming of the latter occurs (possibly in the nature of a partial inhibition), while a series of rhythmic contractions are set up in the uterus and vagina, constituting sexual orgasm. This particular type of female orgasm is sometimes called by women an "internal orgasm". It represents consummation of active inducement response toward the male which has culminated in the capturing of sufficient allied stimuli to counterbalance for the moment, at least, the menstrual period stimuli evoking passive submission. This overwhelming of external genital excitement is only temporary, even three or four "internal" orgasms in succession failing to abolish the aIpS set, which lasts for as long a time as the after discharge of menstrual stimuli remains active.

Male Body Suited For Passion Stimulation Only

Since the internal genitals of the male can at no time be directly stimulated by contact with the female, the male's overt response throughout the sex relationship is one of *active submission* evoked by cumulatively increased stimulation of his *external* genital organ, which is completely surrounded (captured ?) by the woman's internal genital organ, the vagina. We noted, in Chapter XI, that erection of the penis was a submissive type of reaction, made possible by the allied motor stimuli (from tickling,* stroking, etc.), which were able to direct the motor self into this sacral channel of discharge, because superior to the motor self in possessing strength to overcome the usually operating cortical inhibition. We have just observed, in the present paragraph, that further stimulation of the penis evoking submission, occurs when the penis is kept within the vagina of the woman. *But, in order to keep it there, a continuous increment of increase must be maintained by the motor self, sufficient to maintain erection.* This increment of increase of the self continuously extends the part to be stimulated, thus inviting and making possible the stimulation of this part by the only appropriately constructed part of the woman's body. *Such increase of motor self to procure further stimulation to submission constitutes passive inducement.*

It is exactly the same type of response that the child makes in extending its feet and hands to be further tickled and stimulated, cited in the last chapter as evidence of passive inducement in infant love behaviour. It is the same type of response, also, made by the freshman girl who held out her hands to invite a sophomore to place more bonds about them thus evoking further submission. Extension of the penis, to receive stimulation is simply a specialized type of this general passive inducement behaviour, suitable as an inducement only to a specialized type of captivating organism, namely the internal genitals of a woman.

Throughout the inter-sex love act, then, the male expresses passive inducement (increase of motor self) sufficient to render his body stimulable by the woman's body. He simultaneously expresses active submission in movements of the penis and body evoked by pressure of the vagina surrounding his external genital organ. *This simultaneous compounding of active submission and passive inducement constitute physical passion emotion.*

Climax of Male Response Is Active Love

The male sexual orgasm is quite different from the female " internal orgasm " just described. The male orgasm, appears, it would seem, when such a large increment of the male's motor self has been released by external genital stimulation, that the total strength of the self is greater than the total strength of the motor stimuli which had hitherto been compelling the self to submission. When'this shift in the balance of strength between the two integrative elements occurs, the motor self assumes control of the situation, and immediately returns to its qwn reflex balance. This balance, according to our foregoing analysis, calls for a preponderance of motor discharge to the internal genitals. When the motor self returns to this balance, therefore, carrying with it, by *active* inducement, the newly captured, allied motor stimuli, to which it had formerly been submitting, the internal genitals are contracted clonically, a series of rhythmic muscular spasms is set up, and this series of spasms ejects the spermatozoa, contained in their appropriate fluid medium.

During the male orgasm, it is obvious that the phase of love emotion expressed has shifted from passive to active. The male's passive inducement has become active inducement. His motor self, which has been permitted only to increase sufficiently to keep the penis erect, is now increased so greatly that it returns to its own predetermined balance, carrying the newly captured motor stimuli with it. That is to say, the male now *actively* induces the female to a wholly new emotional response of *creation*, by ejecting active generative agents into her body.

At the same time, the active submission of the male changes to *passive* submission. He no longer permits his motor self to discharge its efferent energy under the control and direction of the motor stimuli evoked by the female's vagina. But the male, nevertheless, during the orgasm, *passively* submits to the woman, in that he permits her internal genital organs to induce in his the muscular spasms necessary to the procreative act. That is to say, the motor self of the male remains sufficiently under the control of the motor stimuli previously evoked by vaginal stimulation of his external genital organ to condition the active inducement to direct its total, induced stimuli primarily toward the internal genital organs, rather than toward any one or all of the large number of motor self channels to the skeletal muscles and adjoining viscera, now freely opened (though the excitement spreads, considerably, to the clasping muscles, also).

Thus it is, that the male shifts his love expression, at its very climax, from passion to captivation. It is a captivation designed, however, not to captivate the female responses for his own control, but rather to captivate them for the control of the child to come, created as a result of this culmination of the male's passionate submission to the female.

The chief difference between the female's " internal orgasm " and the male orgasm is one of similarity or contrast to the previously existing type of emotional response controlling the subject. The woman has been expressing active love, or captivation, and this active love emotion culminates in an inducement of menstrually evoked motor stimuli so complete that the latter, for a brief period, are overwhelmed, and are compelled to join in activating the internal genital muscles to clonic contraction. But it is very easy for the female organism to return to its previous state of active love, since only a slight relaxation of the climactic intensity of internal genital stimulation is necessary to permit the temporarily induced motor stimuli to resume their previous rôle of inducers to passive submission by discharge again, into the clitoris. But it is not so easy for the male to return to a condition of passion response. His newly acquired active love set must be precisely reversed before passion response can again control the male organism. To accomplish this result, further stimulation of the external genitals from without the body must take place, and must continue until a large enough increment of the motor self is again determined to the penis, by means of its submission to the motor stimuli evoked, to maintain the external genital organ in a state of erection, or passive inducement. This process may require a considerable interval of quiescense, between the active love climax and the restoration of submissive passion set, once more. Thus a much briefer period of recovery is required between one " internal orgasm " of the female and another (perhaps no interval at all), than the quiescent period elapsing between active love orgasm of the male and renewed passion response.

Woman is capable, as before mentioned, of experiencing both phases of love emotion. By means of clitoral stimulation by another woman (or by some artificial stimulation such as tongue or hand), passion response may be evoked in exactly the same way as it is called forth from the male by stimulation of his penis. The orgasm may follow this passion emotion, in exactly the same way that it follows the passion of the male ; in which case, the orgasm represents the same transition from passion to captivation. (Evidently because the creation emotion character of this climactic active love expression, terminating passion, is perceived by the love-trained consciousness of women having this type of love relationship, it is frequently regarded with a sort of worship, as an emotional experience inviolably sacred, a feeling seldom attained by males during the same behaviour). This type of orgasm is frequently called, by women, the " external orgasm ". The female external orgasm seems likely to persist somewhat longer than its male counterpart, and to be followed by a physical state of more profound lassitude, and inertia.

Some women subjects report that they receive a considerable amount of stimulation of the clitoris during an ordinary act of coitus. Other women subjects can detect little or no stimulation of the clitoris during physical contact with a male. The question seems to be one of relationship between the position of the clitoris and the other structures involved. Women seldom experience an orgasm of the external type as a result of stimulation of the clitoris during relationship with the male. Such external genital stimulation as they do receive, however, frequently leaves female subjects in a condition of passion response after consummating the physical love contact with the male. This passion response cannot be gratified, apparently, by any number of orgasms of internal type.

Men Like To Confuse Love and Appetite

In considering the love seeking behaviour of both women and men, the fact must constantly be borne in mind that appetite emotion is inextricably confused with love responses in the emotional equipment of nearly all subjects. We have already cited a number of cases showing the tendency, especially in the male, to confuse inducement with dominance and captivation emotion with appetitive desire seeking satisfaction. The popular terms for love responses reveal clearly, not only the unconscious confusion between appetite and love, but also the dominant delight which many male authors seem to take in perpetuating this confusion.

To call love " appetite " places it at once in a category which the male can understand and dominate. If even active love, or captivation emotion be recognized as a reaction during which the subject must be wholly controlled by alliance with the interests of the person captivated, the response becomes repugnant to the average male because it means that *he is not getting, but giving*, and the only justification for giving, to the minds of most males, is the possibility of a larger getting to follow. It is dominantly satisfying to a male to think of the love responses as a mere additional source of pleasure, which he can obtain in the ways he is accustomed to obtain appetitive satisfaction ; that is, through the exercise of dominance and compliance.

If love emotions are thought of as depending wholly upon the degree to which a male is willing to submit to another person, especially a woman, the realization at once follows that he, the male, is no longer able to rule, by his dominance, this love half of life which he knows to be by far the most pleasant. If love is recognized for what it is, it means that the *male can never obtain a place of real superiority in love except by learning to become more submissive in proportion to his dominance than is woman.* All this is not consciously thought out, of course, but it will be found to exist, I believe, to some degree, as an emotional undercurrent, in the attitude of nearly all males toward love.

As a consequence of this typical male set, we find, in both popular and scientific literature, which has, for the most part, been written by men not controlled by women, or by women closely controlled by male standards and conventions, a series of more or less deliberately devised misnomers for the love responses. Active love, for example, becomes in male nomenclature " desire " ; passive love, or passion response is designated as an " appetite ", and is further separated from such commendable though somewhat anaemic states of emotional consciousness as " love of virtue ", by characterizing physical love as a " sex appetite ". The inference is plain. The members of each sex are represented by this simple mischaracterization of love as seeking to devour one another, and to possess one another dominantly, each for his own appetitive satisfaction. Persons who insist upon perpetuating their own confusions between love and appetite by defending such a conception are simply engaged in a dominant attempt to escape reality.

Love, Used For Appetite, Must Nevertheless Be Love

As we have seen in the case of inducement response used as a tool to procure appetitive satisfaction, the love response must remain a non-dominant reaction in its entirety if it is to evoke a corresponding love response from the stimulus person, no matter what may be the eventual result of this succession of love reactions. Those who would use love for appetite must first learn to love ; and after that, they must be willing to love sincerely, during the entire period necessary to establish absolute possession over the thing they want to get from the person Judasaically loved. If the seeker starts to dominate the other individual just a few minutes or a few seconds too soon, his ultimate purpose is lost. The love response cannot be termed an appetite, therefore, except in prospect or in retrospect ; that is before the love response is initiated, at which time the ultimate appetitive benefit is being selected and planned, and the period immediately succeeding the termination of the love response itself, when appetitive satisfaction of the result gained is being enjoyed.

Of course, during the persistence of the love response itself, appetitive reactions may mingle in the total behaviour pattern. But in so far as appetite does so mingle with love, the responses evoked from other persons will similarly contain a mixture of appetitive self seeking. Therefore, the efficiency of the love response as a tool for dominance and appetite must be diminished by just so much. *The love seeking of one individual by another is not to be thought of as a desire to eat or to possess the loved one. It can only properly be described as a seeking to establish a relationship with that other individual wherein the seeker may give himself more completely to the person sought, by allying himself more closely with the other's interests.*

It is customarily asserted that women " desire " to captivate males for their own pleasure, even if there is no more sordid financial motive in establishing the relationship. A woman who does seek her own pleasure in captivating a male cannot obtain that pleasure in the manner sought because no love relationship can ever be established. Or, to put the matter in a more positive way, if a woman captivates a male in a true love relationship with herself, she does so by evoking a true passion response from the male. In order to evoke this response, the woman must continually study the male's emotional mechanisms, and stimulate him only in strictest accord with these mechanisms. Furthermore, *she must stimulate the male more effectively, that is, in a way which will give him more pleasure, than any other influence then exerted upon him is able to do.* In short, to captivate a male, a woman must evoke within his organism the greatest possible pleasantness. Her pleasure must consist only in effectively increasing his.

The moment there enters into the woman's total response pattern a desire which seeks to compel the male to stimulate her in some way temporarily pleasant to her but not pleasant to him, at that moment the captivation of the male by the female is diminished by a corresponding amount. The desire gets just what it seeks, that is, an appetitive satisfaction which the male continues to deliver to the female during the length of time that the previous love influence of the woman persists and captivation endures. She has begun to reap an appetitive reward, obtained as a result of a preceding love response. But the love response itself is no longer working, so the woman can only seize as much as she is able before the effect of her previous love response upon the male wears off. If she would gain further appetitive rewards by the prostitution-of-love method, she must abandon again all desire for her own pleasure and seek to evoke, again, the greatest possible pleasantness in the male's consciousness. There may be, of course, deliberate deceptions on the part of a captivating woman (see Chapter XVII) and misinterpretations of the woman's behaviour on the part of the male, but such misinterpretations do not in the least alter the essential quality of the stimulus to which the male is reacting, the only issue being whether the adequate stimulus actually exists in the woman, or whether it merely exists in the man's own central nervous system only.

The following results of love behaviour have no exceptions : *Neither captivation emotion nor passion emotion contains desire or satisfaction in any form. Love emotion contains no appetitive response in any form. Admixtures of desire or satisfaction responses with captivation and passion responses, when controlled by the two appetitive elements, result in the supplanting of captivation and passion by desire and satisfaction.*

Overt Love Behaviour Prior To Sexual Union

The woman's period of passive love, or passion response ends, as we have seen, at the close of the menstrual period.

Thereafter the normal and uninhibited woman begins to seek a male in order to captivate him. The adult male's love responses do not, as a general rule, begin until he has been initially stimulated by a woman or by some correspondingly adequate stimulus. The man's reactions from the first are those of passive love response, or passion.

Some of the frankest and clearest-cut types of captivation of males by women are those accomplished by chorus girls and dancers. The theatre offers a stimulus situation sanctioned by society, wherein a woman passively submitting to her own inner urges (intraorganic stimuli resulting in stimulations of external genitals) reacts toward the man in the audience in such a way as to stimulate his organism, to the maximum extent, with display and movement of her own body. The girl on the stage, in strict accordance with the nature of captivation emotion, observes and analyses the male emotional mechanisms to the best of her ability (or the theatrical producer does this for her); and she practices assiduously to stimulate these male mechanisms in such a way as to evoke, through them, the maximum amount of pleasure in the male. As soon as this stimulation begins to be effective in evoking passion response in the male consciousness, which is, of course, intensely pleasant, to the man, a motor discharge from this passion type of integration immediately results in a series of active submission responses on the part of the male, to the woman's psycho-physical mechanisms.

The first of such active submissions may consist of sending flowers, and of securing an introduction to the woman in order that he may pay verbal tribute to her beauty and captivation powers. These responses, in turn, evoke further captivation behaviour from the woman, which again cumulatively increases the male's passion, with its overt active submission element. The male becomes a constant attendant upon his captivatress, obeying her spoken commands and seeking to submit to her inarticulate emotional nature in every way possible. Of course, this programme may partially degenerate into a process of purchase and sale; but if so, the male gets only what he buys, an appetitive satisfaction without any love relationship. When eventually the woman's captivation response, and the male's passion emotion control their organisms to the degree of establishing a physical love relationship, the captivation stimulus actually evokes changes in the male's body desighed to enable the woman's body to capture it physically, as we have already noted.

Love Union of Sexes

The woman's body by means of appropriate movements and vaginal contractions, continues to captivate the male body, which has altered its form precisely for that purpose. Thus the responses of captivation and passion are cumulatively enhanced up to the moment when the sexual orgasm occurs in one or the other subject. It seems possible from the nature of the structures involved that the female orgasm should be allowed to occur first. The greatly intensified contractions of the vagina, during this occurrence, coupled with greatly increased muscular pressure exerted upon the male by the female seem designed to call forth a culmination of passion from the male. It is quite certain that the female orgasm is likely never to occur at all, if the male orgasm is permitted to occur first. A large number of married women report that they never have experienced an orgasm since marriage for this very reason.

When the seemingly normal sequence of responses is followed, the male experiences a brief period of active love, or captivation emotion, immediately following the culmination, and consequent cessation of the woman's captivation response. At this moment, as we have already noted, the excitement from incidental stimulation of the clitoris is likely to be the prevailing stimulus within the woman's body, changing her own emotional response momentarily at least, from captivation to passion. This passion emotion like the male's culminating captivation response with which it coincides, is not to be considered as part of the initial love response sequence, but rather represents the beginning of a new *creation* response series, having for its purpose the creation and nourishment of a child to come.

Need For Training of Male in Coitus Reservatus

The sequence of love responses suggested as most nearly normal are by no means most frequent of occurrence in ordinary inter-sex love relationships. Up to the point of physical contact between woman and male, the behaviour just described is fairly typical, especially in those instances where the woman has received previous captivation response training, such as that given dancers' and chorus girls in their preparation for passion-stimulating stage spectacles. After bodily relationship is established, however, the outstanding feature of male response is apt to be an attempt to assume the rôle of captivatress as expeditiously as possible. Physically, this takes the form of usurping the woman's rôle of love aggressor as much as possible and hastening the act to its conclusion by what amounts to masturbation ; that is, using the woman's vagina, instead of the hand as a stimulating surface against which to move the penis. The average male's notion of physical love relationship seems to be to obtain a sexual orgasm as quickly as possible. The result of this behaviour is well known. The male orgasm occurs long before the woman has received sufficient vaginal stimulation to bring her captivation response to its climax. The woman, therefore, is deprived of a major proportion of her love experience, and of its final culmination. The male who thus prematurely terminates his own passion as well as the woman's captivation behaviour effectively limits and in time destroys altogether his enjoyment of bodily passion.

Such writers as Havelock Ellis, and H. W. Long, M.D., recognize the necessity for coitus reservatus on the part of the male. " The orgasm ", says Long, " is not the desideratum in this case."[1] Ellis gives a brief history of communities in which the males have been trained, by women, to practice coitus reservatus, with no deleterious physical results, and with great enhancement of pleasantness for both women and males.[2] It is a well recognized fact[3] that the consummation of the woman's physical captivation emotion by means of an internal orgasm requires a much longer period than is necessary to produce the male orgasm, where the male permits himself unrestrained physical movement with consequent self stimulation.

In order to adjust the time sequence of captivation and passion responses, as well as to secure maximal pleasantness and completeness of emotion throughout the physical love relationship, it is obvious that the passion response must be controlled by the captivating stimulus at all times. In other

---

[1] H. W. Long, *Sane Sex Life and Sane Sex Living*, Boston, 1919, p. 129.
[2] Havelock Ellis, *Studies in the Psychology of Sex*, Philadelphia, 1922, vol. VI, p. 552 ff.
[3] H. W. Long, *ibid*, p. 70.

words, the male after learning coitus reservatus, must place himself completely under the control of the woman during physical love relationship, just as he had done, perforce, during courtship when only passion response would suffice to bring about the longed for love relationship with the woman who has captivated him.

Dr. Long advises the male to lie beneath the woman, instead of in the more common position expressive of male dominance. He says : " It is now the *woman* and not the *man* who has *full control* of such meeting, and so can regulate it to her *liking and needs*."[1] Long further emphasizes the fact that the greatest mistake of all marital life is the supposition, " by both an uninitiated husband and an innocent wife, that all the motion should originate with the husband, while the woman should lie still and let him do it all ".[2] After further pointing out the awkwardness and unnaturalness of the physical position with the male superior, Long maintains that it is the woman and not the male who should initiate all the movements of both parties to the relationship. The male's movements should only occur as responses to the woman's, and when permitted by her. In this admirable advice, the doctor recognizes the necessity for the woman's captivation response to prevail throughout the relationship.

Margaret Sanger, who has had practical opportunity to study a very large number of cases of inter-sex love relationships in the course of her work on Birth Control, writes : " Here is the crux of the marital problem. For centuries women have been taught by custom and prejudice, especially in countries in which the Puritanic tradition dominates, that hers should be a passive, dutiful rôle—to submit but not to participate. Likewise men have been schooled by tradition to seek mere selfish gratification. This lack of constructive experience is responsible for the thousands of unhappy marriages and the tragic, wasted lives of many wives, cheated by thoughtlessness and ignorance of their legitimate right to marital joy.

" Much would be accomplished if women were taught to be active and men to check the tumultuous expression of their passion."[3]

[1] H. W. Long, *Sane Sex Life and Sane Sex Living*, Boston, 1919, p. 107.
[2] H. W. Long, *ibid*, p. 81.
[3] Margaret Sanger, *Happiness in Marriage*, New York, 1926, pp. 139-140.

Dominance Controlling Love Thwarts Both Love and Appetite

It is undoubtedly a product of the chronic male control of love by dominance that has led to the curious method of physical love relations between women and males prevalent in Western civilization. In the Orient, where love is practised as an art the necessity of woman's comple te control of physical love behaviour is recognized freely, no matter whether the woman be wife or slave girl. We find numerous evidences in such literature as the Arabian Nights, that Oriental potentates, while indulging in love, are sufficiently intelligent to surrender their bodies completely over to the ministration and control of their captivatresses.

The influence of dominant suppressions and appetitive perversions of natural love behaviour have had a profound and devastating effect upon Western civilization, so far as the development of subtler emotional and " spiritual " values are concerned. The reason that Main Street lacks æsthetic value is primarily the fact that Main Streeters of both sexes turn their love as completely into appetite as possible. They tend to regard it as " wicked ", and " immoral " for women to devote their time and attention deliberately to the learning of captivation emotion, while males, thus deprived of passion at home, seek it elsewhere.

With the appetitive supremacy which an average man gains at marriage, it is expected that the woman's previous captivation attitude toward the male will suddenly conform to the appetitive situation, and will convert itself into passion. The male, on the other hand, tries to regard himself as the captivatress from the moment he obtains unhampered physical access to contact with the woman's body. But the natural emotional rôles for which the two bodies are fitted by reason of sex differences of structure, cannot be reversed in this highhanded fashion. The result of attempting to reverse them is simply a cessation of physical love. At best, there may be a partial substitution of mutual enjoyment of appetitive satisfactions, in the way of home comforts, property and social activities. At worst (and this is more usual) there ensue quarrels over money and appetitive amusements,

Judge Lindsey reported[1] many cases observed by himself, personally, in which a woman and man lived together in completely pleasant love relationship, until the marriage ceremony was performed. Thereafter, appetite replaced love until a divorce was sought. In one case reported, the couple resumed their previously happy love relationship, under the belief that a divorce had been granted, although, as a matter of fact, Judge Lindsey had not signed the papers. Upon learning this fact, both the woman and the man begged the Judge to sign their decree, so that they would not have to separate again ! In such cases, it seems very clear that the male could not continue to feel himself wholly captive to the woman in their love relations when he had, as a matter of fact, assumed supreme control of the partnership by supplying all the money. *While the woman, also, was working, and was paying her part of the expenses, it was borne in upon the man's consciousness continually that his relationship with the girl was by her suffrance only.* She could terminate their relationship at any time she chose, and would undoubtedly do so if the male ceased to submit to her love captivation responses. This seems to be the plain, emotional fact in the matter, however much dominant resistance the majority of males may feel to acknowledging that their bodies are devised for passion response, while women's bodies are designed for the capture of males and not for submission to them.

Woman's Passion

A further problem presents itself in connection with women's expression of passion emotion in relationship with other women. I am free to confess that when I undertook to study this type of love relationship, I had not the slightest idea of its importance in the emotional life of women, nor of the prevalence of such relationships among women whose love conduct happened to be relatively uninhibited, due either to previous experience, or captivation and passion relationships between upper class college girls and freshmen, where no genital organ stimulation occurred. I was aware from personal observation that young women living together in a home might evoke from one another extremely pleasant and pervasive love responses, of both

[1] Judge Ben B. Lindsey and W. Evans, *The Companionate Marriage,* New York, 1927.

types, without bodily contact or genital excitement. Upon investigating, with the invaluable aid of my collaborators, the love relationships between girls and women outside the influence of college authorities and home life, however, I found that nearly half of the female love relationships concerning which significant data could be obtained, were accompanied by bodily love stimulation.

Among cases of women dancers studied, physical love relationships with other women seem to be the rule rather than the exception. In several cases, well-adapted love relationships with husband and children were not felt to be sufficient, without supplementary love affairs with other women. The husband, in one case (an actor) reported that his own physical love contacts with his wife were more enjoyable after passion responses had been evoked from her by another girl. In this case, also, love relationships between the mother and her two children seemed to be enhanced rather than diminished at such times, so far as one could observe. Girls and women who indulge in this form of love expression appear to feel no abnormality or unnaturalness about it, and, in fact, frequently are not restrained from free physical love contact with the woman lover even by the presence of other people. A male psychologist once reported to me a case of two girl lovers, who had been separated from one another for some weeks by the college authorities. These girls performed the love act unhesitatingly in his presence, manifesting intense passion and captivation emotion respectively. According to this report, the girls regarded their love relationship as something peculiarly sacred, and though they were both reported as forming love relationships with males shortly after this occurrence, these relationships with men did not appear to detract in any way from their love for one another.

Verified instances of the same type have come to my attention in connection with love affairs of Parisienne dancers with both males and other girls. In one instance a girl begged her male lover to be allowed to perform a physical love act with another girl at the conclusion of her relationship with him, and in his presence. Recently an extremely able and eminently practical business-man told me with complete tolerance and lack of surprise, that two girl employees had been seen enjoying physical love relationship with one another, in a public portion of the office building, where the act was almost certain to be witnessed by other women workers. In reporting the general trend of female love relationships of this type, I have selected merely those cases illustrating the apparent supremacy of passion over other influences which might be thought to have had the strongest inhibitory effect upon the physical love relationship between one girl and another. So long as a woman possesses two distinct love mechanisms, both stimulable from the environment by stimulus persons of different types, it seems highly probable that she will continue to enjoy both types of love relationship whenever possible, despite attempted social prohibition of one or both varieties of love behaviour.

With regard to the possibly deleterious effect upon women's physical health of this type of love relationship with other women, I have been unable to verify a male medical opinion, given me at the beginning of my investigation, that such love affairs between girls were always injurious to their physical health. Some deleterious results appeared, however, in cases where the women who were carrying on the physical relationships in question were members of a segregated group in a penal institution. In this group of female prisoners studied, some twenty women or more, out of the total prison population (both white and negroes) of ninety-seven, were known to be carrying on love affairs with other women. Two of these women had shown loss of weight and general physical deterioration, as a result, seemingly, of the excessive amount of passion response repeatedly evoked by their female lovers, under circumstances preventing the women thus expressing passion from obtaining any counterbalance of love captivation excitement from relationships with males. In the other cases, the prison matrons and physician could determine no symptoms of physical deterioration traceable in any way to a love relationship. In several instances, on the other hand, the emotional attitude of both women lovers toward prison discipline and compulsory work, was shown to have improved after the beginning of the love affair. Other cases of captivation-passion relationships between girls which have been reported to me, where medical examinations were available, the cases being, of course, outside segretegad or institutional groups, seem to indicate that no emotional or physical results of a deleterious nature could be detected.

Love (pIaS + aIpS) Has Characteristic Complex Emotional Quality

During our discussion of appetite emotion, we observed that the simultaneous mingling or compounding of the already compound enlotions desire and satisfaction, produces an entirely new emotional quality, clearly recognized during smell and taste of food while hungry, and termed *appetite emotion.* In the same way, we may now note *that the successive blending of passion and captivation,* with captivation gradually replacing passion, produces a new and more complex emotion, love.

We have already noted, in the study of male genital mechanisms, how passive inducement changes to active inducement, and active submission to passive submission at the beginning of the orgasm. Although this shift from passive to active love appears suddenly, in male behaviour, its onset must be gradual, beginning almost at the beginning of sexual union. In female love behaviour, seeking physical relationship with a male, the change from passive to active love occurs, probably, when the woman first finds a male who responds to her active inducement, following the cyclic period of intra-organic passion stimulation, or perhaps the change occurs near the close of the period itself. Throughout inter-sex love relationship, there seems normally to be some blending of passion and captivation just as throughout the total appetitive behaviour pattern, there appears a blending of desire and satisfaction. Just as desire must yield gradually to satisfaction and must remain in complete adaptation to satisfaction, throughout appetite, so, in love, passion must be adapted to captivation throughout, and must, at some point, yield to it.

The conscious characteristic of this successive blending between passive and active love is uumistakable to anyone who has once experienced it, and seems to be identical in men and women. It is exquisitely pleasant, subtle, and delicate, yet, at its height, love is ecstatically intense and pervasive, completely blotting out all other emotions from consciousness for the time being. In love between the sexes, with mutual genital stimulation, the love phases of captivation on the part of the woman, and passion on the part of the male, may remain quite unblended, if conditions are maximally favourable, during a major portion of the entire relationship, the full love blend appearing only near the climax of both responses.

Genital Mechanisms are Teachers of Love

It must be remembered, however, that genital organ stimulation, spontaneously initiated in inter-sex behaviour by the automatic menstrual love stimulation cycle of the woman, does not represent the sole source of love. The cases considered in a preceding chapter brought out the fact that all aspects of love actually were evoked from members of both sexes by stimulus persons who did not contact or stimulate the genital organs in any way. Just as the stomach mechanisms connected with hunger pangs are to be regarded as a natural teacher of appetite emotion, and as a possible model for its further constructive development, *so genital organ stimulation, automatically initiated by the female cycle, is to be regarded as a natural teacher and model for love responses.*

The integrative relationships, however, constituting captivation and passion emotions are capable of being evoked by divers stimulus situations throughout life. During many of these love responses, when no genital stimulation whatever is occurring, a person of either sex, if properly trained in love behaviour, may frequently experience that simultaneous compounding of passion and captivation which constitutes the peculiar and unmistakable quality of pure love emotion.

CHAPTER XVI

CREATION

APPETITE and love emotions are relatively independent in the emotional organization of some subjects. But, with a majority of individuals, appetite and love appear to manifest an intricate, and often inextricably confused relationship, in the total behaviour pattern. Human beings are, of course, extremely complex organisms. It is useless to attempt, in a preliminary analysis such as this book represents, anything like a systematic presentation of the extended series of appetite-love relationships which appear in the clinical cases studied. It seems best, therefore, to emphasize the normal and efficient pattern of creation responses, combining love and appetite, which appear to be enforced upon human beings and animals in the course of reproduction. For just as the hunger mechanisms automatically evoke the natural integrative combination of desire and satisfaction into appetite emotion, and as the menstrual function automatically evokes the maximally efficient integrative combinations of passion and captivation responses into love emotion, so, in the same way, do *the reproductive mechanisms automatically evoke a natural integrative combination of love and appetite into an emotional behaviour pattern which may aptly be termed " creation ".*

Types of Physiological Relationships Between Mother and Child During Pregnancy

We have noted that at the termination of physical love relationship between woman and man, the male completes his series of love responses with a brief expression of active love, while the woman simultaneously begins a new series of love responses on her own part, by a corresponding passive love reaction. It would seem that this passive love reaction on the woman's part, consisting, it will be remembered, of the period immediately following an internal type of orgasm, is biologically designed to accompany reception of spermatazoa

342

within the vagina, the uterus eventually receiving the male germ cells without resistance. When a spermatazoon encounters the ovum, however, a process that might be described as physiological captivation of the male cell by the ovum immediately occurs. In other words, there is a mutual physiological attraction between these two cells, the ovum eventually drawing the spermatazoon into itself, and completely surrounding it. Thereafter, in the continued alliance between the two cells, the volume of the ovum predominates throughout, though it might be held that the energy of the male element precipitates the ordered series of cell divisions, shortly resulting in the appearance of the embryo.

It is the mother's responses, however, that we are primarily concerned with, rather than with the genetic origin and history of the infant.

As soon as the fertilized ovum, with its protective tissues and membranes begins its process of further development within the uterus, nutritional connections are made with the blood stream of the mother, and a definite type of relationship is set up between mother and the embryo. In this relationship, throughout the nine month period preceding birth, the embryo and fetus may be regarded as submitting to the mother, by dominating the nutritional substances furnished by the maternal organism for embryonic growth and development. This nutritional supply is placed in contact with appropriate absorptive tissues of the fetus, which must acquire or *dominate* these substances so long as it remains responsive to control by the mother's body. The mother organism, on the other hand, *complies* actively with the food materials taken into it through the stomach, for the purpose of *inducing* the fetus to grow and mature. The mother's body must comply with food from the environment and not only is the usual measure of compliance necessary to furnish materials for her own organism, but also she must comply in new ways, appropriate to the manufacture of materials necessary to the development of the new organism within her own.

This, then, is the first physiological set of relationships established between mother and child. The *mother complies actively with food from the environment in order to induce the fetus to grow. The infant organism dominates the materials furnished by drawing these materials into its own body in order to submit to the mother's inducement.*

A second set of physiological relationships seems also to be present. The mother submits passively to the presence of the other organism within her own, by passively dominating all environmental influences which might tend to injure or attack the unborn child. *Passive dominance*, in short, on the part of the mother, consists in protecting the infant organism from environmental opponents. This passive dominance is simply a means or method of carrying out the response of passive submission to which her body is impelled by its inability to function in a way divergent from the need of the smaller organism, so long as the latter is held incorporated within the mother's body. Similarly, the infant, in order passively to induce this protection from the mother, must passively comply with the physical limitations of the protective tissues and other materials placed around it. If the fetus, for instance, at a late stage in its growth, should move in such a way that the umbilical cord became twisted or a rupture in any tissue occurred, sustenance might fail the fetus, or protection might no longer be obtained from various inimical influences, probably resulting in ultimate destruction of the fetus. In simplest terms, then, *the unborn infant passively complies with the restrictive tissues with which it is surrounded, for the purpose of passively inducing the maternal organism to permit continued presence of the infant within the mother. The mother protects the unborn babe by passively dominating its antagonists for the purpose of continuing passively to submit to the needs of the infant.*

Active Creation (pAaL) Defined in Terms of Physiological Relationships

When we put these two sets of physiological relationships together, we find the following completed behaviour pattern. The mother is passively submitting and actively inducing, simultaneously. We have already seen that this particular compounding of responses constitutes *active love* or captivation response. Furthermore, the mother simultaneously is actively complying and passively dominating. This combination of responses as we have seen, constitutes *passive appetite*, or satisfaction response. Since the appetitive satisfaction attained, however, is not for the mother's own desire but for the desires of the infant, a new character of emotion is produced. *This new type of response, then, consists of passive*

appetite compounded with and adapted to active love (pAaL).
This new response compound may be termed active creation.

Passive Creation (aApL) Similarly Defined

The infant organism reacts simultaneously with passive compliance and active dominance responses. This constitutes *active appetite* or desire. At the same time, however, the unborn infant is reacting with passive inducement and active submission simultaneously. This compound response has been shown to constitute *passive love* or passion. Yet in this case, where appetitive desire is felt only for the sake of consummating passive love, we must again postulate a new type of compound emotion. *This compound response, which consists of active appetite compounded with and adapted to passive love may be termed passive creation (aApL).*

As previously emphasized, the reactions analysed in the preceding paragraphs are physiological, a major portion of the adjustments of the maternal body, and practically all adaptations of embryonic and fetal growth to maternal stimuli, being mediated through the blood, which carries appropriate hormones. Nevertheless, there must be a considerable volume of inter-uterine stimulation adequate to motor discharge back again to the internal genitals, with changes, also, in appetitive stimulations. The resulting integrative picture possibly approximates pAaL, though the integrations evidently occur, for the most part, at sub-cortical levels, giving little introspectively discernable love emotion, and certainly no new creation emotion consciousness which the subject herself is able to observe and report upon.

Active Creation of Mother After Birth of Child

Immediately after birth, however, the situation is changed. The infant, normally, is now nourished at the mother's breast. The mother, therefore, receives stimulation of the nipples from the child's mouth, and some manipulation of the breast itself by the child's hands. Watson, and others, have observed that the resulting experience to the mother is of an erotic variety. That is, in our own terms, a captivation reaction seems to appear, evoked by breast stimulation, plus the other stimulations of holding the child against the body, and perception of the child's behaviour indicating need of nourishment with subsequent satisfaction of the need by means of milk supplied by the mother. There is considerable evidence that the breasts of the mother are intimately connected with the internal genital organs, since the breasts are particularly sensitive, and occasionally painful just before and during menstrual periods. It seems a good guess, therefore, that the motor discharge, following stimulation of the breasts by the child's lips, finds its way to the internal genitals. It will be remembered that this type of motor discharge is to be regarded as evidence that the motor stimuli evoked are in submission to the motor self, and constitutes, therefore, an active inducement reaction. The child, in other words, is being controlled and held in alliance with the mother through stimulation of its lips with her breast. Perception of the child's need of nourishment evokes from the mother a passive submission response which consists of giving up all other activity which might conflict with feeding the child. The simultaneous compounding of these two responses evokes in the mother's central nervous system an integrative pattern of true captivation response. Observations of the general emotional expression of mothers during the nursing of their infants, as well as their verbal reports of introspection indicate that an extremely pleasant type of captivation emotion, qualitatively distinct, can frequently be introspected by the mother herself.

At the same time there are two other groups of stimuli which the mother is reacting to by obvious motor responses. First, there are the stimuli arising from the child's weight, size, etc., which must be supported and placed in position by the mother in order to bring the child to a comfortable posture for feeding. Later in life, when the dominance of the child has developed to the point where it can sit at table and feed itself, the compliance response of the mother will be directed toward the food materials, instead of toward holding the child himself in position to eat. In both cases, however, the essential nature of the reaction seems to be the same. *The mother is complying with certain objects or materials which, when complied with, are capable of satisfying the child's need (pD).* Whether the mother holds the baby up to her breast, therefore, or whether she later cooks and prepares food materials for the child, she is performing an act of active compliance for the purpose of satisfying the inner need of the infant organism. This need, hunger, is evidenced in the child's behaviour in various ways such as crying, making restless movements or making facial grimaces indicating the unpleasantness it is experiencing. These stimuli inform the mother of the child's need. That is, they inform her of the hunger stimuli which are dominating the infant organism and causing unpleasantness in the baby's consciousness. By means of the compliance which the mother expresses toward the child's weight in holding it against her breast, or preparing nourishment in a form which the child can easily dominate, the mother passively dominates the infant hunger pangs.

Thus she simultaneously experiences active compliance with the means of satisfying the pangs and passive dominance toward the hunger pangs themselves in the process of removing them. *This combination of active compliance* and *active dominance constitutes the compound emotion which we have designated as passive appetite or satisfaction.* Mothers, while nursing or feeding their children frequently report a feeling of " intense gratification ", or great satisfaction in being able to provide satisfactorily for the child's need, and in observing in the child's behaviour, the cessation of unpleasantness which it previously had manifested.

Conscious Characteristics of Active Creation Emotion

The mother, therefore, while compelling the child to eat for its own good, and preparing both child and food in such a way that the child's hunger is removed, *experiences simultaneously active love and passive appetite. This complex emotion we have already designated active creation.* Active creation emotion appears to possess a distinct type of consciousness, which can easily be distinguished, and is freely reported upon because it is considered socially admirable in every way. It is sometimes described as " taking vicarious pleasure in doing something for another person ", or as " gratification in having made him do what was good for him ". In the first of these characterizations of active creation, the emphasis appears to be in the satisfaction, or passive appetite emotion. In the last instance, the emphasis seems just as clearly to be placed upon captivation emotion. A considerable list of popular terms and introspections in the subject's own words might be given, describing active creation emotion. All these terms and introspections will be found to include, to some degree, both captivation and satisfaction ; and all might be divided, roughly, into one of two classes according to the emphasis placed upon the active love element, or upon the passive appetite element.

Sex Differences in Active Creation Response

Active creation is an emotion, apparently, which " generous " men experience rather frequently, in bringing toys to their children, buying clothes for their wives and daughters, or bringing presents to their sweethearts. Active creation seems to be the preponderant emotional response. There appears to be, however, a more or less marked difference between active creation reported by mothers of comparatively young children, and active creation as experienced by adult males. The male experience of active creation contains, as a rule, a somewhat more passive love element than true captivation. Mothers whose behaviour I have observed, appeared to derive fully as much pleasure from expression of captivation emotion toward their daughters, especially, as from the satisfaction which they were enabled to give their children.

Males are apt to accept the wish, or demand of a woman or child at its face value, bringing to the loved one the particular thing demanded. Thus when the gift is presented, the chief joy of the giver lies, perhaps, in very extensive satisfaction in the cost, or special virtue of the article presented. This emotion is frequently described as a feeling of " pride " in being able to " give my girl the best there is ". The love emotion element is more markedly submissive than inductive. It would frequently spoil the pleasure of the generous male altogether, if he felt he had persuaded the recipient of the gift to accept a different sort of thing from that which she originally desired, even though the change in choice might obviously suit her much more effectively. Thus the male reaction which comes nearest to being active creation is likely to exhibit a submissive element which is much more active than passive. The satisfaction increment, however, is apt to be so strong in this male emotion, that the love response portion does not clearly assume the aspect of passion emotion.

A mother, on the other hand, very frequently loses a considerable degree of her own pleasure in buying her daughter a dress if the daughter succeeds in selecting the frock spontaneously, without the mother's direction. If the youngster has heart set on a blue frock, however, and the mother, fully confident that she is best able to judge what colours are becoming to the child, persuades the girl to accept a green costume, the mother appears to experience keen delight in having induced the daughter to take (dominate) the green dress as an expression of active submission to the mother. Occasionally a male of peculiarly acute 'perceptions in matters feminine uses this ability to re-educate a girl's taste in clothes, literature, and other esthetic matters. During this process, such a male may actually experience a very vivid and clear-cut type of active creation emotion. Since the subject is a male, his total response is still apt to contain more active submission than does the creation emotion of the average mother. For this very reason, such a rarely gifted male is likely to select the most appropriate avenues of expression for the girl's development, free from his own personal prejudices ; whereas the mother, with a minimum of passive submission, may frequently substitute her own dominance for true love inducement, actually pleasing herself rather than looking out for the daughter's interests. In the main, however, males who undertake the development or education of daughters or sweethearts are either over-submissive, or selfishly dominant. In an instance of the latter sort, a young man attempted to compel the girl to whom he was engaged to learn to play the violin, simply because the boy himself was absorbed in musical interests. The music teacher to whom the girl was sent, after a few hectic attempts, refused to give her further instruction. The girl " couldn't tell one note from another ". Yet her fiancé continued to insist that the girl's one means of salvation lay in learning to become an accomplished musician.

Passive Creation (aApL) Evoked From Child

The emotional responses of the child, on receiving nourishment and other appetitive benefits from the mother, have still to be considered. As previously mentioned, psychoanalysts have made much of the erotic emotion supposedly derived by the infant from stimulation of its lips with the nipple of the mother's breast. A number of writers who do not espouse psycho-analytical theories agree that the so-called " sensitive ", or " erogenous " zone is by no means limited to the infant's genital organs, but also includes its lips and other portions of the body.

Judging by adult behaviour and experiences, the lips do actually contain receptor organs for stimuli ultimately evoking all four types of primary emotional response. Certain types of nourishment, notably liquids, are partially dominated with the lips. Temperature, touch, and possibly taste stimulations of the lips may initiate reflexes tending toward increased salivary secretions, and abolishing of hunger pangs ; that is, active compliance response to food. Tickling or kissing the lips may give rise, in both male and female, to erection of the external genital organs, which we have interpreted as an active submission response. Finally, use of the lips by a woman to arouse passion in a lover, may very possibly result in motor discharge to the woman's internal genital organs, which has been construed as an active inducement response.

Which of these four types of primary emotional responses occur in an infant while nursing at the mother's breast is problematical, to say the least. I have heard of alleged observations of erection, in male children, which occurred, it was said, during stimulation of the child's lips by the nipple of the mother's breast. But it seems to me that some allowance must be made for the extraordinary enthusiasm of persons psycho-analytically inclined, regarding the matter of bringing to light love (" sex ") responses hidden to other eyes. I can only say that I have never succeeded in verifying the reports cited. In the absence of such finding, it seems impossible to assume with any confidence, that active submission response of this particular variety is elicited from the child by lip stimulation at the breast.

There are some other evidences of active submission, however, such as cuddling responses, and various vocal sounds, which may very possibly indicate some sort of submissive attitude toward the mother It is also true that the child is taught to respond by suckling at the breast with its lips, even though no hunger pangs may be motivating him at that particular moment. This probably represents a certain more or less mechanical type of submission integration in the child's nervous system. We may guess, as a result of these secondary behaviour symptoms, that there is some submission response concerned with the act of suckling at the mother's breast.

Dominance response would seem more definite and easily observable, however, during this infant reaction. When the infant's lips are first taught to react, as is frequently necessary, by pressing a finger against them until they begin to contract, the tonic reinforcement of lips and jaw musculature can easily be detected. It would seem evident that the child is reacting to an opposition stimulus, pressed antagonistically, though with comparative gentleness, into its mouth, by increasing its motor self to dominate the stimulus in a manner appropriate to the portion of the body stimulated, that is to say, the mouth. When milk has actually been drawn into the mouth by this dominance reaction, there ensue certain gulping and voluntary swallowing reactions which are clearly of a dominant nature. It would seem probable, therefore, that *the infant organism experiences a rather emphatic variety of dominance reaction in taking the food from the proffered breast, simultaneously with a simpler and less marked degree of submission response toward the mother.*

The passive compliance with hunger pangs, occurring prior to and during the act of nursing, needs no especial comment, since presumably this passive compliance response closely resembles that of an adult who is forced to give up all other business during his quest for food. Passive inducement expressed toward the mother by the infant's holding up its lips to be stimulated with food, and by its various behaviour expressions of helpless solicitation of whatever the mother may choose to give it, like the active submission element involved in taking the breast between the lips, seems somewhat problematical so far as the infant is concerned. The variety of inducement by which a healthy child does actually attract the mother's attention is crying and screaming.

Appetitive Elements Predominate in Child's Responses to Mother

These types of behaviour, no doubt, represent dominance responses on the child's part. It would seem, therefore, that *both the love elements requisite to distinct passion emotion are of such minimal occurrence in the infant consciousness, as to merit little weight in comparison to the appetitive elements composing active desire for food.* Moreover, passive appetite also gives every evidence of controlling the infant's total consciousness, after the swallowing of milk begins to abolish his hunger pangs. If facial expressions and general relaxation of body tension give any indication of what is going on within the infant organism, a great deal of satisfaction emotion is felt by the infant as his hunger pangs are quelled. It would seem that this appetitive satisfaction has little, if any, connection with emotional responses toward the mother. A common sense view of the matter, therefore, based upon the infant's behaviour without, of course, any available infantile introspection, would suppose that the infant while feeding is chiefly concerned with appetite emotion, experiencing, perhaps, a slight admixture of passion response toward the mother.

As the child grows older, and its dominance behaviour becomes more varied as well as more active, a type of situation begins to arise, much more frequently, in which the child experiences desire for some plaything or sweetmeat which it is impossible to obtain without the mother's consent and co-operation. Moreover, when the toy or other object is attained, the child begins to dominate it actively, thus continuing to express desire response rather than relaxing into such placid satisfaction emotion as that manifested by the feeding infant.

Although it is the average adult's chronic point of view that appetitive desire is the primary need of human behaviour, with love and submission used largely as a means to obtain the object of desire, it seems to me still an open question as to whether the child learns submission to the mother through desire for objects which the mother alone can give, or whether *the normal child develops submission response as an intrinsically pleasant method of behaviour scuffiiently powerful to curb and control dominant desire.* So many mothers employ the method of teaching the child obedience by bestowing appetitive rewards for obedient conduct that it seems to me quite likely this use of obedience or submission to serve desire has its origin in the method of training rather than in the natural unfoldment of the child's own responses. Certain it is that submission, once learned as an appetitive technique, is not worth very much to the mother, even as a method for temporarily keeping the child quiet and out of the parent's way. The child who learns submission for its own sake does not continually return to the parent to inquire whether or not the submission period has been long enough to merit the promised reward.

Moreover, from the child's own point of view, the child who learns to enjoy submission for its own sake attains a double pleasantness in receiving an object of desire given it by its mother. I have observed a number of cases of the relationship between child and mother which give considerable evidence that a *passion response is evoked from the child by the mother, with desire emotion very clearly subsidiary to and frequently compounded with the passion response.* The very common type of child response which consists of begging the mother to be allowed to help her in household tasks, or to go out into the garden and pick her favourite fruit or berries, and bring them in to her, appears to represent the normal blending of passion response and desire emotion, with passion for the mother distinctly in control of the reaction. Were desire the predominating element, the child might beg to paint the house, or to pick his own favourite kind of fruit, permitting the mother to share these objects of desire as a mere incident to the total response. This type of reaction is frequently seen in the behaviour of adolescent boys whose appetite development has begun definitely to predominate over their love response. But in normal children of both sexes prior to adolescence, it would appear that *desire to obtain an appetitive object as an expression of passion emotion for the mother comprises the normal attitude on the child's part toward the parent.* This simultaneous compounding of desire emotion and passion response, with desire adapted to passion may be termed *passive creation emotion.* (aApL).

Mothers Evoke Passive Creation From Daughters

Girls, during the adolescent period, frequently develop an exaggerated passive creation emotion for their mothers. This attitude on the part of the girl appears to give a mother whose attention is not predominantly occupied with other pursuits, the most concentratedly pleasant experience of her entire life. Full play is given to the older woman's preponderant captivation response, and if the family means are sufficient, the mother also obtains enormous satisfaction in dressing the child prettily, and training her in the technique of social conduct (the female's appetitive battle ground). In fact, the active creation which the mother is able to express toward her exaggeratedly passionate daughter, during this period, frequently yields such consummate pleasure to the mother that she is unwilling to relinquish this relationship with the girl at a subsequent period, when it is necessary for the girl to begin to live her own life free from the mother's control.

The habits of emotional bondage which the girl may have formed during her phase of concentrated passive creation emotion are likely to persist throughout a major portion of the daughter's life if they are not boldly broken by the girl herself upon the completion of adolescence.

I have had two cases, in clinic, of college girls who were still under this type of maternal constraint, with very great detriment to the girls in question. In one instance, the mother undoubtedly realized that her period of maximally efficient active creation emotion toward the girl was over, yet clung to her control over the daughter as a frankly selfish pleasure to herself.

In the other case, the mother seemed not to realize that she had passed the limit of her own ability to actively create further development in her child. When induced squarely to face this fact, the mother's creative attitude did not pass over into appetite, but compelled her to release the daughter from the emotional control no longer helpful to the girl's mature development. This mother showed true love, and by this very action renewed her love relationship with the girl, the mother now assuming a more passive rôle, and the girl a more active one.

The personnel officer of one of the largest corporations in America, who has spent twenty-five years or more in making a sympathetic, yet eminently clear-headed study of the needs and personalities of employees ranging from $40,000 a year sales managers to unskilled girl clerks barely of legal age, informed me, in personal conversation, that one of his most pressing problems with respect to women employees is this very relationship of complete emotional control exercised by mothers over their daughters. In several instances, women over fifty years of age are still held rigidly confined to the needs and commands of a querulous, and perhaps thoroughly incompetent mother, who originally gained control over her daughter through the extraordinarily intense creation relationship consummated during the daughter's adolescence. Such cases seem to present evidence of the tremendous emotional strength of active creation response on the mother's part, and of the strength of the original passive creation emotion experienced by the daughter. These cases serve, also, to point the danger of continuing this creation emotion relationship, after the mother has ceased to be able to further her daughter's development or well being in any way. From this point on, *the relationship maintained by habit and force of social custom and law inevitably develops into appetitive dominance on the mother's part, and indifferent or unpleasant compliance* on the part of the daughter.

Artistic Creation Expresses Passive Creation Emotion

Perhaps the most important expression of passive creation in adult life is that of artistic production. Observation of a considerable number of artists, together with analysis of their introspection and other verbal responses, has led me to conclude that the popular term " passion for art " is an apt description of the complex emotional response which motivates artists who are capable of producing true art. Too great an admixture of active creation emotion in male artists, at least, seems usually to result in substitution of dominance for inducement. " Freak " art, or perverted, destructive art, of any sort, is inevitably produced in consequence of this controlling dominance emotion. Perhaps it is too sweeping a statement to say that all great works of art have been produced as an expression of passion response to some woman, real or imagined who has strongly captivated the artist. But I can say that in all the cases where I have had opportunity personally to observe and to analyse male artists' emotional responses, I have been able to establish beyond reasonable doubt that passion for a woman or women (sometimes imaginary women) is the *sine qua non* of artistic creation.

Varying degrees of dominance and compliance may appear in the active appetite or desire which impels the artist to gather his materials, and to dominate them successfully in the form desired. Some indubitably great artists are extremely dominant, scorning any considerable amount of compliance preparation for the work to be produced. The results of such artists appear to be bold and strongly compelling. Sarah Bernhardt, Cyril Scott, Leo Ornstein, and other artists who have always insisted upon creating a new vogue in their particular field of art rather than complying with the concept of character portrayal or harmonics conventionally espoused by their predecessors, probably exemplify this strongly dominant type. At the other extreme we find artists who possess an enormous amount of compliance in the appetitive portion of their artistic response, producing as a result very great delicacy and subtlety of artistic creation. Such artists, also, are apt to comply with the current technique and conventions in their own particular field of art.

But whichever type of dominance-compliance emphasis may obtain in the appetitive portion of the artist's emotion, strong passion expressed toward the model or imagined captivatress who is regarded, perhaps "subconsciously", as dictating an ideal pattern, would seem to control the entire creation responses of all true artists from first to last. In landscape painting, or lyric poetry, this passion for captivating women, real or imagined, is less obvious than in sculptures made from nude models, and poetry directly dedicated to the feminine object of adoration. It is my suggestion, however, that artistic portrayals of "nature" represent a certain type of transfer of the passion response, from a human or idealized woman to the beautiful or harmoniously powerful aspects of inanimate objects and forces. The verbal responses of artists of this type give considerable evidence of a sort of animistic attitude toward "mother nature", or "nature the beautiful" which lead one to believe that the artists' response toward nature is one of active submission rather than an attitude of aesthetic compliance. In the case of artists like Edgar Allen Poe, the controlling element of the creative emotional pattern which enabled him to write a lyric poem of unsurpassed beauty such as "Bells", seems clearly revealed by this man's other poems, directly revealing passion for beautiful women. In his "Philosophy of Composition", Poe maintains that the beauty of women is incomparable, the death of a beloved and beautiful woman the supreme loss, "and the most poetical topic in the world". And this from a lyric poet! "With me", says Poe, "poetry has been not a purpose, but a passion ".[1]

It seems a notable fact, also, that a large majority of creative artists prior to the present age have been men. True passion, as we have already noted, is the type of love response for which the male organism is pre-eminently fitted. Any passive creation is, therefore, the type of emotional creation response which might be expected to predominate in the spontaneous behaviour of male artists. We have also observed, however,

---

[1] Preface to the *Poe Collection of* 1845, signed "E.A.P."

that the human female organism possesses a double physiological love endowment, capable of building up both active and passive love emotion patterns. While a majority of women might be expected, therefore, to devote themselves to captivation emotion, for which woman alone possesses an adequate mechanism, the female passion response when, and if devoted to artistic creation might be expected to prove itself unusually potent, and delicate in its form of expression. Such seems to have been the result in the cases of those well known women artists whose work is directly comparable with that of male artists. One might mention, in this connection, the works of Sappho, Le Brune, Laurence Hope, George Sand, Elizabeth Barrett Browning, and Christina Rossetti. Woman's passion, when expressed in artistic creation, frequently, appears to contain a much larger proportion of pure passion element than is the case with the majority of male artists. The writings of Sappho and Laurence Hope serve to illustrate this point. In general, *creative artists of both sexes seem motivated by desire adapted to passion, or passive creation emotion.*

Active Creation Motivates Physicians, Teachers, Clergymen

The most important expressions of active creation in adult life would appear to be of the type represented by the professions of the teacher, physician, and clergyman. The latter is by far the most frank and thorough-going attempt to express combined captivation emotion and passive appetite response. The theory of priesthood, in nearly all religions and civilizations, has consisted of active supervision by the priest over the behaviour of the people with resultant duty on the priest's part to supply spiritual or physical sustenance, or both, to meet the needs of the persons submitting to him. This appears to be the essence of active creation response. Under the political theories of church and state which obtained in Europe throughout the early middle ages, the head of the priesthood exercised appetitive as well as love control over the conduct of human kind. Though the appetitive control of the priesthood over the lay citizenry has been theoretically abolished, there still remains a considerable amount of appetitive power residuent in the supposed male love leaders of the people, though this power must now be exercised through control of social customs and conventions. It is not profitable to attempt to discover to what degree it is possible for a male in a position of leadership of this priestly type, to exercise a true love captivation response over other males, and over women who place themselves under his power and control.

In the case of male leaders in politics, and industry, as we have already noted, the amount of true active love response likely to be exercised, spontaneously, toward employees or underlings, is comparatively slight. Dominance and appetite creep in and control the intended love response, despite the best intentions of the male leader, for dominant appetitive emotion "is the nature of the animal". Perhaps this is otherwise in the case of male church leaders. I have not ventured to make any personal investigation of their emotional patterns of behaviour. In the case of male teachers and physicians, however, the active creation results most helpful to their students and patients are most often obtained when the person submitting to instruction or medical treatment chances to satisfy the appetitive interests of the male teacher, or doctor to a considerable degree. A maximum amount of attention is apt to be paid to persons who can be taught or healed without any unusually altruistic alteration of attitude becoming necessary on the part of the male who is attempting to play the rôle of active creation. I have personally analysed many cases, however, in which a male teacher or physician reacted to another's need with a creative response undoubtedly controlled, in the main, by its love element, though this love element could scarcely be called captivation emotion. As in the cases before mentioned, where male lovers or parents gave gifts to their loved ones, so in the love controlled behaviour of men physicians and teachers, active submission to the existing needs and desires of the stimulus person appear largely to replace the active inducement to *change* the stimulus person's desires or conduct, which is so characteristic of the love behaviour of a mother toward her daughter, or of a woman captivatress toward her lover. In the main, I have encountered no evidence which leads me to believe that any but the most peculiarly gifted male is psycho-physiologically capable of sustaining an attitude of true love captivation for any length of time, toward persons of either sex.

Summary

Love and appetite are found combined, simultaneously, in a complex emotional response, termed creation emotion.

This emotion expresses itself in a mother's responses toward the child to whom she gives birth, and for whose nourishment and protection she later provides. The mother's response is active creation, consisting of captivation emotion toward the child, simultaneously compounded with satisfaction emotion expressed toward the satisfaction of the child's needs. In the child's responses toward the mother, during this same relationship, the child's response is passive creation consisting of passion response toward the mother simultaneously compounded with active appetite toward the food, or other appetitive benefit in the mother's possession.

During active creation each of the appetitive primary emotional elements is adapted to and used for the consummation of a corresponding primary element of the love emotion. In the mother's response of active creation she complies actively with the food materials, in order to actively induce the child to dominate the materials. The mother passively dominates influences inimical to the child's welfare, in order to passively submit to the child's needs rather than her own.

In the child's response of passive creation, the individual reaction elements are arranged in the same way, each separate appetitive element being adapted to and used for the consummation of a corresponding love element. The child passively complies with its hunger pangs or other need by giving up all other pleasurable occupations, in order passively to induce the mother to give her attention to the child. The child then obeys or actively submits to the mother, by dominating whatever food she directs.

The natural physical relationship between mother and child seems to furnish a training mechanism and pattern for the type of integration composing creative emotion just as the bodily mechanisms of hunger and menstruation furnish training mechanisms and patterns for appetite and love respectively.

Active creation emotion appears to reach a height of extreme intensity and pleasantness in the normal love behaviour of a mother toward her adolescent daughter, while passive creation may reach a similar degree of pleasantness and extensity in the relationship of the daughter to the mother at this period.

True artistic creation seems to represent one of the most important expressions of passive creation during adult life. The artist, whether male or female, being motivated by desire to dominate his materials in such a way as to produce a work of art consummating most perfectly his passion response to a captivating woman, real or imagined.

Professions like that of the clergyman, the teacher, or the physician, seem to represent important adult expressions of active creative. emotion. Males who essay the career of teacher or physician are seldom able because of their bodily limitations and training, to maintain pure active love response, with true captivation emotion toward their students or patients. They are apt, on the one hand, to exchange inducement for dominance, and to use those who submit to them for their own purposes, or, on the other hand, to substitute active submission for inducement in the love portion of their creative responses, and thus approximate the type of passive love response which male parents and lovers frequently manifest in giving gifts to children or loved ones. Women teachers, whose pupils are of appropriate age, may, like mothers, express true active creation toward their pupils ; and it would seem possible that women physicians also might express true active creation in their professional relationships at least, toward other women and children.

CHAPTER XVII

Reversals, Conflicts, and Abnormal Emotions

We have noted that efficient functioning of dominance and compliance, either in simultaneous or successive combination, requires a certain definite relationship between those two types of primary emotional reactions. Compliance is the preliminary, preparatory response. Its value in, the general behaviour pattern is to act as a sort of first assistant to dominance. Compliance response is used to select the most efficient portion of the motor self to be reinforced, and also as a sort of escape valve to permit the discharge of over-intense antagonistic motor stimuli which might otherwise destroy some part of the motor self. To serve these functions, compliance must precede a compensating dominance response, and it must be adapted to the dominance reaction which brings the organism back to its natural reflex equilibrium.

Sherrington[1] has recently stated that he finds no tonic reinforcement mechanisms in the flexor muscles of limbs whose natural anti-gravitational posture is maintained by tonic discharge to the extensor muscles. We have then a situation where compliance response must first inhibit the normal tonic (motor self) discharge to the extensors, and must then contract the flexor muscle. This flexor contraction, then, draws the limb into an unnatural condition of balance, not suited for holding the animal erect against the influence of gravity. Unless this compliance response is compensated for, and terminated by an equal and opposite dominance response, the animal can no longer stand erect, or maintain a balanced posture. The compliance response, then, must be allowed to occur only in a limb the reaction of which can be balanced temporarily, by the tonic positions of the other limbs ; and the compliant flexing of the limb moved must be allowed to proceed only to the point of maximal efficiency for the

[1] C. S. Sherrington, *Lecture given before the New York Academy of Medicine*, October 25th, 1927.

application of the dominance response to follow. If the dominant extensor movement of the limb be interrupted by flexor, or compliant inhibition before the dominance response is completed, then this secondary, or intervening flexor response must again be terminated, and compensated for by a dominant extensor reaction especially paired with it. In short, we may lay down the rule that a dominance response can never be paired with a compliance reaction which follows it, and controls it, without loss of equilibrium to the entire organism. *Compliance must always be adapted to dominance ; dominance may never be adapted to compliance without injury to the subject.*

The normal, efficient relationship, then, between these two fundamental appetitive responses, indicates that the very life of the organism itself depends upon the continuous supremacy of the motor self, and the selection of such compliant responses that these acts of compliance will enable the motor self again to rule supreme over the motor stimuli temporarily complied with. *The environment must be adapted to the organism, not the organism to the environment. Preliminary adaptations of the organism to environment are only for the purpose of better compelling the environment to serve the needs of the organism by nourishing it and complying with it in a multitude of other ways.* In terms of tonic and anti-tonic innervations, the animal complies with environment by drawing back its foot, but only for the purpose of being able to extend its foot a little further than before, and thus to dominate its environment more completely. The idea of adaptation to environment has been so strongly emphasized, in theories of biology and evolution, that it is difficult, at first, to realize that *adaptation to environment is a means only, and never an end of human or animal action.*

It is when adaptation to environment becomes the chief end of existence, to which the vital activities of the organism itself are adjusted, that destruction of the organism really begins. *The only animal completely adapted to its environment is a dead animal,* the tissues of whose body have substantially decomposed, thus returning once more to chemical forms of energy completely adapted to the chemical energy forms of its environment. Adaptation, in short, is efficacious and constructive for just so long as it is used to enable the animal to compel the environment to adapt itself to the uses which the animal organism seeks to make of the environment. It is the old question of mechanistic-type cause versus vitalistic-type cause. The environment represents a mechanistic-type cause, and the human or animal a vitalistic-type cause. The mechanistic-type cause must be allowed to alter the behaviour of the organism sufficiently to generate in the organism, as it were, sufficiently potent forms of energy to act as vitalistic-type causes exerting greater influence upon the environment than the environment is exercising upon the organism. In terms of primary emotions, *the organism must adapt its compliance to its dominance at all times.*

When dominance is adapted to compliance, the resulting relationship of primary emotional responses may justly be termed a reversal. Reversals of the normal relationship between successive dominance and compliance responses may be brought about either by too much dominance or by too much compliance. That is to say, dominance may flare up against a compulsory compliance reaction for the purpose of removing it, and so may prevent the organism from adopting a new type of compliance response which is adapted to dominant control and, therefore, could be used to bring the organism back to its normal, dominant balance, once more. This type of situation may be termed *over-dominant reversal.* It is a ram butting his head against an immovable wall with furious determination to destroy this particular obstacle for the very reason that the wall has already compelled him to compliance by stopping him in his course. A *conflict* is inevitable, as a result. *It is a conflict wherein dominance attacks compliance.*

The opposite type of reversal relationship between dominance and compliance may be brought about by too much compliance. Compliance may run riot in the central nervous system, preventing the organism from adopting a new dominance response which tends to limit, in any way, the magnified compliance responses already evoked. During this integrative condition, only those dominance responses are made which are completely adapted to the controlling compliance reactions. This type of situation may be termed *over-compliant reversal.* It is a child running away from his shadow, with terrified abandon of every desire save that to run toward a place where his invincible opponent is not. A continuous series of conflicts between compliance and dominance emotions results,

with compliance always holding the whip hand. *These are
conflicts wherein compliance attacks dominance.*

Over-Dominant Reversals—Rage

The line of demarcation between mere over-dominance
and over-dominant *reversal* falls just between mere *stubbornness* and *rage.* When one holds the arms of an infant, the
baby responds with sheer dominance so long as his motor self
merely calls upon every available reinforcement to throw off
the restraint imposed upon the child's normal, spontaneous
movements. The baby is over-dominant, or stubborn. But
when the baby begins to cry, or to howl with an impotent
but revengeful note in his voice, or otherwise manifests a
baffled behaviour element, it is the signal that his compulsory
compliance with a superior opponent has been forced into his
emotional consciousness, and that his dominance, thenceforth,
seeks partially at least, to injure his opponent rather than to
restore his normal freedom of movement. The baby has been
compelled partially to comply. He no longer strives solely
to adapt his compliance to his dominance. *He adapts, rather,
the whole dominance of his being to attacking and destroying
this one, particular compliance response. The baby is experiencing rage.*

Rage is an abnormal emotion, which occurs all too frequently
in adult life. Since rage customarily springs from over-
dominance, as in the behaviour of a new-born infant. just
considered, it is an emotion that is mistakenly thought by
many people to be normal and even advantageous. Aside
from the destructive disorganization of the subject's emotions
which rage produces, however, and aside from the physical
injury to the subject's body which frequently results from
physical expression of rage (the ram's skull broken against
the offending wall), rage is not efficient nor beneficial in
eliminating the opponent and restoring the normal, successful,
dominance of the subject over his environment. If the enraged subject does, eventually, dominate his environment, it
is the unbaffled dominance which accomplishes this result
successfully, and not the baffled dominance which has given
itself up solely to the attack upon an opponent which has
already beaten the subject. If this superior opponent is to
be destroyed, as a measure of restoring the subject's supremacy over his environment, the destruction will actually be

accomplished by a new series of compliance reactions, designed to select the vulnerable places in the antagonist and to dominate those places. This proceeding may require dominance raised to such a pitch of intensity and violence that the subject himself thinks of it as rage. But *any such series of successful attacking reactions can be shown to be composed of a series of compliance responses properly adapted to succeeding dominance reactions.* There is no rage at all in such behaviour, though, of course, rage may be superadded, with corresponding loss of efficiency. The rage part of the response is always futile, and is, therefore, abnormal.

Another source of confusion, in the popular mind, between rage and the successful dominance with which it may be mixed, springs from the fact that men and animals who possess extraordinary dominance also tend to permit this dominance to break over, frequently into rage. That is to say, a man more powerful than his opponent can indulge in rage without suffering defeat. The unanalytical conclusion tends to follow, in the average mind, that it was rage that produced the victory. The superior, intense, dominance power is obvious to all, and this may be identified, unthinkingly, with the baffled determination to rid himself of all compliance immediately, at whatever cost to himself. When an opponent ultimately appears who is intelligent enough to perceive this rage as a weakness, and to take advantage of it accordingly, the person of superior dominance is defeated. Such cases may be found in the heavyweight boxing contests between Dempsey and Tunney. The former champion, Dempsey, could hit harder, and attack more aggressively. He was by far the more dominant fighter. But he indulged frequently in rage ; he liked to fume and flail about, trying to get rid arbitrarily of all enforced compliance with his opponent. Tunney, an unusually compliant and intelligent boxer, almost literally cut Dempsey's face to ribbons with punches delivered during Dempsey's raging moments of anti-compliant attack. Though tremendous dominance power is frequently found associated with rage, and though such powerful dominance frequently succeeds over weaker opponents despite its handicap of lapses into rage behaviour, it may be stated as an infallible rule that *supremacy over antagonists is only attained by adapting compliance to dominance, and is never attained by adapting overdominance to compliance, as in rage.*

There is a considerable series of abnormal emotions which take their origin from over-dominant reversals of this same general type. Thwarted dominance, irritability, " bad temper ", revenge, and depression may be mentioned as members of this series. Manic depressive insanity may also be traced to over-dominant reversal, whatever physiological or other physical cause may be shown to be responsible for the reversal of response relationships in these extreme cases of obvious abnormality. But the present volume, as its title implies, is devoted primarily to normal emotions, and further consideration of this abnormal series must be reserved, therefore, for discussion elsewhere.

Over-Compliant Reversals—Fear

The line of demarcation between over-compliance and over-compliance *reversal* may be found between the experiences of *startle* and *fear*. When one clashes a dishpan with a stick close behind an infant's ear, a visible start, jump, or startle may be evoked. This response consists, it would seem, of an over-sudden and over-extensive inhibition of the motor self, with its outflowing tonic energy being cut off abruptly. The compliant, anti-tonic motor discharge which thus conquers the motor self, finds expression in the quick, uncontrollable jerk of appropriate anti-tonic muscles. This initial startle response may be followed immediately, after the infant has learned the proper C + D relationship of primary reactions, by crawling or walking away from the source of the startle stimulus. In this case there need be no reversal, and consequently no fear. There is, perhaps, a certain amount of over-compliance. The child moves farther and more quickly than he need do in order eventually to dominate the startling stimulus. But the compliant movements, though over-extensive, are well adapted to place the child in a position where his dominant reactions can supersede, once more, the compulsory compliance, and so restore the normal, dominant supremacy of the child over his environment. So far, compliance remains adapted to dominance.

If, however, the child cries, closes its eyes, or falls down, as reported by Watson[1] in his fear experiments with children, we find responses occurring which are in no way adapted to ulti-

[1] J. B. Watson, *Behaviourism*, p. 121.

mate dominance. In these reactions, there not only appears to be over-compliance with the superior antagonist, but there is also a failure to select those compliance responses which will lead to dominance behaviour capable of replacing them. Instead, reactions like closing the eyes and crying are indulged in, which represent types of dominant behaviour selected only because they are capable of co-existing with the over-compliance responses. The one dominance response which might serve to re-establish the subject's supremacy over environment, that is, walking or running away, is inhibited by compliance with the superior antagonist, and the child falls down. A small amount of dominance, in short, is adapted to a very large amount of compliance, and even such dominance as may be left is attacked and partially defeated by compliance. *Dominance no longer seeks to terminate and replace compliance ; it seeks only to adapt itself in such a way as to avoid conflict with the over-compliance response completely controlling the organism's behaviour. In this process, necessarily, dominance is attacked and largely destroyed (weakened) by over-compliance. The baby is experiencing fear.*

Some years ago, I called attention to the fact that James' famous suggestion that we are afraid of the bear because we run from it must be amended so as to read : " We are afraid of the bear because we do not run away from it fast enough ".[1] We must now amend James' statement about the bear still further. *We do not run away from the bear fast enough because we are trying to suit the bear and not ourselves. If the running psychologist cared not a whit about whether he was conforming sufficiently to the bear's movements but was conscious only of a strongly dominant determination to beat that bear by hook or by crook, he would undoubtedly escape—if not from the bear, at least from all fear of the bear. For fear comes only when dominance tries to adapt itself to its mortal enemy, over-compliance.*

A great deal of foolishness has been written about fear. The source of fear has been sought in " sex ", in the " libido ", in childhood " suppressions ", and in a thousand other obscure and unlikely places. Fear is really a very simple reversal of primary emotional responses, with the cart put before the horse, and that is all there is to it. It is this reversal relation-

---

[1] W. M. Marston, " A Theory of Emotions and Affection based upon Systolic Blood Pressure Studies," *American Journal of Psychology*, 1924, vol. XXXV, pp. 469-506.

ship of responses that is learned in childhood, and not specific fears of this and that.

Mrs. Jones has shown the " spread " of child fears, from loud noises to furry annimals, etc.[1]; and the assumption has been almost universally adopted that each fear became " conditioned " as a response to some new object, by means of some hypothetical associative connection between the first *stimulus* to fear and the new object evoking fear. I would rather say that the first fear response teaches, to some extent, a reversed adaptation of dominance to compliance during reactions to objects bearing a certain relationship to the child's organism ; that is, objects antagonistic and of superior strength. Then the child is further taught (by associations in time or sensory qualities) that other kinds of objects fall into this class. Each new fear response, then, not only tends to classify another object or group of objects in the antagonistic-superior class, but also enhances more and more the reversal of primary response relationship in reactions to this class of stimuli in general. Thus *fear, each time it is evoked, " spreads " both in respect to the number of stimuli able to evoke it, and also, more importantly, in respect to the tendency for the reversed relationship of dominance adapted to compliance to be evoked whenever either one of these responses occurs throughout life.*

This may mean, before adolescence has passed, that the subject lives in an almost perpetual condition of fear, whenever he or she tries to contact " the world " without some protecting guardian to dictate the subject's actions. It does mean, oftentimes, that the reversal between dominance and compliance becomes a chronic one, with fear initially evoked, nearly always, by new and unknown situations and people ; and with compensatory rage likely to follow hard upon the heels of fear, whenever the subject gets away by himself, free from the compulsion of the person or thing felt as superior and antagonistic.

No elaborate and mysterious series of " suppressions " and " complexes " need be worked out, (except, possibly for propaganda purposes, in treating the subject). It doesn't make the least difference, in any of the cases I have studied, whether the person first learned the over-compliance type of reversal giving rise to fear from a barking bull-dog or from

[1] Mary C. Jones, " The Elimination of Children's Fears," *Journal of Experimental Psychology,* 1924, p. 328,

being left alone in a dark room at the age of three. However he learned the reversed relationship between dominance and compliance, he has two tasks now before him : First, to unlearn the reversal ; second, to learn the correct relationship, (C + D). One need never mention the word " fear ", unless for convenience in restraining the subject. *Fear vanishes, automatically, when the subject has learned to adapt his compliance to his dominance in all responses, to all objects.*

I have accomplished this retraining, in a few cases, in ten minutes. In other cases, I have worked for years without nearly completing the retraining apparently necessary. It is all a question of studying the individual subject, establishing a sufficiently submissive relationship of subject to trainer, and then using the symbology and terminology, and primary emotional stimulations which mean most to the particular subject being treated. One generality may be indulged in, however. *Removing the mystery from fear is nine-tenths of the battle. So long as any person thinks of fear as some great, hidden, cosmic force that is ready to jump down his throat anytime, from the great beyond, from the " libido ", from the evolutionary history of the race, or even from his own childhood " complexes " and " repressions," the clinical psychologist hasn't one chance in a million to get rid of it for him. Those concepts, in my experience, constitute precisely the most effective teachers of over-compliance reversal and fear, that it is possible to administer.*

Worry, timidity, retreat from reality, seclusiveness, and " inadequate personality ", as well as outright terrors and phobias, all find their roots in over-compliance reversal. This book, however, is not the place for their further discussion, since *all fears are abnormal emotions.*

Dominance and Fear in Deception Tests

In 1917, I reported to the literature discovery of the so-called systolic blood pressure deception test.[1] My results indicated that the systolic blood pressure tends to rise in a characteristic curve whenever a subject who was to deceive the experimenter concerning some alleged " crime " of which he was accused, was asked a crucial question by the cross-examiner. Increase of systolic blood pressure evidently

[1] W. M. Marston, " Systolic Blood Pressure Symptoms of Deception," *Journal of Experimental Psychology*, 1917, pp. 117-163.

accompanies increase of the motor self, that is, increased tonic motor discharge through sympathetic autonomic channels. There appears to be, therefore, a marked access of power put forth by the organism to meet the challenge of a crucial question which threatens to defeat the subject's self-assumed task of deception. , Following the terminology current among physiologists and psychologists, I termed the emotion thus revealed " fear ". It should actually be called *dominance*.

The nature of this dominance response during deception was further revealed in a subsequent series of experiments during which we measured the reaction time during deception, with the extra time required for additional mental work of deception eliminated from each series of reaction time measurements. This research revealed a distinct type of deception subject who reacts more quickly when lying than when telling the truth.[1] Goldstein later published results showing that a still greater proportion of subjects were of negative reaction-time type during deception when no more mental work was required during deception than during truth telling.[2] In a subsequent unpublished experiment, E. H. Marston and I measured association reaction times of subjects of both sexes, allowing the subjects time to think up any association word they chose, after hearing the stimulus word, and before being called upon to respond with the word they had selected. (Blood pressure was simultaneously recorded with Tycos sphygmomanometer). Comparisons of reaction times when the subject was given the true word (printed on a list given to the subject) and reaction times when he was attempting to deceive the experimenter by substituting a word of his own, were then made. *The results of this experiment finally convinced me that the active emotional response element characterizing deception is not " fear ", but rather dominance.*

Though it is dominance which betrays the deceiver in the two tests mentioned, however, there is probably a good deal of fear actually present in the consciousness of nearly all subjects under examination for alleged deception, whether in the laboratory situation or in the court room. *Fear it is*

---

[1] W. M. Marston, " Reaction-Time Symptoms of Deception," *Journal of Experimental Psychology*, 1920, pp. 72-87.

[2] E. R. Goldstein, " Reaction-Times and the Consciousness of Deception," 1923, *American Journal of Psychology*, pp. 562-581.

that renders the attempted deception less efficient in many ways ; while it is the most successful type of liar who betrays himself most readily in breathing and blood pressure changes symptomatic of dominance (as previously pointed out by Benussi[1] and myself). The inactive, weak liar may frequently reveal himself by lengthened reaction times, disclosure of guilty knowledge in association responses, and self-betrayals under cross examination.

Of course, the weaker type of deceiver, although more subject to fear, still responds dominantly to crucial questions and so may be betrayed by rises in systolic blood pressure. But this dominance is of lesser extent, is more easily overwhelmed, and betrays itself by a more erratic, less smoothly progressive series of rises in systolic blood pressure. Wherever fear exists in the responses of a would-be deceiver, it is found to express itself in symptoms of conflict between ineffective attempts on the subject's part to conceal what he knows and compulsory over-compliance with the demands of the cross examiner. *Fear, during deception, gives experimental proof of its true nature. It consists of enfeebled dominance trying to adapt itself to over-compliance with a stimulus (the cross examiner) which is antagonistic and of superior strength to the subject ; with the subject's dominance, thus reversed, in constant conflict with his compulsory compliance, and constantly being partially defeated by it.*

This conclusion concerning the nature of the subject's emotional responses while he is being tested for deception leads to the discovery that there are two distinct types of so-called " Deception Test ". First, there are tests of the dominance used by the liar to tighten his grip on the secret knowledge in his possession, which the examiner is trying to pull away from him. Second, there are tests of defeats of this dominant reaction (fear), by over-compliance evoked by over-intensity of stimulation applied by the cross-examiner. The dominance test is applicable to all subjects without exception ; the fear test is applicable only to those subjects who are habitually addicted to the over-compliance reversal of relationship between D and C, or who can be forced into this reversal by the conditions of the test. *The dominance test reveals the subject's deceptions by detecting each increase*

---

[1] V. Benussi, " Die Atmungsymptome der Lüge," *Archiv. fur die Gesampte Psychologie*, 1914, pp. 244-271.

of effort that he makes to withold the truth ; the fear test reveals deception only at those times when the subject yields to torture by relaxing his grip, slightly, on the concealed facts. The dominance test situation must encourage the subject to lie just as strenuously as he wants to ; the fear test situation must seek to defeat the subject's deception at every turn.

The dominance tests for deception are : rise in systolic blood pressure (Marston) ; change in ratio of expiration to inspiration (Benussi, Burtt) ; and *shortening* of reaction times (Marston). Fear tests are : *lengthening* of reaction times, guilty associations (Wertheimer, Jung) ; self-betrayal by inconsistencies of verbal responses, or by confusion of statements or confession under torture. H. E. Burtt[1] and other reliable investigators, report most successful and consistent results with the systolic blood pressure tests, and the breathing ratio test, under laboratory conditions. These are both tests of dominance. H. S. Langfeld[2], Jung[3], and others, report good results with lengthening of reaction time test, under similar conditions. This is distinctly a fear test. Burtt, Troland, and myself,[4] in testing various types of deception test for war purposes, in court and laboratory, found the blood pressure test most useful, and the lengthening of reaction time tests least valuable, especially in actual court cases. J. A. Larsen, who has used deception tests of all types, in court cases, upon more than a thousand suspects, has omitted the association-word and reaction-time tests from his later technique, depending chiefly upon the systolic blood-pressure test, " while retaining the breathing curve as a check ".[5] Larson is quoted by C. T. McCormick[6] who has recently made a most careful and painstaking study of the present status of deception tests in America, as stating that his technique has been used successfully in the Police

[1] H. E. Burtt, " The Inspiration-Expiration Ratio During Truth and Falsehood," *Journal of Experimental Psychology*, 1921, vol. IV, p. 18.
[2] H. S. Langfield, " Psychological Symptoms of Deception," 1920, *Journal of Abnormal Psychology*, vol. XV, pp. 319-247.
[3] C. G. Jung, " The Association Method," *American Journal of Psychology*, 1910, vol. XXI, pp. 219-269. See also *Brain*, 1907, vol. XXX, p 153.
[4] W. M. Marston, " Psychological Possibilities in the Deception Tests," *Journal of Criminal Law and Criminology*, vol. XI, no. 4, pp. 112-131.
[5] C. T. McCormick, " Deception Tests and the Law of Evidence," *California Law Review*, September, 1927, p. 491.
[6] Ibid, p. 491-492.

Department of Los Angeles, Oakland, Duluth, and Evanston. Which means, apparently, that the *dominance type of deception test, in actual practice, turns out to be by far the most reliable.*

Reversed Relationships Between Submission and Inducement

Reversals of the normal relationship between submission and inducement are responsible for conflicting and thwarted love emotions in exactly the same way that reversals of relationship between dominance and compliance are responsible for conflicting and thwarted appetitive emotions. We have already noted, in chapters XIII and XIV, that the efficient, normal relationship between submission and inducement response consists of *adaptation of* inducement response to submission emotion. That is to say, in terms of conscious organization of emotional responses, the normal and efficient attitude in all love responses consists of inducing another individual only for the purpose of submitting to him. The final state of resting equilibrium between inducement and submission responses depends upon a final submission response equal to and controlling whatever inducement reaction may have preceded it.

Love is an emotion which is precisely opposite to appetite in the relationship which it establishes between subject and stimulus. In appetitive responses, no matter whether active or passive, compliance with the stimulus must only be a means used to dominate that stimulus for the advantage of the subject organism. Appetite is essentially ego-seeking or self-enlarging, and unless the subject's own organism, at the end of the response, is in a completely dominant relationship to its environment, then appetite has not accomplished its purpose. In the case of love responses, however, quite the opposite relationship is sought. Here, the subject endeavours to place himself under the control of another individual for the purpose of giving himself or some part of himself to the other person.

Inducement must always be the preliminary to this process of giving one's self to another, since it is no part of love to thrust upon another individual something that he does not want. The prospective recipient of a submissive service or gift, therefore, must first be induced to accept it willingly and gladly. For unless submission of one's self to another can be made pleasant and acceptable to the other individual, the ultimate giving ceases to be a true submission. Thus it is easy to see that *inducement must always precede and be wholly adapted to submission response if the total response is to be true love behaviour.*

Reversals of the normal relationship between successive inducement and submission responses may be brought about either by too much submission, or by too much inducement. Submission may be present so predominantly in the subject's existing behaviour, that when the necessity for inducement arises, in order to make continuance of submission possible, the subject tries to go on submitting even though he is compelled by the situation to *want to induce.* This integrative mix-up closely resembles the attempt which over-dominance may make to go on dominating, even after it has suffered defeat by compulsory compliance, by turning vengefully upon the compliance stimulus. So, in the present instance over-submission pushes, helplessly and unpleasantly, at the stimulus which has compelled unwilling inducement response. This type of situation may be called *over-submission reversal.* It is a male lover, gnawing silently and painfully at his moustache, while his mamorata captivates a more attractive man. A most unpleasant conflict is taking place between involuntary inducement wish to win back the girl's attention, and an oversubmission to the girl's charms which is determined, as it were, not to give way to the inducement interruption already tacitly recognized. *This is a conflict wherein submission attacks inducement.*

The opposite type of reversal relationship between submission and inducement may be brought about by too much inducement. When a person whose ultimate aim in all relationships with people is to establish an inducement control over them discovers that the submission which he has preliminarily employed as bait on the inducing hook is, after all, insufficient to make the other person submit, his inducement may flare up at this sudden resistance with consummate virulence. Over inducement is attacking the stimulus person toward whom further submission is required if the ultimate inducement is still to be accomplished. In other words, over-inducement is attacking compulsory submission. This variety of abnormal integration may be called *over-inducement reversal.* It is a woman who, having thrown herself at her former lover's feet to induce him to come back to her, winning but a contemptuous laugh as response, hurls herself upon the man, tearing at his face with her hands in a paroxysm of destruction. A *conflict* is taking place in the woman's central nervous system, between over-intense inducement and enforced submission. *This is a conflict wherein over-inducement attacks submission.*

Over-Submission Reversals—Jealousy

The line of demarcation between over-submission and over-submission *reversal* falls between *unbalanced absorption in the loved one's companionship* and *jealousy.* Watson failed to evoke jealousy, experimentally, by presenting various situations wherein a younger child was loved by the mother in the presence of the older brother, while the older child received less attention than before.[1] It seems probable, perhaps, that love had not reached a height of development, in the child subject, which could result in over-submission to the mother. Also, it seems likely that there was not sufficient love stimulation of the child actually in progress at the time the younger child was introduced. I have evoked jealousy from a three-year-old girl, however, while the mother was ' cuddling " and caressing the little daughter in her arms, by bringing in an older boy to whom the mother turned and talked, though she still kept her daughter in her arm meantime. The little girl at first responded normally, with inducement, by pulling at her mother's dress to attract attention again to herself, and by " snuggling " closer against the mother's body. When this produced only an admonitory " Keep quiet, Bee ! " from the mother, the child made a gesture as though to push the boy away from her mother and then buried her head against the mother's breast and began to cry quite softly, evidently in order to obey the mother's injunction to remain quiet. Neither mother nor child knew that any experiment or behaviour observation was being made.

In this case, the little girl's active submission to her mother was at its height when interrupted. The interruption created a stimulus situation which should normally evoke inducement response from the little girl in order to resume her interrupted submission to her mother. A slight inducement reaction

[1] J. B. Watson, *Behaviorism*, pp. 149-154.

was, in fact, evoked. But when it proved initially unsuccessful, the child's existing over-submission cut short her inducement behaviour. In that process, the child *reversed* the normal relationship between submission and inducement, and actually adapted her over-submission to the abortive inducement response, by submitting to the mother as well as she could while the inducement response was still uncontrollably activating her organism. In short, there was a conflict between submission and inducement, each partially thwarting the other. Submission was compelled to adapt to inducement because it *couldn't* wholly eliminate it, and *wouldn't* give way to it. The result was the abnormal emotion of *jealousy*, probably making its earliest appearance in this child's consciousness.

Consider how an older person possessing normal emotional relationship between submission and inducement, might have solved this emotional problem without suffering reversal, conflict and jealousy. Inducement must be kept in adaptation to submission. That would mean, in a situation similar to the one under discussion, that complete submission to the mother must be maintained continuously, whatever other reactions might be going forward. How to keep this submissive relationship, then, becomes the only issue. There is only one type of emotional response that is capable of influencing the mother to accept further submission, and that is inducement. An inducement programme which will accomplish this end most successfully, then, must be selected. *Inducement must be adapted to submission.* If the boy visitor is giving the mother pleasure, then the would-be inducer must find some way of giving the mother *more* pleasure from the boy's visit. A question might evoke some response from the boy pleasing to the mother, or the boy might be given a cookie or an apple. Such an action toward the boy would constitute an inducement of the mother to accept this new submission, the added pleasure she derives from the boy's presence, at the hands of her daughter. Inducement, on the daughter's part, adapted to submission, has enabled her to submit continuously and actively to her mother. Under the situation produced by the advent of the boy visitor, physical caresses were no longer a submission to the mother. Therefore, a wholly new series of true inducement reactions must be discovered capable of influencing the mother to accept the new submissions. *Inducement would then be adapted to submission, throughout, and there could be no reversal, no conflict, and no jealousy.*

A considerable series of over-submission reversal conflicts might be described, each producing its characteristic, abnormal emotion. Among these might be mentioned sorrow, grief, loneliness (when living in midst of social group), shyness, and melancholy (including psychopathic states of this type). Since this book is devoted to a study of normal emotions, we shall not discuss this abnormal group further here.

Over Inducement Reversals—Hate

The line of demarcation between over-inducement and over-inducement *reversal* falls between *unbalanced determination to control another person's actions,* and *hatred.* There seem to be at hand no well authenticated instances of true hatred responses evoked from children. Clearest examples of hatred on a vast scale are to be found in hatreds between races, especially, of course, during war. The "men in the street" of one nation are convinced, largely by newspaper propaganda, inspired sometimes by politicians but oftener by private appetitive interests of one sort or another, that citizens of another country have "insulted the flag" or "violated the rights of our citizens". When the Spanish war was begun by American newspapers, it was the rights of suffering Cubans that furnished the magic touchstone capable of evoking American hatred. To carry out the love response apparently felt by Americans toward the injured Cubans, America must *induce* the Spaniards to alter their treatment of their oppressed subjects. Americans did not intend to *submit* to the Spanish, on any other basis whatever than that which America proposed to induce Spain to accept. Yet as long as the Spanish continued to treat the Cubans harshly, which it was within their power, for the moment, to do, America was *compelled* to submit, despite the utmost intensity of attempted inducement to the contrary. There resulted a conflict, then, in the American consciousness, between enforced submission to Spain, and over-inducement which was trying to adapt this submission to itself by controlling the actions of the Spanish, and making them adopt the particular course of action to which Americans were willing to submit. So long as the Spaniards refused to yield to America's inducement, therefore, they evoked hatred from every American who suffered from the over-inducement reversal taught by misunderstood patriotism. Until the citizens of one nation are willing to induce another nation only for the purpose of being able better to submit to the interests of that other nation, national hatreds must inevitably spring up upon any occasion when one nation is compelled to submit to the actions of another, despite its utmost efforts to induce the other nation to adopt some other action which the first nation prefers, for its own reasons, to submit to.

In such horribly disastrous international hatreds, where millions of individuals are deliberately taught to experience the most abnormal of all emotions, the primary emotional reversal is identical with that which is responsible for the most transitory private hatred, between two individuals only. And this reversal springs, in both cases, from the same cause. The individual who hates, or the national group of individuals who hate another group, are so determined upon inducing other people to do one particular thing, that they fail to perceive that they can easily induce the other individual or national group to do some other thing that *can be submitted to* by the inducers. Devastating dominance quickly enters the picture, once the offending nation resists being induced, and the offender then becomes an antagonist, not to be induced any longer, but to be knocked out, and thus compelled, not to submit, but to comply. Thus in the end, no matter how successful the war victor may be, *he never attains his original purpose of inducing the other person to submit ; at best, he can only dominate an enemy and compel compliance.* If the original end of inducing submission is to be gained, then inducement must be adapted to submission. Which means, specifically, that some course of action on the offending nation's part must be found to which the inducer is willing ultimately to submit, and which the inducer has the present power to induce the offender to submit to. In short, each must ultimately submit, and each must select an inducement which will bring about acceptance of the submission which each is prepared to make. This is " compromise ", " fellowship of nations ", and *peace*. Inducement *must* be kept adapted to submission, or people become things and destroy one another. Hatred is the abnormal emotion that accompanies destruction of *human things* by *human things.*

Though inducement gives way largely to dominance, during war, enough of the reversed S and I remain to keep active the background of motivating hatred, without which such futilly unproductive dominance would soon die down. And hatred is easily distinguishable from dominance throughout. The background wish is not to make the enemy *comply* but to make him *submit ;* and he is to be made to submit to one specific inducement, selected arbitrarily by the over-inducer. Therefore, there is the constant, motivating drive to make the inducement (now metamorphosed into destructive dominance) more and more and more intense, so that the victim will *feel it sufficiently to submit.* The reversed over-inducer fails utterly to realize that the power of inducement lies not at all in antagonistic intensity, but *allied* intensity. If there is the slightest injurious element felt in the over-intensity of the would-be inducer, all power of such hoped-for inducement to evoke submission is taken from it. But, of course, the attacker does not realize this ; his S and I are in reversal. Therefore, to make his motivating inducement more powerful he seeks to *hurt* the object of hatred personally to the greatest extent possible. This gives hatred quite a different conscious quality from dominance, which seeks only to compel the stimulus object into alliance with the self, or to remove it altogether as an obstacle from the subject's path. Dominance is intense, ruthless, but impersonal. Hatred is deliberately cruel, even more intense than dominance, and concentratedly personal.

Resentment, so called " thwarted sex " or sex anger,[1] certain types of personal malice, certain paranoid states, and many other peculiarly dangerous reversal emotions undoubtedly belong with hatred in the series of over-inducement reversal emotions. But they are abnormal emotions, and therefoie cannot be discussed further in the present volume.

---

[1] I formerly attempted to devote the term " anger " exclusively to this variety of emotion calling it " true anger ", contrasting it to thwarted over-intense dominance, which I termed rage or fury. Criticisms upon this article showed, however, that the term " anger " could not be divorced in the public mind from dominance and its reversals. Therefore, it seems best to emphasize the word hatred in connection with reversal emotion containing submission and inducement in mutually conflicting and ultimately baffled condition.

Summary

Compliance must be adapted to. dominance, and inducement to submission, if human beings wish to remain normal. Reversals of these relationships invariably result in conflicts between primary emotions.

It is beyond the powers of the organism to adapt certain compliance reactions to any superceding dominance responses which the organism is equipped to make. If the subject is over-dominant, he may nevertheless insist upon attempting the impossible, even though there are many other compliance responses available which might easily be adapted to and replaced by ultimate dominance. Such over-dominant subjects merely succeed in adapting their dominance to the unconquerable compliance response by continuing to hammer at it, yet all the while with a dominance partially baffled by recognition of the futility of the attack. *This situation is called over-dominance reversal, and its typical abnormal emotion is rage.*

There may be compliance reactions going on which the organism is fully capable of adapting to appropriate superceding, dominance responses. But if the subject is over-compliant he may not attempt ·the possible. Such over-compliant subjects permit their dominance to be forced into destructive adaptation to their compliance emotion, with the awareness, all the time, that dominance is being progressively defeated. *This situation is called over-compliance reversal, and its typical abnormal emotion is fear.*

There may be submission responses going on which the organism is fully capable of continuing, if appropriate inducement responses are selected, and are adapted to the submission which the organism seeks to attain. But if the subject is over-submissive, his submission may prevent him from choosing and expressing such properly-adapted inducement reactions. The result is that the submission must adapt itself to whatever futile inducement reaction the subject is capable of making, with the constant awareness that his submission is being progressively defeated by its inability to use adequate inducement tools. *This situation is called over-submission reversal, and its typical abnormal emotion is jealousy.*

It is beyond the power of the organism to adapt certain inducement responses to the organism's ultimate submission. Nevertheless, an over-inductive individual may continue to attempt the impossible by refusing to give up this futile·inducement and to select another inducement reaction capable of being adapted to, and superceded by submission response. Such over-inductive subjects merely succeed in adapting their submission to their futile inducement by continuing the ineffective inducement response more and more intensely, though all the while with the awareness of having their submission hopelessly baffled by its adaptation to unsuccessful inducement. *This situation is termed over-inducement reversal and its typical abnormal emotion is hatred.*

Love-Appetite Reversal Emotions

In the course of previous discussion we have noted both the normal and the reversed relationships between love and appetite. The normal relationship consists of complete adaptation of appetite to love. Any life which is both successful and happy must adapt its successes to its happiness. Certain types of individuals who habitually attempt to adapt happiness to success ultimately fail in both. There seems even to exist a predisposing emotional trend, in certain racial types of human beings, toward what might be termed a chronic reversal between love and appetite. Probably nearly all human beings on the planet, however, suffer more or less from this form of reversal and conflict between love and appetite. The Freudian system of psycho-analysis seems to be based, for the most part, on the most fundamental of all discoveries, to wit, that appetite should be adapted to love, whereas in modern life social laws and conventions compel the adaptation of love to appetite. The value of this discovery in the hands of the psycho-analysts, however, has been negated by the defining of love itself in appetitive terms. The prospective lover is told that he has an " appetite " or a " desire " for the body or companionship of his loved one. Love itself is described as " sex emotion ", and its so-called " normal " expression, therefore, is limited to " sexual appetite " between members of opposite sexes. The reversal relationship between love and appetite, with love adapted to and controlled by appetite, which is recognized by some psycho-analysts as the theoretical source of all emotional conflicts, is perpetuated and enhanced by such depictions of love emotion in terms of eating and digesting the alleged loved one.

If the normal and efficient emotional relationship between

love and appetite is to be understood, it is first of all necessary to understand the true nature of love itself, since love, in its normal relationship with appetite, must be the controlling response to which appetite is completely adapted. Love is a giving, and not a taking ; a feeding, and not an eating ; an altruistic alliance with the loved one, and not a selfish conflict with a " sex object ". *Whatever the organism has acquired during the expression of its appetitive emotion must be given away again in the expression of love, and " everything " includes the organism itself.* " Giving away ", however, does not mean destruction or depreciation of the giver. It means only a submission of everything that the giver possesses, including his own body, to the service and needs of the loved one. Such an understanding of love presents an extreme contrast to the description of mixed and conflicting emotional states suggested by the term " sex appetite ".

The normal relationship consisting of appetite adapted to and controlled by love emotion, is made compulsory upon the female organism, at least, during the process of procreation. The emotion of creation which this process teaches necessitates, as we have already seen, the use of appetite solely for love purposes. The female organism is not individually depleted during this process, since the woman herself must remain strong, and physically and mentally efficient for the very accomplishment of the love purpose of serving her child. A human being or animal in order to adapt completely to environment must die and undergo chemical decomposition. But a human being or animal in order to submit to and serve the need of the loved one must become more healthily alive than before. Any deterioration or dimunition of the active creatress injures or diminishes her creation by a corresponding amount. Thus it is that complete adaptation of appetite to love is maximally efficacious, even from the point of view of enlargement of the lover. Adaptation of appetite to love cannot become self sacrificial so long as love is actually in control. Only when the reversed relationship of adaptation of love to appetite creeps in, does any emotional conflict appear between love purposes and appetitive needs.

Preliminary study of all the multitudinous reversal emotions to which control of love by appetite gives rise in human behaviour would require a volume or more devoted to such analysis. But in so far as these reversal emotions exist in human or animal behaviour, they represent real abnormalities of emotion, and therefore fall, for the most part, outside the scope of the present book. A number of these reversal emotions, however, may be somewhat sketchily suggested here, for the sake of the light which they shed upon normal emotional attitudes and relationships.

Reversal Emotions Between Active and Passive Love and Active and Passive Appetite

Active love, when adapted to and controlled by active appetite, gives rise to a type of complex emotional behaviour made famous in America under the term " gold digging ". Chorus girls, night club entertainers, younger sons who marry for money, and " gigolos " whose haunt is the tea-house, whose victims are usually middle-aged women with no longer ardent husbands, and whose method of approach is a position as dancer, all are professional gold diggers. Amateur gold diggers, however, abound on every side. In certain " society " and college circles it is difficult, in fact, to find a girl or young woman who has not, in her emotional make-up, some attributes of the gold digger.

Gold digging is particularly attractive, apparently, because nothing need be given in exchange for appetitive benefits received. Active love consists of captivating the person selected as a prospective source of appetitive supply. When this individual is certain to be under sufficient love control, active appetite is turned on, as it were, to take the supply away from the love-captured individual, and to appropriate it conclusively to the possession of the captivatress. Neither active submission nor compliance, which appear to be the two most difficult emotions for human beings to learn and to express, are required in this process of gold digging. As we have noted, active love and active appetite are held in continuous conflict when the love is controlled by and used for appetite emotion. Active love is definitely terminated altogether, each time the gold digger begins a definite digging, or active appetitive response. If this dominant extraction of money or property from the captivated person can be done very deftly, or very quickly, captivation may again be turned on, and another appetitive reward thereby gained. There is always a definite limit, however, to the series of successive captivations and acquisitions, the length of the series depending upon the proportion of love to appetite in the emotional organization of the victim. Older men, whose appetite emotion is pretty much satiated, and whose love reactions, thus freed from inhibitory restraint, assert an unbalanced emotional control of behaviour in an effort to compensate for total absence of love in the man's previous life, seem to constitute the most susceptible victims for this type of reversed emotional stimulation. Though a woman gold digger may start her reversal activities with an unusually strong equipment of active love emotion, this emotion inevitably dwindles, and becomes thwarted and perverted under the conflicting influence of appetitive control, until, eventually, her power of love captivation is completely gone, and her career as a gold digger automatically çeases.

Active love when adapted to and controlled by passive appetite is popularly termed " *seduction* ". The ultimate object of seduction is not to obtain enrichment from the persons captivated, but rather to compel the love captive to give sensual enjoyment to the seducer, in the same way that delicate food or enjoyable entertainment might evoke satisfaction emotion from the subject.

Passive love, when adapted to and controlled by passive appetite, is frequently referred to as " *sensuality* ". In this case the individual, male or female, wishes to be captivated for the purpose of experiencing passion ; which in turn, is enjoyed as an intensely pleasurable form of appetitive satisfaction.

When passive love is adapted to active appetite the resulting behaviour is legally termed " *prostitution* ". In this case, a love response which, at the beginning, is genuine passion, is adapted to and controlled by desire for obtaining money, and other forms of payment, from the physical captivator to whom the subject submits. All marriages wherein one or the other individual, though experiencing passion for the other person, nevertheless adapts this passion to the acquisition of money or position, and allows this passion to be controlled by this active appetite purpose, may properly be classified under this heading. I have observed, also, a number of instances where boys and young men appear to manifest a real passion response for an older male, whom they admire and " hero worship ". In every case, these young men used their passive love response toward the older and more powerful man, for the purpose of obtaining from him the maximum possible appetitive benefits in the way of position, salary, and professional preferment)

Reversal Emotions Between Active and Passive Love and Dominance

When active love is adapted to and controlled by active dominance, the resulting emotional expression in its abnormal extreme is termed " sadism ". The wish to captivate another person is controlled by the actively dominant purpose of destroying the love captive. In other forms of sadism with which we have been made familiar by the Marquis de Sade, himself, active dominance is used as in war, with the intent to compel the victim to become utterly submissive to the will of the over-inducer-dominator. In this form of sadism, the dominance response imposes various tortures upon the body of the person subjected, revealing the fact that the subjected person is regarded, for the time, as an inanimate antagonistic object, which must be compelled to ally itself with the dominator. The pleasant emotional experiences derived from the exercise of sadism are active love captivation responses springing from whatever spontaneous, voluntary feelings of love captivity and passion may be evoked from the person subjected. Thus a notorious American sadist, a few years ago, compelled a boy whom he whipped mercilessly to write a dictated " submission ", meanwhile, reciting the feelings of abject love captivity which it gave the sadist delight to imagine the boy to be experiencing. Mild whipping, spanking, or other forms of subjecting force applied to the body of the person captivated may not, necessarily, constitute sadism *provided that the individual subjected is not injured physically or emotionally, and provided that the captivatress seeks to subject the other individual only in those ways which will evoke maximum pleasantness in the other individual.* Wherever dominance gains control of active love, a diminution of pleasure and passion in the love captive immediately results, and the captivation excitement and pleasantness in the captivatress is correspondingly diminished. Thus the attempt to adapt love to dominance only results, with sadism as with other forms of reversal emotion, in mutual conflict and diminution, or complete inhibition of love emotion. No male is physically equipped to act as a captivatress. Whenever a man attempts to· use dominance to captivate either a woman or another male, his dominance almost certainly controls his captivation, making him temporarily a sadist. Whenever a man " mauls " a girl, or his wife, or mistress, he may begin as a captivatress, but he almost invariably breaks over into sadism at the climax of his excitement.

Passive love when adapted to and controlled by active dominance, is popularly termed " *treachery* ". The individual who submits actively to another person, passively inducing the other to form an intimate personal relationship of confidence and trust, and then uses the information or power thus obtained to dominate his victim, is said to be " treacherous ". In treachery, the passive love attitude is wholly adapted to and controlled by a dominant determination to destroy the betrayed individual, as an obstacle to the other's purposes, or to compel the betrayed person to ally himself with the other for the purpose of furthering the latter's interests.

Reversal Emotions Between Inducement and Submission and Appetitive Primaries

When active submission is adapted to and controlled by active dominance, or, in fact, by any of the normal appetitive combinations of dominance and compliance, the resulting response is properly termed " *hypocrisy* ". A certain amount of genuine regard for the needs and interests of another, individual is used in this series of reversal emotions, to cloak or disguise the underlying, controlling dominance of the person who would use another individual for his own ends. Inducement, also, may enter the composite integrative picture of hypocrisy. Certain types of hypocrisy behaviour manifest all the elements of creation emotion, in fairly well ordered form, the creative elements being used severally and collectively for the furtherance of appetitive purposes. " Reformers " who receive large salaries and international publicity as a result of their professional " reform " activities seem frequently to typify the extreme of this reversed adaptation of creation emotion to their own appetitive desires. Sometimes such a person's ultimate purpose represents an almost pure dominance response, while upon other occasions the pecuniary reward sought would indicate that active appetite in its entirety is the ultimate controlling response, to which

inducement, submission and perhaps active creation emotion is adapted.
When inducement is adapted to and controlled by dominance or appetite, some form of "deception" results. Active inducement is employed to evoke submission from the person deceived, for the purpose of utilizing the deceived one's submissive behaviour for a dominant or appetitive interest of the deceiver. The combination of primary emotions which results in the initial act of deception is not to be confused with the situation in which the deceiver is being cross-examined by a lawyer or psychologist intent upon revealing the deception which has already been perpetrated. The latter condition, which constitutes the deception test situation, consists, chiefly, of a relationship of attacker and attacked between the cross-examiner and the individual accused of the deception. Probably some admixture of inducement ultimately may be found in the total emotional responses of the subject under examination, if he is lying. But, for the most part, the examinee is merely attempting to defend himself, to the extent perhaps, of his liberty or his life, against what he feels to be the dominant attempt of the examiner to take away from him the secret information which he is with-holding. In actual court room procedure, the situation is somewhat altered by the fact that the witness must induce the judge or jury to believe his story, at the same time that he defends himself against the attack of his enemy or antagonist, the prosecutor, or cross-examining attorney. However this situation may ultimately be analyzed, the emotional responses of the subject under such conditions have very little to do with the fundamental reversal emotions which supply the motivation for initial deception.

Active inducement may be used to accomplish an ultimate end of active appetite over the property of another person. In other words, the property owner may be induced to behave in a manner enabling the deceiver to dominate his possessions without giving compensation therefor. This may be called *deception to obtain property under false pretences.*

Active inducement, again, may be adapted to and controlled by passive appetite emotion. This is the situation in which a person who has committed a crime or indiscretion uses active inducement to evoke submission to himself from the prosecutor, or other person having authority to visit punishment upon the culprit. The submission obtained takes the form of accepting the deceiver's story as an accurate compliance with fact, and a consequent searching elsewhere for the culprit. This type of deception, in a society which punishes all offenders against its arbitrary rules with a savage severity all out of proportion to the offence committed, is generally considered to be a more or less excusable type of reversal behaviour. Thus adults are stimulated to deception reversal by laws which themselves embody male sadism and hypocrisy, just as children are stimulated to deception reversal by parents who similarly adapt love to appetite in their treatment of their children.

Finally, the more simple type of deception, wherein active inducement is adapted to and controlled by simple active dominance, may be mentioned. In this type of behaviour, the deceiver succeeds in dominating the opponent in games, or in a contest involving personal prestige of some sort, by inducing his rival to submit by acting in a manner which will enable the deceiver to dominate him. Traps of all kinds, when set for human beings or for animals, are examples of this type of reversal between active inducement and active dominance. In various sorts of so-called sporting contests, this reversed use of inducement to gain the ends of dominance is considered extremely clever and highly commendable. This type of reversal behaviour is sometimes termed " deceptive trickery ". In games, however, where certain types of deception behaviour are permissible under the rules, it is true that both contestants are fairly warned to be on their guard. That part of the game, therefore, becomes a deception-contest furnishing effective training in the abnormal adaptation of inducement to dominance.

CHAPTER XVIII

EMOTIONAL RE-EDUCATION

No matter how normal a person may be, he has been taught, from earliest childhood, to evaluate his own behaviour by the measuring stick of convention. What his father did before him, and what his neighbours are now doing around him, constitute the standard of normalcy. And this ridiculous method of evaluation is, to a considerable extent, sanctioned by the so-called "social scientists" of to-day—evidently because psychology, so far, has failed to furnish any tangible description of a normal human being, save a statistical one. A bold psychiatrist, not so long ago, frankly stated that if a young girl attended a school where a majority of the other girls smoked and drank, she would be eligible for psychiatric examination if she refused also to smoke and drink. I take it that the eminent doctor who made this assertion did not mean to suggest smoking and drinking as a test of social submission to girl friends, but rather as an emphatic laying down of the rule that average behaviour of a given group constitutes a proper standard by which the normalcy of any member of the group may be scientifically measured. No principle for study and improvement of the individual could be more pernicious than this.

People Only See the Least Normal Part of Other People's Behaviour

It is pernicious for several reasons, but principally for this. The part of the behaviour of any member of a group of human beings which any other member of the group is able to observe, constitutes a small and unrepresentative fraction of the other person's total conscious activities. The part of any individual's behaviour which he permits other individuals to observe is that part which he believes will find most merit in the observer's eyes and, therefore, will probably procure the

389

maximum benefit, of one sort or another, for the person observed.

People are taught, from earliest childhood, that the " right thing to do " is what they are told to do by those who are able to give them rewards. Children tend, therefore, to behave, in the presence of their parents, according to the rules of behaviour set by the parents. With other children, their behaviour is quite different. Still, their responses are not wholly normal, because they have already learned to shape their actions in such a way as to produce the effect upon other children most advantageous to themselves. In absolute secret, however, with no other individuals present, the child behaves in a radically different manner. This secret conduct is most normal. Yet the child quickly learns to regard it as most abnormal. As the individual grows older, his explicit behaviour becomes more and more controlled by what he thinks other people will approve of, and will reward him for most handsomely. His own normal self, determined as it is by his physical body structures, continues to express itself in secret, but gradually this normal behaviour becomes almost wholly implicit, in order not to reveal itself in some action not beneficial to the subject in the eyes of his fellows. Thus human beings, by adhering to the general type of *observable* behaviour in their own group, learn to regard more than one half of their normal selves as abnormal. In order to continue to be thought normal, they must continue to regard their own natural, secret behaviour as abnormal. Moreover, though they may have a shrewd suspicion that other members of their particular group are behaving in secret very like themselves, they quickly learn to regard such secret normalcy of their fellows, whenever discovered, as disgustingly abnormal also. Upon learning that neighbour John Smith is secretly enjoying a true love relationship with a woman who could not advantageously be presented as Mrs. Smith, each secretly normal individual quickly denounces Smith's conduct with all the virulence at his command. Another stone has been added to the burden of abnormality under which humanity is labouring.

The " Inner Conviction " of Abnormality

All of which means, so far as emotional re-education goes, that the stupendously difficult task confronting the clinical psychologist is to convince normal people that the normal part of their emotions is normal. The more normal they are, the more people tend to entertain an " inner conviction " of abnormality. It is very easy, therefore, to detect some normal love longing which the subject already believes to be utterly abnormal, and to convince him (or more likely her), that his secret emotion must be " sublimated " into learning to play church music, or writing essays on art, which will never be published. But it is ridiculous to suppose that these so called " sublimations " will really do anything more than deprive the woman of part of her normal self which, prior to the " analysis ", she had at least a fighting chance of ultimately expressing overtly in a normal way.

Psycho-Neural Normalcy of Behaviour Does Not Depend Upon What One's Neighbour Does

The only practical emotional re-education consists in teaching people that there is a norm of psycho-neural behaviour, not dependent in any way upon what their neighbours are doing, or upon what they think their neighbours want them to do. People must be taught that the love parts of themselves, which they have come to regard as abnormal, are completely normal. More than this, people must be taught ultimately, that love (*real* love, not " sex appetite "), constitutes, in the human organism, the ultimate end of all activity, and that to gain this end appetite emotion must first, last, and always be adapted to love.

When this teaching is suggested, the emotional re-educator is at once faced with the problem of freeing the individual sufficiently from the existing standards of appetite-controlled society to permit him to express his psycho-neural self normally. Emotional abnormalities perpetuate themselves principally through compulsory compliance with *things*. Modern appetites are monstrously developed. To satisfy them, even partially, we must have things, and more things, and to get things we are obliged to comply with the people who now possess them. They set the standards. And they set standards, naturally, which enforce compliance with their own thing-getting activities, and which tend to make those activities more successful. The doctrine of taking the average, observable behaviour of any group as the definition of normal behaviour, really means that the degree of compliance with

things which any person manifests is the measure of his normality. What an astounding doctrine ! You are normal, according to this doctrine, in proportion to the amount of yourself that you are willing to give up, or to consider abnormal, *in order to get more things.*
How, then, can we free the normal part of our subject from the necessity of complying with an abnormal standard in order to satisfy his appetite ? People must be taught, first of all, that the compliance required for the getting of things is not a compliance with the abnormal parts of the thing-possessors, but with the normal appetitive portions of these individuals. These men, themselves, or their ancestors, won their possessions by never complying with any superior 'antagonistic force, except in a way calculated to dominate that very opponent. Applying this first rule of appetitive success to the very problem of over-coming the false standard of normalcy which owners of things seek to enforce, the person who would be normal must be advised to regard such individuals not as superior allies, to whom it is necessary to submit, but as temporarily superior antagonists, with whom it is necessary to *comply* in order ultimately to dominate them.

Appetitive Leaders Are Not Love Leaders

The fact is that persons of appetitive superiority have usurped the position of love leaders by virtue of their superior appetitive strength. They assume to dictate not only what other people must do in order to receive a share of their wealth and power, but also what the public in general must do, supposedly for its own good, without any hope of sharing in the spoils. It is impossible for a man who has spent his life in appetitive activity, or whose pre-eminent position depends upon successful maintenance of vast possessions, to prescribe any rules of conduct other than appetitive rules. It is likewise impossible for him to avoid using his dominant supremacy to compel less powerful people to act in a way favourable to his own interests. If, then, the public at large accept men of this type, not only as appetitive dictators but also as supposed love leaders of humanity, the present utterly abnormal suppression of love must continue.
If, however, it is within the power of the emotional re-educator to teach people in general that they should comply

with rules of conduct dictated by appetitive leaders, only to a sufficient extent to dominate the source of supply, and obtain independent meåns of their own, there is hope. Then people will be free to recognize their own normalcy, and to establish, gradually, a new code of conduct, based upon love supremacy and appetitive subserviency. I have tested this programme in the cases of male clinical subjects sufficiently to know that it can be made to work.

But what happens to the man during this process of re-education ? By the time he has acquired his first appetitive success, he is well on his way to the same dominant inhibition of all love emotion that obtains in the controlling emotional set of all thing-getters and possessors. There is, apparently, no dependable intra-organic love stimulation within the male organism. There is a strong intra-organic appetitive stimulus mechanism, hunger pangs, operating several times each day. As a result of this physical condition of affairs successful males invariably acquire a tremendous over balance of appetitive emotion response. By the time this appetitive drive is employed to the point of becoming successful in competition with other males, the preponderance of appetite over love has become still further exaggerated, and no amount of love stimulation administered by a woman, or women, under ordinary conditions, seems able to restore love to the place of importance which it may have held in the man's total emotional pattern when he was less successful.

In those rare instances were this does not occur, and where the man, after becoming successful, seeks to alter the appetitive code to permit some part of love to be recognised as normal, he is quite likely to suffer appetitive disaster as a result of his temerity in championing love. A case in point seems to be that of Judge Ben Lindsey, of Denver, who recently lost his judgeship, apparently as a result of his activities directed toward freeing love from appetitive control.[1] As a result of my own observations so far, I have reached the tentative conclusion that male love leadership is virtually impossible, for the two reasons stated. First, a man's body is not designed for active love, and does not, therefore, keep him sufficiently love stimulated to control his over developed appetite. Second, if he attains appetitive

[1] Judge Lindsey's opinions on the subject are to be found in his two books, *The Revolt of Modern Youth*, and *The Companionate Marriage*.

leadership, he is unable to turn this into love leadership, because other people will not submit to him sufficiently.

Qualifications of a Love Leader

What are the qualifications of an active love leader, in the situation under discussion ? There are four requisite attributes. First, an organism whose intra-organic stimulus mechanisms cause active love emotion to be evoked, preponderantly over passive love (passion), or any phase of appetite emotion. Second, sufficient appetitive power for self-support, without dependence, directly or indirectly, upon the persons who submit to the leader's direction. Third, a person with sufficient wisdom to understand all the emotion mechanisms 'of the adult organism. Fourth, a person with sufficient practical knowledge of existing social and economic institutions to be able to adapt the necessary measures of social reorganization, so as to evoke a maximum normalcy of emotional response from the public.

These four requirements probably cannot be met by any one in the world to-day. But they represent a wholly practical pattern of personality, which can be evolved, within a few generations, if emotional education is directed specifically towards the training and development of love leaders ; and simultaneously, toward development of a corresponding attitude of passive love on the part of the people who are in need of love leadership.

Emotional Re-education of Women To Become Love Leaders

Where can the emotional re-educator look for persons capable of being trained toward ultimate love leadership ? We have already seen that males cannot be counted on, unless the male organism changes radically. The only possible candidates for love leader training, therefore, are women. But of the four qualifications specified above, women of the present day possess only the first, namely, an organism containing adequate intra-organic love stimulus mechanisms.

It seems to me by far the most hopeful symptom of emotional evolution within the period of recorded human history, however, that women are beginning to develop both the power and willingness to support themselves. When this power is developed to three or four times its present capacity, some women, at least, will have acquired the second essential attribute of active love leadership, namely, appetitive self reliance. The necessity for such appetitive independence in a real love leader should be emphasized again at this point. It is by virtue of appetitive supremacy, alone, that males have ruled the world during the major portion of our racial history.

Presumably, it is because women so vastly preferred love responses to appetitive activity that they refrained so long from developing dominance to the point of appetitive self dependence. For example, I asked a class of thirty girls, recently, to express their preference between having an ideal love affair and possessing a million dollars. These girls are students in a physical training school, and have shown themselves, in other tests, to be much more dominant than the average female group. Twenty-five expressed preference for the love affair, and five for the million dollars. Despite this preference for love, however, modern women are realizing, at last, that love relationship in the home is utterly impossible, so long as they must use their love for appetite in obtaining support from husband or lover. They are equipping themselves accordingly; and there is great hope that love will begin to free itself from its present abnormally reversed relationship to appetite, as soon as women not only win sufficient dominance power to support themselves, but also demand the right to continue to support themselves throughout all relationships with males. The creation of children is not justifiable in a majority of unions between the sexes; but when the creation responses are justifiably undertaken, there is sound psychological ground for advising the woman to provide, before-hand, sufficient funds of her own to carry both herself and the child through the period of her physical incapacity for appetitive work. There is sound psychological ground, also, for requiring the male to share equally, at least, in the home work and the care of children.

Woman's attainment of the last two qualifications for love leadership is still far in the future. The emotional re-educator, however, must take the responsibility for discovering and describing human emotional mechanisms, and for instructing women carefully in their meaning and control. In my experience, at least, I have found that whatever practical knowledge we already possess, especially concerning the love and creation mechanisms, is intellectually assimilated far more rapidly by girl students than by men. The reverse is true, of course, at the present time, with regard to knowledge of the appetitive mechanisms. But when women require this knowledge, also, for the purpose of teaching their own children (the existing type of female love leadership), they seek it eagerly, and study it diligently, as evidenced by the extraordinary growth of " Child Study " organizations in recent years.

The final requirement for active love leadership of humankind by women, namely, that of a practical knowledge of political and social methods and present institutions, should develop from woman's increased dominance development, and from her consequent active participation in appetitive activities of all kinds. Women have already undertaken participation in public life, though not yet with satisfactory results, at least in America. It should be an important part of the emotional re-educator's constructive programme for women, to offer emotional analyses of existing political and social methods and procedures.

Emotional Re-education of Men and Women to Follow Love Leadership

It seems apparent that the second part of the suggested programme of emotional re-education, namely, the training of males and less actively developed women in passion response to the active love leaders, must be left to woman herself. No task could be found more compatible with woman's normal emotional equipment, once its normalcy is publicly acknowledged. But woman must be taught to use her love power exclusively for the benefit of humanity and not for her own destructive, appetitive gratifications, as so many women are doing, under the present appetitive regime.

Men dislike intensely the idea of submitting to women. Yet, at the same time, they exert themselves to the utmost to establish just such passionately submissive relationships with women who have captivated them. If, when such a relationship is accepted by the woman, she has been taught to continue her captivatress' love supremacy throughout the entire duration of her love relationship with the male, great happiness must result for both. The man's passionate enjoyment of submission can be evoked continuously, throughout the relationship, instead of lapsing, lugubriously, as now happens so frequently, when the woman is compelled to shift to a submissive rôle after marriage.

Compliance, if it springs from submission, may be pleasantly learned. This is an incidental benefit to be derived from such an emotional re-education programme as that suggested. For both compliance and dominance, if exercised for the sake of carrying out a passion response, gain all the pleasantness of the passion in place of their previous unpleasantness, without losing their appetitive efficacy in the slightest degree. The emotional re-education programme suggested, therefore, nolds the potentiality of appetitive success as well as love happiness. For, in place of the reversed conflict relationship of happiness adapted to success, which, at the present time, partially defeats both, *success must be adapted to happiness*.

INDEX

INTERNATIONAL LIBRARY

OF

PSYCHOLOGY, PHILOSOPHY,

AND

SCIENTIFIC METHOD

Edited by *C. K. Ogden, M.A.*, of Magdalene College, Cambridge.

Demy 8vo, dark-green cloth.   Prices from 5s. to 25s. net.

The purpose of the International Library is to give expression, in a convenient form and at a moderate price, to the remarkable developments which have recently occurred in Psychology and its allied sciences. The older philosophers were preoccupied by metaphysical interests which for the most part have ceased to attract the younger investigators, and their forbidding terminology too often acted as a deterrent for the general reader. The attempt to deal in clear language with current tendencies whether in England and America or on the Continent has met with a very encouraging reception, and not only have accepted authorities been invited to explain the newer theories, but it has been found possible to include a number of original contributions of high merit. The attention of Librarians is drawn to the comprehensive character of the volumes (nearly seventy in number) now available as a uniform series ; the standard maintained may be judged from the following list.

LONDON
KEGAN PAUL, TRENCH, TRUBNER & CO., LTD
BROADWAY HOUSE : 68-74 CARTER LANE, E.C.
1928

INTERNATIONAL LIBRARY OF PSYCHOLOGY

VOLUMES PUBLISHED

PHILOSOPHICAL STUDIES. By *G. E. Moore, Litt.D.*, author of " Principia Ethica ", editor of " Mind ".
15/- net.
"Students of philosophy will welcome the publication of this volume. It is full of interest and stimulus, even to those whom it fails to convince ; and it is also very undogmatic. Dr Moore is always anxious to bring out the arguments against those in favour of the positions to which he inclines, and cares to refute not persons but false doctrines."—*Oxford Magazine.*
" A valuable contribution to contemporary philosophy."—*Spectator.*

THE MISUSE OF MIND : a Study of Bergson's Attack on Intellectualism. By *Karin Stephen,* formerly Fellow of Newnham College, Cambridge. Preface by *Henri Bergson.*
6/6 net.
" This is a book about Bergson, but it is not one of the ordinary popular expositions. It is very short ; but it is one of those books the quality of which is in inverse ratio to its quantity, for it focusses our attention on one single problem and succeeds in bringing it out with masterly clearness. The problem is the relation of fact to explanation. So stated it may sound dull ; but the moment its import is grasped, it is seen to deal with the fundamental difference between two rival methods in philosophy."—*Times Literary Supplement.*

CONFLICT AND DREAM. By *W. H. R. Rivers, M.D., Litt.D., F.R.S.* Preface by *Professor G. Elliot Smith, F.R.S.*
12/6 net.
" In his last book Mr Arnold Bennett claims for W. H. R. Rivers a place among great men. As traveller, healer, and experimenter Rivers had that kind of commanding vigour that is one of the marks of genius. Nothing could be more fascinating than to watch him separating the gold from the alloy in Freud's theory of dreams. His book is as different from the usual Freudian book on the same subject as is a book of astronomy from a book of astrology."—Robert Lynd, in *Daily News.*

PSYCHOLOGY AND POLITICS, and Other Essays. By *W. H. R. Rivers, F.R.S.* Preface by *Professor G. Elliot Smith.* Appreciation by *C. S. Myers, F.R.S.*
12/6 net.
" In all the essays in this volume one feels the scientific mind, the mind that puts truth first. Each of the essays is interesting and valuable ; perhaps the most arresting is that in which he discusses and defends, in the light of recent research, the conception of society as an organism."
—*New Leader.* " This volume is a fine memorial of a solid and cautious scientific worker."—Havelock Ellis, in *Nation.*

MEDICINE, MAGIC, AND RELIGION. By *W. H. R. Rivers, F.R.S.* Preface by *Professor G. Elliot Smith.*
Second edition, 10/6 net.
"It is principally an attempt to interpret the ideas that inspired primitive medicine. But the penetrating mind of a seeker such as Rivers inevitably went beyond that : it is disclosure of the principles by which primitive societies lived. No more important contribution to ethnological knowledge has been made during the past twenty years."—*Adelphi.* "Dr Rivers' book is one long array of fascinating illustration, linking up his subject with the most modern forms of neurosis, a contribution of quite exceptional value to medicine and history alike."—*Northern Review.*

3

INTERNATIONAL LIBRARY OF PSYCHOLOGY

THE MEANING OF MEANING : a Study of the Influence of Language upon Thought and of the Science of Symbolism. By *C. K. Ogden* and *I. A. Richards.* Supplementary Essays by *Professor B. Malinowski* and *F. G. Crookshank, M.D., F.R.C.P.*

Second edition, 12/6 *net.*

" The authors attack the problem from a more fundamental point of view than that from which others have dealt with it, and at last some light is thrown on the factors involved. The importance of their work is obvious. It is a book for educationalists, ethnologists, grammarians, logicians, and, above all, psychologists. The book is written with admirable clarity and a strong sense of humour, making it not only profitable but also highly entertaining reading for anyone who wishes to address any remark to a fellow creature with the intention of being understood."—*New Statesman.*

SCIENTIFIC METHOD : an Inquiry into the Character and Validity of Natural Laws. By *A. D. Ritchie,* Fellow of Trinity College, Cambridge.

10/6 *net.*

" The fresh and bright style of Mr Ritchie's volume, not without a salt of humour, makes it an interesting and pleasant book for the general reader. Taken as a whole *Scientific Method* is able, comprehensive, and, in our opinion, right in its main argument and conclusions."—*British Medical Journal.* " His brilliant book."—*Daily News.*

THE PSYCHOLOGY OF REASONING. By *Eugenio Rignano,* Professor of Philosophy in the University of Milan.

14/- *net.*

" Professor Rignano's elaborate treatise, which completely surveys all the chief types of reasoning, normal and abnormal, is a valuable contribution to psychological literature."—*Weekly Westminster.* " The theory is that reasoning is simply imaginative experimenting. Such a theory offers an easy explanation of error, and Professor Rignano draws it out in a very convincing manner."—*Times Literary Supplement.*

CHANCE, LOVE and LOGIC : Philosophical Essays. By *Charles S. Peirce.* Edited with an Introduction by *Morris R. Cohen.* Supplementary Essay by *John Dewey.*

12/6 *net.*

" It is impossible to read Peirce without recognizing the presence of a superior mind. He was something of a genius."—F. C. S. Schiller, in *Spectator.* " It is about the clarification of our ideas that Mr Peirce makes his most interesting remarks ; it is here that one sees what a brilliant mind he had and how independently he could think."—*Nation.*

SPECULATIONS : Essays on Humanism and the Philosophy of Art. By *T. E. Hulme.* Edited by *Herbert Read.* Frontispiece and Foreword by *Jacob Epstein.*

10/6 *net.*

" With its peculiar merits, this book is most unlikely to meet with the slightest comprehension from the usual reviewer. When Hulme was killed in Flanders in 1917, he was known as a brilliant talker, a brilliant amateur of metaphysics, and the author of two or three of the most beautiful short poems in the language. In this volume he appears as the forerunner of a new attitude of mind, which should be the twentieth century mind."—*Criterion.*

THE NATURE OF LAUGHTER. By *J. C. Gregory.*

10/6 *net.*

" Mr Gregory, in this fresh and stimulating study, joins issue with all his predecessors. In our judgment he has made a distinct advance in the study of laughter ; and his remarks on wit, humour, and comedy, are most discriminating. The writer's own vivacity of style suits his subject admirably."—*Journal of Education.*

THE PHILOSOPHY OF MUSIC. By *William Pole, F.R.S., Mus. Doc.* Edited with an Introduction by *Edward J. Dent* and a Supplementary Essay by *Dr Hamilton Hartridge.*

New edition, 10/6 *net.*

" This is an excellent book and its re-issue should be welcomed by all who take more than a superficial interest in music. Especially should it appeal to those of a musical or scientific frame of mind who may have pondered upon the why and the how of things musical. Dr Pole possessed not only a wide knowledge of these matters, but also an attractive style, and this combination has enabled him to set forth clearly and sufficiently completely to give the general reader a fair all-round grasp of his subject."—*Discovery.*

INDIVIDUAL PSYCHOLOGY : its Theory and Practice. By *Alfred Adler.* Translation by *Dr Paul Radin.*

18/- *net.*

" Dr Adler is the leader of one of the more important schisms from the original Freudian school. He makes a valuable contribution to psychology. His thesis is extremely simple and comprehensive : mental phenomena when correctly understood may be regarded as leading up to an end which consists in establishing the subject's superiority."—*Discovery.*

" Suggestive and stimulating."—*Morning Post.*

THE PHILOSOPHY OF ' AS IF '. By *Hans Vaihinger.* Translated by *C. K. Ogden. M.A.*

25/- *net.*

" The most important contribution to philosophical literature in a quarter of a century. Briefly, Vaihinger amasses evidence to prove that reality and thought are out of key. Reason was never an instrument, he holds, for the understanding of life. We can arrive at theories which work pretty well by ' consciously false assumptions.' We know that these fictions in no way reflect reality, but we treat them *as if* they did. Among such fictions are :—the average man, freedom, God, empty space, point, matter, the atom, infinity, the absolute. All abstracts, classifications, comparisons, general ideas, are fictions. All the sciences and arts depend upon fictions."—*Spectator.*

THE NATURE OF INTELLIGENCE : a Biological Interpretation of Mind. By *L. L. Thurstone,* Professor of Psychology in the University of Chicago.

10/6 *net.*

" Prof. Thurstone distinguishes three views of the nature of intelligence. He names the first Academic ; the second the Psycho-analytic ; the third the Behaviourist. Against these three views, though not in opposition to them, Prof. Thurstone expounds his thesis that conscious-ness is unfinished action. He contends that it is not inconsistent with any of the three views, while in a sense it interprets each of them. His book is of the first importance. All who make use of mental tests will do well to come to terms with his theory."—*Times Literary Supplement.*

INTERNATIONAL LIBRARY OF PSYCHOLOGY

THE GROWTH OF THE MIND : an Introduction to Child Psychology. By *Professor K. Koffka* of the University of Giessen. Translated by *Professor R. M. Ogden.*
Third impression, 15/- net.

His book is extremely interesting, and it is to be hoped that it will be widely read."—*Times Literary Supplement. Leonard Woolf,* reviewing this book and the following one in a *Nation* Leading Article, writes : " Every serious student of psychology ought to read it [*The Apes*], and he should supplement it by reading *The Growth of the Mind,* for Professor Koffka joins up the results of Kohler's observations with the results of the study of child-psychology."

THE MENTALITY OF APES, with an Appendix on the Psychology of Chimpanzees. By *Professor W. Koehler,* of Berlin University.
Cheaper edition, with 9 plates and 19 figures, 10/6 net.

" May fairly be said to mark a turning-point in the history of psychology. The book is both in substance and form an altogether admirable piece of work. It is of absorbing interest to the psychologist, and hardly less to the layman—especially the lover of animals. His work will always be regarded as a classic in its kind and a model for future studies."
—*Times Literary Supplement.*

TELEPATHY AND CLAIRVOYANCE. By *Rudolf Tischner.* Preface by *E. J. Dingwall.*
With 20 illustrations, 10/6 net.

" Such investigations may now expect to receive the grave attention of modern readers. They will find the material here collected of great value and interest. The chief interest of the book lies in the experiments it records, and we think that these will persuade any reader free from violent prepossessions that the present state of the evidence necessitates at least an open mind regarding their possibility." —*Times Literary Supplement.*

THE PSYCHOLOGY OF RELIGIOUS MYSTICISM. By *Professor James H. Leuba,* author of ' A Psychological Study of Religion,' etc.
15/- net.

" The book is fascinating and stimulating even to those who do not agree with it, and it is scholarly as well as scientific."—*Review of Reviews.* An extension and development of the views outlined in James's *Varieties of Religious Experience* with much new material. A section is devoted to mystical experiences produced by drugs.

THE PSYCHOLOGY OF A MUSICAL PRODIGY. By *G. Revesz,* Director of the Psychological Laboratory, Amsterdam.
With many musical illustrations, 10/6 net.

" For the first time we have a scientific report on the development of a musical genius. Instead of being dependent on the vaguely marvellous report of adoring relatives, we enter the more satisfying atmosphere of precise tests. That Erwin is a musical genius, nobody who reads this book will doubt."—*Times Literary Supplement.*

PRINCIPLES OF LITERARY CRITICISM. By *I. A. Richards*, Lecturer at Magdalene College, Cambridge. *Second edition*, 10/6 *net.*

" A mine of really suggestive ideas. It has real originality."—*Daily News.* " An important contribution to the rehabilitation of English criticism—perhaps, because of its sustained scientific nature, the most important contribution yet made. Mr Richards begins with an account of the present chaos of critical theories and follows with an analysis of the fallacy in modern aesthetics. The principles enunciated are pursued with clear zest and consequent elucidation. Parallel applications to the arts of painting, sculpture, and music form the subject of three chapters." —*Criterion.*

THE METAPHYSICAL FOUNDATIONS OF MODERN SCIENCE, with special reference to Man's Relation to Nature. By *Professor Edwin A. Burtt.* 14/- *net.*

" This book deals with a profoundly interesting subject : the uncritical assumptions which were made by the founders of modern physics, and through them became part of the unquestioned apparatus of ordinary thought. The critical portion of this book is admirable . . ." Bertrand Russell, in *Nation.* " He has given us a history of the origin and development of what was, until recently, the metaphysic generally associated with the scientific outlook. This is what Professor Burtt has quite admirably done."—*Times Literary Supplement.*

PHYSIQUE AND CHARACTER. By *E. Kretschmer.* *With* 31 *plates,*15/- *net.*

" This volume of the steadily growing *Library* will bear comparison with any of its predecessors in interest and importance. It gives scientific validity to much ancient doctrine and folk-psychology. It professes to be merely a beginning ; but, even so, the author has established certain conclusions beyond reasonable doubt, conclusions of great significance and pregnant with possibilities of almost infinite extension." —*Weekly Westminster.* " His notable work [on] the relation between human form and human character."—*British Medical Journal.*

THE PSYCHOLOGY OF EMOTION : Morbid and Normal. By *John T. MacCurdy, M.D.* 25/- *net.*

" There are two reasons in particular for welcoming this book. First, it is by a psychiatrist who takes general psychology seriously. Secondly, the author presents his evidence as well as his conclusions. This is distinctly a book which should be read by all interested in modern psychology. Its subject is important and its author's treatment interesting."—*Manchester Guardian.* " A record of painstaking and original work in a direction that promises to illuminate some of the fundamental problems of psychiatry."—*Lancet.*

THE PSYCHOLOGY OF TIME. By *Mary Sturt, M.A.* 7/6 *net.*

" An interesting book, typical of the work of the younger psychologists of to-day. The first chapter gives a clear summary of metaphysical views of time ; later chapters describe practical experiments ; while the last chapter sets forth the writer's view that time is a concept constructed by each individual. The clear, concise style of writing adds greatly to the pleasure of the reader."—*Journal of Education.*

INTERNATIONAL LIBRARY OF PSYCHOLOGY

PROBLEMS OF PERSONALITY : a Volume of Essays in honour of *Morton Prince.* Edited by *A. A. Roback, Ph.D.*
18/- *net.*
" Here we have collected together samples of the work of a great many of the leading thinkers on the subjects which may be expected to throw light on the problem of Personality. Some such survey is always a tremendous help in the study of any subject. Taken all together, the book is full of interest."—*New Statesman.* Contributors include G. Elliot Smith, Bernard Hart, Ernest Jones, C. S. Myers, C. G. Jung, Pierre Janet, W. McDougall, William Brown, T. W. Mitchell, and numerous others.

THE MIND AND ITS PLACE IN NATURE. By *C. D. Broad, Litt. D.*, Lecturer in Philosophy at Trinity College, Cambridge.
16/- *net.*
" Quite the best book that Dr Broad has yet given us, and one of the most important contributions to philosophy made in recent times."—*Times Literary Supplement.* " Full of accurate thought and useful distinctions and on this ground it deserves to be read by all serious students."—*Bertrand Russell,* in *Nation.* " One of the most important books which have appeared for a long time . . . a remarkable survey of the whole field of psychology and philosophy . . . a piece of brilliant surgery."—*Discovery.*

COLOUR-BLINDNESS : with a Comparison of different Methods of Testing Colour-Blindness. By *Mary Collins, M.A., Ph.D.* Introduction by Dr James Drever.
With a coloured plate, 12/6 *net.*
" Her book is worthy of high praise as a painstaking, honest, well-written endeavour, based upon extensive reading and close original investigation, to deal with colour-vision, mainly from the point of view of the psychologist. We believe that the book will commend itself to every one interested in the subject."—*Times Literary Supplement.*

THE HISTORY OF MATERIALISM. By *F. A. Lange.* New edition in one volume, with an introduction by *Bertrand Russell, F.R.S.*
15/- *net.*
" An immense and valuable work."—*Spectator.* " A monumental work, of the highest value to all who wish to know what has been said by advocates of Materialism, and why philosophers have in the main remained unconvinced. Lange, while very sympathetic to materialism in its struggles with older systems, was himself by no means a materialist. His book is divided into two parts, one dealing with the times before Kant, the other with Kant and his successors."—From the *Introduction.*

PSYCHE : the Cult of Souls and the Belief in Immortality among the Greeks. By *Erwin Rohde.*
25/- *net.*
" The production of an admirably exact and unusually readable translation of Rohde's great book is an event on which all concerned are to be congratulated. It is in the truest sense a classic, to which all future scholars must turn if they would learn how to see and describe the inward significance of primitive cults."—*Daily News.* " The translator and publishers are to be congratulated on rendering this standard treatise accessible."—*Adelphi.*

INTERNATIONAL LIBRARY OF PSYCHOLOGY

EDUCATIONAL PSYCHOLOGY ; its Problems and Methods. By *Charles Fox, M.A.*, Lecturer on Education in the University of Cambridge.
Second edition, 10/6 *net.*
" A worthy addition to a series of outstanding merit. There are interesting sections on heredity and on mental tests. The chapter on fatigue is excellent. The bibliography is valuable."—*Lancet.* " Certainly one of the best books of its kind."—*Observer.* " An extremely able book, not only useful, but original."—*Journal of Education.*

EMOTION AND INSANITY. By *S. Thalbitzer*, Chief of the Medical Staff, Copenhagen Asylum. Preface by *Professor H. Höffding.*
7/6 *net.*
" A psychological essay the material for which is provided by a study of the manic-depressive psychosis. It is a brief attempt to explain certain mental phenomena on a physiological basis. This explanation is based on three well-recognized physiological laws. . . . Whatever the view taken of this fascinating explanation, there is one plea in this book which must be whole-heartedly endorsed, that psychiatric research should receive much more consideration in the effort to determine the nature of normal mental processes."—*Nature.*

PERSONALITY. By *R. G. Gordon, M.D., D.Sc., M.R.C.P.Ed.*
10/6 *net*
" The book is, in short, a very useful critical discussion of the most important modern work bearing on the mind-body problem, the whole knit together by a philosophy at least as promising as any of those now current."—*Times Literary Supplement.* " His excellent book. He accepts the important and attractive theory of Emergence."—*Observer.* " A significant contribution to the study of personality."—*British Medical Journal.*

BIOLOGICAL MEMORY. By *Eugenio Rignano*, Professor of Philosophy in the University of Milan. Translated, with an Introduction, by *Professor E. W. MacBride*, F.R.S.
10/6 *net.*
" Professor Rignano's book may prove to have an important bearing on the whole mechanist-vitalist controversy. He has endeavoured to give meaning and content to the special property of ' livingness ', which separates the organic from the inorganic world by identifying it with unconscious memory. The author works out his theory with great vigour and ingenuity, and the book deserves, and should receive, the earnest attention not only of students of biology, but of all interested in the age-long problem of the nature of life."—*Spectator.*

COMPARATIVE PHILOSOPHY. By *Paul Masson-Oursel.* Introduction by *F. G. Crookshank, M.D., F.R.C.P.*
10/6 *net.*
" He is an authority on Indian and Chinese philosophy, and in this book he develops the idea that philosophy should be studied . . . as a series of natural events by means of a comparison of its development in various countries and environments. After a lengthy introduction on the method, and a chronological table, he illustrates his thesis by chapters on the stages in the evolution of philosophic thought in general and on comparative logic, metaphysics, and psychology."—*Times Literary Supplement.*

THE LANGUAGE AND THOUGHT OF THE CHILD. By *Jean Piaget*, Professor at the University of Geneva. Preface by *Professor E. Claparède.*
10/6 *net.*
" A very interesting book. Everyone interested in psychology,education, or the art of thought should read it. The results are surprising, but perhaps the most surprising thing which this book makes clear is how extraordinarily little was previously known of the way in which children think."—*Nation.* " Fills a gap in the study of the subject."—*Lancet.*

CRIME AND CUSTOM IN SAVAGE SOCIETY. By *B. Malinowski*, Professor of Anthropology in the University of London.
With 6 plates, 5/- *net.*
" In this first-hand investigation into the social structure of a primitive community Dr Malinowski has broken new ground. It is probably no exaggeration to say that the book is the most important contribution to anthropology that has appeared for many years past. Its effects are bound to be far-reaching. . . . It is written by an anthropologist for anthropologists ; but it should be read by all who have to deal with primitive peoples and by all who are interested in human nature as manifested in social relationships, which is to say that it should be read by everyone."—*Outlook.*

PSYCHOLOGY AND ETHNOLOGY. By *W. H. R. Rivers, M.D., Litt. D., F.R.S.* Preface by *G. Elliot Smith, F.R.S.*
15/- *net.*
" Gives us most fascinating evidence of the many-sidedness of Rivers's interests, and of his actual scientific methods. . . . This notice in no way exhausts the treasures that are to be found in this volume, which really requires long and detailed study. We congratulate the editor on producing it. It is a worthy monument to a great man."—*Saturday Review.* " Everything he has written concerning anthropology is of interest to all serious students of the subject."—*Times Literary Supplement.*

THEORETICAL BIOLOGY. By *J. von Uexkull.*
18/- *net.*
" It is not easy to give a critical account of this important book. Partly because of its ambitious scope, that of re-setting biological formulations in a new synthesis, partly because there is an abundant use of new terms. Thirdly, the author's arguments are so radically important that they cannot justly be dealt with in brief compass. No one can read the book without feeling the thrill of an unusually acute mind, emancipated from the biological conventionalities of our time."—*J.* Arthur Thomson, in *Journal of Philosophical Studies.*

THOUGHT AND THE BRAIN. By *Henri Piéron*, Professor at the Collège de France. Translated by *C. K. Ogden.*
12/6 *net.*
" A very valuable summary of recent investigations into the structure and working of the nervous system. He is prodigal of facts, but sparing of theories. His book can be warmly recommended as giving the reader a vivid idea of the intricacy and subtlety of the mechanism by which the human animal co-ordinates its impressions of the outside world. His own clinical experience is considerable, and he has a wide acquaintance with the literature of his subject, but he carries his erudition lightly. Nearly one quarter of the book is devoted to a learned and penetrating study of aphasia."—*Times Literary Supplement.*

CPSIA information can be obtained at www.ICGtesting.com
Printed in the USA
BVOW050059281011

274548BV00001BA/115/A

9 781406 701166